The Persian Prison Poem

Edinburgh Historical Studies of Iran and the Persian World

Published in association with Elahé Omidyar Mir-Djalali, Founder and Chair, Roshan Cultural Heritage Institute

ROSHAN CULTURAL HERITAGE INSTITUTE

Series General Editor: Stephanie Cronin, Elahé Omidyar Mir-Djalali Research Fellow, University of Oxford

Series Advisory Board: Professor Janet Afary (UC Santa Barbara), Professor Abbas Amanat (Yale University), Professor Touraj Atabaki (International Institute of Social History), Dr Joanna de Groot (University of York), Professor Vanessa Martin (Royal Holloway, University of London), Professor Rudi Matthee (University of Delaware) and Professor Cyrus Schayegh (The Graduate Institute, Geneva)

Covering the history of Iran and the Persian world from the medieval period to the present, this series aims to become the pre-eminent place for publication in this field. As well as its core concern with Iran, it extends its concerns to encompass a much wider and more loosely defined cultural and linguistic world, to include Afghanistan, the Caucasus, Central Asia, Xinjiang and northern India. Books in the series present a range of conceptual and methodological approaches, looking not only at states, dynasties and elites, but at subalterns, minorities and everyday life.

Published and forthcoming titles

The Last Muslim Intellectual: The Life and Legacy of Jalal Al-e Ahmad
Hamid Dabashi

The Persian Prison Poem: Sovereignty and the Political Imagination
Rebecca Ruth Gould

Remapping Persian Literary History, 1700–1900
Kevin L. Schwartz

Religion, Orientalism and Modernity: Mahdi Movements of Iran and South Asia
Geoffrey Nash

Muslim–Christian Polemics in Safavid Iran
Alberto Tiburcio

edinburghuniversitypress.com/series/ehsipw

The Persian Prison Poem

Sovereignty and the Political Imagination

Rebecca Ruth Gould

EDINBURGH
University Press

Edinburgh University Press is one of the leading university presses in the UK. We publish academic books and journals in our selected subject areas across the humanities and social sciences, combining cutting-edge scholarship with high editorial and production values to produce academic works of lasting importance. For more information visit our website: edinburghuniversitypress.com

Edinburgh University Press Ltd
The Tun – Holyrood Road
12 (2f) Jackson's Entry
Edinburgh EH8 8PJ

Typeset in 11/15pt Adobe Garamond by
Cheshire Typesetting Ltd, Cuddington, Cheshire, and
printed and bound by CPI Group (UK) Ltd,
Croydon, CR0 4YY

A CIP record for this book is available from the British Library

ISBN 978 1 4744 8401 5 (hardback)
ISBN 978 1 4744 8403 9 (webready PDF)
ISBN 978 1 4744 8404 6 (epub)

Contents

List of Illustrations vi
Terminology, Transliteration and Sources vii
Acknowledgements ix
A Prison Poem Lexicon x
Chronology of Poets, Rulers, Texts and Critics xiv
Map of Ghaznavid South and West Asia xvi

Introduction: The Persian Poet's Bodies: Towards a Corporeal Poetics 1

1 The Prison Poem and the Politics of Genre 30

2 The Lyric Poet's Body 59

3 Borderland Conflicts, Cosmological Complaints 87

4 The Prison Poet as King and Prophet 125

5 Crucifixion as Critique 156

6 The Sovereign and the Poet's Body 207

Epilogue: Incarceration, Metonymy, Modernity 251

Appendix: Khaqani's Six Prison Poems 258
List of Abbreviations 260
Bibliography 262
Index 287

Illustrations

Figures

I.1 Rostam rescues Bijan from the well. Ferdowsi, *Shahnama* (British Library, MS Add. 27258, fol. 257v) 23
I.2 Rostam rescues Bijan from the well (S1986.267) 23
5.1 The *zunnar* worn by non-Muslims 169
5.2 'Ancient Ctesiphon', in John Philip Newman, *The Thrones and Palaces of Babylon* 184
5.3 Cover of *Aiwan-i Mada'in* 186
5.4 Depiction of the Ctesiphon Arch in *Aiwan-i Mada'in* 187

Diagrams

1.1 An overlapping typology of genre 42
1.2 The Persian genre system 44
6.1 Power as representation 238

Table

Table 1.1 A tripartite typology of genre's three dimensions in Persian poetics 34

Terminology, Transliteration and Sources

This book has benefited from 'Balaghas Compared: Comparative Poetics in the Islamic World', a collaborative anthology (currently in preparation) that is among the major outputs of the ERC-funded 'Global Literary Theory: Caucasus Literatures Compared' (GlobalLIT) project (ERC-2017-STG Grant Agreement No. 759346). I have cited in this book from several major works of Persian literary criticism and theory in the (as yet unpublished) translations of the project postdocs Michelle Quay and Nasrin Askari. It is my hope that this anthology will be a great resource for specialists and non-specialists alike in the year to come.

Another project related to this work is 'The Persian Prison Poem: An Anthology from South Asia to the Caucasus', funded by the British Institute of Persian Studies. For this project, Kayvan Tahmasebian and I have gathered together a wide range of prison poems. The Persian texts for all the prison poems discussed here (and more) are given in full in this forthcoming anthology, along with their English translation.

In the interest of reaching a wider audience I have used more simplified transliterations as compared with my previous scholarly work. Diacritics and macrons are used in the notes for Persian and Arabic texts and names, but omitted from the main body of the text. Hence, ʿArūḍī becomes ʿAruzi. Persian transliteration has been retained for Persian texts and Arabic for texts transliterated from Arabic. I have used transliteration here as a guide to writing rather than pronunciation, in order to support those who plan to consult the original texts.

I have used Persian terms such as ghazal without italics, recognising that they are already part of the English language. My use of the word "verse" refers to the Arabo-Persian term *bayt*, consisting of two distiches (*misras*), as further explained in 'A Prison Poem Lexicon', below.

This book discusses a wide range of prison poets, with its most extended focus on Khaqani. Given that premodern Persian poems do not bear titles, I have assigned numbers to six of his poems that are most explicitly about prison, and refer to them as prison poem one, prison poem two, and so on. These six poems are listed in the Appendix. This is intended as a preliminary means of orienting the reader of this book, rather than an absolute typology. Future research (including the above-mentioned anthology) will propose a more extensive classification for prison poems; my aim here is simply to introduce this genre to the reader who has never encountered it before.

The abbreviation system for journals and primary sources detailed on pp. 260–1 has been implemented. Titles are cited in the footnotes in abbreviated form and given in full in the Bibliography. Portions of Chapter 5 appeared in different form in 'Wearing the Belt of Oppression: Khāqānī's Christian Qaṣīda and the Prison Poetry of Medieval Shirvān', *Journal of Persianate Studies* 9(1) (2016): 1–44.

For funding that supported the work that shaped this project, I am grateful to the British Institute for Persian Studies, the European Research Council, Central European University's Institute for Advanced Studies, and the Medieval Academy of America, which granted a Charles Wood Dissertation Award to an early version of this project.

Acknowledgements

For help with various aspects of this and other projects pursued while working on this book, I am indebted to Hebah Alheem, Muhammad Asif, Muhsin al-Musawi, Asil Ateeri, Mona Baker, Wiebke Denecke, Ziad Elmarsafy, Roja Fazaeli, Bruce Grant, Haidar Khezri, Pranav Prakash, Paul Manning, Asghar Seyed Gohrab, Kayvan Tahmasebian, Nathanial Tarn and Khachig Tölölyan. Muzaffar Alam, Mona Baker, Georgi Derluguian and Javed Majeed have all been outstandingly generous with their time and wise with their counsel. At Birmingham, I have been particularly grateful for the companionship and insights of Christopher Markiewicz, Karen McAuliffe, Charlotte Ross, Emmanuelle Santos, Lyndsey Stonebridge, Lynn Wadding, Aengus Ward, Erin Withers and Simon Yarrow. I have benefited greatly from working with Nasrin Askari, Kristof D'hulster, Nila Namsechi and Michelle Quay during their time with the GlobalLIT project.

Of all who have engaged with this work, my debt to Kayvan Tahmasebian is most profound. His work on Persian literature has been a tremendous inspiration to me and I look forward to seeing more of it in the world. As with all of my books, my mother Brenda Gould and my sisters Kate and Beth Gould accompanied me at every step of the journey.

This book – and the PhD project from which it derives – may not have existed at all without Sheldon Pollock. Had I not encountered him during my first day at Columbia University, in search of a non-Eurocentric way of doing comparison, it is hard to say what would have become of me as scholar. Perhaps I would have persisted in the anthropology programme I entered, even though it could not fulfil my dreams of studying premodern and precolonial literatures. More than anyone else, Sheldon Pollock made these dreams possible. He made it possible for me to become a scholar. He has changed my life, as he has changed so many others, and my debt to him is eternal.

A Prison Poem Lexicon (And Other Relevant Terms)

ʿajam – non-Arab; literally, 'inarticulate', on analogy with βάρβαρος (barbarian); commonly used to refer to Persians.

aya (pl. ***ayat***) – verses from one of the 114 *sura*s of the Quran; literally, 'signs'.

band – translatable as 'chain', is arguably (along with ***zanjir***, which means chain, and ***zindan***, which is prison), the single most common topos of the prison poem.

badiʿ – trope, innovation; refers to a poetic style based on the use of fresh imagery; morphologically, if not always semantically, related to *bidʿa* (heresy).

bayan – 'elucidation'; a branch of rhetoric along with *ʿilm-i maʿni and ʿilm-i badiʿ*.

bayt (pl. ***abyat***) – verse or distich; equals two ***misra***ʿs; related to the Arabic word for house (*bayt*).

divan – collection of poems, usually posthumous; also used to mean any official register.

dhimmi (=***ahl al-dhimma***, 'people of the book') – non-Muslim 'protected' peoples, including Christians, Jews and sometimes Zoroastrians; generally restricted to those subscribing to monotheistic faiths.

dubayti – literally 'two verses'. Translated here as 'quatrain'. Similar to the *rubaʿi* in that it comprises two verses, with the difference that the first syllable is short rather than long. The earliest recorded Persian prison poem was categorised as a *dubayti*.

fakhr – boasting; commonly deployed in the pre-Islamic *qasida* and also in the prison poem.

ghazal – love poem that originates formally in the ***nasib*** section of the ***qasida***; soon broke off from the ***qasida*** to constitute an independent formal genre.

habsiyyat – the standard Persian term for the prison poem genre, derived from the Arabic root meaning 'suffocation'; alternative terms in modern Persian include *zindannameh* and *sorud-i az zindan* ('song from prison').

hija' (=***hajv***) – invective, often directed by one poet against another; sometimes contrasted to.

hadith – sayings and teaching by the Prophet or Shi'a Imams; second in authority to the Quran.

iham – literally, 'the creation of doubt'; a literary trope that juxtaposes a word's proximate meaning (***ma'ni*** *qarib*) with its distant meaning (***ma'ni*** *ba'id*, ***ma'ni*** *gharib*), and that aims to evoke this proximate while the distant meaning is the intended one.

imam – in Sunni Islamic political theory (such as al-Mawardi), the standard term for the caliph (***khalifa***), or any temporal ruler.

jizya – a tax historically levied on non-Muslim subjects of states governed by Islamic law in order to fund public expenditures of the state, in place of the taxes that Muslims are obliged to pay (*zakat*). Also known as a poll tax.

khalifa – caliph; vice-regent, representative; the institution whereby an *imam* represents the Prophet Muhammad who in turn represents God; the normative form of political power for the 'Abbasid period; fell into decline in the eleventh century onwards with the ascendancy of the Buwayhids and the consolidation of the Ghaznavid and Saljuq sultanates. ***Khalifa*** occurs in the Quran at 2:30 and 38:26.

lafz (pl. ***alfaz***) – sound, the phonemic counterpart to ***ma'ni*** in the constitution of the poetic unit.

ma'ni (pl. ***ma'ani***) – sense, the semantic counterpart to ***lafz*** in the constitution of the poetic unit; in other usages: topoi, motifs, themes.

madih – the second section of a Persian *qaṣida*; literally, 'praise' directed towards the patron; sometimes contrasted to ***hija'/hijv***.

marthiya (=***ritha'***; pl. ***marathi***) – elegy; a genre dating back to the pre-Islamic period; distinct from the *qasida*.

masnavi – poetic form using rhymed couplets; often used for Persian narrative.

mazmun (pl. ***mazamin***) – tropes, motifs.

misra' – hemistich; two ***misra'***s comprise a couplet (***bayt***); also means 'folding door' in Arabic.

nasib – erotic prelude; one of the three sections that comprise the tripartite ***qasida***; formal ancestor of the ***ghazal***; also referred to as *tashbib*.

nazm – poetry; literally 'ordered discourse'; contrasted to *nathr* (prose).

Nay – the name of one of the Ghaznavid fortresses where Mas'ud Sa'd was imprisoned. *Nay* is a polysemic word that also refers to the pen with which poets write, to a flute and to sugarcane. These many meanings were all used in prison poetry.

New Persian – the literary language of Islamic Central Asia and parts of the Caucasus, as well as Khurasan and other parts of what is now Iran. Based on the Persian spoken at the time of the Islamic conquest, New Persian was given written form through the Arabic script. The Persian prison poem was invariably written in New Persian.

qasida (pl. ***qasa'id***) – the normative formal genre of poetic composition in Arabic and Persian; often, but not always, panegyric in content; classically comprising three sections: ***nasib*** (also called (*tashbib* or *taghazzul*); ***takhallus*** (also called *gurizgah*); and ***madiḥ***. Follows the rhyme pattern a a/b a/c a/d a.

qafiya – rhyme. Classical Persian poems are organised into ***divan***s in alphabetical order, according to their ***qafiya***.

qit'eh – literally, 'fragment'; follows the rhyme pattern a b/c b/d b.

radif – the technical name given to one or more independent words placed after the rhyme at the end of hemistichs or verses, which are repeated at the end of every line throughout the poem.

ruba'i (pl. ***ruba'iyyat***) – quatrain with end rhyme in AABA or AAAA; sometimes referred to in Persian as ***dubayti*** ('two couplets').

tazkira – biographical compendium (often of poets)

sariqat – literary appropriation; plagarism.

sukhan – speech, poetic discourse (unique to Persian; comparable to the Arabic *kalam*).

sura – division of the Quran; there are 114 *sura*s in the Quran in total, which are in turn divided into ***ayat***.

takhallus – the name by which a poet refers to himself in his poetry; also the transition section of a ***qasida*** that bridges the middle section to the main body of the poem.

topos (pl. ***topoi***) – sometimes used interchangeably with 'theme'. The concept of topos is useful in literature because it simultaneously has a material dimension (the term in Latin means 'place') and a conceptual aspect.

verse – the term used here to render *bayt*. Consists of two hemistiches.

zindan – literally translatable as 'prison', ***zindan*** is, along with ***band*** and ***zanjir*** (both translatable as 'chain'), one of the most common topos of Persian prison poems.

zunnar – yellow belt worn by ***dhimmi*** peoples to signify their non-Muslim status; a calque from the Greek *zōnarion* (ζωνάριον=belt); later came to refer to the Brahman's thread (Sanskrit: *yajñopavīta*). A trope in many prison poems, and a symbol of divergence from Islam.

Chronology of Poets, Rulers, Texts and Critics

Poets

Rudaki (858–941)
Nasir Khusraw (1004–1088)
Mas'ud Sa'd (1046–1121)
Sana'i of Ghazna (1080–1131)
Falaki (1108–1157)
Mu'izzi (d. 1127)
Nizami Ganjevi (1141–1209)
Mujir al-Din Baylaqani (d. 1190)
Abu al-Ma'ali Nasrollah Munshi (d. *c*. 1204)
Khaqani Shirvani (1120–*c*.1199)
Minhaj Juzjani (1193–1266)
Dante Alighieri (1265–1321)
'Amid al-Din Lumaki (thirteenth century)
Muhammad Taqi Bahar (1886–1951)

Rulers

Nushirvan (Khosrow I) (r. 531–579)
Ghazanavid Sultan Mahmud (r. 999–1030)
Ghazanavid Sultan Ibrahim (r. 1059–1099)
Saljuq Alp Arslan, better known as Malekshah (r. 1072–1092)
Ghazanavid Sultan Mas'ud III (r. 1099–1114)
Saljuq Ghiyath ad-Din Muhammad b. Malekshah (r. 1105–1118)
Ghazanavid Sultan Shirzad (r. 1114–1115)
Ghazanavid Sultan Arsalan Shah (r. 1115–1117)
Ghazanavid Sultan Bahramshah (r. 1117–1157)
Shirvanshah Manuchihr III (r. 1120–1160)
Shirvanshah Akhsitan I (r. 1160–1197)

Critics and their Works

Nizam al-Mulk, *Conduct of Kings* (between 1086 and 1091)
Nizami ʿAruzi (d. 1127), *Four Discourses*
Rashid al-Din Vatvat (d. 1182/3), *Gardens of Magic*
Muhammad ʿAwfi, *Pith of Essences* (1221)
Shams-i Qays, *Compendium on the Rules of Poetry in the Persian East* (1221)

Key Texts

ʿUmar's Covenant, putatively authored by ʿUmar b. al-Khattab (r. 634–644)
Ferdowsi, *Shahanama* (*c.* 1010)
Khaqani, Christian Qasida
Khaqani, Aivan Qasida

Dynasties

Sassanians (224–651)
Umayyad Caliphate (662–750)
ʿAbbasid Caliphate (750–1258)
Samanids (819–999)
Ghaznavids (977–1186)
Ghurids (also known as the Shansabanids), vassals of the Ghaznavids (*c.* 879–1215)
Saljuqs (1037–1194)
Shirvanshahs, vassals of the Saljuqs (861–1538)

1088: Masʿud Saʿd enters prison, where he remains for the next ten years.
1172: Khaqani embarks on the pilgrimage based on which he wrote the Aivan Qasida.
1192: Shirvanshah capital moved from Shemakhi (near Shirvan) to Baku, after an earthquake.
1258: collapse of the caliphate, following the Mongol conquest of Baghdad.
1933: Bahar composes *Prison Feats* (*Karnameh-yi zindan*) from prison.

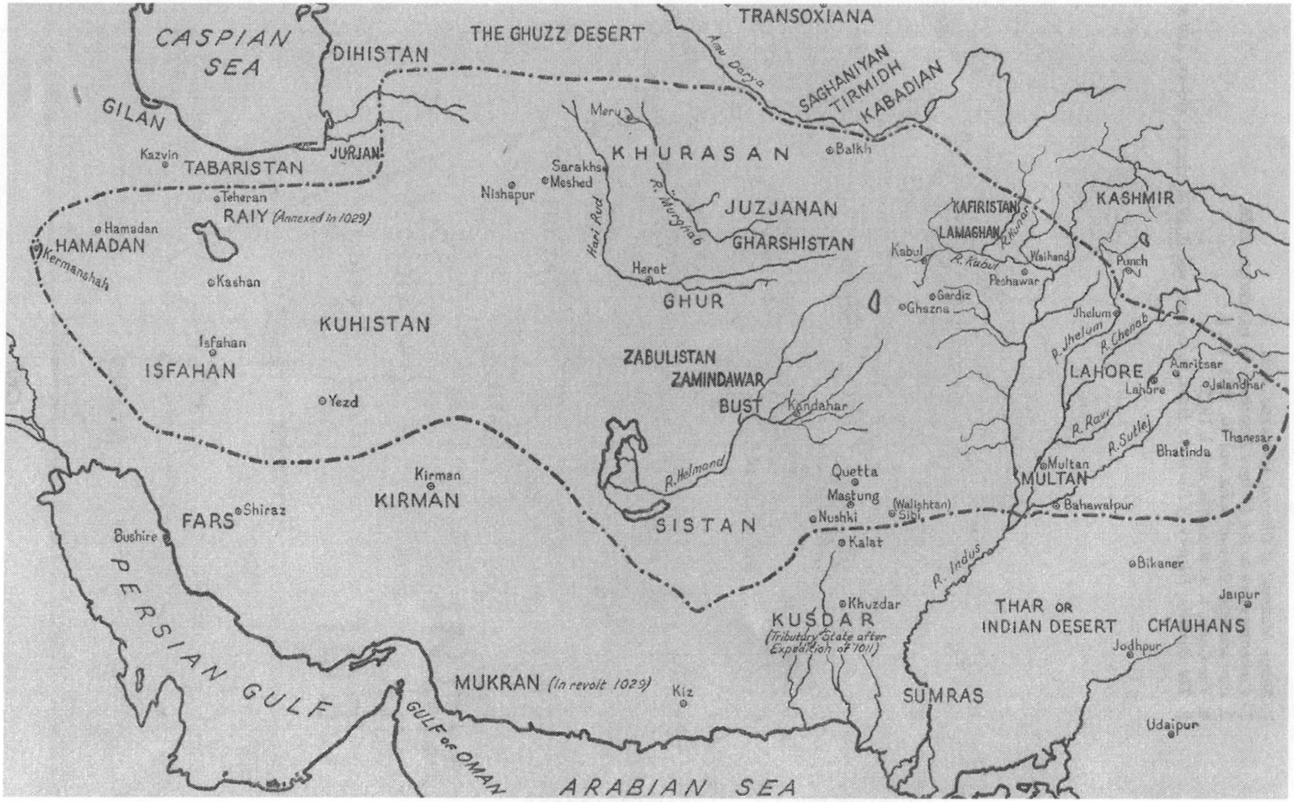

Map of Ghaznavid South and West Asia

Source: C. Collin Daves, *An Historical Atlas of the Indian Peninsula* (Oxford: Oxford University Press, 1949), 25.

If everything in the world were banned:
the right to breathe, to open doors,
to insist that life will persist,
and that people, like judges, will judge.
If they dared enchain me like a wild beast –
flinging my food on the floor –
I'd neither stay silent nor dull pain's edge.
I'd say what I'm free to say by choice –
swinging from the wall like a naked bell,
awakening the enemy's dark corner.
I'd yoke ten oxen to my voice
and sweep the dark with the plough of my hand.

Osip Mandelshtam, 'If Our Enemies Took Me'

All great works of literature either establish a genre or dissolve one.

Walter Benjamin

For Kayvan

Introduction

The Persian Poet's Bodies: Towards a Corporeal Poetics

In his classic study of kingship, *The King's Two Bodies* (1957), medieval historian Ernst Kantorowicz examined how the theory that the king was possessed of two bodies – one comprising his mortal flesh and the other epitomising his sacred and immortal status – shaped medieval and early modern literature and political thought.[1] Kantorowicz's study is bookended by two distinct, yet closely intertwined, narratives. First, 'the Christological origin of secular constitutionalism in Shakespeare's England'. Second, 'the secular religion of humanity best articulated by Dante'.[2] Although it is a work of historical scholarship, the chronological order of presentation is inverted in *The King's Two Bodies*: it opens with Shakespeare's *Richard II* (1597) and ends with Dante's *Divine Comedy* (1320). Kantorowicz deftly navigates conceptual and literary history as he traces the shifting contours of medieval European sovereignty, from Christ-centred kingship during the eleventh century, to law-centred kingship under Frederick II of Sicily (1198–1250), to polity-centred kingship, following which the sovereign's body replaced the mystical body of the church.[3]

Scholars have engaged critically and productively with Kantorowicz's work, while proposing revisions, extensions and new applications.[4] Although it is a work of historical scholarship, *The King's Two Bodies* goes beyond the remit of traditional historiography; its narrative derives from the scaffolding of literature. While producing a historiography of medieval kingship, Kantorowicz plots the interaction of law and literature from Dante to Shakespeare.

Within the field of literary studies, many scholars have picked up on Kantorowicz's insights into the workings of kingship in medieval and early modern literature. David Lee Miller dedicated a book-length study to Spenser's *Faerie Queene* (1590), an epic poem he takes to exemplify an emergent concept of 'the poem's two bodies'.[5] Victoria Kahn looks at the role of legal fiction in constructing the concept of the king's two bodies.[6] Lorna Hutson develops Kahn's interest in legal fictions to reveal how 'the fiction-making that dominated the common-law thinking' in sixteenth- and early seventeenth-century England generated the 'subversive constitutionalism' of early Stuart England.[7] Pivoting to more recent times, Graça Capinha traces the metaphysical entelechy of the king's two bodies as it is manifested in the poetics of the modern American poet Robert Duncan.[8] Stephanie Elsky reads the concept of the king's two bodies as a metaphor for the humanities at large.[9]

In line with such critical and creative engagements with medieval political theology in its interaction with poetry, this book explores the vision of the poet's two bodies that developed within the Persian prison poem. The main term for the Persian prison poem (*habsiyyat*) derives from the Arabic root for confinement (ح ب س).[10] As I document, the concept of the poet's two bodies was intimately linked to changing structures of power and in particular to the increasing authority accorded the poet's voice amid a decline in the caliph's power following the collapse of the Abbasid empire and the decentralisation of Islamic empires. Using their credentials as poets, Persian poets claimed for themselves a unique authority to expose through their poetry the sultan's abuses of power. They made poetry from, with and about their bodies, often from within prison cells. Embodied prison poetry was born from a variety of wounds: metaphysical (inflicted by the cosmos); personal (inflicted by the beloved); political (inflicted by the king); and physical (inflicted by imprisonment). The eleventh-century poet Nasir Khusraw (1004–1088) was among the inaugurators of this tradition. As Nasir Khusraw wrote in one of his poems, written from exile in Yamgan, high in the Pamir mountains:

> If my body is changed, it is no surprise:
> the body ages in this rotating dome.
> I have not changed the faith inscribed in my soul
> because my soul is not like my body under the skies.

گر دگر گشت تنم نیست عجب زیراک
از تن پیر در این گنبد گردانم

از ره دین که به جانست نگشستستم
زانکه در زیر فلک نیست چو تن جانم [11]

Nasir Khusraw's near contemporary Mas'ud Sa'd Salman (d. 1121) transposed the poetry of exile into a poetics of incarceration, in verses such as the following:

If they put what my body endures on the mountain
and if they place what is in my heart on the sea,
the pearl will melt in the shell from that heat,
and the ruby encased in granite will bleed from that weight.

گر آنچه هست بر این تن نهند بر کهسار
ور آنچه هست درین دل زنند بر دریا
ز تابش آب شود در در میان صدف
ز رنج خون شودی لعل در دل خارا [12]

In this brilliant image of the imprisoned poet's body, the ruby encased in granite becomes redder the longer it remains within the larger stone. Surrounded by dark prison walls, the poet compares his immured body to a piece of ruby which becomes purer the longer it is interred.

In another prison poem, Mas'ud Sa'd Salman dwells on his decaying imprisoned body:

To me with this frail body and insomniac eye,
the world is like crow's feathers. The heart is like the feathers of a fly.
The lamp is my companion in the dark of the night
The book is my companion, brightening my heart.
My face is yellow like an astrolabe's. Its skin,
torn by my fingernails, is like the astrolabe's web.
My two eyes are open like two holes day and night:
they receive neither the sun's nor the moon's light.

مرا ازین تن رنجور و دیده بی خواب
جهان چو پر غرابست و دل چو پر ذباب
ز بهر تیرگی شب مرا رفیق چراغ
ز بهر روشنی دل مرا ندیم کتاب
رخم چو روی سطرلاب زرد و پوست بر او

ز زخم ناخن چون عنکبوت اسطرلاب
دو دیده همچو دو ثقبه گشاده ام شب و روز
ولیک بی خبر از آفتاب و از مهتاب (1:64)

These verses depict the poet's body in a prison cell, confined in such a dark space that the holes in the prison cell – metaphorically, his eyes – receive no light from the world outside.

Not every poem that Masʿud Saʿd wrote about his body takes place in prison. Many, however, do. What matters for this book is how the poetics of the body and of the prison came to be intertwined over time. I examine the multiple sources of affliction articulated by Nasir Khusraw, Masʿud Saʿd (the focus of Chapter 2), and the many other poets who followed in their tradition, including Khaqani Shirvani (the focus of Chapters 3–5).

My account of the Persian poet's suffering and incarcerated body is embedded in a medieval cosmology that spanned Asia and Europe. Kantorowicz's ideal monarch, Frederick II of Sicily, began his reign a year before the death of this book's primary protagonist, Khaqani. Kantorowicz insists throughout his work that 'the KING's TWO BODIES is an offshoot of Christian theological thought and consequently stands as a landmark of Christian political theology' (*TKTB*, 506). As we will see, many Persian prison poems partake of a broadly medieval dualistic anthropology of the body, which divides it into an earthly and a spiritual half. Yet, whereas Kantorowicz emphasises sacralised notions of medieval kingship, this book considers how the prison poem elevated the status of poets – rather than sovereigns – through its corporeal poetics. This book shows how Persian prison poets use the materiality of the prison to promulgate a dualism of the body that realigned earthly and spiritual realms in favour of poetry. This division was political–theological in the sense proposed by political theorist Carl Schmitt, who famously claimed that 'all significant concepts of the modern theory of the state are secularised theological concepts'.[13] Schmitt was drawing on a long-standing tradition of political reflection on the state and its relation to the creaturely realm, which begins with the Roman antiquarian Varro, if not earlier, is further developed by Augustine, and extends to Spinoza and beyond. Political theology has a related yet parallel trajectory within the Islamo-Persian tradition.[14]

This book uses twentieth-century insights concerning the synchrony of the sovereign and the sacred to elucidate a world that brought the poet into conflict with the sovereign. While a study of the medieval poet's body may appear at first glance to mark a radical departure from the theory of the king's two bodies, the example of Dante, discussed below, shows its relevance. As Kantorowicz recognised, the thesis of the king's two bodies involves a specific vision of the body generally. In the Islamo-Persian context, the poet's body is bifurcated by the closely intertwined institutions of poetry and kingship. The prominent place of poetry in the twelfth-century Persianate world, and above all in the Persian prison poem, a literary genre that records the emergence of the poet as a newly dissident subject, contesting abuses of power by the sultan and the suppression of dissent, gives new meaning to this division of bodies. In the prison poem, political theory was channelled into poetry. In the process of generating a corporeal poetics from the poet's body, the Persian prison poem developed a unique conception of the body as a nexus of the conflict between worldly and poetic power. It thereby introduced a new element into the traditional Islamic duality between faith-based authority (*din*) and earthly sovereignty (*dawlat*).

This book traces this transformation in two stages. First, in the poetry of Ghaznavid-era poets such as Masʿud Saʿd, who infused his depictions of the poet's suffering body with a lyric dimension. Masʿud Saʿd used the imagery and experience conferred by his eighteen years of imprisonment to develop the *shikwa* (complaint) tradition exemplified by earlier Persian poets such as Rudaki and Nasir Khusraw, who wrote in non-carceral contexts and at greater physical removes from the court. The second stage in the prison poem's corporeal poetics transpired in the Caucasus, most notably in the poetry of Khaqani, the pre-eminent master of the prison poem genre. Taken together, these two stages in the prison poem's evolution produced a corporeal poetics that filtered Christian anthropology through an Islamic and Persianate lens to sacralise the body of the suffering and persecuted poet.

Before delineating the stages of Persian prison poetry's transformation of the poet's body through the experience of imprisonment across the twelfth century, a closer examination of the role of global medieval and early modern poetry in mapping the body of the poet onto that of the sovereign is in order. One achievement of Kantorowicz's account of medieval political theology is to have made Dante's intervention in world literature foundational to political theology. This book attempts a similar feat with regard to the twelfth-century Persian prison poem.

Making the Poet Sovereign

Many critics have remarked on Kantorowicz's unique use of literature to elucidate political history. 'Kantorowicz unmasked the intellectuals in the institutions', argues Schiller, by exposing their subservience to the rulers of the age, while vindicating the poets.[15] Similarly attesting to the unique role allotted to poets in Kantorowicz's political theology, Kahn argues that 'Kantorowicz's reading of Shakespeare and Dante' reveals literature's 'capacity for ideological critique and for enabling fictions of human community'.[16] According to this hermeneutic tradition arising from *The King's Two Bodies*, literary texts generate political form.

Kantorowicz's prooftexts are poems, along with legal documents. Yet, within this hermeneutic tradition, the specific work of poetry in generating political theology remains by and large unaccounted for. In an article published four years after his famed monograph, Kantorowicz himself outlined how 'the offices of *poet* and, by transference, of painter and artist at large' are strengthened by the concept of the pope's prerogative (*plenitudo potestatis*).[17] In his reading of Dante, Kantorowicz makes this point directly. It was Dante who, according to Kantorowicz, 'visualize[d] the very tension of the "Two Bodies" in man himself', and made *humanitas* 'the sovereign of *homo*' (*TKTB*, 495). In bringing into focus the high valuation placed on poetry within medieval Persianate society, I develop a political-theological framework for understanding poetry as a means of political critique and as a tool of social transformation in the Persianate world and beyond.

Dante's political poetics mark a pivotal moment in global medieval literature: he is the poet who introduced 'an image of kingship which was merely human and of which MAN, pure and simple, was the center and standard – MAN, to be sure, in all his relations to God and universe, to law, society, and city, to nature, knowledge, and faith' (*TKTB*, 451). Writing in a similar vein three decades earlier, the German philologist Erich Auerbach described Dante as a 'poet of the earthly world', for whom eternity and immanence were inextricably intertwined.[18] By uniting the polarities of perpetuity and contingency, the poet's body reconfigures the political-theological realm. Dante's centring of kingship on the body also reconfigured the role of the poet. In his 1961 article, Kantorowicz also locates the beginnings of the equation between 'poet and emperor or king – that is, of the poet and the highest office representing sovereignty' in Dante.[19] This book examines this equivalence as it unfolded a century earlier, in the Persian prison poem. I show how this genre brought pre-Islamic Persian discourses of sovereignty into conversation with Arabo-Persian concepts of poetic inspiration to generate political agency for a newly sovereign subject.

Let us dwell a bit longer on Dante's transformation of the poet's social role, in order to better grasp the specificity of the two bodies paradigm. In the *Inferno*, Dante beholds Homer with sword in hand, and declares: 'He is Homer, sovereign poet [*quelli è Omero poeta sovrano*].'[20] Midway through the poet's journey, in *Purgatorio*, Dante offers an extended account of the transference in the locus of sovereignty from the ruler to the poet. The poet's investiture takes place through a formal ritual. Virgil crowns Dante and pronounces the famous words: 'I crown and mitre you over yourself' (*Purgatorio*, 27:142). As with medieval kings such as Frederick, whose methods of governance borrowed heavily from his Norman and Roman predecessors, and the Shirvanshahs of the Persianate Caucasus, who imitated pre-Islamic Persian kings in their names and regalia, Dante's ascent to power is conferred by the authority of antiquity.[21] As a result of the Virgilian '*translatio* of authority', Dante evolves from a mere personage (*personaggio*) to a poet.[22] Meanwhile, the idea of the poet acquires new – or rather, old – meaning. Finally, in *Paradiso*, the sovereign and the poet are equated when Apollo's laurel is declared the reward of 'a Caesar or a poet' (*Paradiso* 1.29).[23]

Further insight into the poet's negotiation of contingency and perpetuity is found in Hegel's characterisation of Dante's epic in his *Aesthetics* (1835). 'Here, in the face of the absolute grandeur of the ultimate end and aim of all things, everything individual and particular in human interests and aims vanishes,' writes Hegel, 'yet there stands there, completely epically, everything otherwise most fleeting and transient in the living world, fathomed objectively in its inmost being, judged in its worth or worthlessness by the supreme Concept, i.e. by God.'[24] Hegel's reading is not without flaws. Notably, it omits Dante's focus on the contingency of the poet's body. This Hegelian mode of literary criticism inaugurated a tradition of reading Dante as a poet of pure immutability which reached its fulfilment in philosopher Benedetto Croce's 1921 study.[25] These limits notwithstanding, Hegel's reading of Dante marks a turning point in the political theology of the poet's body.

Readers prior to Kantorowicz had recognised the significance of the poet's investiture in the *Divine Comedy*. But Kantorowicz's reading of Dante situated this medieval poet within a political theology cognate to the Persian prison poem. Based on Dante's narration of his acquisition of kingly authority, Kantorowicz reasons: 'philosophically speaking, the king as King, or as Crown, is full actuality – perpetually and at any moment – whereas the individual body natural is mere potentiality' (*TKTB*, 495). Kantorowicz adds that this formulation offers 'the philosophical explanation for other features of the king as King: that he never dies; that he is free from the imbecility of infancy and the defects of old age; that he cannot sin or do wrong' (495). The king, argues Kantorowicz, is the 'perpetual actualization of all royal potencies'; he is manifested 'sometimes in terms of the two-natured God, sometimes in the sense of Justice and Law, and sometimes on the basis of People and Polity'. His body is the essence of sovereignty.

This dual-bodied identity is not exclusive to the king. Rather, it functions as an allegory of a generalised and universal human body. In his final gloss on Dante's coronation as a poet, Kantorowicz recognises the inadequacy of purely political readings of the king's two bodies which factor out the poet's mediation. 'It remained, however, to the poet,' Kantorowicz concludes, 'to visualize the very tension of the "Two Bodies" in man himself, to make *humanitas* . . . the sovereign of *homo*, and to find for all those intricate cross-relations and interrelations the most complex, terse, and simple, because most human, formula: "I crown and mitre you over yourself"' (495).

A poet who acquires a second body attains not only to immortality but also to what Kantorowicz calls 'full actuality'. The 'full actuality' of kings lies at the foundation of the divine right of governance. And yet it is also the case that 'mere potentiality' enables the poet to speak through their bodies and to write poems that acquire their unique posterities. For Dante, as for all the poets discussed in this book, the capacity to write poetry intersects directly with the duties and responsibilities of governance. The poet is by nature a political being, and the prison poem is among the poet's most effective instruments of political critique. While poetry's political force is widely registered throughout world literature, this book shows how Persian prison poetry crafted a body for the poet from the rhetoric of sovereignty. In order to savour this unique distinction of Persian poetics, we must first reckon with some of the Persian poetic texts about the body that preceded the advent of the Persian prison poem.

Persian Poets' Bodies before the Prison Poem

Centuries before Dante brought the poet's body into alignment with that of the sovereign, Persian poets crafted a corporeal poetics that was also a political theology. The earliest poems written in New Persian, the literary language that followed the Islamic conquest of Central Asia, initiated the work of memorialising the poet's suffering body. Often such poems took the form of *hasb-i hal* (literally 'account of a condition'), which can refer to any kind of autobiographical writing in verse.[26] The Central Asian poet Rudaki (859–941) is distinctive among early Persian poets for his exploration of the poet's self through the poet's ageing body. As he declares in a famous *qasida* (ode) lamenting his physical decay:

> My teeth are all worn down and falling out.
> They weren't just teeth, they were as bright light,
> They were silvery white, coral and pearls,
> bright as raindrops or as the morning star.
> None remained of them all, worn down and fallen.
> How ominous it was! It was indeed Saturn's omen.

مرا بسود و فرو ریخت هر چه دندان بود
نبود دندان لا بل چراغ تابان بود
سپید سیم زده بود و در و مرجان بود
ستارهٔ سحری بود و قطره باران بود
یکی نماند کنون زآن همه بسود و بریخت
چه نحس بود! همانا که نحس کیوان بود [27]

Having lamented the decay of his body, the poet waxes nostalgic for his youth, referring to himself in the third person:

Gone are the days when his skin was silken-soft.
Gone are the days when his hair was raven-dark.
Beauty was once his dear guest and friend:
A dear guest who'll never come back when gone.

شد آن زمانه که رویش به سان دیبا بود
شد آن زمانه که مویش به سان قطران بود
چنان که خوبی مهمان و دوست بود عزیز
بشد که باز نیامد عزیز مهمان بود

Its pathos notwithstanding, in this early Persian poem, the poet's lament is not explicitly political. In the above verses, the poet is simply a mortal creature like all others. Unlike later Persian prison poems, his death does not intimate a crisis of governance.

From his exile in the Pamir mountains of Badakhshan, Nasir Khusraw located his ageing body within the genre of complaint:

Pearls dropped down round this black silk,
hanging with the hands of the unfaithful world from my two cheeks.
Everyone rejoices over pearls and silk except me,
whose silky cheeks are adorned with pearls.
I cry on the narcissus that opens on my face:
the narcissus grows when it's watered.

فرو بارید مروارید گرد این سیه دیبا
که بر دو عارض من بست دست بی وفا عالم
به مروارید و دیبا شاد باشد هر کسی جز من
که دیبای بنا گوشم به مروارید شد معلم
بگریم من بر این نرگس که بر عارض پدید آمد
مرا، زیرا که بفزاید چو نرگس را بیاید نم [28]

These verses cultivate a passive corporeal poetics. The poet compares the pearls on his clothing to the tears rolling down his cheeks. Although the poet speaking here is miserable, he is no more of a dissident than was Rudaki. Viewed from the vantage point of the prison poem, what is most striking in these early poems is the absence of political consciousness.

More obviously relevant to the Christological anthropology of the prison poem, Masʿud Saʿd of Lahore, writing from a South Asian periphery of the Ghaznavid empire, indirectly compares his body to that of the crucified Jesus through an elaborate metaphor that revolves around his pen. First describing his pen as 'Jesus son of Mary', he then rehearses the biography of Jesus, the Christian saviour and Islamic prophet, who, in his words, 'had a mother but no father'. From there, we learn how the pen conducts itself like Jesus:

[The pen] rejuvenates every dead meaning –
behold its wondrous power and success!
How amazing! look how the pen
forms a cross with the fingers.

همه معنی مرده زنده کند
عجب قدرت و کامگاری نگر
شگفتی نگه کن که کلکش همی
چلیپا نماید به انگشت بر [29] (1:228)

Like Jesus, the pen is crucified:

Like Jesus they mean to kill it.
Every hour, they lop off its head.
But when it is crucified on the fingers,
its position and rank are exalted.
It reaches that lofty heaven:
there is no path for the soul beyond that.

چو عیسی به کشتنش دارند قصد
که هر ساعت او را ببرند سر
و لیکن چو بر دار انگشت شد
فزون گرددش قدر و جاه و خطر
بر آن آسمان بزرگی شود
که ره نیست جان را ازین پیشتر (1:228)

Another poem by Masʿud Saʿd forcefully illustrates the poet's obsession with his body, as well as his isolation from his prison cell:

My body is weak: my heart has been disabled.
The one who feeds on sorrow will find his heart disabled.

I sleep with insomnia. Separation lives with me.
They do not depart even for a moment from my eyes or body.

زانم ضعیف تن که دلم ناتوان شدست
دل ناتوان شود کش از انده بود غذا
هم خوابه ام سهر شد و هم خانه ام فراق
یک لحظه نیستند ز چشم و تنم جدا (1:31)

Such verses involve the poet projecting an image of his subjective self. The impersonal voice of the traditional panegyric is rejected, even though such lamentations can also be found within the panegyric. Yet, although they mark a new trend within the Persian tradition, none of these verses by Masʿud Saʿd claim prophetic gifts for the poet. Nor do they insert the poet's body into the political realm. Even when Nasir Khusraw uses prison metaphors in his verse, as in the following example, his words lack a political charge:

O God! Now that all people are drunk and in love,
why do I remain in my prison cell?

گر بیدل و مست خلق شد یا رب
چون است که ماندهام به زندان من [30]

Such relatively tepid complaint should be compared to the firebrand voice of a prison poet like Khaqani, writing a century later:

In the clime of speech, there's no king better than I.
To govern the kingdom of speech befits only me.

نیست اقلیم سخن را بهتر از من پادشا
در جهان ملک سخن راندن مسلم شد مرا [31]

Just as salient as these poetic insistences on the poet's sovereignty are the minute associations, in other poems by Khaqani, between the poet and Jesus. One particularly striking comparison (discussed in the next section) links the poet's body to Mary's folded thread in one verse and then to Jesus' needle in the next verse.

Such shifts in the poet's voice correlate with broader political transformations that were shaping Persianate conceptions of kingship during these centuries. The succession crisis that accompanied the decline of the caliphate yielded to a series of regional sultanates, until its total collapse in 1258 with the Mongol invasion. This development coincided with a third phase in the Persian prison poem, that witnessed its circulation across South Asia, often in poems that appear to have been modelled on the prison poems of Khaqani. One striking case is the thirteenth-century Indian poet ʿAmid al-Din Lumaki, who held the position of chief accountant (*mushrif al-mamalik*) under Sultan Nasir al-Din Muhammad of Delhi.[32] ʿAmid al-Din is the author of two prison poems which use many of the same tropes used a few decades earlier by Khaqani. In this prison poem, he begins by imagining himself as different kinds of birds. He then shifts immediately to the prison context, and expatiates on his eloquence and unjust imprisonment in terms that recall the above-cited verse by Khaqani.

> I am an eloquent parrot, not a goshawk
> The parrot's leg has been trapped by mistake.
> Please do not keep me waiting for release
> The chain has turned my blood into water from waiting.
> The fame of my eloquence crosses from west to east.
> Is it just to keep this famed man in chains?

من طوطی سخنورم آخر نه جره باز
بر پای طوطیان غلط آمد شکار بند
چندین مدارم از پی تخلیص منتظر
خونم چو آب کرد در این انتظاربند
نامم ز شرق و غرب گذشت از سخنوری
واجب کند بپای چنین نامدار بند؟ [33]

While the avian tropes used here are familiar from many prison poems, the last verse, expressive of the poet's conviction concerning his literary excellence, is particularly expressive of prison poem poetics.

Another prison poem by the same poet offers an even more densely intertextual engagement with the genre's tropes and metaphors. Although it is not explicitly Christological in its orientation, the poem uses imagery also found in Khaqani's influential Christian Qasida (discussed in Chapter 5). For example, the hemistich 'I'm like a thread: my place is in the needle's eye', closely intersects with Khaqani's parallel verse. Both verses allude to the thread of Mary, who is depicted as a spinner of purple thread in Byzantine iconography, and the needle of Jesus.[34] Poems like these belong to a long history of poetic engagement with threads, needles, chains and belts in prison poem poetics.

The lurking hawk of God's wrath pawed me.
That's why I'm nestled in a corner like a dove
They led me to this windowless tower but
I have dug seven ways out with my ambition.
A tower like my heart, even smaller than my heart.
I'm like a thread: my place is in the needle's eye.
I deserve the golden throne of the sun.
Now I'm seated on an iron seat.
The seven-headed serpent hid itself in fear of the
double-headed snake I have concealed in my robe.
I'm offered a prison like Bijan's in the well of injustice,
although I've never seen Manijeh or committed the crime of Bijan.

شاهباز غیرت حق از کمین زد پنجه‌ای
زان کبوتروار در یک گوشه مسکن کرده‌ام
ره درین یک برج بی‌روزن نمودندم ولی
من بهمت ره برون از هفت روزن کرده‌ام
برجی آنگه چون دلم بل کز دل من تنگ‌تر
رشته‌ام، گویی مکان در چشم سوزن کرده‌ام
مسند خورشید زرین تخت می‌زیبد مرا
حال را من تکیه بر کرسی آهن کرده‌ام
در گریبان سر فرو برد اژدهای هفت سر
تا من این مار دو سر در زیر دامن کرده‌ام
بند بیژن میکنندم عرض در چاه ستم
نی منیژه دیدم و نی جرم بیژن کرده ام [35]

Alongside the allusions to the Christian Qasida and the imagery of threads, chains, belts and needles, we find here a series of avian allusions, which also characterise the prison poem (as established in Chapter 4). Also, as in many prison poems, there is a special place for serpents (*azhdaha*, also translated as 'dragon'). For example, Masʿud Saʿd writes in one of his prison poems:

Although goodness guided me like a staff,
the serpent of the skies became a serpent for my soul.
Deceit and magic attacked me and coiled
around my mind and talent like a serpent.

گشت اژدهای جان من این اژدهای چرخ
ورچه صلاح رهبر من بود چون عصا
بر من نهاد روی و فرو برد سربه سر
نیرنگ و سحر خاطر و طبعم چو اژدها (1:22)

Yet another feature of prison poetry's repertoire on display in Lumaki's poem is the comparison between the poet and Bijan, an Iranian knight immortalised by Ferdowsi in the *Shahnama.* Bijan falls in love with Manijeh, the daughter of Afrasiab, the king of Turan, who is Iran's greatest enemy. When Afrasiab learns of the romantic liaison between his daughter and a member of an enemy people, he orders that Bijan be thrown into a well. Manijeh sits by the edge of this well, lamenting her fate. The image of Bijan trapped in a well (see Figures I.1 and I.2, as well as the cover of this book) is often used to evoke the condition of the imprisoned poet in Persian prison poems.

Early laments against the tyranny of the age (*jawr-i zamaneh*) recur across the centuries in the works of Persian prison poets. A quatrain (*ruba'i*) composed from prison by the Safavid poet Khan Ahmad Gilani uses the 'tyranny of the age' in a provocative pun on the name of his prison, Qahqaheh. The name Qahqaheh happens to coincide with the verb to laugh (*qahqaheh zadan*). Thus, the final hemistich of his quatrain lends itself to two legitimate yet different translations. One version would read:

I cry from the topsy turvy world.
Observe how I cry from the tyranny of the age.
With my back bent like a decanter night and day.
I am in Qahqaheh but I weep blood.

از گردش چرخ واژگون می گریم
از جور زمانه بین که چون می گریم
با قد خمیده چون صراحی شب و روز
در قهقهه ام ولیک خون میگریم [36]

In the above verse, *qahqaheh* signifies both the name of the poet's prison and the act of laughing. This is a rare case of a prison poem which elicited a poetic response from the object of its critique. An alternate translation of the final hemistich of Gilani's verses could read 'in my laughter, I cry blood'. In responding to the poem, Khan Ahmad Gilani's jailer and ruler, Shah Isma'il (r. 1501–1524), himself a renowned poet, demonstrates that rulers had also internalised the political valences of the prison poem:

> You used to laugh [at the government].
> You thought it would last only a hundred months.
> Cry today in Qahqaheh [prison].
> That laughter [*qahqaheh*] put you in this Qahqaheh [prison].

آن روز که کارت همگی قهقهه بود
با رای تو رای سلطنت صد مهه بود
امروز درین قهقهه با گریه بساز
کان قهقهه را نتیجه این قهقهه بود

As this exchange attests, the prison poem genre was created by poet and rulers, who were also jailers and patrons. The re-signifying process through which literary discourse reconstitutes the world was set in motion by certain features of Persian poetics, specifically the ability of literary signs to function according to the principle that the least discernible meaning is the dominant poetic meaning. In the case of this poetic exchange, the political content of the prison poem genre was laid bare by puns and double entendre (known in Persian as *iham*).

Khaqani Shirvani is the main force behind the transformation of the prison poem into a political-theological genre. His transformation of the prison poem into a vehicle of political and prophetic critique is narrated in this book in a degree of detail that it has not received before in literary history, even in Persian. Like Dante, Khaqani's prison poems mark a turning point in world literature. New political themes were introduced through Khaqani's verse, which in turn extended poetry's political relevance.

The next six chapters document these successive transformations of the prison poem. They detail how this genre developed the tension between the poet's two bodies – one material and imprisoned, imbued with mortality, and the second spiritual and endowed with a unique capacity to critique the sultan's injustice amid his imprisonment. Before embarking on this narrative, I will briefly consider the shared political-theological currents that united medieval Islamic and Christian worlds. In the process, they laid the groundwork for the Persian prison poem.

Christology and Persian Political Theology

Khaqani was born in 1121, the year of Masʿud Saʿd's death, in Shirvan, a region of the Caucasus near Georgia and not far from Daghestan, to a mother who had converted from Nestorian Christianity to Islam. The Caucasus of Khaqani's birth is located at the crossroads of multiple civilisations and has long served as a cradle for ancient religions, including Christianity and Zoroastrianism.[37] The prison poems of Khaqani's predecessor Masʿud Saʿd use Christian imagery, as noted above, but Khaqani's links to Christianity were deeper than those of any other Persian poet during this period. I will return to the Christian Qasida in Chapter 5, but for now let us dwell on the poet's comparison of his body to Mary's thread:

> My body is folded like Mary's thread.
> My heart is one like the Jesus' needle.
> I am shackled with ropes in this cell,
> as Jesus was pinned down by a needle.

تنم چون رشتهٔ مریم دوتا است
دلم چون سوزن عیساست یکتا
من اینجا پای‌بند رشته ماندم
چو عیسی پای‌بند سوزن آنجا [38]

The poet's body is bent in two (*duta*) like the thread of Jesus' mother Mary, known in the Christian Apocrypha for her skill as a seamstress. Yet his soul remains as whole (*yekta*) as Jesus. As explained in the nineteenth-century Indo-Persian dictionary *Succourer of Language* (*Ghiyath al-Lughat*), the thinness of Mary's thread (*rishteyeh Maryam*) was indicative of her skill as a seamstress; her threads were 'so thin that that they could be seen only when folded [*duta*]'.[39] This dictionary comes from a later period, but both sources use the same terminology to describe Mary's thread: *duta*, which literally means 'folded', and is derived from the word for two (*du*). This etymology underscores the binary logic that structures the poem, and specifically its antithesis between one and two, the straight and bent, the one who resists and the one who submits. The same contrast between the poet standing straight and hunched over occurs later in the poem (v. 20), with a multilingual (Persian and Arabic) pun on the words for 'blame' and 'I submit' that alludes to the letters that comprise these words:

> I am standing before and behind the blame (طعن)
> in such a way that alifs of 'I submit' (اطعنا) have stood.

چنان استاده‌ام پیش و پس طعن
که استادست الف‌های اطعن

Here too there is an antithesis between a body that is bent and a body that stands straight, as between a body that rebels and a body that submits.

This Christian theme was continued two centuries later by the Timurid poet Barandaq Khujandi (d. 1431) in another poem explicitly modelled on Khaqani's Christian Qasida, which also reproduces the avian imagery of other prison poems:

> I'm shedding the blood of my heart from my eyes,
> as clear as as the Holy Spirit's breath.
> My tongue is a sweet-talking parrot
> that eloquently intones the oneness of God.

مرا خون دل از دیده روانست
مصفا چون دم روح معلا
زبانم طوطی شکرفشانست
که در تکرار توحیدست گویا [40]

As we have seen from Masʿud Saʿd's earlier poem comparing the imprisoned poet to Jesus, the prison poem's Christology did not begin with Khaqani. But Khaqani developed it in a new direction, towards a conception of the poet-as-prophet. He thereby tapped into the hitherto untapped potential of Christ's immortal body for prison poetry. The comparison of the imprisoned poet to Jesus' secular body preceded Khaqani, but the habit of comparing Christ's immortal body to the imprisoned poet belongs to him. What is of interest from the vantage point of prison poem poetics is less Khaqani's erudition than the way in which he used Christian anthropology – in particular its understanding of the hypostatic body of Jesus Christ – to develop a political theology based on the tension between the poet's two bodies. Anticipating Dante, Khaqani laid bare his understanding of the politics of poetry and the poetry of politics in his prison poetics. When he used his body to memorialise the trope of incarceration, the contingent realm of earthly power and the spiritual realm of transcendent authority were brought into a new alliance that was then fortified across the centuries by the prison poem genre.

In medieval European and classical Persian poetry alike, the dualistic concept of the body was informed by Christian theology. Specifically relevant to both contexts is the long history of the debate, much of which transpired centuries earlier in nearby Constantinople (modern Istanbul), around which proportion of the body of Jesus Christ was divine and which proportion was mortal, and how to reconcile the apparent antinomy between these two dimensions of his sacred body. These conflicts were at the heart of the Nestorian Christian tradition that inspired the pioneer of the prison poem, Khaqani. Equally, they provided the conceptual framework for the political theology of medieval Europe, from the concept of the divine right of kings in the early Middle Ages to early modern state sovereignty. As Kantorowicz notes, we 'need only replace the strange image of the Two Bodies by the more customary theological term of the Two Natures [of Christ]' in order to clarify how medieval political speech and legal discourse 'derived its tenor in the last analysis from theological diction' (*TKTB*, 16). Persian political theory similarly helped to structure medieval Persian poetics, as documented in Chapter 6.

Analogously to Dante's creative refashioning of Christian theology and the theory of sovereignty to elevate poetry, the prison poetry of Khaqani manifests a crypto-theological theme: it transfers the authority of a prophet, Jesus, onto the poet. There are, of course, notable differences. Whereas in medieval Europe, Christological links were inevitable, Khaqani's use of Christian tropes is surprising and unexpected. Yet, as I argue in subsequent chapters, these tropes are central to his political theology, as well as to his literary vision, which emphasises the materiality of the verbal sign in its pursuit of corporeal poetics (see especially Chapters 4 and 5). Arguably, Jesus' entirely human – while still prophetic – status within Islam made the tropes associated with his divinity more readily available to poets for creative appropriation. Statements and images that would have been seen as blasphemous within medieval Europe could be poetically generative in the Islamic world.

Just as medieval European poets such as Dante turned to the authority of classical antiquity in order to bolster their claims for the sovereignty of the poet, poets from the Islamic world enjoyed greater poetic licence with regard to the foundational tropes of Christian theology than they had when working exclusively within an Islamic tradition. Basing his case for the poet's sovereignty on pre-Christian poets such as Homer and Virgil enabled Dante to evade accusations of blasphemy, as well as competition with Christian rulers and Catholic popes. Similarly, basing his case for the poet's sovereignty on Christian theology and anthropology enabled Khaqani to develop a prison poetics – and a poetic challenge to earthly sovereignty – centred on the imprisoned poet's body.

The generality of the king's two bodies should not come as a surprise, for the medieval European concept is deeply rooted in both Christian and Old Testament political theology, much of which was shared with the Islamic world. The anonymous Norman author of a treatise in defence of a Catholic conception of kingship at the turn of the twelfth century could have been speaking for his Persian contemporaries when he wrote of his king that:

> We thus have to recognise a twin person, one descending from nature, the other from grace . . . One through which, by the condition of nature, he conformed with other men: another through which, by the eminence of [his] deification and by the power of the sacrament [of consecration], he excelled all others. Concerning one personality, he was, by nature, an individual man: concerning his other personality, he was, by grace, a Christus, that is, a God-man.[41]

At the same time, the path towards establishing the sacrality of the king's body within medieval Europe diverged from that followed in the Islamic world. But the conclusion, and the political agenda underwriting it, was the same: medieval political theorists had to find a way of demonstrating how a mortal creature could legitimately be endowed with the authority to rule over everyone in his domain. This could be done only by acknowledging his mortality, on the one hand, and by insisting on his immortality – his divine mandate – on the another. For the anonymous Norman author quoted above, as for many Muslim political theorists, certain kings of the Old Testament (such as David and Solomon) were prefigurations of medieval rulers. While the political legitimacy of these rulers derived from ancient religious precedent, the shift towards secular notions of kingship required a new political theology. The Persian prison poem is among the most eloquent testimonies in world literature to what happened to kingship when the sovereign's body was exposed as mortal and poetry's impermeability to space and time was thereby demonstrated.

In their conceptualisations of the poet's two bodies, both medieval European and Persian engagements with Christian imagery provided crucial theological precedents for new materialist accounts of the literary imagination and specifically its bridging of immanence and contingency. Unmoored from its medieval European and Persian origins, the poet's two bodies reverberate across world literature, all the way to late twentieth-century American poetics. While he was a student of Kantorowicz, American poet Robert Duncan (d. 1988) discovered 'the prophetical dissidence in the position taken by the poet' by reflecting on the king's two bodies in medieval literature.[42] This book develops the duality that inspired Duncan and countless other modern poets by examining poems from a tradition outside Europe, which was nonetheless impacted by Christian concepts of the body.

As in my prior work, the disciplinary orientation through which I pursue this book's agenda departs from established paradigms.[43] In part, this is a study of a medieval literary genre that intervenes in contemporary literary theory. My material is densely historical, but it is not treated in ways that most historians might expect. My focus throughout is on prison poems as texts, more than on their social and historical contexts. At the same time, my readings of these texts call for in-depth engagement with their historical, cultural and political milieus, beyond what would typically be encountered in a work of contemporary literary theory. These chapters abound in dense empirical detail, which is however marshalled towards the non-historical goals of literary exegesis and political critique. In contrast to Kantorowicz's study (although in the spirit of its subtitle, 'a study in medieval political theology') *The Persian Prison Poem* is not intended as a work of history, literary or otherwise. Rather, I offer a political theology of a literary genre, and tie the shifts I have observed in the trajectory of this genre over the course of the eastern Islamic world's long twelfth century to changes in the structures of medieval sovereignty.

While a comparative approach may frustrate readers in search of more conventional literary historiography, this approach can also benefit our understanding of the Persian prison poem. As this book shows, Persian prison poems were used in many different social contexts and for varying political and aesthetic ends. Numerous studies have shown that imprisonment was common in the medieval Persianate world, yet first-hand accounts of imprisonment are strikingly absent.[44] Medieval manuscripts are notably lacking in visual renderings of prisons, fortresses and similar fortifications from this period, perhaps because the art of this period was uninterested in documenting historical reality. Aside from a few representations of Bijan stuck in a well in illustrations of Ferdowsi's *Shahnama* (Figures I.1 and I.2), I have been unable to locate any extant rendering of a medieval prison in Persian visual art. Similarly, while historical chronicles record many prison sentences for rebellious poets, insubordinate subjects and unlucky rulers, efforts to document the psychic impact of incarceration in prose are few and far between.

In order to learn about the medieval experience of imprisonment, we must turn to the prison poem. A deep engagement with this genre will inevitably frustrate the historian, for prison poems are strikingly uninterested in documenting historical reality. In order to understand the work these texts do in the world, we must be attuned to their social contexts, while also recognising the many ways in which these texts break free from the chains of realistic representation. While the oppression described in their poems was real, prison poets also exaggerated their suffering and sometimes invented their imprisonment, particularly as the genre became more sophisticated, more intertextual and more capable of reflecting on itself. Sometimes, exaggeration was among prison poets' aesthetic goals. It was through this aestheticising process that the prison poem genre made poetry political. Far from regarding poets' departures from the historical record as flaws, this divergence from history – and indeed from empirical experience – marks the genre's beginnings. My relationship to the prison poem is not that of an historian seeking

Figure I.1 Rostam rescues Bijan from the well. Ferdowsi, *Shahnama* (Isfahan, 1628). British Library, MS Add. 27258, fol. 257v.

Figure I.2 Rostam rescues Bijan from the well; Arthur M. Sackler Gallery. S1986.267 (detail). Ferdowsi, *Shahnama*.

a clear depiction of an empirical world. Rather, it is that of a lover, translator and creator of poetry, who seeks to shed light on the political impact of poems written from prison on the world outside the prison cell.[45]

How to Read this Book

Establishing the political role of poetry in the world requires following a circuitous path. It means beginning with relatively technical issues in the classification of genre, even when the appeal of the prison poem reaches well beyond genre theory. Scholars without a specific interest in literary genres may wish to skip ahead to the historical development of the genre, discussed in Chapters 2 and 3, and its politics, explored in Chapters 4–6. Readers who are drawn to the politics of prison writing should be aware that the political dimensions of the genre are not fully revealed until Chapters 4 and 5, as the accumulated weight of poets' oppression explodes into poems that advance political claims that had never before been articulated in Persian poetry. In order to grasp the development of the prison poem's political idiom, it is necessary to begin with less obviously political lyric poems, and to trace the emergence of the poet's subjectivity across these early works. Readers less interested in poetry's aesthetic dimensions may choose to orient their reading accordingly. Having offered some guidance regarding how to read this book, I will conclude with an overview of its contents.

Over the course of the six chapters that follow, the Persian prison poem is revealed as an early Persian prototype for the 'prophetic dissidence' Kantorowicz discovered in Dante, and from a domain of world literature in which such forms of resistance are rarely sought. Chapter 1 introduces the 'body' of the poem as a genre in three dimensions: formal, topical and discursive. I show how the prison poem is distinctive within the classical Persian literary system: it operates at all three dimensions of genre, not only at the level of form. I further show how, by introducing a new corporeal poetics through the prism of genre, the prison poem uniquely reveals literature's role in constituting and reconstituting sovereignty.

Chapter 2 examines the prison poem as a special kind of formal genre. Introducing a neologism, I call this genre, as developed most notably by Mas'ud Sa'd, the lyric ode. I examine the emergence of the lyric ode in relation to the corporeal poetics that developed from the earliest Persian prison poems. As with the poems discussed above by Rudaki and Nasir Khusraw, I document the relatively symbiotic relationship with the sovereign in the earliest prison poems in order to establish, by way of contrast, the political tensions that emerged following the prison poem's migration to the Caucasus a few decades later.

Chapter 3 examines how Persian poets competed with each other through their literary output as they vied for patronage when the prison poem came into fashion in Shirvan, under the aegis of the Shirvanshahs. Khaqani was at the centre of the Caucasus' borderland literary culture, but he was far from the only prison poet in his milieu. The tensions that circulated around him, and related signs of animosity among poets that affected the intellectual atmosphere of literary Shirvan, were rooted in a range of factors: competition for resources and patronage from the Shirvanshahs; multi-confessional tensions among Muslims, Christians and Zoroastrians; transformations in the locus and meaning of sovereignty as an older concept of a sacred caliphate ceded ground to a secular concept of the sultanate; and the increasing authority of the poet that followed from these transformations.

Chapters 3–5 Five discuss the poet who is the genre's leading voice and the protagonist of this book: Khaqani of Shirvan. Chapter 4 examines the prophetic imagery that recurs frequently in Khaqani's prison poems and considers its implications for the prison poet's doubly-constituted body, as his verse oscillates between contingency and perpetuity. Having discussed Khaqani's use of prophetic tropes and imagery in Chapter 4, my primary prooftext for Chapter 5 is Khaqani's famous Christian Qasida, which has been studied by a range of scholars, but never specifically as the crowning achievement of Persian political theology or of carceral poetics. The Christian Qasida, I argue, shows how the poet's imprisoned body was reshaped by the use of imagery relating to the body of Jesus.

The translation of the prison poet's doubly-constituted body across Islamic, Persian and medieval European contexts and cultures is brought into further relief through an examination of the pre-Islamic sources for twelfth-century Persian political theology in Chapter 6. Alongside its readings of political theory, this chapter also engages with the literary-theoretical texts that shaped the canon of classical Persian poetics and which framed the emergence of the prison poem. This chapter concludes with the dialectic between the prophetic language of prison poetry and the discourse of worldly sovereignty. Persian political and ethical treatises, including by the first critic of the prison poem, Nizami ʿAruzi (referred to in this book simply as ʿAruzi), were the mainstay of this tradition. Bridging contingency and perpetuity like the prison poet's body, these literary-theoretical texts situate prison poem poetics within a philosophical context that also grounds the genre's political theology. Conceptualising this body of work across poetry, literary theory and political theology, and tracing its transmission from South Asia to the Caucasus and beyond, I show how twelfth-century Persian prison poems introduced into world literature a new way of understanding the poet and his incarcerated body. Through this process, the genre revealed a new way of experiencing the politics of poetry.

Notes

1. Ernst H. Kantorowicz, *The King's Two Bodies: A Study in Mediaeval Political Theology* (Princeton, NJ: Princeton University Press, 1957). Future references to this work are given parenthetically and abbreviated as *TKTB*.
2. Victoria Kahn, 'Political Theology and Fiction in *The King's Two Bodies*', *Representations* 106(1) (2009): 77–101 at 79.
3. Here I follow the account in Ralph E. Giesey, 'Ernst H. Kantorowicz: Scholarly Triumphs and Academic Travails in Weimar Germany and the United States', *Leo Baeck Institute Year Book* 30 (1985): 196.
4. Critiques include David Norbrook, 'The Emperor's New Body? Richard II, Ernst Kantorowicz, and the Politics of Shakespeare Criticism', *Textual Practice* 10 (1996): 329–57.
5. David Lee Miller, *The Poem's Two Bodies: The Poetics of the 1590 Faerie Queene* (Princeton, NJ: Princeton University Press, 2014).
6. Kahn, 'Political Theology and Fiction in *The King's Two Bodies*', 77–101.
7. Lorna Hutson, 'Imagining Justice: Kantorowicz and Shakespeare', *Representations* 106(1) (2009): 118–42.
8. Graça Capinha, 'Robert Duncan and the Question of Law: Ernst Kantorowicz and the Poet's Two Bodies', in *Robert Duncan and Denise Levertov: The Poetry of Politics, the Politics of Poetry*, Albert Gelpi and Robert Bertholf (Stanford, CA: Stanford University Press, 2006), 18–31. Kantorowicz's influence on the Berkeley poets is further detailed in Kelly Holt, '"In the Sense of a Lasting Doctrine": Ernst Kantorowicz's historiography and the serial poetics of the

Berkeley Renaissance', PhD dissertation, University of California, Santa Cruz, 2009.

9. Stephanie Elsky, 'Ernst Kantorowicz, Shakespeare, and the Humanities' Two Bodies', *Law, Culture and the Humanities* 13(1) (2017): 6–23.
10. While *ḥabsīyyāt* is the standard term (in plural form), this genre has also been referred to as *zindānāmeh* (from the Persian word for prison, *zindān*) and *surūd-i az zindān* ('songs from prison') in most recent times. Persian prison literature is broader than the specific genre of primarily premodern poetry considered in this book.
11. Nāṣir-i Khusraw, *Dīvān-i ash'ār-i Ḥakīm-i Nāṣir-i Khusraw Qubādiyānī*, eds Mujtabā Mīnovī and Mahdī Muḥaqqiq (Tehran: Mu'assasah-'i Muṭāla'āt-i Islāmī, 1978), 196.
12. Mas'ūd-i Sa'd-i Salmān, *Dīvān-i ash'ār-i Mas'ūd-i Sa'd-i Salmān*, ed. Mahdī Nūriyān (Isfahan: Inteshārāt-i Kamāl, 1985), 1:8 (henceforth cited without notes, in the body of the text).
13. Carl Schmitt, *Political Theology: Four Chapters on the Concept of Sovereignty*, trans. George Schwab (Chicago, IL: University of Chicago Press, 2005), 36.
14. For an approach to the subject focused on modern Islamic thought, see Andrew F. March, *The Caliphate of Man: Popular Sovereignty in Modern Islamic Thought* (Cambridge, MA: Harvard University Press, 2019).
15. Kay E. Schiller, 'Dante and Kantorowicz: Medieval History as Art and Autobiography', *Annali d'Italianistica* 8 (1990): 406.
16. Kahn, 'Political Theology and Fiction in *The King's Two Bodies*', 81.
17. Ernst Kantorowicz, 'The Sovereignty of the Artist: A Note on Legal Maxims and Renaissance Theories of Art', *Essays in Honor of Erwin Panofsky* (New York: New York University Press, 1961), 279. Emphasis added.
18. Erich Auerbach, *Dante als Dichter der irdischen Welt* (Berlin: de Gruyter, 1929).
19. Kantorowicz, 'The Sovereignty of the Artist', 276.
20. Dante, *Divine Comedy*, ed. and trans. Charles Singleton (Princeton, NJ: Princeton University Press, 1980), *Inferno* (4.88). Further citations from the *Commedia* are given parenthetically and refer to this edition, with translations modified.
21. See David Abulafia, 'Kantorowicz and Frederick II', *History* 62(205) (1977): 193–210, for Frederick II's debt to Norman (p. 210) and Roman (p. 206) precedents.
22. Albert Russell Ascoli, *Dante and the Making of a Modern Author* (Cambridge: Cambridge University Press, 2008), 330. For further commentary on this passage, see Singleton, *Divine Comedy*, 2:665.

23. See Kantorowicz, 'The Sovereignty of the Artist', 276.
24. G. W. F. Hegel, *Aesthetics: Lecture on Fine Arts*, trans. T. M. Knox (Oxford: Oxford University Press, 1975), II:1103–4.
25. Benedetto Croce, *La poesia di Dante* (Bari: Laterza, 1921).
26. For further on this genre (also discussed below in Chapter 1), see Daniela Meneghini Correale, *Studies on the Poetry of Anvari* (Venice: Libreria Editrice Cafoscarina, 2006), 80, and Zayn al-ʿĀbidīn Mu'taman, *Shiʿr wa adab-i fārsī* (Tehran: Chāpkhana-i Tābish, 1953/1332), 252–7.
27. *Dīvān-i Rūdakī*, ed. Manūchihr Dānish'pazhūh (Tehran: Tus, 1995), 37. The renderings of Rūdakī are amended from Sassan Tabatabai, *Father of Persian Verse Rudaki and his Poetry* (Leiden: Leiden University Press, 2010), 66.
28. Nāṣir-i Khusraw, *Dīvān-i ashʿār-i Ḥakīm-i Nāṣir-i Khusraw Qubādiyānī*, 80.
29. My translation follows with modifications Sunil Sharma's in his *Persian Poetry at the Indian Frontier* (Delhi: Permanent Black, 2000), 143, who also discusses the poem.
30. Nāṣir-i Khusraw, *Dīvān-i ashʿār-i Ḥakīm-i Nāṣir-i Khusraw Qubādiyānī*, 327.
31. Khāqānī Shirvānī, *Dīvān-i Afẓal al-Dīn Bedīl b. ʿAlī Najjār Khāqānī Shirvānī*, ed. Ziyā' al-Dīn Sajjādī (Tehran: Zuvvār, 1388), 17.
32. For further biographical details on this poet, see Iqtidar Husain Siddiqi, *Perso-Arabic Sources of Information on the Life and Conditions in the Sultanate of Delhi* (New Delhi: Munshiram Manoharlal Publishers, 1992), 65–73. Lumakī is referred to as ʿAmīd Loīkī (or Lamīkī or Lowīkī) Sunamī in South Asian scholarship. *EI*[2] includes an article by I. H. Siddiqui in which the poet is called 'Amīd Tūlakī Sūnāmī'.
33. The Persian text is taken from Nazir Ahmad, 'Amid Loiki: A Seventh Century Poet', *Indo-Iranian Studies*, ed. Fathulla Mujtabi (Delhi: Indo-Iran Society, 1977), 7–8.
34. On Mary's thread, see Maria Evangelatou, 'The Purple Thread of the Flesh: The Theological Connotations of a Narrative Iconographic Element in Byzantine Images of the Annunciation', in Antony Eastmond and Liz James (eds), *From Icon and Word: The Power of Images in Byzantium. Studies Presented to Robin Cormack* (Aldershot: Ashgate., 2003), 269–85.
35. Persian text in Ahmad, 'Amīd Loiki', 7–8.
36. See Reẓā Qūlī Khān, *Majmaʿ al-Fuṣāḥa'*, ed. Maẓāhir Muṣaffā (Tehran: Chāp-i Mūsawī, 1960), 5:3–5, both for Khān Aḥmad Gilānī's poem and for Shāh Ismāʿīl's answer. Qahqaheh was a Safavid prison located in the Karabakh region and known for its horrifying conditions (Ẓafarī, *Ḥabsīyyah*, 21).

37. The cosmopolitan Caucasus is further discussed in Alison Vacca, *Non-Muslim Provinces Under Early Islam: Islamic Rule and Iranian Legitimacy in Armenia and Caucasian Albania* (Cambridge: Cambridge University Press, 2017); Rebecca Ruth Gould, 'The Persianate Cosmology of Historical Inquiry in the Caucasus: 'Abbās Qulī Āghā Bākīkhānuf's Cosmological Cosmopolitanism', *Comparative Literature* 71(3) (2019): 272–97.
38. Khāqānī Shirvānī, *Dīvān*, 24. See Chapter 3 (below) for further analysis.
39. Muḥammad b. Jalal al-Dīn Ghiyāth al-Dīn, *Ghiyāth al-Lughat* (Bombay: n.d., n.p), 139.
40. Cited in *Zindān-nāma-hā-yi Fārsī az qarn-i panjum tā pānzdahum*, eds Muḥammad Riẓā Yūsufī and Ṭāhirah Sayyid Riẓāyī (Qum: Dānishgāh-i Qum, 1391/2012–13), 181.
41. H. Böhmer, *Kirche und Staat in England und in der Normandie im XI. und XII. Jahrhundert. Eine historische Studie* (Leipzig: Dieterich, 1899); cited in *TKTB*, 46 (translation follows Kantorowicz with minor emendations).
42. Capinha, 'Robert Duncan and the Question of Law', 24.
43. In prior work, I have developed a 'literary anthropology' that integrates literary analysis with fieldwork. While that is not precisely my approach here, traces of that methodology can be discerned. For an elaboration of this method, see Rebecca Ruth Gould, *Writers and Rebels: The Literature of Insurgency in the Caucasus* (New Haven, CT: Yale University Press, 2016), 22–9.
44. For the historical work on premodern imprisonment in the Islamic world, see Rebecca Ruth Gould, 'Prisons Before Modernity: Incarceration in the Medieval Indo-Mediterranean', *Al-Masāq: Islam and the Medieval Mediterranean* 24(2) (2012): 179–97. More recently, see Petra Sijpesteijn, 'Policing, Punishing and Prisons in the Early Islamic Egyptian Countryside (640–850 CE)', in Alain Delattre, Marie Legendre and Petra Sijpesteijn (eds), *Authority and Control in the Countryside: From Antiquity to Islam in the Mediterranean and Near East (6th–10th Century)*, (Leiden: Brill, 2018), 547–88. The most important study in English remains Christian Lange, *Justice, Punishment, and the Medieval Muslim Imagination* (Cambridge: Cambridge University Press, 2008).
45. A Pushcart Prize-nominated poem of mine in this tradition is 'Constellations', *Chiron Review* 118 (2020): 48, republished in Rebecca Ruth Gould, *Cityscapes* (Monee, IL: Alien Buddha Press), 9.

1

The Prison Poem and the Politics of Genre

The concept of genre has changed so much over time that some have argued for its irrelevance to the classical literatures of the Islamic world. In contemporary popular culture, genre refers to the commodification of art within pre-established themes and conventions. Broadly, genre converts experience – and everything else that has yet to be shaped by an aesthetic sensibility – into art. It is a tool through which art and literature can be evaluated and contested. Genre is the language through which art – particularly literature – speaks. Just as language homogenises unique ideas into words, genre imposes a generality of discourse onto the unique experience of the artwork. Although scholars of premodern literature have by and large preferred to avoid genre as a category of analysis for fear of anachronism, the trajectory of the prison poem shows that literature as such is inconceivable apart from genre. Genre is therefore the foundation of this book.

But what is genre? The task of defining genre in Persian (or Arabic) terms has only just begun. Admittedly, the genre systems of modern and premodern literature, as well as European and non-European literatures, are worlds apart. Anachronism awaits anyone who breaches these boundaries. The pages that follow court anachronism in certain respects. They compare the incomparable, in the belief that such juxtapositions are a necessary prelude to a post-Eurocentric world literature. Before embarking on this analysis, we would do well to begin with a formulation of Walter Benjamin which, like so many of his statements, reaches well beyond its immediate context: 'a major work either establishes a genre [*Gattung*] or abolishes it. A perfect work does both'.[1]

What did Benjamin mean? He later provided a further gloss on this comment in his commentary on Proust: 'All great works of literature establish a genre or dissolve one.'[2] For Benjamin, genre is the most important tool at the artists' disposal and the measure by which a work of art can ultimately be evaluated. This evaluation should be made not according to how a literary work conforms to a genre, but rather with respect to how it diverges from and transforms it. Genre imposes constraints on the work of art, and the path through these constraints is the path towards liberation. We will find that the prison poem has a particular affinity for transgressing established genre norms. The rigid application of Eurocentric genre paradigms can certainly do more harm than good. Yet, given that all comparative inquiries depend on taxonomies, and literary forms such as prison poetry can be understood only within the framework of a concept of genre, the question is not: do we speak in terms of genres, but in terms of what genres do we speak and what are those genres' terms?

Literature cannot be conceived without a theory of genre, which, simply put, is a taxonomy of literature's component parts. The task of reshaping this rubric of literary analysis in terms adequate to classical Persian poetics and the specific genre of the prison poem is the challenge faced in this book. One thing that will need to be done is to replace the long-standing division of all poetry into lyric, epic and drama with a genre system grounded in the specificities of Perso-Arabic poetics.[3] Given the nascent state of the inquiry into classical Persian genre systems, it is necessary to begin by outlining the challenges faced by the would-be genre theorist of the Persian prison poem. Because genre is, among other things, a theory of reading – and reading is in part a theory of genre – a peremptory discussion of genre must precede close readings of prison poems. The relevance of genre (and hence of this chapter) to the prison poem may become entirely clear only in retrospect, but I would argue that there can be no politics of literature apart from genre, which enables works of art to speak across time and space, and to generate a community around a specific discourse. Even if these postulates seem opaque at present, I hope that you will be persuaded by the end of the book.

The main point to bear in mind for now is that the prison poem presents a quandary from the point of view of its classification: it lacks an established position within any genre system. Because genre was not a central theoretical concern within premodern Islamicate poetics, the path to establishing the genre of the Persian prison poem is necessarily circuitous. In the sense that there is no established tradition for its formal classification, the prison poem recalls the *zajal* in Andalusian poetics, a form of oral strophic poetry that emerged as a 'sub-literary genre' from 'colloquial dialects and non-classical formal features'.[4] Both genres are external to established literary canons, yet central to our understanding of the politics of literature. My aim in this chapter is to show that, rather than being a difficulty to be suppressed in the interest of analytic clarity, the anomalous status of the prison poem from the point of view of genre is central to the dialectic of politics and aesthetics that it introduced into world literature.

Whereas recent work on European prison literature delineates many different 'metaphors of confinement', this book focuses on how imprisonment shapes literary form as metonym, through modalities of contiguity and association.[5] In Perso-Arabic as in European poetics, metaphors operate according to a logic of difference: a characteristic is transferred from one object to another, thereby bringing them into relation.[6] Metonyms operate according to a logic of association and proximity. For a literary genre that was born from confinement, it is unsurprising that imprisonment would manifest itself as metonymy more readily than as metaphor. Whereas many prison literatures position freedom and confinement as polar opposites, Persian prison poets considered imprisonment to be part of their everyday lives.

A second distinction between the Persian prison poem and other prison literatures is that, rather than being a free-floating category that ranges across a literary canon, the scope of the Persian prison poem is defined by its subject *and* by its form. Hence, a study of the prison poem need not wander aimlessly across an amorphous range of autobiographies, biographies and other prosographic sources in search of an authentic originary text. The genre has been defined in advance for us by the tradition that created it.

This book reveals how genre interacted with politics in creating the Persian prison poem (*habsiyyat*), while also showing how the prison poem extended the scope of genre beyond a formal rubric. The Persian prison poem is distinctive within genre theory because it is a topical (theme- or image-based) genre within a literary system that did not formally prioritise topical genres. With regard to its anomalous topicality, the prison poem joins other analogues in Persian and Arabic literature, including wine poems (*khamriyyat*), hunting poems (*tardiyyat*) and ascetic poems (*zuhdiyyat*).[7] Yet it is the only topical genre that developed a political theology.

For the distinctive relationship it inculcates between politics and form, and specifically its inversion of panegyric norms, the prison poem is a key document in the intersection of aesthetics and politics – and of culture and power – in premodern world literatures. By way of clarifying its global relevance, I begin by first locating the concept of genre in terms of global literary systems, before returning to the classical Persian context.

What is Genre?

Before considering the genre of the prison poem on its own terms, it is necessary to dwell on one of literary theory's most vexing questions: what is genre? Are genres discrete entities or contiguous overlapping frameworks? Within contemporary poetics, genres are often regarded as 'fetters from which we are duty-bound to escape, or brands of an unimaginative establishmentarianism, or . . . self-made prisons in which we acquiesce'.[8] The association with confinement in these words is more than serendipitious; across world literature language and imprisonment are closely aligned, and this has implications for the theorisation of literary form.[9]

By way of developing a more comparative approach to genre, this chapter synthesises three major schools of literary theory: Bakhtin's concept of speech genres; Jameson's concept of the ideology of form; and Adorno's account of the relationship between poetry and experience. While Bakhtin and Jameson are clearly aligned with the theory of prose, Adorno's paradigm is closely linked to poetry. While reformulating Bakhtin, Jameson and Adorno's foundational approaches to genre theory, I also draw on modern genre theorists, including Alastair Fowler, Northrup Frye and Ralph Cohen, to clarify distinctions between genre and form. By way of integrating the Persian genre system into world literature, I introduce three dimensions through which genre is manifested in Persian poetics: as form (*naw'*), theme (*mazmun*) and discourse (*sukhan*). At once overlapping and mutually implicating, these three dimensions respond to Ralph Cohen's call for a 'generic reconstitution of literary study' that reflects the full extent of poetry's engagement with the politics of form.[10] As the chapters that follow show, the prison poem is ideally suited to lead such a reconfiguration.

As a genre that traverses poetics and politics, the prison poem calls on us to develop a multidimensional account of genre. Merging the Perso-Arabic and European understandings, we can provisionally define genre – *anva'-i adabi* in Persian – as *what happens when empirical data or imagined premises* (muqaddamat) *are transmuted into literary form* (sheikl) *through the literary imagination.* This definition already suggests the overlapping nature of genres, and indicates that literary texts achieve their ends by transgressing the norms of the genres they help to establish. Table 1.1 presents a schematic representation of genre that corresponds to this account.

Table 1.1 A tripartite typology of genre's three dimensions in Persian poetics.

	ROUGH TRANSLATION	EXAMPLE	FEATURES	THEORISTS
1. FORMAL	*asnaf, anva'*	A ode (opposite of lyric) *qasida* (opposite of ghazal) quatrain (*ruba'i, dubayti*) fragment (*qit'eh*)	A meter rhyme scheme length use of the *radif*	A Raduyani Vatvat Shams-i Qays
2. TOPICAL	*mazmum* (pl. *mazamin*)	B prison poems wine poems hunting poems ascetic poems	B topos (pl. topoi) lexicon authorial voice imagery	B Jonathan Culler Earl Miner Nizami 'Aruzi
3. DISCURSIVE (not a genre, but a relation)	*nazm* *kalam* *sukhan*	C *Cannot be categorised by example. Not a genre in itself; it is the relation between formal and topical dimensions.*	C *Always reaches beyond the formal vs thematic/topical genre rubrics.*	C Jurjani Bakhtin Benjamin Adorno Jameson

Let us now break down Table 1.1's components parts, in order to better understand how the Persian prison poem uniquely integrates two of genre's dimensions – form and topos – into the third, discursive, dimension. A poem operates within genre's formal dimension through its meter and rhythm (1A). A poem operates within genre's topical dimension through its topos (*mazmum*), which is to say its theme. Sometimes used interchangeably with 'theme', the concept of topos is useful for the corporeal poetics of the prison poem due to its materiality (the term in Latin means 'place'). A topos denotes a certain style of thought, or logic of argumentation, that fits well with the prison poem genre.[11] In Persian and Arabic poetics, common topoi (plural of topos) include prison, wine drinking, hunting and asceticism (2B). The formal and thematic (topos-based) dimensions of a poem's genre are clear; harder to define is a poem's discursive dimension (3C). Yet this dimension, which combines the formal and thematic, is an essential component of its genre.

As in many classical literatures, the formal dimensions of genre are prioritised within the Persian genre system. Certain genres, such as the panegyric ode (*qasida*), are canonised by a formal genre system, while others, such as the quatrain (*ruba'i*) and the fragment (*qit'eh*) occupy the margins.[12] A poem's form can be gauged by its appearance on the page. In modern Iranian literary criticism, Sirus-i Shamisa's discussion of the Persian genre system focuses on literary genres (*anva'-i adabi*). As such, it is among the closest approximations within Persian literature to a theory of kinds, such as that proposed by Alastair Fowler.[13] Yet there is also a difference: the Perso-Arabic genre system prioritises the multivalent sign more explicitly than modern European poetics.[14] We should pause here over a specific example, by the Indo-Persian poet 'Amid al-Din Lumaki discussed in the Introduction. In one of his lengthy prison poems, Lumaki creatively deploys a multivalent refrain (*radif*): *band*, meaning 'chain'. In the first half of the poem, the sultan's *band* is represented as good and just. Here are two verses from this section which display the range of *band*'s meanings:

A hundred thousand chains [*band*] of violet around your jasmine!
Your ruby lips form a chain [*band*] round your pure pearls.
His Majesty, Muhammad Balban whose noose of wrath
enchains [*band*] the rebels in the time of battle.

ای از بنفشه بر سمنت صد هزار بند
وز لعل تست بر گهر آبدار بند
والا محمد بلبن کز کمند قهر
بر سرکشان نهد بگه کارزار بند

In the second half of the poem, the topos, of the chain is transformed. The poet complains of the injustice of the sultan's chains. The panegyric becomes a complaint, as the poet reflects on his own imprisonment:

You've put the learned in chains.
Alas, do not hold learned ones in chains.

فرموده‌ای که بند نهند اهل فضل را
هی هی، بر اهل فضل منه زینهار بند

As these verses show, the same word – *band* – can carry radically different associations, even in the same poem. While what in Persian would be called the *lafz* (utterance) of *band* remains stable, its *maʿni* (sense) changes over the course of the poem. This distinction reveals how the refrain (*radif*) shifts over the course of the text, pushing against the limits of its genre, even while its form is unchanged. To restate this re-signifying process in Anglophone terms, the poet's skilful manipulation of the formal structures of the *qasida* (panegyric) form underscores the duality of the sovereign's power. While Lumaki's use of the refrain *band* to manifest the tension between sense and utterance does not constitute a theory of genre, this device often structured the genre of the prison poem.

One advantage of constructing a genre system around poetic forms is the simplicity and symmetry of such classification. An ode, a quatrain or a fragment can easily be classified, simply by noting the presence or absence of a few formal traits. Such taxonomies are relatively free of ambiguity. The disadvantage of such a system is also linked to this simplicity: seemingly transparent demarcations of form obscure the changing relations of sense and utterance, and conceal what Fredric Jameson calls 'the ideology of form'.[15] When a text's genre membership is determined solely by its conformity to a pre-established form, it becomes difficult to recognise new genres in their emergence, and to watch great works of literature transgress genres, generating aesthetic experience from this cross-genre movement. A model of genre exclusively based on poetic forms also simplifies the relation between form and content by obscuring how movement among and within themes and topoi shifts genre membership. With his multivalent refrain, Lumaki adds a new genre dimension to his poem. Because it belongs to the formal genre of the *qasida*, which is typically a panegyric, we would have expected a eulogistic tone. The genius of the poem consists in its ability to subvert our expectations for this genre by skilfully transforming the meaning of the word *band*.

Finally, a purely formalistic approach to genre conceals the fluidity of genre membership. Walter Benjamin articulated this fluidity in axiomatic terms when he argued that 'a major work either establishes a genre [*Gattung*] or abolishes it'. Bakhtin made a similar point when he stated that 'the transfer of style from one genre to another . . . violates or renews the given genre'.[16] Far from having their content predetermined by their formal classification, compelling works of art shape the genres within which they are classed. They establish or abolish genres, and sometimes do both, in the same instant. Benjamin and Bakhtin's insights into genre membership as a rule-breaking process captures the prison poem's political aesthetic. In the absence of a reckoning with genre in all of its dimensions, a purely formal account of genre would obscure the intersection of aesthetics and politics in the prison poem.

The second dimension of genre in Table 1.1 is 'topical'. 'Topical' can also be denominated 'thematic', since themes or topics, as well as motifs, are involved. The topical dimension functions as a counterpoint to the formal dimension, and corresponds more closely to genre in the modern sense. A genre's topicality aligns with its materiality; this is what links it to the prison poem's corporeal poetics. The materiality of the prison poem in its topical dimension is manifested in its depiction of the poet's body, its Christology, its concern with the sartorial signs of oppression (explored in Chapter 5), and its relationship to other genres, including the *qasida* (panegyric ode), the *hasb-i hal* (autobiographical writing in verse) and the *hajv* (invective).

Novels exemplify the genre's topical dimension. While the novel genre possesses a fixed and definite form – it is expected to be prose and longer than a short story – it has attracted the greatest share of literary attention not for its form but for its themes, including growing up, growing old, falling in and out of love, the urban cityscape, poverty and wealth, the fragmentation of everyday life, the 'homelessness' of modern experience, alienation, and the increasing pace of modern life.[17] While the novel has been involved in many formal innovations, even in the aftermath of Bakhtinian polyphony, it is for its *themes* that the novel is regarded as the paradigmatic genre of literary modernity, even more than for its form.[18] Although attempts to identify premodern counterparts to the modern novel have broadened the genre's definition to include nearly any kind of narrative prose, modern literary theory nonetheless treats the novel as a topical genre, with its criteria of membership and exclusion determined more by content than by form.[19] The classification of texts as heterogeneous as the Chinese *Journey to the West* (1592), *Madame*

Bovary (1856) and Vikram Seth's verse novel *The Golden Gate* (1986) within the same genre is a result of this topical focus. Premodern genre systems tend to taxonomise according to form. Modern genre systems by contrast classify texts according to their themes and topoi. Form is an afterthought in relative terms for much of contemporary poetics. The Persian prison poem is not adequately comprehended by either approach; this genre requires prioritising both dimenions: the formal, inasmuch as most prison poems are panegyric *qasida*s, and the thematic, in that these *qasida*s often break with the generic expectations that accompany the panegyric form. It is due to this anomaly of content and form that is unique to the prison poem that I introduce the concept of discursive genre, which helps us to account for the specific genre status of the prison poem within both the classical Persian genre system *and* contemporary poetics.

Discursive dimensionality, which is the third aspect of genre in Table 1.1, captures the pressure that the prison poem exerts on both formal and thematic conceptions of genre. Whereas the formal and thematic rubrics refer in part to pre-existing types of genre that often overlap, 'discursive' refers not to a type but to a *modality* of genre; it is the co-existence of the formal and thematic within a given text. The discursive dimension of genre is captured well by ʿAbd al-Qahir al-Jurjani's concept of *nazm*, a term that is here denominated by discourse, and that can also be translated as order.[20] *Nazm* refers to the equilibrium whereby utterance and sense are held in tension, together constituting discourse.[21] The discursive dimension of genre signifies neither its form nor its content, but their interrelations of these two dimensions. Al-Jurjani holds that it is in this interchange, rather than in specific words or meanings, that the miracle of poetry is made manifest. Since this book argues that it is only by tracing the interrelations of formal and topical, of form and content, and of utterance and sense, that the prison poem can be enjoyed in its fullness, it follows that the prison poem genre is best read through the prism of its discursive dimension.

The discursive dimensionality of genre has gained in recognition thanks in large part to Bakhtin and the Russian formalists who were concerned to understand the specificity of literary discourse in relation to non-literary language.[22] Although the discursive dimension of genre is the most difficult to track, this as yet untheorised dimension is, I argue, key to identifying the prison poem as a genre. Bakhtin is the pre-eminent theorist of genre as discourse, a concept he analyses through the rubric of speech genres (*rechovykh zhanrov*). Bakhtin registered well how the formal and topical dimensions of genre interact with the discursive dimension when he described how every utterance within a given genre 'refutes, affirms, supplements, and relies on' the other utterances with which it is necessarily in dialogue (196). Framed in these dialogic terms, genre is that which constitutes the prison poem as a political, as well as an aesthetic, force. Part of the analytical difficulty we face here is that there is no discursive genre as such; everything is or can be made into a discourse. However, it is precisely the ubiquity of discourse that made it so useful to prison poem poetics. By engaging with genre in this malleable sense, prison poets could praise *and* condemn their sovereigns simultaneously with the same set of words.

In contrast to both the formalist and topical approach, Bakhtin is interested in the interface between the genres of everyday existence – including dialogue, letters, speeches – and the genres that structure literary texts.[23] He denominates the genres of everyday life as primary genres, while literary genres are classified as secondary and ideological (161). Bakhtin's contribution to genre theory hinges on his account of the relations between these two types of genre, the first referring to everyday speech and the second to literary expression. This discursive approach to genre enables Bakhtin to bring aesthetics into conversation with everyday politics. It also illuminates the role of genre in the making of the prison poem, for, as Bakhtin clarifies, language becomes expressive – which is to say, political – through its generic transmutation.

For Bakhtin, poetics does more than deploy language in its dictionary meaning; a text's genre status depends on its political role. Every secondary genre depends on the primary genres that constitute it. As with the example of *band* above in the prison poem by ʿAmid al-Din Lumaki, words with positive connotations can acquire negative meanings in the context of a poem and vice versa. That which is sad can signify as 'comically joyful' (*shutlivo-vesyolii*), in Bakhtin's phrase. The re-signifying work done by poets generates new genres while pushing forward the socio-political horizon of the possible. For example, comic epitaphs, Bakhtin points out, originated in classical tragedy (192).

Bakhtin's analysis of the work of speech genres in transforming meanings – making the sad comically joyful – has striking precedents in Persian literary theory, most notably in the *Four Discourses* (1155–1157) of literary critic Nizami ʿAruzi. As the first text to explicitly identify the Persian prison poem as a genre, *Four Discourses* figures centrally into any account of the Persian prison poem. In this work, ʿAruzi argued that poetry makes an 'insignificant idea significant [*maʿni khurd ra buzurg*]' and a 'significant idea insignificant [*maʿni burzurg ra khurd*]'.[24] This dialectical process relies on genre's three-dimensionality to aestheticise the utterance through form and theme, and to confer on it world-making capacities.

Bakhtin's concept of genre as discourse moves considerably beyond genre's formal and topical dimensions. Whereas the formal dimension of genre can easily be mapped onto established forms in Persian poetics such as the *qasida* and ghazal, and the topical dimension of genre can be mapped onto prisons and their associated topoi, the discursive dimension of genre is more elusive. Whereas, as noted in Table 1.1, both *nazm* and *kalam* are Arabic approximations for discourse, the corresponding Persian term would be *sukhan*.[25] *Sukhan* also signifies literary discourse, just as *nazm*, which can also mean 'composition', can also refer to the specific relation between meaning and form that constitutes poetry. The discursive dimension of genre also manifests the political power that the prison poem wielded within its literary and cultural milieu.

What is Genre in Arabo-Persian Poetics?

The topos of imprisonment appears only rarely in classical rhetorical manuals, yet it is a common trope in twelfth-century Persian poetry. How should we account for this discrepancy? As Lara Harb has shown in her work on the concept of wonder in Arabic poetics, just because a term was rarely defined or under-theorised within a literary tradition does not mean that it was insignificant.[26] It simply means that contemporary critics and theorists must work harder to draw out the full critical potential of these unarticulated concepts. We need to think about genre before modernity in ways that neither thoughtlessly project modern categories onto premodern materials nor which are limited to technical formalities while ignoring poetry's wider impact the world.

Medieval poets adopted a topical approach to genre at a time when critics and rhetoricians prioritised the formal dimension of genre that best suited their taxonomic agendas. This discrepancy also serves as a reminder that we should not always take critics – whether classical or modern – as the final arbiters, particularly when the poetic tradition provides contrary evidence. Sometimes even Persian rhetoricians mischaracterised the literatures they assessed, or neglected important genres, such as the prison poem. We must be willing to engage with the Perso-Arabic tradition in order to track the position of the prison poem, while also moving beyond it when Perso-Arabic literary–critical paradigms prove insufficient. But first we have to establish what these patterns were, and how they relate to world poetics.

Genre is but one iteration of the broader issue of the relation between form and content, a matter which has deep resonance across the literatures of the Islamic world. The form–content relation is central to understanding the dialectic between utterance (*lafẓ*) and sense (Persian *maʿni*; Arabic *maʿna*) in Arabo-Persian poetics, which is among the most frequently recurring concerns of that tradition. While genre in its contemporary meaning is used to classify entire works (books, movies, plays), utterance and sense in classical Persian were used to classify smaller verbal units, such as words and figures of speech. Understanding the prison poem as a genre means extrapolating the classical distinction between utterance and sense onto the poem as a whole.

Table 1.1 identified three dimensions of genre: the formal, the topical and the discursive. Whereas the formal and the topical can be mapped onto specific genres, the discursive dimension corresponds to an equilibrium between form and theme. Diagram 1.1 considers these three rubrics from the point of view of their overlaps and intersections, in the form of a Venn diagram. Here we see the same three dimensions of genre introduced in Table 1.1 – formal, topical and discursive – but from the vantage point of their convergences. Every work of literature participates in genre's three dimensions: through their form and theme, and the conjunction of these two typologies, which produces literary discourse. Viewing prison poems dialectically across these three dimensions reveals how this genre channelled the sovereign's power, thereby extending the political scope of poetry across the eastern Islamic world

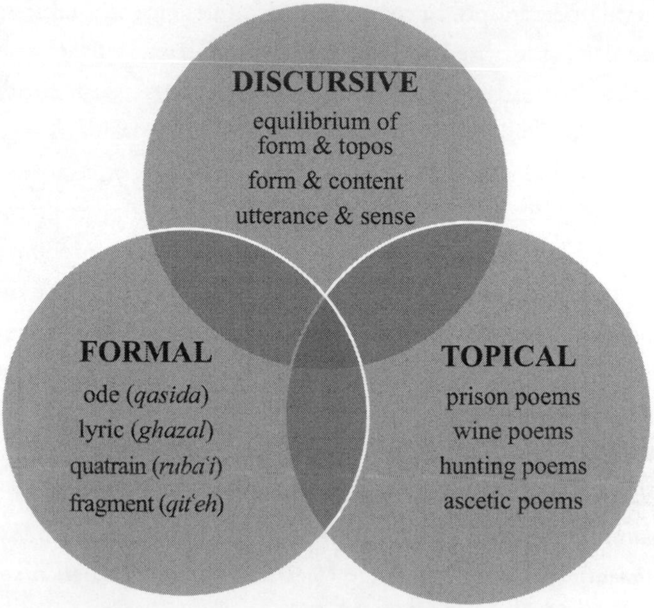

Diagram 1.1 An overlapping typology of genre.

In one of the first extended discussion of the classical Arabic genre system, Gregor Schoeler broadened the genre concept (*Gattungsbegriff*) to encompass the classical literatures of the Islamic world. 'A literature is unthinkable,' writes Schoeler, that 'does not divide [literary] works into their outer and inner forms [*ausseren und inneren Form*] that constitute them.'[27] Saussure's account of linguistic signification as a 'system of differences without positive terms' supports this view.[28] As such theoretical defences suggest, genre is more useful as a method for comparison than as a means of safeguarding rigid literary taxonomies.

The Persian prison poem was preceded by an Arabic literature of captivity that developed primarily along the Byzantine border with the captivity poems of Abu Firas al-Hamdani.[29] Numerous other world prison literatures should also be brought into comparison with the Persian prison poem.[30] Yet the *habsiyyat*'s twelfth-century trajectory from South Asia to the Caucasus (as chronicled in the following chapters) is *sui generis*. With respect to Arabic poetry, Schoeler asks 'whether the prison poem can be classified as a genre of its own in Arabic poetry; it rather concerns a theme which, as a rule, is linked with other (mostly superordinate) themes'.[31] Schoeler writes with reference to Arabic rather than Persian; the Persian literary record tells a rather different story.

Meanwhile, the Persian tradition categorises classical Persian poetry through a range of what I have identified as formal and topical genres. Diagram 1.2 adapts the schema of one scholar who works within this tradition, Bo Utas, to my tripartite system.[32] Utas begins with the formal features of classical Persian poetry (short versus long, followed by *qasida*, ghazal and other formal rubrics). He then shifts to topical genres, thereby confirming the perception that formal genres are primary and topical genres are secondary. As we will see, this framework is challenged by the trajectory of the prison poem, which is characterised by a fluid relationship to specific formal genres across the centuries. Although most of the poems discussed in this book are *qasidas*, they rebel against the conventional expectations attached to this form. Furthermore, as the centuries progressed, Persian prison poetry reached well beyond the *qasida* form. Hence, the prison poem can be understood only when it is the topos and theme, rather than the form, that is regarded as determinative.

As Diagram 1.2 registers, a formal genre like the *qasida* overlaps with a number of different topical genres, such as the panegyric, threnody, homiletic and mystical poem. The ghazal similarly overlaps with multiple topical genres. By contrast, the quatrain (*ruba'i*) is a self-contained form with a relatively fixed set of topics. In this dualistic theory of genre, the relationship between the formal and topical dimensions of genre is one of hierarchical dependency. Conceiving of genre as a discourse that combines form and theme moves beyond such binary distinctions. Genre as discourse implies an overlapping of form and content, utterance and sense, and the formal and topical dimensions of genre (as in Diagram 1.1). Genre as discourse also provides an infrastructure for tracking the prison poem's political aesthetics.

Further light is shed on the discursivity of genre by Bakhtin and Medvedev in their classic critique of formalist aesthetics, subtitled 'a critical introduction to sociological poetics'. Echoing the distinction between utterance (*lafz*) and meaning (*ma'na*), as well as in Latin between *res* and *verba*, Bakhtin and Medvedev argue that 'the thematic unity of the work and its actual place in life grow together organically in the unity of genre'.[33] Genre is the process through which 'the unity of the factual reality of the word [*slova*] and its meaning [*smyisla*] are most fully realised'. The new word-utterance

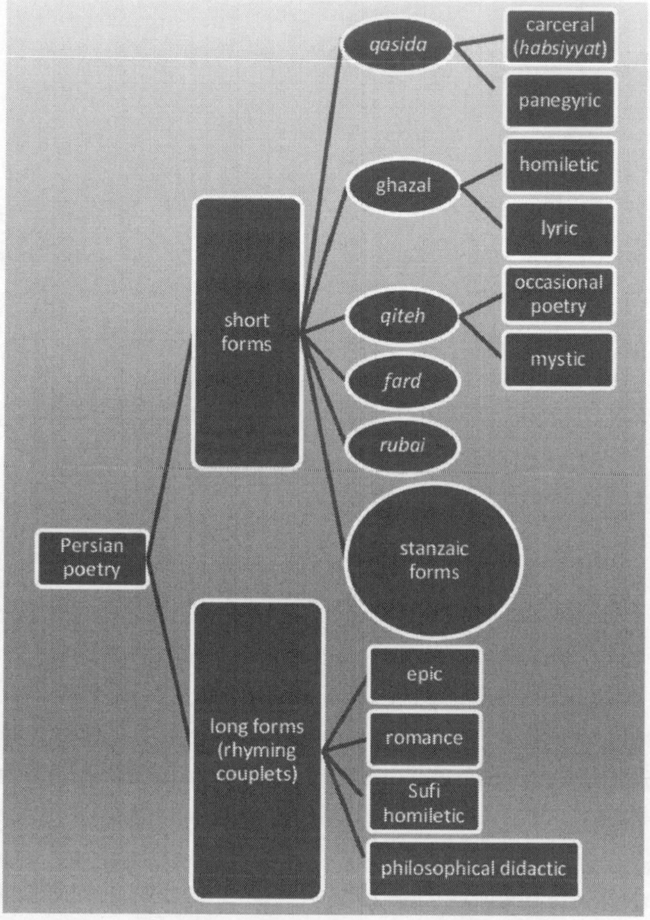

Diagram 1.2 The Persian genre system (diagram adapted from Utas, '"Genres" in Persian Literature 900–1900', 231 and 224).

(*slova-vyiskazivanie*) brought about by genre's unification of word and meaning is discursive and therefore political. Adorno gestured in this direction when he insisted that 'there is no material content, no formal category of an artistic creation, however mysteriously changed and unknown to itself, which did not originate in the empirical reality from which it breaks free'.[34] Adorno had in mind primarily the discursive work of genre when he outlined the complex dialectic between history and the imagination. His assertion that all artistic creation originates in 'the empirical reality from which it breaks free' captures the dialectic between form and topos, and utterance and sense, that is brought into acute relief by the prison poem.

'Genre', Bakhtin and Medvedev conclude in a rare gloss on the topical dimension of genre, 'is the organic unity of theme and of what lies beyond it'. To the extent that it belongs to a genre, every literary text is entrenched in the world of non-literary discourse and in the empirical realities from which it strives to break free. Echoing the Bakhtinian yoking together of utterance and meaning, Guillén proposed that 'generic models, to a greater degree than rhetorical or stylistic norms, postulate . . . the emergence, beyond *res* and *verba*, of a unified artistic whole'.[35] In their dialectical approaches, both Bakhtin and Medvedev and Guillén create a framework for the prison poem's ideology of form.

For Arabist Jaroslav Stetkeyvich, the *qasida* becomes an 'Arabic lyrical ode' when it formally incorporates the *nasib*, the Arabic version of the *captatio benevolentiae* ('winning of goodwill') and the ghazal's formal ancestor.[36] This is suggestive of the dialectical relation between formal and thematic genres that is constitutive of genre's discursive dimensionality. For Kerstin Eksell, writing from the vantage point of early Arabic poetics, 'of the three grand genres, or modes, defined by Aristotle – epic, drama and lyric – the Arabs do not really count any other than the lyrical one'.[37] Both scholars underscore the discontinuous taxonomies that complicate efforts to integrate the classical Arabo-Persian genre system into contemporary literary theory.

Consider Stetkevych's criticism of an anthology of Arabic poetry edited by the Orientalist A. J. Arberry. He complains that the only distinction Arberry permits in his anatomy of Arabic poetry is between the *qasida* and the *qit'eh* (fragment), 'as if no further classification were possible' within classical Arabic genre systems. Stetkevych warns that, in the absence of genre criticism, Arabic poetry will become 'an amorphous conglomerate of verse, with its chronological arrangement giving the impression of a mere accident'.[38] By contrast, a dialectical approach to genre will 'account for literary change more adequately than histories based on themes, ideas, periods and movements'.[39] Literary studies organised by genre have advantages that periodisation lacks, constrained as it is by what Eric Hayot calls 'institutional time'.[40]

Some critics call topical genres like the prison and wine poem subgenres, with the same relation to the formal dimension of the *qasida* as the 'Udhri love lyric has to the ghazal; these are parts of larger wholes. Eksell, for example, situates the 'motif' (her rendering of *maʿna*) 'beneath' genre, and connects the growth of motif-dominated 'subgenres' to the 'diversification of poetry in the growing, urban society'.[41] While the sociological turn is promising, the genre–subgenre typology perpetuates the reductive approach to genre as a mere taxonomy, which dominates premodern literatures. At its worst, this approach can perpetuate the illusion that the only legitimate genres are the formal ones because these are most amenable to classification.[42] In reducing all genres to their formal dimensions, this approach inhibits the recognition of the topical and discursive dimensions of premodern genres such as the prison poem. Genres like these are born from the transgression of formal genres. Hence, a dialectical approach to genre recognises the perpetual overlapping of form and topos within genre as discourse (as in Diagram 1.1).

Following the example of nineteenth-century Orientalist Wilhelm Ahlwardt, who studied the organisation of the *divans* (poetry collections) of Abu Nuwas and Ibn al-Muʿtazz in order to learn about medieval Arabic conceptualisations of genre, Schoeler examines the editing principles that governed the works of al-Suli (d. 916) and Hamza al-Isfahani (d. 961), who collected, edited and arranged the poems of the Abbasid poets Abu Nuwas, Abu Tammam and al-Buhturi. Schoeler also examines *divan*s from as late as the fourteenth century (of al-Mutanabbi by al-Halabi), and of poets from the thirteenth century such as al-Hajiri (d. 1235) and Safi al-Din al-Hilli (d. 1349).

By tracing the development of genres in their topical dimensions across these poetry collections, Schoeler demonstrates how they were shaped by local transformations in literary norms. According to Schoeler, the primary distinctions for medieval anthologists were not among formal genres (*qasida*, ghazal, *qitʿeh*). Rather, topical genres such as the wine poem, hunting poem (*tardiyyat*), praise poem (*madih*), satire (*hijaʾ*), mourning poems (*marathi*), ascetic poems (*zuhdiyyat*) and poems of reproach (*ʿitab*) were the dominant organising rubrics. Whereas Orientalist scholarship reduces the classical Arabo-Persian literary canon to formal genres, poets working within these traditions understood that the formal and topical dimensions of genre were perpetually overlapping and mutually reinforcing.

Within Utas' typology, the *qasida* is a formal genre (similar to a ghazal, *qit'eh*, *ruba'i*), while the prison poem is a topical genre, belonging to the class that includes *khamriyyat*, *tardiyyat* and *zuhdiyyat*. What is not captured within this paradigm is the concept – central to the prison poem – of poetry as an oppositional discourse, and as a critique of power.[43] If the formal dimension of genre is taxonomic and the topical dimension is methodological, then genre as discourse – which is not a kind of genre but rather the relation between formal and thematic genres – is ontological. These overlapping dimensions were registered in Arabo-Persian poetics in terms of a widely varying group of lexemes, including *aghrad*, *asnaf*, *arkan*, *anva'* and *aqsam*. Frequently, form, topos and discourse were mixed, as when Ibn Rashiq (d. 1064) divides literary expression into four pillars (*arkan*): encomium (*madih*), invective (*hija'*), erotic poetry (*nasib*) and elegy (*ritha'*).[44]

A genre, notes Cohen, 'cannot be defined by its own terms'.[45] Like language in the Sausurrean system of differences, genres can be grasped only in relation to each other.

E. D. Hirsch echoes this point: 'A type can be entirely represented in a single instance,' he clarifies, 'while a class is usually thought of as an array of instances.'[46] Genre as used in this book is more akin to a class than a type. A prison poem need not invoke the entire thematic apparatus of incarceration in order to participate in this genre. This pertains particularly to the topical dimension, which is synecdochic in structure. Chains, grey hair, tears, toothless mouths, mouthless teeth and other tropes of the aging body are all found in prison poems, such that the presence of one topos implies the presence of others, whether named or not. To cite an example from a prison poem of Mas'ud Sa'd, who is the focus of the next chapter:

> Blessed Allah! Look at this fate and this life.
> From here to death, prison is my home.
> My spleen became like a comb's teeth from this regret
> when I saw a white strand of hair on my comb.

تبارک الله ازین بخت و زندگانی من
که تا بمیرم زندان بود مرا خانه
چو شانه شد جگرم شاخ شاخ ز انده آن
که موی دیدم شاخ سپید در شانه [47]

These verses are dense with prison poem topoi. First, there is the literal prison (*zindan*), which, along with chains (*band*), is an indisputable genre marker of the prison poem. Second, we find the poet's body in decay, with his spleen resembling a comb's teeth, striated by grief. Finally, prison assumes a metonymic function within these verses: it at once amplifies and reflects the poet's suffering. If prison is his home, this implies that his existence is a prison sentence.

Prison in these verses is not precisely a metaphor in the sense that metaphor carries in the Arabo-Persian tradition, entailing an ontological difference between the two objects being compared.[48] Instead, we can discern here the metonymic logic of the Persian prison poem, whereby the poet's imprisoned body is a sign of his mortal status. Although Masʿud Saʿd is not the sole paradigm for what prison poetry is and can be, he is presented as the first such poet to inaugurate this tradition. Considered alongside their appearance in the rhetorical tradition discussed in the next chapter, these verses reveal the genre's refashioning of the poet's body. These verses achieve their effect through their topoi even more than through their form.

The Prison Poem as a Transgressive Genre

Having presented a typology of genre in three dimensions, I will now return to the political-theological themes of the Introduction, which can now be enriched with the tools of genre theory. This genre's undermining of the king's authority was symptomatic of a shift in the locus of twelfth-century sovereignty in the eastern Islamic world, following the re-territorialisation of power that followed from the decline of the Baghdad-based caliphate under Abbasid rule. The transformation transpired across centuries. The Abbasid caliphate was nominally still in power when the most significant prison poems were written in Persian.

Nonetheless, the prison poem genre was shaped by the weakening of caliphal power alongside the growth of new dynasties during the eleventh and twelfth centuries.[49] Under the new sultanates that spread through Central Asia and the Caucasus, politics became a realm of 'poetics, even fabrication', along the lines of what Kahn discerns in early modern Europe.[50] A growing awareness of the fragile foundations of the ruler's sovereignty coincides in twelfth-century Persian poetics with the desacralising shift away from the language of the Quran, increased reliance on New Persian as a language of literary discourse, the decline of the caliphate, and the proliferation of multiple, fragmented sultanates from South Asia to the Caucasus.

To paraphrase Adorno's statement quoted above, artistic creations resist the contingency of their material existence just as prison poets resist their confinement in verse. A political theology of genre rooted in premodern Middle Eastern literatures should explore the dialectic between the prison poem's topoi and its forms, be these the *qasida*, quatrain or ghazal. Such an account, which is also a theory of reading, should reveal how the poet's imprisoned body is reconstituted by genre, in new discursive, topical and formal dimensions.

As noted above, Bakhtin and Medvedev define genre as 'the organic unity of theme with what lies beyond it'. Genre for these authors and formalises non-literary speech genres into literary discourse. This means that genre conditions are experienced across the temporal and geographic spectrum. Genre shapes the process through which experience is given form. In the case of the prison poem, genre's 'finalisation of utterance' also involves a return to, and transformation of, prophetic history. For Bakhtin and Medvedev, literature's generic transformation culminates in the exhilarating dictum that the artist (*khudozhnik*) must 'learn to see actuality [*deistvitel'nost'*] through the eyes of genre [*glazami zhanra*]': the comprehension of actuality is generated "in the process of ideological social intercourse'.[51] Through this process of genre formation, prison poetry developed a political theology, and political theology acquired aesthetic form.

When the formal, topical and discursive dimensions of genre are studied from the vantage point of their mutual interaction, the politics of genre is made legible. While writers 'compose in genres that resist the restraints the authorities impose', the rulers control 'the production of genres by punishment or threat of punishment', writes Cohen, elliptically evoking the prison poem.[52] Prison poems reveal the contingency of our political existence when they address social tensions through genre. These tensions generate a dialectic between resistance and constraint that illuminates the terrain of the Persian prison poem. Prison poems imposed political obligations, revealed the contingency of worldly power, and replaced the sovereign's sacred imprimatur with the poet's vatic mandate.

The formal dimensions of genre are the most standardised – and standardisable – dimensions of genre criticism. They are also more immediately recognisable and classifiable than are the topical and discursive dimensions of genre. *Qasida*, ghazal, quatrain and *masnavi* can be defined once and forever through their fixed formal properties. Hence, the abundance of studies on the *qasida*, the ghazal and other formal genres, compared with the paucity of studies on the prison poem and other thematic genres.[53] But what is most significant for the politics of prison poem poetics is less the qualities that constitute a given genre than *how* its different dimensions interact to produce a text that intervenes in the world. By accounting for how this equilibrium produces genre as discourse, we come close to addressing the core of Adorno's paradox: literary texts break free from their empirical origins even – and especially – in acts of resistance. These acts cannot be neutral. They must be political.

This chapter has examined genre's genesis across three different dimensions – as form, topos and discourse – in the context of the Arabo-Persian genre system and in order to develop a framework for reading prison poems as political documents. The Arabo-Persian taxonomies listed in Table 1.1 have been mapped onto genre's dimensions, with the *qasida*, ghazal, *qit'eh* and *ruba'i* organising genre as *form*; the *habsiyyat*, *khamriyyat*, *tardiyyat* and *zuhdiyyat* organising genre by *topos*; and the fluid relation among these two dimension corresponding to genre as a political discourse. The categories proposed here are dialectical, reflective of the complex interaction of literature with the world it represents. Every category overlaps and is shaped by its others. These overlaps remind us that no dimension of the genre, whether formal, topical or discursive, comes into being in isolation from its other dimensions.

The overlapping character of genres is most apparent in the case of formal genres. The ghazal is derivative of the *qasida* form (specifically the *qasida*'s opening, the *nasib*); most Persian meters are available to both formal genres. The contingency of every genre's entry into the world is manifested across genre's three dimensions, from the panegyric (*qasida*) to the lyric (ghazal) to the medium of poetry in contrast with prose to literature itself. Recognising that these dimensions of genre always overlap, this book resists the impulse to subordinate the topical dimension of genre to its formal dimension, as much modern scholarship on prison literature does, or the formal to the topical, as Persian modern and premodern critics, tend to do.[54] For the purposes of this book, *any* poem that creatively deploys the topos of imprisonment is a prison poem, regardless of its length, its formal genre or any other feature. And yet the prison poems that have been most successful in shaping the conversations of their time and of subsequent eras around imprisonment and justice tend to be those that have an intimate relationship to a formal genre, such as the panegyric *qasida*, even when they subvert it. A case in point is Khaqani's Christian Qasida, discussed in Chapter 5.

The chapters that follow offer an unprecedently detailed account of how the prison poem was constituted as a genre formally, topically and discursively. This chapter specifically has provided a framework for reading what we will see in the chapters to come: prison poems created the genre of prison poetry as they moved across different formal genres, from the *qasida* and quatrain to the ghazal, the *masnavi* and free verse in modern Iran. It is by *transgressing* formal genres and by engaging with genre as discourse that the prison poem became political. Among scholars of prison poem poetics, the Russian Persianist Ekaterina Akimushkina has concentrated on interactions between the formal and topical dimension of genre with respect to the prison poem.[55] Two decades prior to Akimushkina, the Iranian scholar Zafari produced a still authoritative study of the prison poem as a topical genre, from its beginning up to and including the 1979 Revolution.[56] More thoroughly than any scholar to that date or since, Zafari attended to the many themes and tropes (*mazamin*) associated with prison poem poetics. Lacking a conceptual framework for genre as discourse, Zafari limited himself to discussing the prison poem as a formal and topical genre. His pioneering monograph does not show how the politics of the *habsiyyat* developed through the transgression of existing genres. The chapters that follow aim to do precisely that. They integrate the empirical work of Zafari and Akimushkina into a dialectical understanding of genre as discourse, while also adding to this archive a number of prison poems that have never been discussed before. In so doing they reveal the prison poem's political aesthetic.

The chapters that follow examine genre in each of its dimensions, moving progressively from form to topos to discourse. They reveal the prison poem as a genre capable, in the words of 'Aruzi, of 'causing great affairs in the order of the world' or, as Bakhtin put it, of 'making the sad comically joyful'. Over the course of the long twelfth century, prison poets infused their carceral poetics with prophecy's discursive authority, as outlined in Chapter 5. In developing a political theology on aesthetic foundations, the prison poem extended the remit of genre to cover the relationship between poet and reader as well as between poet and patron. When new poetic genres were born, so too were new audiences created. The poet's body came to symbolise the sultan's oppression, while poems about prison signified the poet's struggle for freedom. Often poets remained in prison in spite of their poetic critiques. Sometimes the prison was a metaphor for something else. Nonetheless, the research presented in this book shows that the prison poem was entangled in a wider transformation of the sovereign's power, and that the changing status of the poet in the medieval Persiante world was a major effect of these transformations. As power was decentralised and desacralised, poets forged a literary community for themselves through this genre. They rediscovered their vocation in a new political and literary landscape.

The sequence of the five chapters that follow abide by genre's three dimensions. Having outlined a dialectical approach to genre in Chapter 1, Chapter 2 focuses on the formal dimensions of the earliest prison poems: the lyric odes of South Asian poet Masʿud Saʿd. Chapter 3 examines the topical development of the prison poem during its journey from South Asia to the Caucasus. Chapters 4–6 probe the discursive politics of the prison poem, as poetic forms are transgressed by, respectively, the rhetoric of prophecy, Christology and sovereignty. Throughout these chapters, the understanding of genre as a political discourse advocated for here reveals the prison poem's intervention in existing structures of political power. The analytical framework outlined in this chapter will clarify how the prison poem inflected the rhetoric of power, producing texts that at once rivalled and undermined the decrees by their sovereigns. As I have argued in this chapter and as the chapters to come will show, the Persian prison poem calls for an approach to genre that is centred on poetry's relationship to power. Grasping the politics of the prison poem genre requires reading poetry against the grain of its own critical tradition and in ways that it has not been read before.

Notes

1. Walter Benjamin, *Ursprung des deutschen Trauerspiels*, ed. Rolf Tiedemann (Berlin: Suhrkamp, 2000), 27.
2. Walter Benjamin, 'On the Image of Proust', *Walter Benjamin: Selected Writings, vol. 2. Part 1: 1927–1930*, eds Michael W. Jennings, Howard Eiland and Gary Smith (Cambridge, MA: Harvard University Press, 1999), 237.
3. See, for example, Peter Szondi, 'Schlegel's Theory of Poetic Genres', in *On Textual Understanding and Other Essays* (Manchester: Manchester University Press, 1986), 86.
4. James T. Monroe and Mark F. Pettigrew, 'The Decline of Courtly Patronage and the Appearance of New Genres in Arabic Literature: The Case of the *Zajal*, the *Maqāma*, and the Shadow Play', *Journal of Arabic Literature* 34(1) (2003): 161–2.
5. Monika Fludernik, *Metaphors of Confinement: The Prison in Fact, Fiction, and Fantasy* (Oxford: Oxford University Press, 2019).
6. For a modern account of the logic of metaphor in Arabic poetics that underwrites this analysis, see Wolfhart Heinrichs, *The Hand of the Northwind: Opinions on Metaphor and the Early Meaning of Isti'āra in Arabic Poetics* (Wiesbaden: F. Steiner, 1977).
7. See Philip Kennedy, *The Wine Song in Classical Arabic Poetry: Abu Nuwās and the Literary Tradition* (Oxford: Oxford University Press, 1997); A. A. al-Zabidī, *Zuhdīyyāt Abī Nūwās* (Cairo: Maṭba'at Kūstātsūmās, 1959).
8. Rosalie Littell Colie, *The Resources of Kind: Genre-theory in the Renaissance* (Berkeley: University of California Press, 1973), 1.
9. See, for example, Fredric Jameson, *The Prison-house of Language: A Critical Account of Structuralism and Russian Formalism* (Princeton, NJ: Princeton University Press, 1974).
10. Ralph Cohen, 'Introduction: Notes toward a Generic Reconstitution of Literary Study', *NLH* 34(3) (2003): v–xvi at xvi.
11. For topos as a mode of reasoning, see Lynette Hunter (ed.), *Towards a Definition of Topos: Approaches to Analogical Reasoning* (London: Springer, 1991). I follow the convention of translating *maẓmūn* as 'theme' (see Dād, 219–20), even though, as noted above, it can be misleading when used interchangeably with topos.
12. These divisions are explored in Rebecca Ruth Gould, 'The Much-Maligned Panegyric: Towards a Political Poetics of Premodern Literary Form', *Comparative Literature Studies* 52(2) (2015): 254–88.

13. Sīrūs Shamīsā, *Anvāʿ-i adabī* (Tehran: Bāgh-i Āyīnah, 1370/1992); Alastair Fowler, *Kinds of Literature: An Introduction to the Theory of Genres and Modes* (Oxford: Clarendon Press, 1982).
14. See Michael Sells, 'Guises of the Ghuk: Dissembling Simile and Semantic Overflow in the Early Arabic Nasib', in Suzanne Pinckney Stetkevych (ed.), *Reorientations: Arabic and Persian Poetry* (Bloomington: Indiana University Press, 1994), 130–64.
15. Fredric Jameson, *The Ideologies of Theory* (London: Verso, 2008), 146, first articulated by Jameson in 'The Ideology of Form: Partial Systems in "La Vieille Fille"', *SubStance* 5(15) (1976): 29–49.
16. M. M. Bakhtin, 'Problema rechevykh zhanrov', in *Sobranie sochinenii v semi tomakh*, ed. S. G. Bocharov and L. A. Gogotishvili (Moscow: Russkie slovari, 1996), 166. For an English translation, see M. M. Bakhtin, *Speech Genres and Other Late Essays*, trans. Vern McGee (Austin: University of Texas Press, 1986).
17. See, respectively, Georg Lukács, *The Theory of the Novel: A Historico-Philosophical Essay on the Forms of Great Epic Literature* (London: Merlin Press, 1978) and Ian Watt, *The Rise of the Novel* (Berkeley: University of California Press, 1957).
18. Among many *locus classici* on Bakhtin's theory of the novel, see Mikhail Bakhtin, *Problems of Dostoevsky's Poetics*, trans. Caryl Emerson (Minneapolis: University of Minnesota Press, 2013). For Bakhtin's concept of the novel from the vantage point of ancient literatures, see Robert Bracht Branham (ed.), *The Bakhtin Circle and Ancient Narrative* (Groningen: Groningen University Press, 2005).
19. See Arthur Heiserman, *The Novel Before the Novel: Essays and Discussions About the Beginning of Prose Fiction in the West* (Chicago, IL: University of Chicago Press, 1977).
20. In this regard, *nazm* bears an uncanny resemblance to Michel Foucault's concept of order as discourse in 'The Orders of Discourse', *Social Science Information* 10(2) (1971): 7–30.
21. Following among others the precedent set by Margaret Larkin, 'Al-Jurjani's Theory of Discourse', *Alif: Journal of Comparative Poetics* 2 (1982): 76–86; Margaret Larkin, *The Theology of Meaning: 'Abd al-Qāhir al-Jurjānī's Theory of Discourse* (New Haven, CT: American Oriental Society, 1995).
22. The *locus classicus* here is Shklovskii's concept of estrangement (*ostranenie*), as explicated in his 1917 essay 'Art as Device', available in *Russian Formalist Criticism: Four Essays*, Lee T. Lemon and Marion J. Reis (trans. and Intro.) (Omaha: University of Nebraska Press, 1965), 3–24.
23. These ideas are also elaborated in Bakhtin's extensive writing on the theory

of the novel, including M. M. Bakhtin, *The Dialogic Imagination: Four Essays* (Austin: University of Texas Press, 1981), as well as his extended studies of two major novelists: *Rabelais and His World* (Bloomington: Indiana University Press, 1984) and *Problems of Dostoevsky's Poetics* (Minneapolis: University of Minnesota Press, 1984).

24. Niẓāmī Samarqandī al-ʿAruẕī, *Chahār maqāleh*, ed. Muḥammad Qazwīnī (Berlin: Irānshahr, 1927), 30. In order to avoid confusion with the poet Niẓāmī Ganjevī (discussed in Chapter 3), I refer to Niẓāmī ʿAruẕī simply as ʿAruzi.
25. For an analysis of *sukhan*, see Bābak Aḥmadī, *Sākhtār va ta'vīl-i matn* (Tehran: Markaz, 1992), 2:712–13.
26. Lara Harb, *Arabic Poetics: Aesthetic Experience in Classical Arabic Literature* (Cambridge: Cambridge University Press, 2020).
27. Gregor Schoeler, 'Die Einteilung der Dichtung bei den Arabern', *ZDMG* 123 (1973): 9. For another account of genre from the perspective of classical Arabic poetics, see Amjad Trabulsi, *La critique poétique des arabes* (Damascus: Institut français de Damas, 1958), 215–38.
28. Ferdinand de Saussure, *Course in General Linguistics*, ed. Roy Harris (London: A&C Black, 2013), 141.
29. For classical Arabic prison literature, see Marzīyah Ābād, *Habsīyyah'sarāyī dar adab-i ʿArabī: az āghāz tā ʿaṣr-i ḥāẕr* (Mashhad: Dānishgāh-i Firdawsī, 2001), and, specifically, in relation to the Persian prison poems of Khaqani, Ramlah Maḥmud Ghanim, *Fann al-ḥabsiyat bayna Abī Firās al-Ḥamdānī wa-al-Khāqānī* (Cairo: Dār al-Zahra lil-Nashr, 1991).
30. For prison poetry in European languages, which flourished after the advent of the Persian prison poem, see Guy Geltner, *The Medieval Prison: A Social History* (Princeton, NJ: Princeton University Press, 2008), esp. 112–21; Joanna Summers, *Late Medieval Prison Writing and the Politics of Autobiography* (Oxford: Oxford University Press, 2004); Linne R. Mooney and Mary-Jo Arn (eds), *The Kingis Quair and Other Prison Poems* (TEAMS Consortium for the Teaching of the Middle Ages, 2005); Ruth Ahnert, *The Rise of Prison Literature in the Sixteenth Century* (Cambridge: Cambridge University Press, 2013). Many of these sources are discussed in Gould, 'Prisons Before Modernity'.
31. Gregor Schoeler, 'The Genres of Classical Arabic Poetry: Classifications of Poetic Themes and Poems by Pre-Modern Critics and Redactors of Dīwāns', *Quaderni di studi arabi* 7 (2012): 243.
32. Bo Utas, '"Genres" in Persian Literature 900–1900', in Anders Pettersson (ed.),

Literary History (Berlin: Walter de Gruyter, 2006), 2:215. Accounts of genre in Middle Eastern literatures include Sīrūs Shamīsā, *Anvā'-i adabī* and the special issue on literary terminology (*qaḍāya al-muṣṭalah adabī*) published by the Cairo-based literary journal *Fuṣūl* 7(3) (1997).

33. M. M. Bakhtin and P. N. Medvedev, *Formal'nyi metod v literaturovedenii* (New York: Hildesheim, [1929] 1974), 180. For *lafẓ* and meaning *ma'nā* in classical Arabic literary theory, see Alexander Key, *Language between God and the Poets: Ma'ná in the Eleventh Century* (Berkeley: University of California Press, 2018), as well as Rebecca Ruth Gould, 'Inimitability versus Translatability: The Structure of Literary Meaning in Arabo-Persian Poetics', *The Translator* 19(1) (2013): 87–96.
34. Theodor Adorno, 'Commitment', in Terry Eagleton and Drew Milne (eds), *Marxist Literary Theory: A Reader* (New York: Wiley-Blackwell), 199.
35. Claudio Guillén, *Literature as System: Essays towards the Theory of Literary History* (Princeton, NJ: Princeton University Press, 1971), 118.
36. Jaroslav Stetkevych, 'The Arabic Lyrical Phenomenon', *JAL* 6 (1975): 57–77 at 72. On the origins of the ghazal in the *nasīb* of the *qaṣīda*, see Thomas Bauer and Angelika Neuwirth (eds), *Ghazal as World Literature I: Transformations of a Literary Genre* (Beirut: Orient-Institut Beirut, 2005).
37. Kerstin Eksell, 'Genre in Early Arabic Poetry', in Anders Pettersson (ed.), *Literary History: Towards a Global Perspective* (Berlin: Walter de Gruyter, 2006), 2:162.
38. Jaroslaw Stetkevych, 'Some Observations on Arabic Poetry', *JNES* 26(1) (1967): 3.
39. Ralph Cohen, 'Genre Theory, Literary History, and Historical Change', in David Perkins (ed.), *Theoretical Issues in Literary History* (Cambridge, MA: Harvard University Press, 1991), 113.
40. Eric Hayot, 'Against Periodization; or, On Institutional Time', *New Literary History* 42(4) (2011): 739–56.
41. Eksell, 'Genre in Early Arabic Poetry', 2:164.
42. For criticism of the purely taxononmic understanding of genre criticism, see Fowler, *Kinds of Literature*, 37.
43. The distinction between formal and topical genres roughly corresponds to Fowler's distinction between kinds and modes. As noted by van Gelder, the latter in turn corresponds to what is usually meant in classical Arabic literary theory by *gharāḍ* (pl. *aghrāḍ*). See Geert Jan van Gelder, 'Some Brave Attempts at Generic Classification in Premodern Arabic Literature', in Bert Roest and

Herman Vanstipout (eds), *Aspects of Genre and Type in Pre-modern Literary Cultures* (Groningen: STYX Publications, 1999), 20–1.

44. Ibn Rashīq al-Qayrawānī, *al-ʿUmda fī ṣināʿat al-shiʿr wa naqdih* (Cairo: Maṭbaʿat al-Saʿādah, 1907), 77–8.
45. Cohen, 'Genre Theory, Literary History, and Historical Change', 97.
46. E. D. Hirsch, *Validity in Interpretation* (New Haven, CT: Yale University Press, 1967), 50.
47. Rashīd al-Dīn Vaṭvāṭ, *Ḥadāʾiq al-siḥr fī daqāʾiq al-shiʿr*, ed. ʿAbbās Iqbāl (Moscow: Nauka, 1985 reprint), 318.
48. In the Aristotelian-derived European tradition, similes are classified a variety of metaphor, as explained by Kayvan Tahmasebian, 'Comparison Beyond Similarity and Difference', unpublished manuscript; Denis Donoghue, *Metaphor* (Cambridge, MA: Harvard University Press, 2014), 80–2)). In the Arabo-Persian tradition by contrast, metaphors and similes have entirely different ontological foundations.
49. For the late Abbasid period in Islamic history, see Eric J. Hanne, *Putting the Caliph in His Place: Power, Authority, and the Late Abbasid Caliphate* (Madison, NJ: Fairleigh Dickinson University Press, 2007); H. Busse, *Chalif und Grosskönig, Die Buyiden im Iraq* (Beirut: Steiner, 1969); V. Minorsky, *La domination des Daylamites* (Paris: Leroux, 1932).
50. Victoria Kahn, *Wayward Contracts: The Crisis of Political Obligation in England, 1640–1674* (Princeton, NJ: Princeton University Press, 2004, 16.
51. Bakhtin and Medvedev, *Formal'nyi metod*, 182–3.
52. Cohen, 'Introduction: Notes toward a Generic Reconstitution of Literary Study', xii–xiii.
53. Alongside Stefan Sperl and Christopher Shackle (eds), *Qasida Poetry in Islamic Asia and Africa* (Leiden: Brill, 1996), outstanding studies include Bauer and Neuwirth's *Ghazal as World Literature*; al-Zabidī, *Zuhdīyyāt Abī Nūwās*; Kennedy, *The Wine Song in Classical Arabic Poetry*.
54. This restrictive methodology is evident in attempts to police the border of what can and cannot legitimately be considered a prison poem that animates some philological scholarship, such as M. R. Turkī, who considers Khāqānī's Christian Qasida a *sogandnāmah* (oath poem) rather than a prison poem (*Naqd-i Ṣiyrafiyān* (Tehran: Sukhan, 1394/2015), 196–200). I have refrained from proposing restrictive definitions of which poems do and do not belong to the genre of the *ḥabsiyyāt*, and have instead aimed for an approach that encompasses the many formal genres in which the topos of incarceration has been expressed.

55. Ekaterina Akimushkina, *Zhanr Habsiyyat v persoiazychnyi poezii XI–XIV vv* (*The Prison Poem Genre in Persian Literature from the Eleventh to the Fourteen Centuries*) (Moscow: Natalis, 2006).
56. Valī Allāh Ẓafarī, *Ḥabsīyyah dar adab-i Fārsī: Az āghāz-i shiʿr-i Pārsī tā pāyān-i Zandīyah* (Tehran: Amīr Kabīr, 1985/6); *Ḥabsīyyah dar adab-i Fārsī: Az āghāz-i dawrah-'i Qājārīyah tā inqilāb-i Islāmī* (Tehran: Amīr Kabīr, 2001/2).

2

The Lyric Poet's Body

Writing from Lahore, a borderland region under Ghaznavid rule, where South Asian dynasties regularly clashed with Muslim rulers, Masʿud Saʿd Salman is considered to be the first prison poet in Persian literary history. He was born in 1046, according to his own testimony, into a family that had risen high in the ranks of the Ghaznavid administration. In his verse, Masʿud Saʿd states that his father served the government for fifty years:

> Did not Saʿd Salman serve for fifty years?
> He laboured hard for this land and estate.

> نه سعد سلمان پنجاه سال خدمت کرد
> بدست کرد برنج اینهمه ضیاع و عقار [1]

Notwithstanding his illustrious lineage, or perhaps precisely as a result of it, the poet's consciousness of social inferiority palpably shapes his experience of imprisonment. The sharp contrast between the poet's privileged social status and his incarcerated condition led to the production of poetry that was intimately linked to his personal experience. Sunil Sharma notes that 'more than any other Persian poet, [Masʿud Saʿd's] biography is inextricably linked to his poetry and in fact much of his work does not make sense without the necessary historical contextualization'.[2] Indeed, it is possible to situate Masʿud Saʿd's poems along a temporal continuum according to their tone, theme and register of complaint.

This chapter introduces the prison poem as a lyric genre produced by the prison poet's corporeal poetics. It traces the beginnings of this genre across what is now Central and South Asia with a consideration of the poetic forms through which the prison poem was established by Masʿud Saʿd and

Nasrullah Munshi, including two different types of quatrains (*rubaʿi* and *dubayti*), and numerous odes (*qasidas*). Concurrently, I review the institutionalisation of the prison poem in the contemporaneous literary criticism of ʿAruzi, ʿAwfi and other literary critics, which contributed to the formation of this tradition. I conclude by briefly considering the South Asian trajectory of the genre inaugurated by Masʿud Saʿd through the extant yet understudied prison poems of ʿAmid al-Din Lumaki and Minhaj Siraj Juzani.

Whereas this chapter focuses largely on South and Central Asian poets, the rest of this book focuses on poets from Iran and the Caucasus. By bringing these diverse literary geographies together, I present the Persian poem as a genre that traversed many different cultural contexts, and which in the process was shaped by multiple non-Muslim religious traditions.[3] Tracing how the lyric poet's body was made into a genre by a poet from Lahore and his interpreters across the eastern Islamic world helps to establish the future itinerary of the prison poem with which the chapters that follow are concerned.

Defining the Lyric

Defining the lyric as a genre is a notoriously fraught endeavour.[4] One place to begin is with Earl Miner's thesis that the lyric is the genre that most closely approximates to a universal across literary cultures. 'The primacy of the lyric,' argues Miner, 'in the emergence of literature confirms its role as the originative or foundation genre for the poetics or poetics systems of *all* literary cultures except the western holdout . . . In all its versions, the lyric-based poetics is affective and expressive in nature.'[5] Miner is a pioneer in his efforts to develop a global poetics of genre. Although his assertion of the lyric's universality homogenises world literature and is open to contestation from many corners, it facilitates the turn away from European paradigms. As we will see, in both the formal and thematic mode, the lyric played an overwhelming role in the formation of the Persian prison poem.

Masʿud Saʿd's affective and expressive aesthetics were underscored by the two critics who contributed the most to the dissemination of his poems, ʿAruzi and Muhammad ʿAwfi. It is not only the affective dimension of Masʿud Saʿd's poetic register that qualifies him as a lyric poet. Masʿud Saʿd's poetry is rich in formal devices that literary theorists working outside the Persian tradition readily ascribe to the lyric. Most notably, he frequently relies on shifting the addressee (*iltifat*), a poetic device which his Central Asian contemporary, Raduyani, defines as 'when a poet . . . shifts from one meaning [*ma'ni*] to another'.[6] In the guise of apostrophe, Anglo-American critics have qualified this device as a condition of possibility for the lyric as such.[7] The most famous among Mas'ud Sa'd's apostrophic poems is his elegy for Lahore, written from prison:

Oh Lahore, woe on you! How are you without me?
How can you be bright without your bright sun?
You were once adorned by the garden of my talent.
With no tulip, violet, or lily, how are you?

ای لاوهور ویحک بی من چگونه‌ای
بی‌آفتاب روشن، روشن چگونه‌ای
ای باغ طبع نظم من آراسته ترا
بی‌لاله و بنفشه و سوسن چگونه‌ای [8]

Although formally a *qasida*, a genre that is commonly translated as 'ode' and sometimes opposed to the lyric, this prison poem might more appropriately be called a lyric ode. The term is not without precedent; during the late eighteenth century, the British poet Peter Pindar, who described himself on the title pages of his books as 'a distant relation to the poet of Thebes', published a series 'lyric odes' which he addressed to 'the Royal Academicians'.[9] Translators of world poetry have also had recourse to the term 'lyric ode'. F. V. Dickins called his translation of the ancient Japanese poetry collection *Hyak Nin Is'shu* (1866), 'Japanese Lyrical Odes', without elaborating on what he meant by this term.[10] While the word 'lyric' is strategically deployed in Dickins' title, it is absent from the book itself, leaving the reader with no clue with regard to the intended meaning of this term. The concept of the lyric ode makes concrete what these previous usages intuited in inchoate fashion: while the term 'ode' captures the genre's politics, prison poems also often have a lyric dimension, which is centred on the poet's subjectivity. For this reason, I avoid here the conventional rendering of *qasida* as 'ode' and instead consider Mas'ud Sa'd's prison poems as lyric odes.

As with many of Mas'ud Sa'd's *qasida*s, apostrophe is written into the very grammar of these verses. The refrain '*ai*' commands the reader's attention and evokes their presence.[11] This apostrophic second-person marker alerts us to a dialogue between the poet and a fictive interlocutor that is bound by the strictures of the lyric to end in isolation rather than communion. It combines what M. H. Abrams called in his study of the Romantic lyric 'the free flow of consciousness, the interweaving of thought, feeling, and perceptual detail, and the easy naturalness of the speaking voice' that characterises this genre, while at the same time grafting onto this lyric form oratorical aspects of the panegyric.[12]

In Masʿud Saʿd's apostrophe to Lahore, the city is speechless. The subject of the lyric ode is the poet's subjectivity, not his interlocutors. Six verses into the poem, the city is infolded within the poet's self. Jonathan Culler intuits Masʿud Saʿd's bifurcated subject when he argues that 'the subjectivity at work in the lyric is a formal principle of unity more than the consciousness of a given individual'.[13] While the rhetorical appeal to an other – whether a patron, a ruler, a lover or a city – frequently precedes the lyric ode's inward turn, the foregrounding of the poet's self over his interlocutors is among the clearest genre markers of the prison poem. Its emergence coincides with the changing conception of selfhood that marks the literature of this period on the global scale, as has been well documented for medieval Europe.[14]

After addressing the city of Lahore in the second person for six verses, the poet turns inward. The dialogue becomes a monologue, of the poet with himself. Notably, the poet compares himself with Bijan, the Iranian knight in the *Shahnama* whose captivity inside a well is a recurring trope of prison poem poetics, as shown in the Introduction. Masʿud Saʿd anticipates the later prison poems of Khaqani and ʿAmid al-Din Lumaki when he writes:

> You're suddenly separated from your dear child.
> In the grief of his absence, in lament and tears, how are you?
> You don't send me a message saying faithfully:
> now that you're enchained in prison, like Bijan, how are you?
> When topsy-turvy fortune drags you down,
> how are you with your head proudly raised?

ناگه عزیز فرزند از تو جدا شده است
با درد او به نوحه و شیون چگونه‌ای
نفرستیم پیام و نگویی به حسن عهد:

کاندر حصار بسته چو بیژن چگونه‌ای
گر در حضیض برکشدت باژگونه بخت
از اوج برفراخته گردن چگونه‌ای

Although the poet appears to speak *in propria persona*, the allusion to Bijan and to the poet's chains show that Mas'ud Sa'd's voice is mediated by impersonal norms of the genre he inaugurated. Far from engaging in unmediated representation, lyricism in this poem is constituted by the 'categorical elimination of experience' which transforms 'the poet's presence into a formal conceit'.[15] Arguably the most famous prison poem of the eleventh century, Mas'ud Sa'd's homage to Lahore begins in a dialogue, while using the device of apostrophe to shift to an internal monologue. The poet's internally bifurcated self lays the foundation for the prison poem's lyric transformation of the panegyric ode.

The poem to Lahore is also paradigmatic of the genre in that, although it begins in separation, has an open and unforetold destination. The absence of a fixed itinerary demonstrates the poet's freedom. This particular text ends in a vocal assertion of poetic selfhood that moves in a different direction from the grief expressed in the opening lines, which was directed outward. Mas'ud Sa'd concludes the poem with verses that forthrightly address his own body:

You could never stand the indifference of a friend;
How are you today with the enemy's blame?
Residing in an airless prison,
How are you, poet, without the open garden?
I was a meadow. You were the lion in the meadow.
How were you with me? How are you without me?

با ناز دوست هرگز طاقت نداشتی
امروز با شماتت دشمن چگونه‌ای
ای دم گرفته زندان گشته مقام تو
بی‌دل گشاده طارم و گلشن چگونه‌ای
من مرغزار بودم و تو شیر مرغزار
با من چگونه بودی و بی‌من چگونه‌ای

Whereas the opening lines are those of a poet alienated from his body who sees in Lahore the very self from which he has been separated, these closing lines are those of a poet who has been reunited to his body, confirming Sharma's point that, in Masʿud Saʿd's prison poetry, the 'increased and ultimately exclusive focus' on the poet's self generates 'constant references to his own versatility and virtuosity' that surpass the boasting (*fakhr*) typical of the panegyric *qasida*.[16] The voice in the beginning of the poem is entirely submerged within another (Lahore); as the poem develops the poet turns inward, focusing solipsistically on his imprisoned body. Judging by its concluding verses, the final lines of Masʿud Saʿd's Lahore poem reinforce the 'non-response of the "you"' as a structural feature of the lyric.[17] Having been separated from his initial self – the free person who resides in Lahore – the imprisoned poet acquires a new body, that resides 'in an airless prison . . . without the open garden'.

The scenario evoked in this poem is many stages removed from the prison poems of Khaqani that more closely correspond to the political-theological model of Kantorowicz. Yet the duality that broadly structures this poem is a familiar feature of the genre: between inside and outside the prison; between a time-space marked by freedom and rooted in Lahore; and a time-space marked by confinement, rooted in the poet's body. Masʿud Saʿd's Lahore poem displays these themes in an early stage; their gradual development and transformation during the eleventh and twelfth centuries into a paradigm for the poet's prophetic body is the story of the prison poem.

Sharma's account of Masʿud Saʿd's poetics is theorised largely through the topos of exile rather than prison or chains. Examining more closely the intersection between the captive body and lyric affect in his poems can shed light on the role of imprisonment in constituting the prison poem as a genre. The role played by the lyric voice within Masʿud Saʿd's aesthetics has as much to do with political conditions along the eastern periphery of the Ghaznavid empire as with the poet's private predilections. Two early works of Persian literary criticism pave the way for a fuller account of why the prison poem emerged when and where it did, the political relations that shaped its genesis and structure, and the implications of these configurations for our understanding of its literary form. The first text is ʿAruzi's *Four Discourses* (introduced in Chapter 1). The second is Muhammad ʿAwfi's *Pith of Essences* (*Lubab al-albab*), widely considered to be the first biographical compendium (*tazkira*) of Persian poets. I turn to each text successively by way of exploring their treatments of the prison poet's lyric subjectivity and of probing the space opened up by prison poetry for political critique.

Inventing a Lyric Subject

What new discursive relations were registered and formalised by the prison poem? The first extant discussion of the genre in Persian prose sheds much light on this question. *Four Discourses* was composed between 1155 and 1157 for the Ghurid ruler Abu Hasan ʿAli b. Masʿud (1148–1215).[18] The Ghurids (also known as the Shansabanids) were vassals of the Ghaznavids (under whose patronage Masʿud Saʿd wrote) who had converted from Buddhism to Islam. Although they spoke a language other than New Persian, the Ghurids were major patrons of Persian literature, much like the Ghaznavids.[19] *Four Discourses* is the first text to integrate the prison poem into Persian literary criticism and to record its genesis in prose. Alongside treatises on Persian poetics such as Vatvat's *Magic Gardens*, ʿAruzi's *Four Discourses* developed an aesthetics specific to the Persian prison poem. Concurrently, if less directly, it generated the framework for the genre's political theology that will be explored in subsequent chapters.

Framing the reception of Masʿud Saʿd's prison poems for a millennium to come, ʿAruzi opens his discussion with a detailed report of the circumstances leading to Masʿud Saʿd's incarceration by Sultan Ibrahim, son of the notorious Mahmud of Ghazna, a ruler remembered primarily as a 'temple raider' and 'destroyer', due to his raids on South Asian territory.[20] He explains that the poet was imprisoned following reports that he had conspired with the sultan's son to desert him and enter into the service of the Saljuq ruler Malikshah in Iraq. As ʿAruzi recounts, Masʿud Saʿd was sent to Jiristan, to a fortress (*qalʿeh*) called Nay, which he was to make famous with his poems. While incarcerated in the fortress, Masʿud Saʿd sent a quatrain (*dubayti*) to Sultan Ibrahim. ʿAruzi presents this poem as the inaugural text in what he was the first to call the *habsiyyat* tradition. Centrally located in the first work of Persian literary criticism, Masʿud Saʿd's quatrain is the first poem to be denominated as a prison poem in Persian literary history. While not his best prison poem, it is arguably his most consequential. The two verses that comprise it are dense with double meanings:

Malikshah should be in your chains,
and your chains wear down the sovereign leg.
He who is born from the loins of Saʿd Salman
cannot harm your sovereignty, even if he becomes poison.

در بند تو ای شاه ملکشه باید
تا بند تو پای تاجداری ساید
آنکس که ز پشت سعد سلمان آید
گر زهر شود ملک ترا نگزاید

These verses have an immediate political goal: insisting on his loyalty to Sultan Ibrahim, the poet denies the allegation that he was planning to switch sides. Yet he does so evasively; his verses yield many different readings. One interpretation would emphasise the power of the ruler, Sultan Ibrahim, who is also the poet's jailer. And yet these verses also yield a rather different, and even opposite meaning: by emphasising the process through which chains (*band*) wear down (*sayad*) the sovereign's crown (*tajdari*), the poem also undermines the ruler's claim to power. Admittedly, this alternative reading is merely latent in the poem, but it persisted as an undercurrent throughout the entire genre, until Khaqani's prison poems brought it out into the open.

Alongside its incipient critique of sovereignty, we find here a subtle insistence on the superiority of the poet vis-à-vis the ruler. Not only does Masʿud Saʿd explicitly state that he will not harm the sultan; the very suggestion of 'wearing down the sovereign crown' that we find in the first verse casts a shadow over the entire poem, suggesting that the very act of imprisoning his subjects weakens the ruler. That the poet is the one to point this out further strengthens his own power and by implication undermines that of the sultan.

The transferability – and hence fragility – of sovereign power is underscored by a pun in the second verse, in which the poet asserts that no one descended from his father will infringe on the sultan's power. The term used here for sovereignty (*mulk*), directly invokes the name of Sultan Ibrahim's rival, Malikshah (*mulk* and *malik* share the same root), as if to suggest that sovereignty belongs to him alone. Although Masʿud Saʿd may have hoped that his poem would secure his release, its primary impact was to highlight the precarious circumstances of the imprisoned poet and to expose the frailty of the ruler's sovereignty.

The preceding reading of these two ambiguous verses emerges from a tradition of prison writing, in which poets turned to Masʿud Saʿd as their inaugural example. A reading produced in retrospect, that narrative was shaped by the subsequent trajectory of the prison poem. Whether Masʿud Saʿd intended to or not, with these verses he set the stage for the more direct critique of sovereign power in the century to come that is documented in subsequent chapters. As these chapters also show, the prison poem's effort to expose the fragility of the sovereign figured heavily in Persian literature's corporeal poetics throughout the long twelfth century.

ʿAruzi denominates Masʿud Saʿd's poem as a quatrain (*dubayti*), thereby fixing the formal dimension of its genre, and creating a framework for a specific relationship between form and topos within the prison poem.[21] Reflecting on the political uses of the quatrain in courtly contexts, scholars have argued that the formal genre of the quatrain was both 'an outsider and an insider to the world of patronage as typified by classical Persian poetry'.[22] The liminal status of the quatrain in courtly milieux provides a context for understanding Masʿud Saʿd's *dubayti*, which is seen by ʿAruzi as the poem that inaugurated the genre. Occasioned by a conflict of interest between poet and patron, the *dubayti* is embedded within courtly politics. Beyond the matter of formal genres, poetry composed in prison has a polemical relation to the ruler. By subversively advocating the imprisonment of a king, Masʿud Saʿd raises questions about the legitimacy of the sovereign's rule. In declaring that he has no intention of harming the sultan's domains (*mulk*), the poet highlights the fragility of the sultan's power. It is the poet – not the sovereign – who dictates the terms of governance in this poem, albeit from the weak position of his prison cell.

ʿAruzi accounts for the emergence of the prison poem's lyric subject by reframing the circumstances of the poet's imprisonment. Stating that Masʿud Saʿd's prison poems move him to tears and make his hair stand on end, he frames the readerly encounter through the prism of genre. He accuses the ruling class, which control the circulation of courtly literature, of lacking the capacity to appreciate poetry. In the following revealing passage concerning the above-quoted quatrain, ʿArudi recounts the very moment when the prison poem was born:

> This quatrain was brought to the king . . . but it had no effect on him, even though all readers with literary taste and impartial judgement will recognise that Mas'ud Sa'd's *habsiyyat* attain to the highest degree of sublimity ['*uluv*] and that they are rich in eloquence [*fasahat*]. Sometimes when I read his poems, my hair stands on its ends and water flows from my eyes. But when these verses were read to the king, he felt nothing and his heart was not warmed. Thus [the king] died, leaving that free man [Mas'ud Sa'd] in prison. (*CM* 64–5)

No other poet, adds 'Aruzi, approximated the splendour of Mas'ud Sa'd's prison poems. 'Aruzi describes the poems as 'brilliant odes' (*qasa'id-i ghurar*) and praises the 'pearl-like rarity' (*nafa'is-i durar*) of their language. He insists on Mas'ud Sa'd's inborn talent (*tab'*) for composing such refined (*masnu'*) poems.[23]

'Aruzi's efforts to situate prison poetics within a broader social and political context contrast with what another literary critic, Rashid al-Din Vatvat, would later describe as Mas'ud Sa'd's uniqueness among the poets of the Persianate world ('*ajam*). The two qualities that distinguished the Lahore poet in Vatvat's view are the beauty of his motifs (*husn-i ma'ani*) and the delicacy of his words (*lut-i alfaz*).[24] In support of his argument for Mas'ud Sa'd's uniqueness, Vatvat adduces another prison poem to exemplify the trope of 'comprehensive discourse [*al-kalam al-jami'*]'.[25] For Vatvat, this trope consists of 'wise thoughts (*hikmat*), teachings (*maw'izat*), and complaints against fate (*shikayat-i ruzgar*)'. He illustrates comprehensive discourse with the verses by Mas'ud Sa'd cited in the preceding chapter:

> Blessed Allah! Look at this fate and this life.
> From here to death, prison is my home.
> My spleen became like a comb's teeth from this regret
> when I saw a white strand of hair on my comb.

تبارک الله ازین بخت و زندگانی من
که تا بمیرم زندان بود مرا خانه
چو شانه شد جگرم شاخ شاخ ز انده آن
که موی دیدم شاخ سپید در شانه

Vatvat develops the formal dimension of the prison poem when he writes that many of Mas'ud Sa'd's poems make use of this literary device, 'especially those composed in prison [*dar habs*]'. These poems are organised by the topos of complaints against fate. The homiletic rhetoric that Vatvat discerns in Mas'ud Sa'd's poetics lays the groundwork for the transgressive genre that Khaqani would pioneer in Shirvan, following the prison poem's migration to the Caucasus.

For 'Aruzi, who is more engaged by literary criticism than by the discipline of rhetoric, artistic greatness is determined by innate talent (*tab'*). For Vatvat the rhetorician, artistic excellence is a function of the poet's style (*shiveh*; *HS*, 318). Whereas style can be acquired – hence, the need for rhetorical manuals like his own – talent is only given or denied. And yet 'Aruzi the literary critic and Vatvat the rhetorician converge in crucial ways. Both envision a rigorous course of training for the aspiring poet. For 'Aruzi, this training includes memorising 20,000 verses from the poetry of the ancients (*mutaqaddiman*) and 10,000 verses from the poetry of the moderns (*muta'akhkhiran*) (*CM*, 48).

The appeal to natural talent (*tab'*) is immediately followed in 'Aruzi's aesthetic theory by an appeal to acquired or artificial talent (*masnu'*, a term frequently contrasted in Arabic poetics to *matbu'*, innate talent).[26] We might expect to find that prison poetry comprises a combination of natural talent (*tab'*) and innate talent (*matbu'*). Instead, we read that talent (*tab'*) and craft are the requisite qualities for the composition of poetry. While 'Aruzi conjoins talent to effort and inspiration to artifice, both critics perceive in the prison poem an emergent literary genre that combines affect with artifice. Equally, both critics regard this genre as one worth recommending to future poets.

'Aruzi was concerned above all to establish the political salience of the genre he first situated in critical discourse, while accounting for Mas'ud Sa'd's persecution:

> That free man [*azad mard*] spent his entire life in prison [*habs*] in their government. This infamy remained in that great dynasty . . . I am doubtful how to account for this: as the sign of a resolute mind, or a negligent nature, or cruelty at heart or evil intention. However this act might be accounted for, it was unworthy of praise. (*CM*, 75)

This is the second time that ʿAruzi juxtaposes freedom and imprisonment. In spite of having spent nearly two decades in prison, Masʿud Saʿd is described as a free man, as if to indicate that no conflict with an earthly sovereign can undermine the poet's innate freedom. The state can, however, govern through oppression. Under such conditions, the good poet spends his life in prison, while the evil man rises to power.

ʿAruzi's patron, Abu'l Hasan ʿAli b. Masʿud of the Ghurid dynasty, was in continual conflict with the Ghaznavids. ʿAruzi's interest in maligning the Ghaznavids is evident in his account of Mahmud of Ghazna's failure to appreciate the work that is widely regarded as the greatest epic of Persian literature, Ferdowsi's *Shahnama*. According to his report, Ferdowsi personally carried his epic poem to Ghazna after working on it for thirty years, and was turned away before he even had a chance to speak to the sultan. Many of ʿAruzi's anecdotes concerning literary culture under Ghaznavid rule seem aimed to demonstrate the corruption of Ghaznavid politics and to shine a light on the more generous Ghurids.

Yet there is more to ʿAruzi's account than a critique of a specific regime. ʿAruzi wrote as a literary figure at the Ghurid court, but also as a key exponent of the political and lyrical ethos of the Persian prison poem. He was also a poet himself. His stance is evident in the indictment of worldly rulers that concludes ʿAruzi's narration of Masʿud Saʿd's life in prison:

> I have never known a wise man who was prepared to praise [the Ghaznavid] dynasty . . . And I heard the king of the world . . . Malikshah say . . . that imprisoning an enemy is a sign of a malicious heart, because there are only two reasons [for doing so]: either he is good [*muslih*] or evil [*mufsid*]. If he is good, it is an injustice [*zulm*] to put him in prison [*dar habs*] . . . that negative reputation [*bad nami*] will endure until the resurrection.

Aware that the Ghaznavid literary ethos understood a person's honour (*nam*) to impinge on the very core of their identity, ʿAruzi uses this concept to blacken the names of rulers who persecute and imprison poets.

ʿAruzi here takes his cue from Ferdowsi, who in his epic poem proclaimed: 'I shall not die henceforth, I'll live long / Because I have sown the seeds of poetry.'[27] With this verse, Ferdowsi connected the durability of poetry with its ability to bring new things into the world. As the first canoniser of the prison poem, ʿAruzi was keenly attuned to the genre's transgression of existing literary norms. His theoretical justification for poetry quoted briefly in Chapter 1 can also enrich the way in which we read the prison poem. I quote it here in full:

> Poetry is a craft [*sinaʿat*] by means of which the poet arranges in order the imagined premises [*muqaddamat*] and knits together resulting analogies in such a way as to make the meaning of an insignificant thing [*maʿni khurd*] significant and the meaning of a significant thing insignificant. [The poet] displays a beautiful thing in a hideous robe and an ugly thing in gorgeous raiment. By means of such ambiguity [*iham*] [the poet] stirs the irascible and concupiscent faculties so that people experience contractive and expansive faculties and thereby cause great affairs in the order of the world. (*CM*, 30)

ʿAruzi's account of the genesis of the prison poem tallies well with the claims he makes for poetry as a disturber of the world's order (*nizam-i ʿalam*). The transformative capacity of the prison poem is attested by its mixture of the ugly and beautiful (*zisht va niku*), the small and the large (*khurd va bozorg*), and the contractive and expansive faculties (*ghazani va shahvani*). Mixing these categories causes readers' hair to stand on end and tears to pour from their eyes. Such reader-oriented formulations codified the prison poem's invention of lyric subjectivity amid the political fragmentation of Ghaznavid, Ghurid and Saljuq empires.

Prison Poetry's Shifting Idioms

Muhammad ʿAwfi, a literary chronicler who began writing a few generations after ʿAruzi, was better informed about the prison poems of Masʿud Saʿd's fellow prisoner, Nasrullah Munshi, author of a Persian version of *Kalila and Dimna* (1141), a work that belongs to the genre of advice for kings, or mirrors-for-princes (also known as *Fürstenspiegel* in the European tradition). Having secured a position as vizier and then fallen into disgrace, Nasrullah Munshi was executed under Khusraw Malik (r. 1160–1186).

ʿAwfi's contribution to the prison poem also begins with his engagement with Masʿud Saʿd, whose native city of Lahore was not far from the court of Nasir al-Din Qubacha in Ucch where ʿAwfi lived and worked until 1258. It was in Ucch that ʿAwfi composed both the first Persian biographical compendium (*tazkireh*), *Pith of Essences* (*Lubab al-albab*) and an extensive collection of stories about the lives of scholars, saints and kings titled *Collection of Anecdotes and Flashes of Tales* (*Jawamiʿ al-hikayat va lawamiʿ al-rivayat*).[28] In the first work, ʿAwfi describes Masʿud Saʿd as a 'rare gem of his age' while punning on the instrument he used for composing poems (*nay*, meaning sugarcane, reed and, by implication, pen, since reeds were used in writing) and the name of the fortress where is was interred, also named Nay:

> [Masʿud Saʿd] was clipped of his wings in the ups and downs of the world and at times, like the sugarcane [*nay*], he sweetened the palate of the world's soul with the sugar of wisdom. At times in the fortress [*qalʿeh*] of Nay he swallowed the bitter poison of events. He performed noble deeds in the land of India [*bilad-i hind*] and spent his life in honour [*be niku nami*] and joy. (*Lubab*, 423)

Although ʿAwfi notes Masʿud Saʿd's imprisonment and praises his erudition, his citations do not go as far as either ʿAruzi or Vatvat in establishing Masʿud Saʿd's reputation as a prison poet.[29] The fragments (*qitʿehs*), poems (*shiʿrs*) and verses (*nazms*) (to follow the classifications used by ʿAwfi) of Masʿud Saʿd's poems that appear in *Pith of Essences* barely indicate the extent of the poet's talents. Nor do they add much to our understanding of the prison poem genre that, as ʿAruzi and Vatvat had noted half a century earlier, Masʿud Saʿd introduced into Persian literature. ʿAwfi includes only two unremarkable poems that are loosely associated with imprisonment. Unlike ʿAruzi, he does not develop the prison poem in all of its dimensions (as form, theme and discourse).

ʿAruzi introduced the prison poem as a genre by revealing its lyric subjectivity to a courtly, patron-oriented, literary culture that had hitherto focused on glorifying the sovereign. Vatvat singled out Masʿud Saʿd's prison poems – without however employing ʿAruzi's term for the genre, *habsiyyat* – by associating them with a specific literary device (*al-kalam al-jamiʿ*), and thereby with a kind of style. Although ʿAwfi mentions Masʿud Saʿd's imprisonment in the fortress of Nay, he does not directly present the prison poem as a genre. The closest ʿAwfi comes to evoking the prison poem as a genre is with his citation of the final line of a fragment (*qitʿeh*), which dramatically evokes the scene of imprisonment: 'the wind was mad and insane / [the sky] wrapped the water in chains'. He also cites a *qasida* by Masʿud Saʿd which uses as a familiar refrain a morphological variation of *band* (chains): *bandam* (*band*, meaning chains, but turned into a verb and conjugated in the subjunctive), beginning:

For how long will I bind my exhausted heart to worries?
Bind others for my faults in blame?

تا کی دل خسته در گمان بندم
جرمی که کنم برین و آن بندم

ʿAwfi closely reproduces ʿAruzi's account of the genesis of Masʿud Saʿd's prison poems. We saw above that ʿAruzi noted that Masʿud Saʿd was imprisoned as a consequence of his ties with Mahmud Sayf al-Dawla. ʿAwfi repeats this detail in different words. For both critics, the Persian prison poem has the same genesis: a poet is accused of affiliating with another king, and his sovereign becomes enraged. Notably, the patron and addressee for many of the poems of Abu Firas, the best known of Arabic captivity poets, also bore the name Sayf al-Dawla.[30] Scholars have noted overlaps in specific tropes and imagery between Abu Firas' poems written during his Byzantine captivity and Masʿud Saʿd's prison poems.[31] Whether the coinciding names of their patrons was known to ʿAruzi and ʿAwfi is impossible to say, but it may have intensified their mutual fixation on the name of Masʿud Saʿd's patron-jailer.

ʿAruzi stresses the sublimity (*ʿuluv*) of Masʿud Saʿd's prison poems as well as their eloquence (*fasahat*). While ʿAwfi's discussion of the prison poem is less conceptually innovative than its predecessors, his way of describing his experience of reading prison poetry evokes a corporeal poetics of the reader's body, as if in response to the poet's imprisonment. While reading these prison poems, ʿAwfi suggests, readers' mouths become so stricken with grief that their upper lips cannot turn upwards to create the sound of the letters b and m:

> In this *qasida* of Masʿud Saʿd [written from prison] there is such elegance of artistry [*sukhan-i sinaʿat*] and golden lustre in their brilliance that while reading it is impossible to locate [the letters] b and m. The upper lip does not descend. (*Lubab*, 424)

This unusual evocation of the reading experience further develops a method for reading prison poetry by associating specific letters with specific emotions. The phonemes *ba* (ب) and *mim* (م) are both formed by the meeting of the upper and lower lips. By preventing the joining of letters conventionally pronounced together, the prison poem gives corporeal form to the experience of imprisonment.

While ʿAruzi dwells on the grief memorialised by prison poetry, ʿAwfi underscores how Masʿud Saʿd's prison poem incapacitates its readers. The prison poem is paradoxically adept at rendering the reader inarticulate. The silence induced by the prison poem attests to its transgressive propensities, for as the next chapter shows, the prison poets of Shirvan added a cosmological and metaphysical transgression to the genre's repertoire. The world of the prison cell was rendered as text and the text of the poem became the imprisoned poet's world.

All extant contemporaneous critical engagements with the prison poem, including the three commentators discussed here (ʿAruzi, Vatvat and ʿAwfi), refrain from making the bold political-theological claims advanced in the poetry itself, as well as in this book. It is perhaps for this reason that ʿAwfi's image of the reader's open mouth – lips ajar, stumbling over words that cannot be pronounced, incapacitated by the feelings the poet has evoked – tells us more about the Persian prison poem than do centuries of literary criticism and history, and indeed much modern scholarship. Rendered mute, the upper and lower lips of the reader of a prison poem are suspended in a state of perpetual astonishment. The reader's lips are ravished by the genre's lyric power, just as the poet's body is incapacitated by his chains.

After introducing *Kalila and Dimna* as among the most useful (*dastmayeh*) books, ʿAwfi recounts the events leading up to Nasrullah Munshi's imprisonment and execution. He recognises that Nasrullah Munshi's fate 'entered a period of decline' as a result of calumnies against him by evil-doers. Ultimately, he continues, 'the star of his good fortune faced a calamity, his condition became inverted, and the descent into misfortune was evident. Due to the tyranny of the age, he became a captive [*muqayyad*] and was imprisoned' (*Lubab*, 87). Reversing ʿAruzi's careless treatment of the poems of Nasrullah Munshi as compared with his sympathetic treatment of Masʿud Saʿd's parallel corpus, ʿAwfi grants Nasrullah Munshi what he denied Masʿud

Sa'd: a thorough and detailed discussion of his prison poetry. Two quatrains are cited, one of which is the following:

> Although we suddenly deserted power's tribunal,
> God be praised, we left in greater wisdom.
> Many have come and many have parted.
> We too will be gone, by God's will.

از مسند عز اگرچه ناگه رفتیم
حمدالله که نیک آگه رفتیم
رفتند و شدند و نیز آیند و روند
ما نیز توکلت علی‌الله رفتیم (143)

The temporal and political allusions that structure this poem set the stage for later prison poems. The tribunal (*masnad*) referred to in the first line (*misra'*) strengthens the theme of judgement. This tribunal is the seat on which a king, judge or vizier sits when he passes judgements. It is the locus of the body politic, as well the physical location of the body of the person who is endowed with the right to judge. This right is provisional, the poet implies, for God will judge all his subjects, including those who rule in his name.

The third line – 'Many have come and many have parted' – alludes to the fleetingness of worldly power, and prefigures the *ubi sunt* (meditation on mortality) style discussed in Chapter 5. These words can be taken as an implicit warning addressed to the sovereign. The poem juxtaposes the contingency of worldly power to the everlasting divine power to which the poet appeals in the second line. While awaiting execution, Nasrullah Munshi evokes in this quatrain a sequence of overthrown tribunals. Inevitably, at some point in this chain, the sultan will be judged.

In his discussion of Nasrullah Munshi, 'Awfi equates poetic inversion (*ma'kus*), with misfortune (*manhus*). Likewise, the condition of the captive (*muqayyad*) and that of the prisoner (*mahbus*) are linked by 'Awfi. Nasrullah Munshi's incarceration is attributed to the injustice or cruelty of time (*awr-i zamaneh*), rather than to a specific transgression and punishment. (Mas'ud Sa'd also frequently used the term *jawr* with reference to his unjust imprisonment.[32]). Although it was expressed in a cosmological lexicon, Nasrullah Munshi's imprisonment was political. Ultimately, it was his death sentence.

His jealous rivals sought to foment suspicion regarding his loyalty in the mind of Sultan Ibrahim of Ghazna, the same ruler who had ordered Masʿud Saʿd's imprisonment.

ʿAwfi's political explanation for Masʿud Saʿd's misfortune is immediately followed by a cosmic retelling of this event: the star of Masʿud Saʿd's fortune (*akhtar-i iqbal*) fell into adversity (*wabal*). Here as elsewhere, event-based and cosmic history merge to generate the prison poem's political theology. The 'banner of polity [*rayat-i dawlat*)]', a term that simultaneously invokes political subjects and the elements of fortune, is said to be inverted (*maʿkus*) like a sun in its ascent. ʿAwfi was surely aware that the juxtaposition of the sun's ascent and its descent was one of Masʿud Saʿd's favourite ways of evoking his imprisonment. The image of the rising sun alludes to the fact that all that he could see from the fortress of Nay where he was confined was the movement of the sun across the firmament.[33]

Like the 'banner of the polity', the polysemous term *dawlat*, which can mean 'fortune', 'fate' or any given political regime, further sets the stage for the prison poem's political poetics. In the prison poems of Masʿud Saʿd and others, *dawlat* and *mihnat* (affliction) often occur together. This polyvalence lays bare ʿAwfi's political aesthetics: the unjustly imprisoned poet suffers from the inversion or reversal of *dawlat*, as if a natural disaster had occurred. The cosmic equilibrium has been violated, and the political order has been subverted. The conceptualisation of injustice as the violation of a natural order precedes the conceptualisation of injustice as a human failure.

In accounting, albeit elliptically, for the emergence of the prison poem, ʿAwfi bears witness to a transition that was taking place in twelfth- and thirteenth-century Persian literary and political culture (and which is presented more fully in Chapter 6) between the two concepts of *dawlat*. A concept of justice grounded in divine authority was gradually yielding to one anchored in an increasingly secularised sovereignty grounded in worldly power. This process parallels the contemporaneous transformation in the idioms of governance (*siyasat*) documented by legal scholars, and their increasing alignment with discretionary punishment (*taʿzir*), most explicitly in the political theory of the Delhi Sultanate.[34]

In a further continuation of ʿAruzi's legacy with respect to the prison poem, ʿAwfi cites a quatrain that Nasrullah Munshi sent to Sultan Ibrahim.

Although the incident closely mirrors what happened to Masʿud Saʿd, in this case the quatrain is called a *rubaʿi*, rather than a *dubayti*. As noted above, ʿAruzi reported that Masʿud Saʿd defended himself against the charge of disloyalty by affirming that neither he nor his successors would ever poison the sultan's domains. Here, in this analogous quatrain, Nasrullah Munshi critiques this same sovereign in strikingly similar terms. This time, however, he is bolder in his critique of the sovereign's abuse of power through imprisonment. Contrasting the temporality of this-worldly power to the temporality of the resurrection (*ruz-i qiyamat*), Nasrullah Munshi warns the ruler that his subjects neither fear nor respect him. Referring as other prison poets had done to chains, he links the ruler's inability to grasp the source of his power to the abuse being inflicted on his body through imprisonment:

> O shah, never do what you might be called to account for
> on a day when you know no one fears you.
> You take no pleasure in the dominion and kingdom God has given you.
> How can I rejoice, being enchained by you?

ای شاه مکن آنچه بپرسند از تو
روزی که تو دانی که نترسند از تو
خرسند نه ای بملک و دولت زخدای
من چون باشم ببند خرسند از تو [35]

Eerily reminiscent of the prison poem of Masʿud Saʿd, Nasrullah Munshi's quatrain anticipates the unmasking of worldly power that was to become the defining feature of the prison poem. Masʿud Saʿd's quatrain offers a close intertext, with a nearly identical opening and ending:

> O shah, you should fear when they call you to account
> in a place where you know no one fears you.
> You take no pleasure in the sovereignty God has given to you.
> How can I rejoice, being enchained by you?

ای شاه بترس از آنکه پرسند از تو
جایی که تو دانی که نترسند از تو
خرسند نیی بپادیشاهی ز خدای
پس چون باشم ببند خرسند از تو [36]

The nearly identical wording of these quatrains, which have the effect of conflating Masʿud Saʿd and Nasrullah Munshi, indicates how the figure of the prison poet was generalised far beyond the life story of one individual poet and his prison poems. Just as he created the genre of the prison poem, Masʿud Saʿd's story served as a paradigm for what was to become a phenomenon. Masʿud Saʿd's saga of his eighteen-year imprisonment became an allegory for the position of the poet across the eastern Islamic world. The three critics discussed here, ʿAruzi, Vatvat and ʿAwfi, were instrumental in turning the lyric quatrains of Masʿud Saʿd and Nasrullah Munshi into templates for subsequent prison poems. Already in its early phases, prison poems could be *qasida*s, quatrains or fragmented forms. The formal genre fixity that characterises much of classical Arabo-Persian is not evident in the case of the prison poem, which is why I have denominated it a transgressive genre.

ʿAwfi's discussion of Nasrullah Munshi's quatrains further anchors the genre within the semantic field of the poet's body. Key terms in this lexicon are *gham* (sorrow), *mihnat* (affliction) and *ranj* (suffering). In these early stages of the prison poem's evolution, these words begin to differentiate themselves from each other. Sorrow (*gham*) conveys a melancholy resignation. Affliction (*mihnat*) communicates perpetual injustice, linked to a cosmic condition. Like its synonym *ranj*, *mihnat* also conveys the sense of physical exhaustion that one finds in the prison poetry of Shirvan a few decades later. The first poet of Shirvan, Falaki (discussed in the next chapter), brought this lexicon together in the first extant prison poem of the Shirvan school:

> I drown in such affliction [*mihnat*],
> that I don't care [*gham*] for this endless suffering [*ranj*].

> غرقه گشتم به محنتی که در آن
> غم این رنج بیکنارم نیست [37]

This poem evokes the physical dimension of this affliction (*mihnat*) by comparing the imprisoned poet with a drowning man. The affliction that renders him passive can be exorcised only by death. Sorrow (*gham*) by contrast abides with the poet for as long as he is in chains.

Writing a few decades after Falaki, ʿAwfi relied on the contrast established by the prison poem between affliction (*mihnat*) and sorrow (*gham*) to narrate Nasrullah Munshi's imprisonment.[38] 'Just as the days of his affliction [*mihnat*] were prolonged and the arrow of his enemies reached its target, intercessions by recourse to his virtue and art reached nowhere, they aimed to kill him,' he writes. Using the imagery of arrow and bow in conjunction with the planet Mercury, ʿAwfi describes how Nasrullah Munshi discerned the plans of his enemies to silence him forever.

Sorrow (*gham*) is a melancholic resignation to a predicament. Affliction (*mihnat*) by contrast denotes a violent reaction against the circumstances that caused the grief. Because sorrow is more closely associated with agency and freedom of the will, prison poems closely associated affliction with the imprisoned poet's body. ʿAwfi's account of Nasrullah Munshi's imprisonment ranges across the entire semantic field of the prison poem's corporeal poetics.

The prison poet's body is further textualised and incorporated into prison poem poetics with Masʿud Saʿd's declaration of his attempt to write a commentary (*sharh*) on his grief:

Here are the many afflictions that I described.
With all these afflictions, I'm always impotent.
Although I'm withered by affliction,
I am a fresh garden in age.

هست این همه محنت که شرح دادم
با این همه پیوسته ناتوانم
هرچند که پژمرده‌ام ز محنت
در عهد یکی تازه بوستانم [39]

Such commentaries made of grief, etched on the body, consolidate the distinctiveness of the prison poem as a genre in all of its political and poetic dimensions. The suffering highlighted by ʿAwfi as a constitutive aspect of this genre correlates to Masʿud Saʿd's aesthetic juxtaposition of the poet's physical weakness to his life-giving verse. The contrast between the poet's vatic power and his incarceration is rendered even more memorably in a *qasida* that not coincidentally shares a refrain with Masʿud Saʿd's elegy to Lahore, which, as seen above, culminates in the poet's imprisonment:

I plead from my heart like a reed from the fortress of Nay.
My ambition declined in this high place.

نالم ز دل چو نای من اندر حصار نای
پستی گرفت همت من زین بلند جای [40]

Later in the same poem, Mas'ud Sa'd plays on the polysemy of *dawlat* in order to associate affliction (*mihnat*) with political oppression:

> O affliction [*mihnat*]! Go only for an hour, before you become a mountain!
> O fortune [*dawlat*]! Stay with me, before you vanish like a breeze.

ای محنت ار نه کوه شدی ساعتی برو
وی دولت ار نه باد شدی لحظه‌یی بپای [41]

Dawlat here is used in the broadest sense to refer to fate as well as a political regime. The political dimension remains as yet muted. At the same time, the poet's inward turn attests to the changing idiom of the prison poem. Specifically, it reveals the historical transition from a concept of passive suffering to a concept of resistance and, ultimately, transgression. Across its frequent deployment in Persian prison poetry, and in related literary criticism, affliction (*mihnat*) gradually distinguished itself from a broader semantic field of corporeal suffering encompassed within other, less politically charged, varieties of grief.

Southern Migrations of Prison Poetry

The poetry of Mas'ud Sa'd and Nasrullah Munshi may have inspired a prison poem by another South Asian author, Minhaj Juzjani (1193–1266). Juzjani is best known not as a poet but as an historian who served under the Ghurids, the same dynasty for which 'Aruzi worked. His history of India, *Generations of the Age of Nasir* (*Tabaqat-i Nasiri*, 1260), 'crafted the first panel in the triptych of Persian historiography in India'.[42] Of greater relevance for the present is the poem he composed when he was imprisoned for a month and a half following his refusal to communicate a message from his ruler threatening war.

Like 'Awfi, Minhaj began his career in the court of Nasir al-Din Qubacha, until he moved to Delhi in search of more stable patronage. Echoing the prison poems of Mas'ud Sa'd, Juzjani's prison poem incessantly repeats the poet's hopeless complaint: 'for how long [*ta kay*]?':

For how long should my crystal tears be coloured coral
by the emerald sky on the amber of my face?
My sighs are like the smoke of aloe wood from Qumar; no wonder,
o my tears, if you're fragrant rose water.
Neither dark secrets nor evil reside in me, so why
am I imprisoned in Mt Sefahbodi?

تا کی بلور اشک مرا چرخ زمردی
بر کهربای روی دهد لون بسدی
آهم چو دود عود قماریست نی عجب
ای آب دیده گر تو گلاب مصعدی
نی شر سیرت سیه و نی بدی چرا
محبوسم و اسیر به کوه صفهبدی [43]

Many recurrent prison poem topoi are condensed into these verses, including secretions from the poet's body ('crystal tears' and 'the amber of my face') and high mountains that reinforce the sense of confinement. In yet another recurrent prison poem metaphor, the poet compares himself with a caged bird, and then puns on his name, Minhaj, which means both 'open' and 'straight':

I'm not Simurgh and this mountain is not Mt Qaf.
It's not pleasant for a parrot to be in prison [*habs*] forever.
Minhaj! You'd better seek your straight path on a journey.
You'll find no open path to dignity in the fortress.

سیمرغ نیستم من و این که نه کوه قاف
طوطی و حبس خوش نبود تا به سرمدی
منهاج راه راست تو در ره گشاده به
بر قلعه راه راست نیاید به مسندی

Imprisonment, Minhaj concludes, is an intrinsically degrading condition, and a violation of his dignity.

Mas'ud Sa'd's prison poems circulated westwards soon after the poet's death, as we know thanks to the poet Sana'i of Ghazna (d. 1131), who collected his master's poetry into a *divan*. Vatvat's inclusion of Mas'ud Sa'd's prison poems in his rhetorical manual also attests to their westward movement. Most of all, however, we know of this migration due to the impact of

Mas'ud Sa'd's prison poems on the prison poetry of Shirvan in the Caucasus, which became the centre of the second phase of the prison poem, discussed in the next chapter.

After its lengthy sojourn in the Caucasus, and its further development by Khaqani (discussed in Chapters 3–5), the genre resurfaced in thirteenth-century Delhi in the poems of figures like 'Amid al-Din Lumaki.[44] As noted in the Introduction, Lumaki authored at least two prison poems of high literary merit. The first develops an elaborate pun on the many meanings of *band*, with verses that play on the ambivalence of world sovereignty, such as:

> With your justice, break up the chains so that
> no chain remains, due to your justice, but the beloved's hair.

> اسباب فتح را ره عدل آن چنان گشای
> کز عدل تو نباشد جز زلف یار بند

In his other extant prison poem, 'Amid al-Din shifts his attention from his ruler-jailer to his own body. 'I'm nestled in a corner like a dove', he writes, and then, 'I'm like a thread: residing in the needle's eye'. The poem sharp evokes the poet's suffering:

> The body in jail needs to be fed. I have prescribed
> a bloody syrup and a meaty heart to quench its fever.

> تن غذاخواهست در بند غم و من را تبش
> شربت از خون و کباب از دل معین کرده‌ام

Thus did the prison poem become internalised, not only within Persian and Central Asian literature, but also within the broader South Asian literary landscape. Concurrently, Mas'ud Sa'd's poetry became part of an autonomous Indo-Persian literary culture. By the early modern period, an Indo-Persian poet of Central Asian origin such as Bidel (1644–1721), would establish a direct lineage from Mas'ud Sa'd's aesthetic to his own style.[45]

When does oppression justify rebellion? What is the role of thc insubordinate poet – and of the poetry of dissent – in resisting the unjust ruler? These questions have long animated prison literature. The earliest Persian prison poems, including those introduced in this chapter, spoke almost from within a patronage nexus, yet they were not subservient to it. Precisely because the imprisoned poet was locked away, sometimes forever, he was free to criticise the sultan. When the prison poet's hopes for freedom were permanently vanquished, prison poetry flourished: the genre was liberated from the pressure to please the patron in the hopes of securing release from prison. This is precisely what happened in the case of Masʿud Saʿd. The more desparate his situation became, the more plaintive was his lyric voice, and the sharper his critique. Although it was a catastrophe for him personally to end his life in prison without having committed a crime, the profound sense of bitternesss and alienation which Masʿud Saʿd infused into his poetry over the course of nearly two deacades of incarceration laid the foundations for the prison poem as a political genre for the next milleanium of Persian literature.

In their early Central Asian phase under Ghaznavid rule, prison poems did not directly subvert the terms of political sovereignty. Ghaznavid's poets' critiques were muted, lyrical and often indirect. This early stage in the prison poem's evolution is vital, however, for tracing its subsequent trajectory. In the new inflections they gave to sovereignty (*saltanat*), poetic discourse (*sukhan*) and politics (*siyasat*) across Ghaznavid and Ghurid domains, the prison poems of Masʿud Saʿd, Nasrullah Munshi, Minhaj Juzjani and their Central Asian contemporaries set the stage for the next phase of the Persian prison poem. This new phase, which followed the westward migration of the genre and its further development in the Caucasus, brought the poet's imprisoned body into conflict with the cosmos itself, as well as with the sovereign. It is to this second phase that the next chapter turns.

Notes

1. Masʿūd Saʿd, *Dīvān*; 1:212, *qaṣīda* 91.
2. Sharma, *Persian Poetry at the Indian Frontier*, 16.
3. For further on these channels of transmission, see Rebecca Ruth Gould, 'The Geographies of *ʿAjam*: The Circulation of Persian Poetry from South Asia to the Caucasus', *Medieval History Journal* 18(1) (2015): 87–119.
4. I pursue this line of inquiry in Rebecca Ruth Gould, 'Russifying the *Radif*: Lyric Translatability and the Russo-Persian Ghazal', *Comparative Critical Studies* 17(2) (2020): 263–84.
5. Earl Miner, "Why Lyric?" in Earl Miner and Amiya Dev (eds), *The Renewal*

of Song: Renovation in Lyric Conception and Practice (Calcutta: Seagull Books, 2000), 13 (emphasis added).

6. Rādūyānī, ch. 38, 'On Shifting the Address', in *Balaghas Compared*, trans. Michelle Quay.
7. Mark J. Smith, 'Apostrophe, or the Lyric Art of Turning Away', *TSLL* 49(4) (2007): 411–37, esp. 412.
8. Mas'ūd Sa'd, *Dīvān*, 2:689.
9. Peter Pindar, *More Lyric Odes to the Royal Academicians* (1789); *More Lyric Odes to the Royal Academicians, by Peter Pindar, a Distant Relation to the Poet of Thebes* (London, 1783); *Lyric Odes, to the Royal Academicians* (London, 1782).
10. Frederick Victor Dickins, *Hyak Nin Is'shu Or Stanzas by a Century of Poets, Being Japanese Lyrical Odes Translated Into English, with Explanat. Notes, the Text in Japanese and Roman Characters* (London: Smith, Elder, 1866).
11. For further discussion on the meaning of the *radīf* and its specific function in Persian poetics, see Franklin D. Lewis, 'The Rise and Fall of a Persian Refrain: The Radif 'Ātash u Āb', in Suzanne Pinckney Stetkevych (ed.), *Reorientations: Arabic and Persian Poetry* (Bloomington: Indiana University Press, 1994), 199–226.
12. M. H. Abrams, 'Structure and Style in the Greater Romantic Lyric', *Correspondent Breeze* (New York: W. W. Norton, 1986), 88.
13. Jonathan Culler, *Theory of the Lyric* (Cambridge, MA: Harvard University Press, 2015), 350.
14. See Charles Homer Haskins, *Renaissance of the Twelfth Century* (Cambridge, MA: Harvard University Press, 1927); Robert W. Hanning, *The Individual in the Twelfth-Century Romance* (New Haven, CT: Yale University Press, 1977); Colin Morris, *The Discovery of the Individual 1050–1200* (New York: Harper & Row, 1972); Carol Walker Bynum, 'Did the Twelfth Century Discover the Individual?' *Journal of Ecclesiastical History* 31 (1980): 1–17. While scholarship on the Islamic world has yet to establish a parallel body of work for this period, the Persian prison poem should serve as a starting point.
15. Stetkevych, 'The Arabic Lyrical Phenomenon', 72.
16. Sharma, *Persian Poetry at the Indian Frontier*, 32.
17. Smith, 'Apostrophe, or the Lyric Art of Turning Away', 415.
18. For the dating of *CM*, see Qazwīnī's remarks in *CM*, pp. ix–x, comm. p. 22 n. 4.
19. Some scholars have argued that the Ghurid language was related to Middle Persian, the official language of the Sāsānians; others (e.g., C. E. Bosworth, *EI*², 'Ghurids') maintain that they spoke a language related to an Eastern Iranian

dialect, such as Yaghnobi or Sogdian. The vassalage status of the Ghurids was to become a recurring feature of texts associated with the prison poem.

20. Manan Ahmed Asif, *A Book of Conquest: the Chachnama and Muslim origins in South Asia* (Cambridge, MA: Harvard University Press, 2016), 50.
21. For the origins of the *dūbaytī*, originally termed *fahlavī*, see Sīrūs Shamīsā, *Sayr-i rubā'ī dar shi'r-i Fārsī* (Tehran: Ferdows, 1996), 300.
22. Olga Davidson, 'Genre and Occasion in the *Rubā'īyyāt* of 'Umar Khayyām', in Beatrice Gruendler and Louise Marlow (eds), *Writers and Rulers* (Wiesbaden: Reichert Verlag, 2004), 133.
23. چندان قصائد غرر و نفائس درر که از طبع وقاد او زاده البته هیچ مسموع نیفتاد (*CM* 72).
24. Rashīd al-Dīn Vaṭvāṭ, *Ḥadā'iq al-siḥr fi daqā'iq al-shi'r*, 318.
25. Raduyani similarly defines it as 'a kind of *balāgha* when the poet adorns his poem with wise thoughts, preaching, complaints against fate' (130–1). Muḥammad Ḥusayn Shams al-'Ulamā-yi Garakanī, *Quṭūf al-rabī' fi ṣunūf al-badī'* ed. Murtaẓā Qāsimī, Aṣghar Dādbih and Badr al-Zamān Qarīb (Tehran: Farhangistān-i Zabān va Adab-i Fārsī, [1843] 2010), 86–7, offers the same definition but with different examples.
26. The most comprehensive study of this issue to date is Mansour Ajami, *The Neckveins of Winter* (Leiden: Brill, 1984).
27. *Shahnāmeh-yi Ferdowsī*, ed. Jules Mohl (Tehran: Sherkat-i sahāmī-yi ketab-hā yi Jibi, 1974), 7:252.
28. On this work, see Muḥammad Mu'īn, 'Tarjuma-yi aḥvāl-i 'Awfī', in his partial edition of *Jawāmī' al-ḥikāyāt* (Tehran: Ibn Sinā, 1340); Iqtidar Hussein Siddiqui, 'Lubab-ul-Albab and lawami-'ul-Hikayat of Sadid-ud-din Muḥammad Awfi', *Perso-Arabic Sources of the Sultanate of Delhi* (New Delhi: Munshiram Manoharlal Publishers, 1992), 1–43; Sayed Hasan Askari, 'Awfi's Jawami-ul-Hikayat', *Patna University Journal* (1966): 9–69.
29. The inadequacy of 'Awfī's account of Persian literary history was noted as early as Mirzā Muḥammad Qazwīnī, in the first critical edition of *Lubāb*, and is repeated by Mumtaz Ali Khan, *Some Important Persian Prose Writings of the Thirteenth Century* A.D. *in India* (Aligarh: Aligarh Muslim University, 1970), 101, with reference to the selections from Khāqānī, Niẓāmī and Ferdowsī, and the wholesale omission of Asadī Tusī, Nāṣir Khusraw, 'Umar Khayyām and Falakī Shirvānī. Also see Sharma, *Persian Poetry* (who dissents from Khan's overall criticism of 'Awfī's aesthetic on p. 148, n. 19); Muzaffar Alam, 'Persian in Precolonial Hindustan', in Sheldon Pollock (ed.), *Literary Cultures in History* (Berkeley: University of California Press, 2003), 140–1.

30. See Joel L. Kraemer, *Humanism in the Renaissance of Islam: The Cultural Revival During the Buyid Age* (Leiden: Brill, 1992), 90, for further on the Sayf al-Dawla who was patron to Abū Firās.
31. Ghulām ʿAlī Karīmī, 'Masʿūd Saʿd va Abū Firās al-Ḥamdānī', *Maʿārif-i Islāmī* 23 (1354/1975): 111–38; Sharma, *Persian Poetry at the Indian Frontier*, 72 and 142.
32. See, for example, his *Dīvān*, 1:479.
33. For example, see Masʿūd Saʿd, *Dīvān*, 1:541.
34. Baber Johansen, 'Eigentum, Familie und Obrigkeit im hanafitischen Strafrecht', *DWI* 19(1/4) (1979), esp. 54–5; Blain Auer, *Symbols of Authority in Medieval Islam: History, Religion and Muslim Legitimacy in the Delhi Sultanate* (London: I. B. Tauris, 2012), esp. 137–42.
35. ʿAwfī, *Lubāb*, 87; also discussed in Ẓafarī, *Ḥabsīyyah dar adab-i fārsī*, 65.
36. Masʿūd Saʿd, *Dīvān,* 2:1050; compare the different syntax in *Dīvān-i Masʿūd Saʿd*, ed. Rashīd Yāsemī, 718.
37. For Falakī's poem, where the word *meḥnat* recurs four times over the course of thirty *bayts*, see Chapter 3.
38. For example, Masʿūd Saʿd, *Dīvān*, 1:451 v. 35; 1:490: v. 29; 1:523 v. 76; 1: 529; 1:535 v. 7.
39. Masʿūd Saʿd, *Dīvān*, 1:490.
40. Masʿūd Saʿd, *Dīvān*, 2:687.
41. Masʿūd Saʿd, *Dīvān*, 2:687, v. 18, reading بپای for بیای.
42. Auer, *Symbols of Authority in Medieval Islam*, 19.
43. Cited in *Ṭabaqāt-i Nāṣirī*, ed. ʿAbdul Hay Ḥabībī (Kābul: Anjuman-i Tārīkh-i Afghānistān, 1963), 2:188. Also see the faulty version cited in Khan, *Some Important Persian Prose Writings*, 134.
44. See Ahmad, 'Amīd Loiki' (two of his prison poems are cited on 7–8), and Gazanfar Iu. Aliev, *Persoiazychnia literatura Indii* (Moscow: Nauka, 1968), 41–7. For a contemporaneous Delhi poet who was influenced by Mujīr but who left behind no prison poems, see Nazir Ahmad, 'Sirajuddin Khurasani', *Islamic Culture* 38 (1964): 107–40; I. H. Siddiqui, 'Life and Poetry of Siraji Khurasani', *Indo-Iranica* 26 (1973): 1–16.
45. See the selection from Bīdil's ghazals in Muḥammad Reẓā Shafīʿī Kadkanī, *Shāʿir-i āʾīnah'hā: barrasī-i sabk-i Hindī va shiʿr-i Bīdil* (Tehran: Mu'assasah-'i Intishārāt-i Agah, 1987), 139, ghazal 33.

3

Borderland Conflicts, Cosmological Complaints

Like Lahore within the Ghaznavid empire, Shirvan within the Saljuq empire was a region at the edges of a vast imperial formation. Ruled by the Shirvanshah dynasty that had once been ethnically Arab yet which invented for itself an ancient Iranian lineage, Shirvan was a provincial literary centre. Like Lahore, it was at once a vibrant cultural capital and far removed from the locus of administrative power within the Saljuq empire of which it was a part. Distance from centralised power in these cases served as a stimulus for literary creation. Although the poets of Shirvan collectively created a local twelfth-century renaissance, this literary culture was marked by acrimony and sometimes by outright hostility. Among the literary genres that flourished in the twelfth-century Caucasus, the most striking and original was the prison poem.

First, the competition was between poets, as in the following verses in which Khaqani claims pre-eminence in both Persian and Arabic poetry:

> Although before this time, across
> the Arab and Persian world, the poetry
> of Shahid and Radaki, of Labid and Buhturi,
> has been in vogue, I'll blow three strikes
> with my unique poem at all those four, in both languages.

> گر چه بدست پیش از این در عرب و عجم روان
> شعر شهید و رودکی نظم لبید و بحتری
> در صفت یگانگی آن صف چارگانه را
> بنده سه ضربه می زند در دو زبان شاعری [1]

Iranian critics have long remarked on Khaqani's high valuation of his own verse. In the mid-twentieth century, Badi' al-Zaman Faruzanfar described Khaqani as 'a scribe [*dabir*], an exegete [*mufassir*], and a critic [*adib*]'.[2] Khaqani, he added, 'considers his Arabic poetry more beautiful than and preferable to [the poetry of] Labid and Buhturi . . . In Persian he is more accomplished than 'Unsuri, Sana'i and Mu'izzi.' Every time he invokes a predecessor or contemporary, Khaqani dwells on his superior talents, with the grounds of his pre-eminence varying according to the rival. Among the many poets with whom he compares himself, Khaqani developed a particular obsession with poets writing under Ghaznavid rule. The earliest poet from this group is the Ghaznavid court poet 'Unsuri of Balkh (d. 1040). Of this most eloquent of poets, Khaqani says:

Where is 'Unsuri, listening to [my] sparkling poetry
until he surrenders his competition with me?

کو عنصری که بشنود این شعر آبدار
تا خاک بر دهان مجارا بر افکند [3]

Attesting to what Riccardo Zipoli describes as Khaqani's '*forza polemica*', such verses indicate that Khaqani saw in 'Unsuri, Mahmud of Ghazna's court poet, a rival in eloquence.[4] And yet Khaqani's keenest competitive instinct was reserved not for the first among the Ghaznavid poets but rather for one of the last: Mas'ud Sa'd. The prison poet from Lahore perturbed Khaqani not merely due to his talent or even eloquence but with his piercing lyric voice, through which he inaugurated the prison poem's corporeal poetics. As the inventor of the genre in which he wished to excel, Mas'ud Sa'd posed a potent challenge to Khaqani's claim to originality. Khaqani responded with the following metapoetic challenge, addressed to himself in the second-person voice, in a sexually charged language that equated masculine virility (*fahl*) with poetic ability:

Mas'ud Sa'd is not a virile poet compared to you,
although everyone who searches his verse finds a precious treasure.
Though 'Unsuri's enemy, he writes in 'Unsuri's style.
[Mas'ud Sa'd's] *qasida*s are drenched in mockery [of 'Unsuri].

مسعود سعد نه سوی تو شاعریست فحل
کاندر سخنش گنج روان یافت هر که جست
بر طرز عنصری رود و خصم عنصریست
کاندر قصیده هاش زند طعنه های چست [5]

In *Magic Gardens*, the treatise on poetics introduced in the preceding chapter, Vatvat praised the sublime tropes (*husn-i maʿani*) and delicate language (*lutf-i alfaz*) in Masʿud Saʿd's prison poems. He did not cite even once from Khaqani, even though he wrote *qasida*s in praise of him (as discussed in the next chapter). Khaqani must have resented this omission by his friend and rival. It is plausible that his satires of Masʿud Saʿd were composed with Vatvat in mind. No doubt Vatvat's high praise for Masʿud Saʿd bristled against the amibitious young poet from Shirvan, who aspired to become not just the greatest Persian poet of his era, but also a poet-prophet.

Resentful of his provincial location, and far removed from metropolitan centres of power, Khaqani could not countenance the prospect of anyone ever surpassing his verse. He demanded pre-eminence over kings and prophets, as well as over his fellow poets. The critiques Khaqani directed against his predecessors and contemporaries reveal a keenly competitive sensibility that set the tone for the often rancorous prison poetry of twelfth-century Shirvan.

Stimulated by the jealousy occasioned by Vatvat's treatise and Masʿud Saʿd's critical reception, Khaqani invented a conflict between ʿUnsuri, Mahmud of Ghazna's court poet, and Masʿud Saʿd. The real enmity however was not between the two Ghaznavid poets but between the poets of Shirvan and Lahore. Before literary critics such as ʿAruzi and ʿAwfi formulated in analytical terms the structure of feeling specific to the prison poem, Masʿud Saʿd revealed it through his lyric verse. To bolster his sense of originality, Khaqani resorted to literary appropriation (a practice known in the Perso-Arabic tradition as *sariqat*). He borrowed literary devices from Masʿud Saʿd and recast them in his own voice. By contrast, Sana'i of Ghazna, the poet from whom Khaqani derived his first pen name (*takhallus*), Haqa'iqi (meaning 'the truthful one'), did not induce anxieties of influence of the same order as did Masʿud Saʿd. Khaqani likely thought that the most effective way of surpassing Masʿud Saʿd was to absorb his genre innovations into his own verse. Hence, he conceptualised the prison poem as a transgressive genre that breached the antinomies of form and theme and which put in their place new literary norms. In Khaqani's hands, the prison poem became the vehicle for a corporeal poetics that transgressed existing political and theological norms.

Khaqani is not always as dismissive of other poets' talents as he is when writing about Masʿud Saʿd. When he writes about his other major Ghaznavid predecessor, Sana'i, his tone is considerably more reverent. Khaqani boasts of his spiritual kinship with Sana'i in his verse:

I entered the world as a replacement for Sana'i.
For this reason, my father called me 'replacement'.

بدل من آمادم اندر جهان سنایی را
بدین دلیل پدر نام من بدیل نهاد [6]

In contrast to his hypercritical attitude towards Masʿud Saʿd and his hometown of Lahore, Khaqani boasts that his hometown Shirvan will meet with the same fate as Sana'i's Ghazna:

When time inscribed the death of Sana'i,
the sky generated an eloquent person like me.
When the sorcerer was buried in the dust of Ghazni,
a new sorcerer was born from the soil of Shirvan.

چون زمان عهد سنایی در نوشت
آسمان چون من سخن گستر بزاد
چون بغزنین ساحری شد زیر خاک
خاک شروان ساحری نوبر بزاد [7]

Khaqani does not mention that Sana'i contributed to the transmission of prison poetry, the genre through which he sought to make his name, by editing Masʿud Saʿd's *divan*.[8] He instead charges Masʿud Saʿd with a lack of originality. Falaki meanwhile asserts his superior style (*tarz-i sukhan*). Both Khaqani and Falaki manifest what has in the context of British Romanticism been called an 'anxiety of influence' and what in terms of this tradition can be framed in relation to theories of literary appropriation (*sariqat*).[9] Khaqani and Falaki both downplayed Masʿud Saʿd's achievements while appropriating his signature genre. The poets of Shirvan also used motifs relating to prophets and prophecy, in particular to the figures of Moses (the Quranic

Musa) and Jesus (the Quranic ʿIsa), as discussed in Chapter 5, to further transform the prison poem.

Home to an astonishing number of innovative poets, Shirvan literary culture was also infected by rivalry. Through their patronage of the poet Nizami Ganjevi, Shirvanshah rulers provided the material conditions for the creation of the most famous *khamsa* – five-part collection of verse narratives – in Persian literature. Combining patronage with oppression, this dynasty also inaugurated a new phase in the prison poem. Masʿud Saʿd's prison poems exerted a formative influence on all the major poets of Shirvan, including Falaki, Abu'l ʿAla' Ganjevi and Khaqani, but his legacy inspired envy more than praise. The most notorious volley in this rivalry is Khaqani's above-cited accusation that Masʿud Saʿd was merely an imitator of ʿUnsuri's style (*tarz*), and that even when seeking to rival the Ghaznavid court poet, he was merely copying his voice.

Even earlier, in the first citation of Masʿud Saʿd by any Shirvan poet, and quite possibly the first citation of Masʿud Saʿd anywhere outside Ghaznavid domains, Falaki ventured to compare his style (*tarz*) with that of Masʿud Saʿd. In keeping with the self-praise (*fakhr*) that is one of the central topoi of the prison poem, Falaki sought with his *tarz* to vanquish Masʿud Saʿd's style:

If Masʿud Saʿd had my style in poetry,
then his spirit would be blessed one hundred times by his father's.

گراین طرز سخن در شاعری مسعود را بودی
بجان صد آفرین کردی روان سعد سلمانش [10]

Dawlatshah (fl. 1487), the most famous *tazkira* writer of the early modern period, introduces these verses of Falaki by way of comparing the poets from Lahore and Shirvan. 'Men of letters and poets of distinction,' writes Dawlatshah, 'have a high opinion of Masʿud Saʿd's verse. Falaki Shirvani, while praising himself, recalls Masʿud Saʿd's poetic speech.'[11] Dawlatshah's statement, which further canonises the prison poem centuries after its early formation, attests to the impact of Falaki's poetry on subsequent conceptualisations of this genre. Ironically, these lines may have been wrongly attributed to Falaki by the critical tradition; nearly identical verses have been found in the *divan* of the twelfth-century poet Adib-i Sabir (d. 1143). The Indian scholar Hadi Hasan reports that a seventeenth-century manuscript of Masʿud Saʿd's *divan* reproduces Dawlatshah's words without attribution and singles out Falaki for his praise of Masʿud Saʿd. Hasan challenges the attribution of this verse to Falaki, on the grounds that the *divan* of Adib-i Sabir contains a close paraphrase:

> If Masʿud Saʿd's verse possessed this beauty and radiance,
> then it would be praised by his father's spirit.

> بدین حسن و طراوت شعر گر مسعود را بودی
> هزاران آفرین کردی روان سعد سلمانش [12]

It is not improbable that Falaki deliberately cited Adib-i Sabir or vice-versa. Although not a prison poet, Adib-i Sabir suffered from the vagaries of sovereign power: during the course of his diplomatic activities in the service of the Saljuqs, the Khwarezmshah ruler Atsïz ordered that the poet be drowned in the Oxus.[13]

Recognising the indeterminacy of the prison poem at this stage in its gestation, the thirteenth-century Persian critic Shams-i Qays praised Falaki for his formal innovation in transitioning from the *madh* (praise section of the *qasida*), into the *taghazzul* (amorous section) within the same *qasida*, as in the following verse:

> Where did he go, who brought pleasure and happiness to my soul?
> With his departure, my heart and eyes withered with wrinkles and sorrow.

> کجا شد آنکه مرا جان بدو خوش وخرم
> که تا شد او دل و چشمم تباه شد زخم و غم [14]

Falaki, whose name itself evokes the heavens (*falak*), was learned in the science of the stars, as Khaqani noted in his elegy on Falaki's death that claimed him as his pupil, even though Falaki was older.[15] Falaki's legacy does not compare with that of Masʿud Saʿd on the prison poem. Nonetheless, as the first prison poet of Shirvan who played a role in the genre's geographic and cross-generational transmission, Falaki role is significant.

Falaki's *divan* is extant only in fragments, but these partial relics indicate the significance of this poet for the prison poem's trajectory. Falaki's most sustained contribution to the genre is a *qasida* comprising two parts. The first part (vv. 1–12) expresses the poet's distress over his incarceration. The second part (vv. 13–27) elaborates an ambivalent plea for freedom from the Shirvanshah ruler Manuchihr III (r. 1120–1160). Over the course of the first part, the poet enumerates the many different ways in which his friends have abandoned him. Punning on the morphological link between madman (*divaneh*) and demon (*div*), he states:

> I drown in chains like a madman [*divaneh*],
> although I am not at war with any demon [*div*].

غرقه در آهنم چو دیوانه
گرچه با دیو کار زارم نیست [16]

He then launches into a tragic refrain that underscores his isolation and loneliness, even within Shirvan's vibrant literary culture:

> No matter how much I ask for help
> from friends, no friend will help me.
> My roots were in this abode,
> but I have no friends here.

چند خواهم ز هرکسی یاری؟
!که کند یاریم، چو یارم نیست
زین دیارم نژاد بود ولیک
!هیچ یار اندرین دیارم نیست

Falaki grieves over his abandonment by his friends and peers. The first prison poem of Shirvan derives its force from the contrast between the imprisoned poet and the world outside his prison cell. Falaki's carceral lexicon – encompassing affliction (*mihnat*), sorrow (*gham*) and suffering (*ranj*) – is so strongly reminiscent of Mas'ud Sa'd's poetry that some medieval sources attributed this poem to him.[17] Although fluid authorial attributions are common across the Persian literary canon, the transferable authorship of many prison poems attests to the genre's wide circulation. As with the conflation of authorship in the case of poems by Nasrullah Munshi and Mas'ud Sa'd noted in the preceding chapter, this fluidity contributes to the prison poem's status as a transgressive genre: transgressing established boundaries of form and theme give the prison poem discursive power. The specific historical circumstances of the authors matter less for these critics than the aesthetic effect of their poems.

In part two, Falaki appeals for freedom to the sovereign. Suddenly a new element is introduced: the lyrical second-person voice that also inflected Mas'ud Sa'd's lyric odes. Prior to its migration to Shirvan, the prison poet's lyric voice operated within a solipsistic vacuum that made the poet both auditor and addressee. Although 'Aruzi's response to Mas'ud Sa'd's poetry after his death was tinged with passion and praise, the contemporary reader is struck by prison poets' isolation from their readers. The solipsism of prison poetry is partly related to its bodily focus on the poet's confinement, which is a sign of his oppression. When the genre migrated to the Caucasus, its political tone intensified, partly as a result of the relatively large number of poets who by now were working in this genre.

For the remainder of the poem, Falaki attributes his suffering to the rivalries that placed him behind bars and in chains. These dynamics become evident when the poet affiliates himself with an elite demographic he calls the 'people of intelligence' (*ahl-i 'aql*). People of intelligence, Falaki notes, are particularly vulnerable targets for punishment, including imprisonment, but there is no shame in that:

> My fear of your punishment [*siyasat*]
> is no scandal among the intelligent [*ahl-i 'aql*].

> گر بترسیدم از سیاست تو
> ببر اهل عقل عارم نیست

Both by focusing on punishment in a formal genre – a *qasida* – that almost by definition celebrates the ruler's glory and in drawing attention to the persecution of the poets of Shirvan, Falaki reveals an emergent discourse about poetry and the persecution of poets taking place in the prison poem.

Although clearly anticipated by Mas'ud Sa'd's lyric ode, Falaki's lament propels the prison poem genre even further away from the panegyric *qasida*. Why does the poet dwell on his persecution when the panegyrics that shaped the aesthetic horizons of Shirvan's literary culture, such as those of 'Unsuri and Anvari of Balkh (in modern-day Afghanistan), disengage from their subjective experience in order to glorify the patron? To take these poets' words in their poems as merely autobiographical statements of historical interest would mean ignoring their aesthetic complexity. Instead, we should attend to the ways in which Falaki moves the prison poem genre forward by negotiating the dialectic between art and experience.

Of even greater importance than Falaki's revelation of his suffering is his effort to separate his poetic persona from his surroundings and to declare his social isolation at poetry's threshold. From its earliest beginnings, the prison poem cleared a new space for poetic selfhood, newly defined in opposition to the ruler's sovereignty. In this first extant prison poem composed in the Caucasus, we observe the beginnings of the discourse of the poet's sovereignty that reached its apotheosis in Khaqani's prison poems (explored in Chapters 3–5). When Masʿud Saʿd inscribed his imprisoned body onto the lyric ode, he lamented his fate rather than critiquing the sovereign. By grafting a critique of sovereignty onto a lyric ode that was in the process of being codified as a genre, Falaki further developed the prison poem's political theology.

'My sole possessions are made of affliction [*mihnat-i man milk umal-i manast*]', Falaki states, asserting his status as a member of the intellectual elite (*ahl-i ʿaql*). The poet's dependence on his patron merges the power of the ruler with the patron's power. Examining the patronage of poetry in the Ghaznavid and Saljuq domains, to which Lahore and Shirvan belonged, according to the changing meanings of sovereignty sheds light on why poets faced imprisonment by the very same sovereigns they so persistently flattered. Mastering the art of rhetoric 'enabled poets to articulate the dynamic quality of patronage and their potential for social mobility within it'.[18]

The aspersions cast by both Khaqani and Falaki on their predecessors attest that great achievements in poetry can be stimulated by rivalry.[19] Even Khaqani's student Mujir experienced a vicious break with his teacher concerning the authorship of their respective poems. Notwithstanding its distance from metropolitan centres, the stakes of literary conflict for the poets of Shirvan were high. Amir Khusraw, the most famous Indo-Persian poet of the subsequent century, anachronistically declared in his *Preface to the Crescent Moon* (*Dibacha-yi ghurrat al-kamal*, 1294) that Khaqani merely imitated the style (*tarz*) of his student Mujir and that Muʿizzi merely imitated the style of Masʿud Saʿd, who was born just two years prior to him.[20] These aspersions show how the spirit of rivalry that animated the poetry composed by the prison poets of Shirvan persisted long after these poets had passed from the world.

Rivalry can only become an organising principle in a literary culture that has institutionalised relations between poets and the court, and which makes of every poem a political act. In such a society, the axis of conflict is not solely between poet and patron. In addition to their accountability to their patrons, sovereigns and jailers, Khaqani, Falaki, Abu'l ʿAla' and Mujir addressed their students, teachers and fellow poets. The role of rivalry in cultivating this literary culture's transgressive poetics explains the dismissive tone of Khaqani's elegy (*marthiyya*) on Falaki's death. It also explains why Khaqani claims in this poem to have been Falaki's teacher. The genre in question is an elegy for mourning the dead; Khaqani's reduction of his teacher to a sneeze (*ʿatseh*) exemplifies the astringent and seemingly ruthless satire in which he excelled:

Falaki was a sneeze of my licit magic.
He understood the mystery of the nine skies in the ten sciences.
He parted this world quickly. A sneeze does not last long.
Alas! What a short life was given to my sneeze.
His life gave a sneeze and abandoned the body.
The angel of death said to him: May Allah forgive you.

عطسۀ سحر حلال من فلکی بود
بود بده فن ز راز نه فلک آگاه
فروشد که عطسه دیر نماند زود
آه که کم عمر بود عطسۀ من آه
جانش یکی عطسه داد و جسم بپرداخت
هم ملک الموت گفت یرحمک الله [21]

These very same verses were later used by Mujir against Khaqani himself. For now, let us further trace the workings of rivalry in Khaqani's oeuvre. Rivalry's vituperative energy permeates the invective in the autobiographical verse narrative *Gift from the Two Iraqs* (*Tuhfat al-ʿIraqayn*, *c*. 1157). Khaqani's pilgrimage extended across the 'two Iraqs,' as Mesopotamia and western Iran were called in premodern Arabic and Persian. By any estimate, *Gift from the Two Iraqs* is among the most compelling autobiographies in all of medieval literature.[22]

While offering an unforgettable rendering of his pilgrimage, Khaqani also narrates his upbringing. He dedicates individual chapters to his father, a carpenter who dedicated his life to ensuring a good future for his son; his mother, a Nestorian Christian slave who was kidnapped while a girl and converted to Islam; his uncle, who taught him mathematics, Quranic hermeneutics, geography and Arabic poetry (*Tuhfat*, 199); and, lastly, his teacher, Abu'l 'Ala' Ganjavi, who gave him his second penname (*takhallus*), Khaqani.[23] Evocative of *khaqan*, the Mongol term for the 'political and military leader of the empire',[24] this portentous penname signalled the poet's ambition of rivalling the sovereign in authority and power.

In spite, or perhaps because, of their mentoring relationship, Khaqani accused Abu'l 'Ala' of depravity. According to his own testimony, Abu'l 'Ala' introduced the young Khaqani to courtly life and launched his career. In the following verses, the teacher curses his belligerent student in unusually coarse language:

Afzal al-din [Khaqani], if you want the truth:
I swear by your soul, I am unhappy with you.
You were known in Shirvan as the carpenter's son.
I gave you the the title Khaqani.
I've done you much good.
I gave you my daughter wealth and fame.
Why do you not respect me because I
who am both your father-in-law and your teacher?
Stop saying I have said such and such.
I don't remember uttering such words.
I said what I said; I didn't say what I didn't say.
I screwed who I screwed. I didn't screw who I didn't screw.

توای افضل الدّین اگر راست پرسی
بجان عزیزت که از تو نشادم
دروگر پسر بود نامت بشروان
به خاقانیت بر لقب من نهادم
بجای تو بسیار کردم نکوی
ترا دختر و مال وشهرت بدادم
چرا حرمت من نداری تو چون من

ترا هم پدر خوانده هم اوستادم
بمن چند گویی که گفتی سخنها
کزین سان سخنها نباشد بیادم
بگفتم بگفتم نگفتم نگفتم
بگادم بگادم نگادم نگادم [25]

Alongside the teacher's bitter reminders to his ungrateful student, we can detect in these words a jealous poet's relish in denigrating his rival's lowly origins, accentuated by the reference to the occupation of Khaqani's father as a carpenter (*durudgar*). This slight to Khaqani's parentage in particular seems to have motivated the attack that followed. It also underscores the role of class tensions in determining the fault lines of Persian literary culture.

Khaqani framed a reply to Abu'l ʿAla' within the satirical genre (*hajv*, *hija'*) in a chapter in *Gift from the Two Iraqs* titled 'In Mockery of Abu'l ʿAla' Ganjavi'. In light of the intensity of the poet's rancour against his peers, the satirical element appears as simply one layer in a text suffused with numerous other anxieties of influence. Khaqani writes of his teacher Abu'l ʿAla' in highly derisive terms. Drawing as he typically did on his vast erudition, Khaqani associates his teacher's mother with the sister of Satan, whom he terms 'Shaykh of Najd'. The label refers to a legend whereby Satan (*Iblis*) appeared in the guise of a shaykh from Najd to the Quraysh, the tribe of the Prophet Muhammad, and sought to persuade them to kill the Prophet. These verses by Khaqani draw on religious rhetoric to condemn his teacher:[26]

When that dog from Ghur was born,
he became the sibling of the Shaykh from Najd.
He lives like a dog and is cunning like any canine.
In short, he is nourished on the milk of dog.
The one who wishes evil on the Jahiz of time
is a denier of faith. May God destroy him!

چون آن سگ غوری از جهان زاد
همشیره شیخ نجدی افتاد
سگزی و چو سگزیان محتال
پرورده شیر سگ علی الحال
آن جاحظ وقت را بدی خواه
وان جاحد دین اباده الله [27]

Such are the angry words Khaqani had for Abu'l ʿAla'. Their mutual hostility drove him to compare Abu'l ʿAla' to a dog. This exchange was preceded by a longer violent exchange in verse, much of which has been lost. Only these verses by Abu'l ʿAla' addressed to his student-rival are extant:[28]

Khaqani, although you know poetry well,
let me offer you free advice:
don't curse a man older than you.
He may be your father without your knowing.

خاقانیا اگرچه سخن نیک دانیا
یک نکته گویمت بشنو رایگانیا
هجو کسی مکن که ز تو مه بود بسن
شاید ترا پدر بود و تو ندانیا

Although it circulated widely in Indo-Persian poetry anthologies well into the Mughal period, Abu'l ʿAla's full *divan* is no longer extant.[29] Khaqani succeeded in wreaking vengeance on his teacher for the latter's mockery of his lowly origins. Alongside his widely disseminated attack on his teacher, Khaqani's critique may have helped his reputation to eclipse that of his teacher. The vituperative rhetoric of Khaqani's autobiography in verse set a precedent for even more caustic texts to come.

Khaqani had many reasons to polemicise with his forbearers and contemporaries. But what of the other prison poets of Shirvan? Khaqani was not the only poet active in formulating the prison poem's aesthetics in this borderland region of the Caucasus. Alongside Falaki, Khaqani's student Mujir al-Din Baylaqani (d. 1190) substantially contributed to this genre. Although the younger poet, Mujir al-Din, eventually parted ways with Khaqani due to their rivals' calumnies, his poems reveal a remarkable continuity of form and content between student and master. Together with the substantial oeuvres of Khaqani and Mujir, extant fragments of the poetry of Falaki and Abu'l ʿAla' amply justify scholars' characterisation of the Persianate Caucasus as a region that cultivated a distinctive literary style on par with Bukhara, Khwarezm and Khurasan.[30]

In both his life and poetry, Mujir reproduced his master's literary trajectories. Just as Khaqani began his literary career with an attack on Masʿud

Sa'd's poetry, so did Mujir inaugurate his career by publicly defaming his teacher. Specifically, Mujir's poetic debut made use of the same idiom that Khaqani had used decades earlier on the occasion of Falaki's death. Khaqani had boasted that Falaki was a sneeze (*'atseh*) of his lawful magic and proposed an analogy between the cat and the lion (*gurbeh va shir*).[31] Mujir constructed his satire on Khaqani around this same idiom. One imitation of his teacher's poem evinces the same contempt towards Khaqani that Khaqani had earlier exhibited towards Falaki. The rhetorical device used here to contrast the reflection on Khaqani's weakness to Mujir's greatness is known as 'beautiful etiology' (*husn-i ta'lil*), meaning the ascription of imaginary causes. Fantastic etiology is here activated through two comparisons (*tashbih*): of Khaqani to a cat (*gurbeh*), and Mujir to a lion (*shir*):

Why should I fear Khaqani's slander and his stupid work?
To me he weighs less than an oat seed.
No wonder if I get offended from him.
A cat bothers a lion no more than the lion's sneeze.

مرا ز غیبت خاقانی و خریش چه باک
چنو به نزد من کم از جوی سنجد
اگر برنجم از و هم شگفت نیست ازآنک
که گربه عطسه شیراست و شیر ازو رنجد [32]

Although these simulacrums of rivalry are best interpreted as expressions of literary ambition rather than as proof of enmity, they are indicative of the politically contentious atmosphere that shaped the second stage of the prison poem.

Mujir's prison poems are few in number. In his seminal essay on this poet from 1946, Iranian scholar Hossein Bastanirad identifies only one poem that he refers to as *habsiyyat*.[33] In terms of my understanding of prison poetry as any poem that deploys tropes relating to confinement, many more poems by Mujir fall under this rubric. Yet the poem identified by Bastanirad as a prison poem does effectively reproduce what had become the genre's core features. This poem opens with praise for the poet's ruler and jailer, Zahir al-Din, a high-ranking official in the court of Atabek Jahan Pahlavan (r. 1175–1186), whom Mujir hopes will act as a mediator and secure his release. It then moves quickly to the topic of the poet's imprisonment. Both Zahir al-Din and the ruler-jailer Jahan Pahlavan are eclipsed by the wheel of fate (*gardun*), a metonym for the cosmos. A few verses earlier, another metonym for the cosmos, the 'blue sky' (*charkh-i azraq*) is said to 'deserve only deceit and lies'. Continuing in the spirit of complaint against an impersonal sky, the poet declares that 'no heart is happy in the grips of its wrath'. He then invokes a trope earlier used by Khaqani, who alludes in the Christian Qasida to a legend about Jesus. In the Muslim tradition, Jesus was prevented from ascending to the fourth heaven (to which God had assigned him) due to a needle in his pocket:[34]

> In the fourth heaven, Jesus called me the pole of meanings.
> He put me in chains because this pole does not deserve wandering.

> مرا قطب معانی خواند بر چارم فلک عیسی
> ببندم کرد یعنی قطب دوران را نمی‌شاید [35]

This complicated image, which relies on the rhetorical device of *husn-i ta'lil* (the ascription of imaginery causes) needs to be unpacked. The imprisoned poet depicts himself as standing like a compass. One foot stands like a pole. The other foot circles around the pole. Mujir says that Jesus (the Islamic prophet rather than the Christian God) called him a 'pole of meanings [*qutb-i ma'ani*]'. He is enchained and prevented from moving as pubishment for his restlessness. Typically, the pole should be stationary.

Finally, Mujir registers a complaint, not just against fate, but against the injustice of his imprisonment:

> It's not the king's order. The order has come from the wheel of fate:
> This eloquent Hassan does not deserve benevolence.
> If you ask the Avesta-reading magus about me,
> he'd say that chain and prison are wrong for this Muslim.

> ز شه در خط نیم زیرا که خطی دارد از گردون
> که این حسان سخن فی‌الجمله احسان را نمی‌شاید
> و لیکن گر تو حال من ز گبر زند خوان پرسی
> بگوید کین مسلمان بند و زندانرا نمی‌شاید

Insisting on his piety, Mujir channels the words of a hypothetical magus – a Zoroastrian priest – to the effect that 'chain and prison are wrong for this

Muslim'. Mujir also alludes in the above verses to the Prophet Muhammad's beloved poet, Hassan ibn Thabit, whose life spanned the period before and after Islam.[36] During his association with the Prophet, Hassan ibn Thabit acted as a kind of diplomat, persuading non-Muslim tribes to accept Islam by producing eloquent invectives against non-Muslim poets.[37] Mujir's invocation of Hassan also alludes to the name by which Khaqani was known: Hassan al-ʿAjam, the Hassan of the Persians (a name taken up in further detail in the next chapter). As soon as he assigns himself this title, Mujir undercuts it, insisting that 'this eloquent Hassan does not deserve benevolence'. While this undercutting may be an act of deference to his teacher Khaqani, who by implication would deserve benevolence on this reading, it is also an assertion of the poet's talent. Even if the poet does not deserve benevolence, the poem implies, his poetry merits comparison with the poetry of Hassan al-ʿAjam, Prophet Muhammad's favourite poet.

Although earlier in the poem he absolved the king of responsibility and attributed his predicament to the wheel of fate, in his concluding verses he pleads with the sovereign, implicating him in the injustice visited on the poet: 'It's fair if the king decides to release me / prison and suffering do not belong in Eid al-Adha.' This verse implores the king to release the poet as a gift, in honour of the holiday (Eid al-Adha, also known as Eid Qurban, is the holiday of sacrifice, when animals are slaughtered as a gift to God). The poet then adds that if the king feels inclined to slaughter him for this holiday, it would be a mistake: the poet is not an animal fit for slaughter.

Like Khaqani, Mujir boasted of his lowly origins. He compares his poems with Turks in a verse that recalls the label that Khaqani applied to himself throughout his poems and in his verse autobiography: 'carpenter's child [*pisar-i durudgar*]'.[38] Mujir then distances himself even further from the ruling class by revealing his foreign origins:

> The children of my talent [my poems] have Turkic faces.
> How wondrous it is then, that my mother was African [*habashi*]

> طفلان طبع من بصفت ترک چهره اند
> وین طرفه تر که از حبشی بود مادرم [39]

Mujir's most recent editor provides an alternate reading for this verse, which suggests that Mujir was Armenian.[40] Traditionally, however, this verse has been taken to mean that Mujir is claiming African descent.[41] Regardless of which reading is followed, and Mujir's actual or perceived ethnic origins, both readings present the poet as an ethnic outsider, of non-Iranian descent and non-Muslim lineage. Together with Mas'ud Sa'd's poetics, forged on Indo-Persian borderlands, and Khaqani's Christology explored in chapters to come, Mujir's self-fashioning as an outsider who is most at home on cultural borderlands and political peripheries reveals the specific appeal of the prison poem for poets whose lives and surroundings were marked by cultural, religious and ethnic difference.

Mujir learned from Khaqani the art of utilising elaborate disciplinary lexicons in his verse, including especially terminology pertaining to backgammon (*nard*). Khaqani and Mujir were among the few – and perhaps the only – twelfth-century Persian poets to use the term *nadab* in the sense of 'staking one's life' (*dastkhun*), for example.[42] This seemingly technical detail elucidates a more significant affiliation between the two poets and their prison poems. While the reasons for Khaqani's imprisonment have been debated, the stimulus for Mujiir's prison poems is even more difficult to ascertain. Like Mas'ud Sa'd, Khaqani was imprisoned at least twice. By contrast, it is not known whether Mujir was ever imprisoned. Were his prison poems responses to actual imprisonment or did the popularity of the prison poem genre in the Caucasus inspire him to claim this mantle for himself as a poet? This genre's shifting relationship to empirical experience confirms Adorno's dictum: every literary genre that resists the conditions of its genesis breaks with its empirical moorings. The more political its aesthetic, the more marked the rupture. Viewed in this light, the prison poem is the pre-eminent transgressive genre of Persian literature.

All that is known of Mujir's trials and tribulations is found in his *divan* and the *divan*s of his contemporaries. He ran into trouble for a poetic satire on the city of Isfahan which was mistakenly attributed to Khaqani and which prompted a falling-out between the two poets.[43] The poem also created problems for Mujir, who denied ever having mocked Isfahan in the following verses:

I never said this and such things didn't enter my head.
No one has witnessed these words from me.

My discourse [*hadith-i man*] is all pure poetry.
I have no business with the discourse of sovereigns.
When my rival lied about me, the king agreed.
Due to the king's anger, I am deprived of his proximity.

نگفتم و نگذشتست بر دلم هر گز
نکرده هیچکس از بنده این سخن اصغا
حدیث من ز مفاعیل فاعلات بود
من از کجا سخن سر مملکت ز کجا
بیک دروغ که حاسد بگفت و شاه شنید
ز خشم شاه فتادم ز صدر شاه جدا [44]

The metapoetic phrase rendered above as 'my discourse is all pure poetry', alludes to the intricacies of Arabo-Persian prosody, which consists of fifteen meters that are categorised according to their morphological variations on the Arabic verb 'to do' (*fa*, *'ayn*, *lam*).[45] The Persian text incorporates one of these Arabic variants (*mafa'ilu fa'ilat*) corresponding to the *mozare'* meter. In this manner, and in the tradition of Khaqani's baroque style, Mujir's bilingual poetics operate at the level of form as well as content. By explicating his position through metapoetic means, Mujir contributes to his own canonisation.

Like Khaqani, Falaki, Mas'ud Sa'd and every prison poet who preceded him, Mujir's prison poetry was conditioned by a genre that was gradually becoming detached from its empirical roots in the experience of imprisonment. As part of this discursive transformation, and like the other prison poets of Shirvan, Mujir disassociated his poetic voice from that of the sultan. 'I have no business with the discourse of sovereigns,' Mujir declares in the above-cited poem. As I argue throughout this book, this new division between the poet and the sovereign that was formed during Persian literature's long twelfth century represents a paradigm shift that is intimately linked to the development of the prison poem.

Was this emerging tension between poet and sovereign dictated by a growing perception, then spreading across the eastern Islamic world, of incompatibility between the sultan's discretionary power and the poet's vatic authority? The fragility of Islamic governance within the centres of Persian literary culture such as Shirvan and Lahore suggests a partial answer. The decline, first, of Abbasid dominion and Baghdad as a centre of power, leading to its conquest by the Mongols in 1258, and then the rise in significance of literary production in eastern Islamic borderlands, filled poets with a new sense of their vocation and inspired them to stand in judgement on the sovereign's power in ways that they had not done before.[46]

The decline of Ghaznavid dominion in Central Asia during the twelfth century overlapped with the ascent of the Shirvanshahs, vassals of the Saljuqs, throughout the region that is now modern Azerbaijan. The Shirvanshahs and the late Ghaznavids shared in common an ambivalent relationship to metropolitan centres of Islamic power, such as Baghdad, and later Isfahan, Qazvin, Merv and Hamadan. The instability of sovereignty runs like a thread through the political theory of the texts written under these regimes. Every new ruler inaugurated a new chapter in the story of the prison poem. The king's body was becoming ever more corrupted, while the poet's imprisoned body acquired new sanctity and authority. While changes in the structure of sovereignty shaped the development of the prison poem, the transformations of literary genres that resulted from these shifts also had an impact. The main lesson that Mujir appears to have gleaned from Khaqani was to view his accusers from the perspective of a carceral and corporeal poetics that exposed the discourse of worldly sovereignty as more transient and ultimately less legitimate than the discourse of poetry.

The Signless Sky

The previous chapter traced the genesis of the prison poem in the lyric odes of Masʿud Saʿd. This chapter has dwelt on how the prison poem was perforated by borderland conflicts, anxieties of influence, and competition among poets vying for literary pre-eminence and patronage. We have not yet witnessed the cosmic apotheosis of the prison poem in the hands of Khaqani. Khaqani is the pivotal figure in the story of this genre: he transformed and transgressed its political and aesthetic dimensions. With Khaqani, prison poetry became more than a literature of exile, and more even than a discourse of oppression. Through his poetic discourse, Khaqani introduced a new way of relating, and of opposing, poetry to its empirical points of reference. Most importantly, Khaqani made the prison poem genre available for appropriation by later poets who had no direct experience of imprisonment. Altering the dialectic between experience and the imagination, Khaqani upended the relationship between the poet and the sovereign. Poetry's world-making capacity came in Khaqani's hands to matter more for prison poem poetics than the sovereign's decree.[47] The poet's imprisoned body that under Ghaznavid dominion had given shape to a lyric self in early prison poems on the borderlands of the Caucasus became an instrument of political critique in the genre's later phase. Breaking with history, Khaqani's vatic utterance linked poetry to prophesy.

Prison poetry did not always or necessarily correspond to or reference an actual experience of imprisonment. Instead, it functioned as a metonym – reflective of a broader political-theological situation – for the poet's condition. A century earlier in the Arabic tradition, Syrian poet Abu'l ʿAla' al-Maʿarri (d. 1058) refers to his imprisonment in Maʿarrat al-Nuʿman in a purely metaphorical sense, without alluding to any actual prisons.[48] Equally, a long tradition of Persian Sufi writing describes the dwelling of the soul within the body as a kind of incarceration. The poetry of ʿAttar Nishapuri offers many such examples, including the following:

> How can the undead parrot of your soul
> get free from this iron cage?
> You're alive today, yet you're in the grave.
> When your body sinks into the grave, the soul will rise from the grave.

> هزار بار به نامرده طوطی جانت
> چگونه زین قفس آهنین تواند جست
> تو گرچه زنده‌ای امروز لیک در گوری
> چو تن به گور فرو رفت جان ز گور برست [49]

Further examples proliferate in Rumi:

> Die! Die! And separate from your body.
> Your body is like chains and you're like prisoners.
> Take an axe and make a hole in the prison walls.
> When you break from the prison, you're all princes and kings.

> بمیرید بمیرید وزین نفس ببرید
> که این نفس چو بندست و شما همچو اسیرید
> یکی تیشه بگیرید پی حفره زندان
> چو زندان بشکستید همه شاه و امیرید [50]

Written into the genre of the prison poem is an ambivalent – and at times oppositional – relationship to history. Given that, to invoke Adorno again, genres require empirical realities from which to break free, the poet who advocates for poetry's authority over and against the king's power must learn to navigate a contentious genre. This tension between freedom and constraint is elucidated through a gambling metaphor in the third of Khaqani's six major prison poems:[51]

Are the times faithful to me? Never
are times faithful to anyone ever.
This sky resembles two blank dice.
It stakes lives when gambling.
With the odds of five to one against you,
your two sixes are counted as two ones.

روزگارم وفا کند هیهات
روزگار این به روزگار کند
این فلک کعبتین بی‌نقش است
همه بر دستخون قمار کند
پنج و یک برگرفت باز فلک
که دوشش را دو یک شمار کند (3:3–5)

As frequently occurs in Khaqani's poetics, these verses condense dense layers of emotion into a discussion marked by unparalleled – and formidable – technical acumen. In this instance, the rules of gambling are used to elucidate the slow passage of time within the prison cell. Instead of a normal sequence, whereby rolling two sixes twice would comprise a year (six plus six equals twelve months), for this prison poem, a roll of six only counts as one month in a prison cell. The deferred temporality – whereby the prisoner's sentence never reaches its end – becomes a commentary on the poet's bad luck in life. Gambling is always uncertain, but the imprisoned poet must contend with particularly unfavourable outcomes. Such deft technical manoeuvres further expose the injustice of the poet's prison sentence.

Along with Khaqani's five other major prison poems, prison poem 3 is a *qasida*. It is bound by its genre to the conventions of praise, and specifically to the glorification of the ruler. At the same time, like Masʿud Saʿd's lyric odes,

Khaqani's *qasida* approximates a ghazal in terms of its lyric motifs, themes and tropes. Although a divine creator (*kirdgar*) makes a cameo appearance in the second-to-last hemistich, and imposes a semblance of order, this poem is dense with the metaphysical indeterminacy that marks the prison poem in its second phase. Just as the compressed calculation of the dice reveals the lengthening of time from within the prison cell, so does the comparison of the horizon of the poet's existence to a role of blank dice – literally a Ka'ba without inscription (*ka'batayn-i bi naqsh*) – reveal the dimensionality of the prison poem genre in the process of its discursive reconfiguration.[52]

Gambling metaphors abound in Persian and Arabic poetry.[53] Specifically relevant to the poetic repertoire used here, comparisons of the sky to dice occur in a verse of the philosopher Ibn Sina (d. 1037), who declared:

> Death is a player and we are pieces of the game.
> The sky is a pair of dice and the world is the board.

اجل نردبازست و ما مهره‌ایم
فلک کعبتین و جهان تخته نرد [54]

Already in this verse, the etymological link between dice and the Ka'ba generates a further association with the heavens: the Ka'ba is figured as a constellation in the sky.

Elsewhere in his poetry, Khaqani plays on this polysemy to signify a surplus of verbal signs.[55] The following verse from a ghazal is a case in point. He says to his beloved:

> When in memory of you, I grab two dice,
> I'll throw a Pleiades on both dice.

چون به یادت کعبتین گیرم به کف
کعبتین را نقش پروین آورم [56]

This love poem compares the attraction of the poet for his beloved with the ties binding him to the cosmos. Throwing a Pleiades (*parvin avaram*) means to throw sixes on both dice. This is the likeliest outcome in the game of backgammon (*nard*) that Khaqani is here describing. In Persian literature, the Pleaiades (*Parvin*) consisted of six stars. Khaqani sees the six dots on the side of a dice as six stars in the sky. By contrast to the certainty of the ghazal, in which the likeliest outcome is the one that comes to pass, in Khaqani's prison poems, the dual Kaʿba is stripped of verbal signs, signifying God's distance from creation. The signless Kaʿba, without an inscription, becomes a paradigm of the poet's imprisoned condition. The lack of signage on the Kaʿba reflects the poet's desperation, his alienation from his fellow humans, his separation from the social and political order, and from creation itself.

Midway through the poem, the focus shifts. Khaqani complains that fate (*ruzgar*) has suddenly changed its face and is now his jailer. The capricious behaviour of fate as construed in this poem mirrors the arbitrary power of Shirvanshah rulers. As Saljuq vassals who turned away from Arabic idioms of caliphal sovereignty while transmuting Arabic into Persianate registers, these secular rulers relied on imprisonment as a mode of punishment on a scale never before encountered in Islamic history.[57] Just as sovereignty was reconstituted by rulers' dynastic and imperial lineages across Central Asia and the Caucasus, so did the changing modalities of punishment shape the discursive world of the prison poem.

Khaqani's engagement with the rhetorical repertoire of backgammon does not end here. While in this context, *kaʿbatayn* refers metaphorically to a pair of dice, the word itself is also the dual plural form of Kaʿba, the most sacred shrine in Islam, and an ancient site of pilgrimage, dating back to pre-Islamic times. The symbology of the Kaʿba features repeatedly in Khaqani's poems, including in the verses that do not belong to prison poems:

The wheel of fate rotates like a dice without inscription.
No one should stake their bet on its faith.

چرخ آمده کعبتین بی‌نقش
کس نقش وفا از آن ندیدست [58]

The above verse is taken from a panegyric to Shirvanshah Akhsitan (r. 1160–1197) and his queen. In another elaboration on this repertoire, Khaqani alludes to Kaʿb, the poet who authored a famous *qasida* praising Muhammad the Prophet:[59]

These two dice [*kaʿbatayn*] without inscription bowed my head to the ankle [*kaʿb.*].
So that I eulogised the two Kaʿbas like [the Arab poet] Kaʿb.

این کعبتین بی‌نقش آورد سر به کعبم
تا بر دو کعبه گشتم چون کعب مدح گستر [60]

The two Kaʿbas in the above verse are not dice but the actual Kaʿba and the Sun, which is described earlier in the poem as a 'world-wandering Kaʿba' (*kaʿba-yi jahangard*). Such verses illustrate how the elaborate rhetorical apparatus adopted by prison poets reverberated across all three of genre's dimensions. The multiple meanings attached to Kaʿb, Kaʿba and *kaʿbatayn* enable the poet to speak as a prophet and sovereign of the vatic realm, while rooting the transfiguration of his body – its metamorphosis from a contingent vessel of mortality into a vessel of prophetic effulgence – within the prison poem genre.

Assisted by such double entendres, Khaqani conjures the spectre of a sky circling the earth, shorn of the signs by which bewildered creatures might orient themselves. Instead of guidance, the poet confronts a signless abyss. This poem exposes the cosmos, as viewed from the poet's prison cell, as a blank textual surface that resists signification. Not only are the dice through which the poet gambles his life equated here with a sacred symbol of Islam; significantly, these dice are blank, devoid of signs (*bi naqsh*). Khaqani introduces a signless Kaʿba that is then compared with a sky on a starless night, with no guidance from above and no light to illuminate the path forward.[61]

Displaying his talent for compression, Khaqani condenses this imagery, rich in metaphysical meanings, into just a few words: *falak kaʿbatayn bi naqsh ast*. Literally this means: the sky is a pair of dice without inscription. These words also suggest that the sky is a Kaʿba, a sacred sign of God's promise to humanity, lacking an inscription. Although there is no sign or inscription in the sky, the dual Kaʿba asserts an alternate kingdom: the realm of the imagination. Within the world created by this poem, constellations simultaneously reveal and contest God's beneficence. These intersecting cosmologies move the genre beyond its empirical origins as the poet laments his imprisonment.

For every this (*in*) there is a that (*an*), the poet declares at the end of his poem, suggesting an endless cycle of repetition. The dice provide no respite – and no promise of justice – to the poet seeking consolation. Rather, they mock the concept of justice celebrated by earlier *qasida*s to glorify the sultan.

This mockery is followed by an ominous conclusion: the stakes on which our lives are waged are rigged against us. The blank dice, like the signless sky, yield no interpretations. They resist the impulse to fabricate meaning from chaos, and leave unsatisfied the prisoner's need to understand the reasons for his imprisonment. Confounding everyday ratiocination, these images present poetry as a discourse that, to quote Nizami ʿAruzi, causes 'great affairs in the order of the world' through its realignment of everyday perception.

Khaqani's signless sky contrasts with the association in Persian poetics of inscriptions with order, beauty and the imprint of the creator. The association of inscriptions with ordered beauty also extends to the use of chronograms (*madda tarikh*) in Persian poetry.[62] Khaqani used chronograms throughout his poetry, including in the Aivan Qasida (discussed in Chapter 5) and in a *qasida* on Isfahan which established the date of his first pilgrimage.[63] In the preface to his third *divan*, the Indo-Persian poet Amir Khusraw, whom we encountered as a critic of the poets of Shirvan, describes inscription (*naqsh*) as the imprint of the creator on the created, the testimony of which is poetic speech. 'The inscriber [*naqqash*] of outward appearance,' writes Amir Khusraw, 'declares "I have gilded [*nigashtam*] humanity's shape [*naqsh-i insan*] and soul with the best of forms [*khubtarin surat*]. This form's best adornment is poetic speech [*sukhan*]."'[64] For Amir Khusraw, the surface on which poets inscribe their poetry is rich with inscriptions, each of which imprints order onto chaos.

In contrast to the chronogram's ordered entelechy, the prison poet's sky is empty of both verbal and visual signs. In prison poetry, language lacks the scaffolding that the compact between the poet and the sovereign traditionally generated. No message is transmitted, either through gambling or prayer, in spite of the poet's longing for meaning. Prison poem number 3 reveals in microcosm how the prison poem relentlessly confronts an omnipotent but indifferent heaven with an incapacitated and incarcerated creaturedom. Khaqani's blank dice (and signless Kaʿba) explicate for his readers the silence of the sky (*falak*) alongside that of fate (*ruzgar*). In prison poem 3, the Kaʿba's silence – and the dice's blankness – extends to the entire created world. In contrast to the traditional *qasida*, this prison poem offers no abundance of meanings for the poet to attend to because the world viewed from the prison cell is bare of signification.

These tropes evoking a signless universe that silently peruses the spectacle of human suffering inspired in Mujir verses reflections kindred to Khaqani's:

No one's hope will ever be realised in this world.
This earth will never heal any heart's suffering.
What good is two-coloured fate and the hypocrite sky,
when all that was good turns bad in the end?
Who finds the shore of happiness' abode?
The one who has not been born to this world.
The world won't cease its treachery for anyone's words.
No one's labours can turn iron into gold.

تا عالمست امید کسی زو وفا نشد
تا خاک بود درد دلی را دوا نشد
دهر دو رنگ و چرخ دو کیسه چه کار کرد؟
کان هر چه بد صواب به آخر خطا نشد
بر ساحل سعادت کلّی که اوفتاد؟
آنکس که از مشیمهٔ عالم جدا نشد
عالم بقول هیچکس از فتنه سر نتافت
آهن به جهد هیچ کسی کیمیا نشد [65]

Like Khaqani's prison poem, these verses take the genre in a new direction, away from lamenting specific instances of imprisonment, as in Masʿud Saʿd or Falaki, and towards a cosmological complaint against the injustice, not only of the ruler, but of the cosmos itself. Both Khaqani and Mujir juxtapose a signless cosmos to a sign-suffused domain of human speech. Mujir suggests that those who search for meaning in chaos by seeking consolation in dust may never find what they are searching for. Language begins in rectitude (*savab*) and culminates in error (*khata*). The contingency of the created world that punctures these poems illustrates how the prison poem intertwined lyric and cosmic poetics on Caucasus borderlands.

Khaqani's cosmic metaphors, similes and metonymies insist that life itself is a gamble that humans are destined to lose. The cosmos (*falak*) will always triumph over creaturely existence. As quoted above in prison poem 3, the cosmos 'stakes lives, gambling / with the odds of five to one against you, / counting two sixes as two ones' (3:5). Life is depicted here as a game of chance against fate that ends inevitably in death's victory. Thus is the sky, and by extension the cosmos, offered up as a dishonest gambler who manipulates whomever it can and inflicts suffering with impunity. Paradoxically, the Ka'ba, the most sacred symbol of Islam, now doubled and rendered signless, is a vehicle for this deception.

The verses that follow intensify the contrast between the poet's vision of justice and the arbitrary power of patron, ruler and jailer, who collude in imprisoning the blameless poet. Khaqani compares himself with two small animals, the bird (*murgh*) and the ant (*mur*). He then reflects on the irony of imprisoning such weak creatures, given that they are powerless to determine the outcomes of battles and to win wars:

I am a mute bird and a hungry ant.
Who imprisons a bird like me?
How can a bird's song move an army?
How can an army of ants decide a battle?

مرغیم گنگ و مور گرسنه‌ام
کس چو من مرغ در حصار کند
بانگ مرغی چه لشکر انگیزد
صف موری چه کار زار کند (3:7–8)

Such rhetorical questions invert the relation between the human and animal world. In this prison poem, animals prey on the poet's captive body. In a series of increasingly grotesque images, the poet's body is devoured by bees, snakes and rabid dogs:

Tumult and turmoil is the bee's business.
Who wants such rumbles?
The sky casts iron rings
like a snake's mouth around my two feet.
These tight toothless mouths
leave the same traces on my two calves
as a saw hacks off a fruit-laden branch
with mouthless teeth all year long.
Has this iron become a rabid dog?
It bites my entire calf.

شور و غوغا شعار زنبور است
شور و غوغا که اختیار کند
بر دو پایم فلک ز آهن‌ها
حلقه‌ها چون دهان مار کند
این دهن‌های تنگ بی دندان
بر دو ساق من آن شعار کند
که به دندان بی‌دهان همه سال
ارّه با ساق میوه دار کند
سگ دیوانه شد مگر آهن
که همه ساق را فکار کند (3:9–13)

At the very moment when Khaqani's poetics appears most rooted in his experience of imprisonment, surreal imagery suffuses the poem. The chain gripping his legs becomes a snake's mouth (*dahan-i mar*). The comparison between chains and a snake's mouth vividly conjures a voracious pair of lips sucking the life out of its victims. The toothless mouth intensifies the predator's surreal, mute brutality.

Other implications of the poet's fascination with serpentine imagery emerge when situated within the rich visual repertoire depicting hell in Islamic culture. One of the most widely disseminated sources of Islamic eschatology is the story cycle that narrates Muhammad's ascent to heaven. One version of this cycle, known as *Story of the Ascent* (*Khabar al-miʿraj*), includes a journey through hell. In this work, the first of the seven floors of hell is populated by creatures with pig-like lips writhing under demons' red-hot forks, while serpents enter their mouths and consume their bodies from within.[66] Serpents also cluster together on the second floor, populated by usurers. Their mountain-like bellies are so weighed down by scorpions that whenever they stand, they collapse on their faces. The surreal movement in prison poem 3 from the chain to a rabid dog recalls the version of Ibn ʿAbbas, wherein the inmates of hell have the faces of dogs.[67] As with the Prophet prior to his ascent (*miʿraj*), Khaqani pays a visit to hell.[68] Elsewhere in Khaqani's corpus (particularly in the Christian Qasida, discussed in Chapter 5), the descent into hell produces a chiasmus – an inverted antithesis – of Jesus' journey to heaven.

Three of Khaqani's six prison poems (2, 3 and 6) deploy serpentine imagery to describe the poet's incarceration. The serpentine imagery of prison poems 3 and 6 together create a surreal effect, transforming animals into objects, as if the poet were reporting on a nightmare, as in the followimg verses:

Have you seen a serpent coiling around a plant?
Now see the snake in the cave of sorrows encircling my plant-like leg.
See the serpent sleeping beneath my clothes.
I do not stir, fearing my serpent will wake.

مار دیدی در گیا پیچان؟ کنون در غار غم
مار بین پیچیده بر ساق گیا اسای من
اژدها بین حلقه گشته خفته زیر دامنم
ز آن نجنبم ترسم آگه گردد اژدرهای من (6:6–7)

Prison poem 2 achieves a serpentine effect through intertextual allusions to Ferdowsi's *Shahnama*.[69] Ferdowsi narrates the transformation of the Arab villain Zahhak, who kills his father Merdas and becomes king in his place, into a three-headed monster. To punish his crime, the sorcerer Ahriman causes the heads of two snakes to grow from his shoulders. To protect Zahhak's head from being devoured by the snakes, they are fed with the brains of young men who are sacrificed daily for this reason. After he is defeated in battle by Faridun, Zahhak spends the remainder of his days in Mt Damavand while snakes feeding on his brain. Further intensifying the prison poem's corporeal poetics (particularly the Aivan Qasida discussed in Chapter 5), Khaqani compares his eyes with Shayegan, the palace of the Sasanian king Khusraw Parviz (r. 590–628), from which precious treasures – including the pearls to which Khaqani implicitly compares his tears – were taken at the time of the Arab conquest of Iran:[70]

Zahhak's snake stayed on my feet.
The treasures of Shayegan left my lashes.
I began to burn like a fish in a pan
from these two whale-like snakes.

مار ضحاک ماند بر پایم
وز مژه گنج شایگان برخاست
سوزش من چو ماهی از تابه
زین دو مار نهنگ سان برخاست (2:15–16)

Following this figural descent into a serpentine hell, the poet's suffering is amplified with another set of surreal images. The snake's toothless mouth suddenly morphs into teeth without a mouth (*dandan-i bi dahan*). And then, just as suddenly, the saw morphs into a rabid dog (*sag-i divaneh*), his teeth bared as he feasts on the fleshly legs of the unjustly imprisoned poet.

In prison poem 5, the infernal serpentine imagery of a toothless mouth (*dahan-i bi dandan*) shifts to the more conventionally poetic image of a mouthless set of teeth (*dandan bi dahan*). Apart from its imagistic quality, this poetic inversion plays on the relation between sentience and suffering. Inasmuch as a toothless mouth can still articulate, sentient speech lies within its discursive domain. By contrast, mouthless teeth are mute. As skeletal, non-sentient objects, they kill and inflict suffering while lacking the capacity to comprehend their actions. Khaqani's mouthless teeth anticipate ʿAwfi's association of the prison poem with the reader's incapacity to bring their upper and lower lips together. As shown in the preceding chapter, the capacity to induce bewildered silence was for ʿAwfi a defining characteristic of this genre.

The muteness induced by the prison poem generates a metaphysical crisis as well as a political critique. More than prior prison poets, Khaqani created a genre that confronted the basic conundrum of political theology: the suffering of innocent creatures, including himself. As the representation of the poet's imprisoned body was transformed into a vehicle of political critique, suffering was politicised by the redistributions of sovereignty across the twelfth-century eastern Islamic world. New modes of punishment accompanied the new alignments of power, generating in turn new roles for poetry. In prison poem 3, Khaqani resolves in his imagination to go to the other side (*ansu*; 3:14), far from his prison cell, knowing full well that such feats are possible only within poetic discourse. In his imagination, Khaqani travels so far that the spectator's eyes must exert themselves to see him. Moving towards closure by repeating his pen name with belligerent force and speaking of himself in the third person, the poet attributes to himself, in a semi-prophetic utterance, the capacity to illuminate all that is hidden from the world by the cosmos:

> Khaqani's sigh complaining of the heavens
> went so far that it disappeared from the eye.

Everything hidden by the veil of the heavens
will be unveiled by Khaqani's sigh.
His problems will not be resolved by this or that.
The creator alone can address his woes.
Khaqani has more enemies than sand.
Death will turn them all to dust.

اه خاقانی از فلک زانسو
رفت چندان که چشم کار کند
هر چه پنهان پردهی فلک است
آه خاقانی آشکار کند
کار او زین و آن نگردد نیک
کارها نیک کردگار کند
گر چه خصمان ز ریگ بیشترند
همه را مرگ، خاکسار کند (3:14–17)

In the very instant when the poet asserts his helplessness (recalling here Falaki's poem that inaugurated the prison poetry of Shirvan), Khaqani informs his readers that the cosmos is on his side. All Khaqani's enemies, who are more numerous than sand (*rig*), will be buried by death. Such prophecies may seem, if not wishful thinking, then at least unsubstantiated by what precedes them. Has not Khaqani just powerfully juxtaposed his suffering to the heavens' indifference? Has he not used the prison poem to announce that fate (*ruzgar*) and the cosmos (*falak*) are against him, and cited his imprisonment as proof? If not an arbitrary cosmos, what determines the poet's fate?

The tension between the poet's lyric and political selves correspond to the prison poet's bifurcated body. The next chapters explore this fissure while tracing the emergence of the prophetic self in the poems of Khaqani. These bifurcations are produced by the panegyric *qasida*, the formal genre in which most prison poems were written. The patronage nexus enabled, and required, that the prison poet dwell in a counterfactual realm, opposing his literary imagination to the increasingly corrupt power of the rulers. The prison poem enabled poets like Khaqani to challenge the subjugation of their bodies and the silencing of their voices. The trope of prison became, in a profound sense, an allegory for the cleavage of their identities. Critique in verse, composed from the prison cell, gave prison poets leverage over the sultan, and empowered their imaginations as they critiqued worldly power. Paradoxically, the corporeal turn within Persian poetics increased the poet's power.

Newly endowed with poetry's capacity to challenge the power of the sultan, Persian poets found in the prison poem a discourse of authority that enabled them to cultivate their voices as sources of a different kind of sovereignty, far removed from the material world. While Khaqani's signless sky exposes the poet's absolute vulnerability, it also reveals poetry's potentiality. Rulers needed poets to consecrate their legitimacy even more than poets needed patrons. The formally transgressive status of the prison poem resulted from the revelation of poetry's power. Khaqani, it has been argued, 'is one of the few poets of this period whose poetry possessed temperament-specific lexicons that could be used to identify his many moods'.[71] The poet's versatility helped him to extend the prison poem across a wide array of disciplines, discourses and psychic conditions. In each instance, prison poems adapted literary forms, such as the *qasida* and quatrain, to their evolving political environments.

With the prison poets of Shivan, the prison poem became a transgressive genre that reached beyond formal taxonomy in order to reveal genre as a discursive process that refashioned empirical experience, and which brought about new alignments among signifiers and signifieds. This genre entered the world, not as a natural development of any given formal rubric or other typology, but rather through the dialectical transgression of form and content in the service of a political and aesthetic effort to replace worldly power with poetic authority. Every prison poem discussed in these chapters represented a subtly different transgression of existing literary norms. Such aesthetic transgressions contributed to the sacralisation of the poet's mortal body.

Notes

1. Khāqānī, *Dīvān*, 425. See the discussion in Naʿimah Ḥassūkī, 'Madḥ-i nabavī dar shiʿr-i Ḥassān-i bin Thābet va Khāqānī-yi Shirwānī', MA thesis, Tarbiat Modares University, 1385, 119.
2. Badīʿ al-Zamān Farūzānfar, *Sukhan va sukhanvarān* (Tehran: Intishārāt-i Khwārizmī, 1350), 625.
3. Khāqānī, *Dīvān*, 140.

4. Riccardo Zipoli, 'Il Khāqāni polemico', in Giovanna Pagani-Cesa and Ol'ga Obuchova (eds), *Studi e scritti in memoria di Marzio Marzaduri* (Venice: Quaderni del Dipartimento di Studi Eurasiatici–Universita Ca'foscari, 2002), 474.
5. Khāqānī, *Dīvān*, 831.
6. Khāqānī, *Dīvān*, 850.
7. Khāqānī, *Dīvān*, 858.
8. On Sanā'ī's philological and editorial activity, see J. T. P. de Bruijn, *Of Piety and Poetry* (Leiden: Brill, 1983), 89–144.
9. Harold Bloom, *The Anxiety of Influence: A Theory of Poetry* (Oxford: Oxford University Press, [1973] 1997).
10. Falakī, *Dīvān*, 112.
11. Dawlatshāh Samarqandī, *Taḍhkira al Shu'arā'*, ed. Edward Granville Browne (London: Luzac, 1901), 47.
12. Hādī Ḥasan, *Falakī-i Shirvānī* (London, 1929), 62. The manuscript cited is Br. Museum, MS Egerton 701, f.1b.
13. 'Awfī, *Lubāb*, 2:117–25.
14. Shams-i Qays, *Kitāb al-mu'jam fī ma'ayīr ash'ār al-'ajam*, ed. Mudarris-i Raḍawī (Tehran: Kitābfurūshī-yi Tehrān, 1338/1959), 392–3.
15. Most scholars accept Khāqānī's assertion that Falakī was his student at face value. However, given the libelous polemic he directed against Abū'l 'Alā' Ganjavī (on which see below), it is possible (if unprovable) that Khāqānī misrepresented the situation. Jāmī (d. 1492) asserts that Khāqānī was Falakī's student, though without good authority. See his *Nafaḥātu'l uns min khaḍarāt al-quds*, ed. Gholām 'Isa 'Abd al-Ḥamīd and Kabīr al-Dīn Aḥmad (Calcutta: W. Nassau Lees, 1859), 281.
16. Falakī, *Dīvān*, 23–4.
17. Hādī Ḥasan, *Falakī-i Shirvānī* (London: Royal Asiatic Society, 1929), 62.
18. Jocelyn Sharlet, *Patronage and Poetry in the Islamic World: Social Mobility and Status in the Medieval Middle East and Central Asia* (London: I. B. Tauris, 2011), 8.
19. See also the polemic between Khāqānī and Athīr al-Dīn, cited in Ḥasan, *Falakī-i Shirwānī*, 53–4.
20. Amīr Khusraw, *Dībācha-yi ghurrat al-kamāl*, ed. Sayyid Vazīr al-Ḥasan al-'Abīdī (Lahore: Nīshnul Kumītī Barāyī Sāt-i Sū Sālah Taqrībāt-i Amīr Khusraw, 1975), 38–41.
21. Khāqānī, *Dīvān*, 918.

22. The oldest extant manuscript (transcribed in 1197, during Khāqānī's lifetime) of *Tuḥfat* bears the title *Khatm al-Gharā'ib* (*Seal of Wonders*) (Vienna: Mīras al-Maktūb and Österreichische Akademie der Wissenschaften, 2006). In his *qaṣīda* in praise of Isfahan, Khāqānī refers to this work as *Khatm al- Gharā'ib*:

آنک ختم الغرائب آخر دیدند
تا چه ثنا رانده ام برای صفاهان

(They saw another seal of wonders [= my book].
[And saw] how much I praised Iṣfāhān.)

Khāqānī, *Dīvān*, 355.

The title *Tuḥfat al-'Iraqayn* appears as early as 'Awfī's *Lubāb* (p. 405). Given my interest here with reception rather than authorial intention, I have adopted the title by which Khāqānī's *masnavī* was best known.

23. These episodes are analysed by A. L. F. A. Beelaert, in *A Cure for the Grieving* (Leiden: Nederlands Instituut voor het Nabije Oosten, 1996). For Khāqānī's journey, see Henri Massé, 'Aspects du pélerinage à la Mecque dans la poésie persane', *Melanges Franz Cumont* (Brussels: Annuaire of the Institut de Philosophie, 1936), 859–65. Also see Rebecca Ruth Gould, 'From Pious Journeys to the Critique of Sovereignty: Khaqani Shirvani's Persianate Poetics of Pilgrimage', in Montserrat Piera (ed.), *Remapping Travel Narratives in the Early Modern World* (Amsterdam: Amsterdam University Press, 2018), 25–47.
24. Michal Biran, 'The Mongol Transformation: From the Steppe to Eurasian Empire', *Medieval Encounters* 10(1–3) (2004): 341.
25. Cited in N. de Khanikof, 'Mémoire sur Khâcâni, poëte persan du XIIe siècle', *Journal Asiatique* 6(4) (1864): 151.
26. See 'Abd al-Malik ibn Muḥammad Tha'ālibī, *Thimār al-Qulūb fī al-Muḍāf wa-al-Mansūb* (Cairo, 1908), 196.
27. For the full Persian text, see de Khanikof, 'Mémoire sur Khâcâni, poëte persan du XIIe siècle', 152–3. The the exchange between Abū'l 'Alā' and Khāqānī has undergone numerous modifications over the centuries. Khanikof's text is neither identical with the text in Yaḥyā Qarīb's edition of Khāqānī's *Tuḥfat*, nor with the version cited in the nineteenth-century commentary by Muḥammad Ismā'il Khān Abjadī, *Sharḥ-i Tuḥfat al-'Iraqayn*, ed. Muḥammad Ḥusayn Maḥvī (Madras: University of Madras, 1954). A comparative study of these different versions is an urgent desideratum.
28. Rostom Pestonji Masani, *Court Poets of Iran and India* (Bombay: New Book Company, 1938), 59. Even more graphic invectives by Abū'l 'Alā' are cata-

logued in Ḥamdu'llah Muṣtafā Qazwīnī's *Tārikh-i Guzīda*, the relevant sections of which are available in Edward Browne, 'Biographies of Persian Poets', *JRAS* 32(4) (1901): 741–2.

29. See the letter from Chandra Bhan Brahman to his Khwaja Tej Bhan that includes Abū'l ʿAlā's poetry in its list of Persian texts necessary for the would-be Mughal courtier to master, cited in Muzaffar Alam, *The Languages of Political Islam: India 1200–1800* (London: Hurst, 2004), 131.
30. See E. E. Bertels, *Nizami i Fuzuli* (Moscow: Nauka, 1962). Bertels adapts the region-based methodology of Bahār's stylistics (*sabkshinasi*).
31. Khāqānī, *Dīvān*, 328.
32. Mujīr al-Dīn Baylaqānī, *Dīvān*, xxii.
33. Ḥossein Bastānīrād, 'Ḥabsiyyeh-ye Mujīr al-Dīn Baylaqānī', *Majalleh Yādgār* 6 (1324/1946): 54–8.
34. This tradition is alluded to in Mohammad Ali Amir-Moezzi, 'An Absense Filled with Presences. Shaykhiyya Hermeneutics of the Occultation', in Rainer Brunner and Werner Ende (eds), *The Twelver Shia in Modern Times: Religious Culture & Political* (Leiden: Brill, 2001), 53.
35. Mujīr al-Dīn Baylaqānī, *Dīvān*, 310.
36. On this poet, see Walid ʿArafat's introduction to his edition of the *Diwan of Hassan ibn Thabit* (London: Luzac, 1971); Jennifer Hill Boutz, 'Hassan ibn Thabit, a True Mukhadram: A Study of the Ghassanid Odes of Hassan ibn Thabit', PhD dissertations, Georgetown University, 2009.
37. Ibn Hishām, *The Life of Muhammad: A Translation of Ishāq's Sīrat Rasūl Allāh*, trans. A. Guillaume (London: Oxford University Press, 1955), 628–31.
38. See, for example, Khāqānī, *Dīvān*, 323 (listed in the Appendix, prison poem No. 6, v. 53).
39. Farūzānfar, *Sukhan va sukhanvarān*, 2:250, n. 5.
40. Muḥammad Abādī, 'Tarjumeh-yi hal o sharh zindagi', *Dīvān-i Mujīr al-Dīn Baylaqān* (Tabriz: Mu'assassah-'i Tārīkh va Farhang-i Irān, 1358), page سه. In his edition, Abādī changes حبشی (African/Abyssian) in the above-quote verse to ارمنی (Armenian). The matter remains unresolved.
41. See, for example, Ẕabīḥallāh Ṣafā, *Tārīkh-i Adabīyāt dar Īrān*, 5 vols (Tehran: Ferdows, 1371/1992), 2:721.
42. Alireza Korangy, 'Development of the Ghazal and Khāqānī's Contribution', PhD dissertation, Harvard University, 2007, 241.
43. See Ṣafā, *Tārīkh-i Adabīyāt dar Īrān* (Tehran: Ferdows, 1371/1992), 2:352.
44. Farūzānfar, *Sukhan va sukhanvarān*, 2:264, n. 2.

45. For a systematic account of the Arabic prosodic system, see D. V. Frolov, *Klassicheskii arabskii stikh* (Moscow: Nauka, 1991).
46. These transformations are documented in Omid Safi, *The Politics of Knowledge in Premodern Islam: Negotiating Ideology and Religious Inquiry* (Durham, NC: University of North Carolina Press, 2006); Lange, *Justice, Punishment, and the Medieval Muslim Imagination*; C. E. Bosworth, *The Later Ghaznavids: Splendour and Decay* (New York: Columbia University Press, 1977); Vladimir Minorsky, *A History of Sharvān and Darband in the 10th–11th centuries* (Cambridge: Heffer, 1958). Also see Chapter 6, below.
47. While the world-making capacity of literature is a cornerstone of contemporary literary theory, the discussion has tended to focus on modern European prose. See, for example, Pheng Cheah, *What Is a World? On Postcolonial Literature as World Literature* (Durham, NC: Duke University Press, 2016); Eric Hayot, *On Literary Worlds* (Oxford: Oxford University Press, 2012).
48. See Abū'l ʿAlā' al-Maʿarrī, *Dīwān luzūm mā lā yalzam*, ed. Kamāl al-Yāzjī (Beirūt: Dār al-Jamīl, 1992), 204.
49. Farīd al-Dīn ʿAṭṭār, *Dīvān*, ed. Badīʿ al-Zamān Fūrūzānfar (Tehran: Negah, 1994), 163.
50. Jalāl al-Dīn Rūmī, *Kuliyat-i Shams-i Tabrīzī*, ed. Badīʿ al-Zamān Fūrūzānfar (Tehran: Sana'i & Sales, 2002), 1:238.
51. My identification of these six poems follows Vladimir Minorsky, 'Khāqānī and Andronicus Comnenus', *BSOAS* 11(3) (1945): 561, with the addition of prison poem 3, not mentioned by Minorsky. The *maṭlaʿ* (opening verse) for each of these six poems is listed in the Appendix.
52. The under-discussed topic of Khāqānī's gambling imagery is examined in Kāmrān Aḥmadgulī and Sajjād Suleimānī Yazdī, 'Sabk-i āzarbāijān va shiʿr-i mitāfīzīk: Shatranj dar shiʿr-i Khāqānī Shirvāni va Abrāhām Kowlī', *Naqd-i zabān va adabiyāt khārijī* 14(19) (1996): 13–32.
53. Franz Rosenthal explores gambling tropes across the Arabo-Persian poetic tradition in his classic *Gambling in Islam* (Leiden: Brill, 1975), 113–37.
54. Cited in Hermann Ethé, *Avicenna als persischer Lyriker*, in *Nachrichten von der K. Gesellschaft der Wiss. und der Georg-Augusts-Universität* (Göttingen, 1875), 566–7.
55. A. L. F. A. Beelaert, 'The Kaʿba as a Woman: a Topos in Classical Persian Literature', *Persica* 13 (1988/9): 107–23.
56. Khāqānī, *Dīvān*, 644.
57. Prior contexts do, however, bear comparison with the culture of imprisonment

in twelfth-century Shirvān. See, for example, S. W. Anthony, 'The Domestic Origins of Imprisonment: An Enquiry into an Early Islamic Institution', *Journal of the American Oriental Society* 129 (2009): 571–96; S. W. Anthony, 'The Meccan Prison of ʿAbdallāh b. al-Zubayr and the Imprisonment of Muḥammad b. al-Ḥanafiyya', in Maurice A. Pomerantz and Aram Shahin (eds), *The Heritage of Arabo-Islamic Learning* (Leiden: Brill, 2016), 2–27.

58. Khāqānī, *Dīvān*, 69.
59. This text is introduced and translated in Michael Sells, '"Bānat Suʿād": Translation and Introduction', *Journal of Arabic Literature* 21(2) (1990): 140–54.
60. Khāqānī, *Dīvān*, 188.
61. In his annotated concordance to Khāqānī's oeuvre, Sajjādī glosses *kaʿbatayn bī naqsh*, referring specifically to this passage, as 'an empty [*khalī o tuhī*] Kaʿba without inscription' (*Farhang-i lughāt va taʿbirāt bā sharḥ-i aʿlām va mushkilāt-i Dīvān-i Khāqānī Shirvānī* (Tehran: Zuvvār, 1374), 2:125).
62. For chronograms in Persian literature, see Paul Losensky, 'Coordinates in Time and Space: Architectural Chronograms in Safavid Iran', in Colin P. Mitchell (ed.), *New Perspectives on Safavid Iran: Empire and Society* (London: Routledge, 2011), 198–219; Paul Losensky, 'The Equal of Heaven's Vault: The Design, Ceremony, and Poetry of the Ḥasanābād Bridge', in Beatrice Gruendler and Louise Marlow (eds), *Writers and Rulers: Perspective on Their Relationship from Abbasid to Safavid Times* (Wiesbaden: Ludwig Reichert Verlag, 2004), 195–216.
63. See O. L. Vil'chevskii, 'Khronogrammy Khakani', *Epigrafika Vostoka* 13 (1960): 59–68, trans. into English by Jerome W. Clinton, 'The Chronograms of Khaqani', *Iranian Studies* 2(2/3) (1969): 97–105.
64. Amīr Khusraw, *Dībācha-yi ghurrat al-kamāl*, ed. Sayyid Vazīr al-Ḥasan al-ʿAbīdī (Lahore: Nīshnul Kumītī Barāyī Sāt-i Sū Sālah Taqrībāt-i Amīr Khusraw, 1975), 9.
65. Mujīr al-Dīn Baylaqānī, *Dīvān*, 375. Also see Farūzānfar, *Sukhan va sukhanvarān*, 278–9.
66. Miguel Asín Palacios, *La escatologia musulmana en la Divina Comedia*[4] (Madrid: Hiperion, 1984), 433. Serpentine imagery in Islamic depictions of hell is further detailed in Lange, *Justice, Punishment, and the Medieval Muslim Imagination*, 150, 176; Roberto Tottoli, 'Tours of Hell and Punishments of Sinners in Miʿraj Narratives', in Christiane J. Gruber and Frederick Stephen Colby (eds), *The Prophet's Ascension* (Bloomington: Indiana University Press, 2010), 11–26.
67. This version is discussed in Frederick S. Colby, *Narrating Muhammad's Night*

Journey: Tracing the Development of the Ibn ʿAbbas Ascension Discourse (Albany, NY: SUNY Press, 2008).

68. For detailed accounts of the *miʿrāj* in Persian visual culture and across the Islamic world, see Christiane Gruber, *The Ilkhanid Book of Ascension* (London: I. B. Tauris, 2010); Christiane Gruber, *The Timurid Book of Ascension (Miʿrajnama)* (Valencia: Patrimonio, 2009).
69. The poem's image also recalls the blood-red serpents that surge towards the shore to attack and ultimately suffocate Neptune's high priest Laocoon and his sons in Virgil's *Aeneid* (2:200–20).
70. Sajjādī, *Farhang-i lughāt*, 1:896.
71. Alireza Korangy, *Development of the Ghazal and Khāqānī's Contribution: A Study of the Development of Ghazal and a Literary Exegesis of a 12th c. Poetic Harbinger* (Wiesbaden: Harrassowitz Verlag, 2013), 271.

4

The Prison Poet as King and Prophet

In tracing the shift from the lyric ode to the cosmic lament within the prison poem genre, the preceding chapters focused on imprisoned poets who sought assurance from a mute cosmos. The poems discussed thus far have been dominated by a pervasive sense of the imprisoned poet's helpless confinement and the perceived incapacity of poetic discourse (*sukhan*) to liberate him from the conditions of his oppression. I have yet to fully examine how, beyond lamenting the poet's incapacity, the prison poem develops an oppositional discourse of sovereignty, and an alternative source of authority, by reconfiguring the poet's body. Now that we are halfway through the book, the remaining chapters focus on the prison poem's political dimensions. Incorporating the political into the literary imagination, I examine this genre no longer as a testimony to the imprisoned poet's helplessness, but rather as evidence of his poetic – hence otherworldly – sovereignty.

In this chapter and those that follow, I shift the focus away from the poet's incapacity and trace the development of a discourse around the imprisoned poet's power. I examine the dialectic between prophetic and poetic gifts by way of demonstrating the sacrality of the poetic utterance. This involves showing how poetry's licit magic confers political substance on poetry's vatic power. The next chapter examines one of Khaqani's most famous poems – the Christian Qasida – through the prism of this dialectic. It concludes by considering how another famous poem, the Aivan Qasida, reconfigures the sovereign's two bodies to shift authority to the poet's doubly constituted body. The final chapter contextualises two important works of medieval Persian political theory in relation to the twelfth-century carceral aesthetics that traversed South, Central and West Asia while tracing the discursive shift away from worldly sovereignty to vatic authority that this aesthetics facilitated. Before engaging with these political and aesthetic transformations, it will be helpful to review the poems that made the case for poetry's prophetic capacities in early Islamic literature before the prison poem, and that set the stage for political aesthetics in a post-caliphal world.

Licit Magic

> I cut therewith the sinews of thy feet, and they were severed, and
> after my satire [*al-hija'*] succeeded you had no more power to rise.
> I smote you with notable verses, full of strange startling words, a
> blow you cowered beneath, and your heart was nearly dead.

قَطَعْتُ بِهِ مِنْكَ الحَوامِلَ فانبرَتْ   فَما بكَ مِنْ بَعدِ الهِجاءِ نُهوضُ
صَعَقْتُكَ بالغُرّ الأوابِدِ صَقْعَةً [1]   خَضَعْتَ لها فالقَلبُ مِنْكَ جَريضُ

Thus writes the sixth-century poet ʿAbid ibn al-Abras, full of faith in the power of his verse. He was addressing his rival Imru al-Qays (d. 545), whose equally stirring verses impressed on his audience the importance of his poetry. Like Khaqani centuries later, ʿAbid ibn al-Abras perceived in satire a weapon in the battle for poetic sovereignty. Centuries of Quranic and post-Quranic reflection on the uses and dangers of poetry made this discourse more sophisticated, but the basic tension between poetry and prophecy remained constant. Given that this tension also influenced the trajectory of the prison poem, it is worth tracing here what in the Perso-Arabic tradition is called poetry's licit magic (*sihr-i halal*).

The sorcerer (*sahir*) hardly holds a position of prestige in traditional Islamic thought. Like his metier, magic (*sihr*), he is relegated to a subterranean existence, unsanctioned by authority and forbidden by doctrine. The Quran is unambiguous: Harut and Marut, the angels who made magic available to humans, were sent by God to Earth where they committed every kind of iniquity and were punished by having their feet suspended in a well in Babylon (Q. 2:102). Equally forbidding are the passages in the *hadith* that sanction retaliation against those who engage in divination. Ibn Hanbal instructs the pious to 'kill every sorcerer [*sahir*]'.[2] Al-Tirmidhi specifies that the sorcerer (*sahir*) should receive as punishment (*hadd*) decapitation by the sword.[3] Abu Muslim and al-Bukhari list magic (*sihr*) among the seven crimes that, together with idolatry (*shirk*), murder, robbing orphans, usury, apostasy and the slandering of faithful women, merit execution.[4]

While these examples suggest a uniformly negative attitude to magic within Islamic legal thought, they are counterbalanced by the wealth of positive allusions in classical Persian poetry, especially prison poetry, to the licit magic that constitutes poetic discourse. Technically, the term *sihr-i halal* refers to the phenomenon when the same poem can be read in two different meters, but its meanings are also broader than it. Whereas, according to J. C. Bürgel, we find 'little religious poetry of real importance written in Arabic, most of the great Arabic poetry being nonreligious or even outspokenly pagan',[5] twelfth-century Persian poetry abounds in poems, particularly prison poems, that appropriate religious discourse in order to criticise the sultan's power. From Central and South Asia to the Caucasus, magic (*sihr*) was the crucible through which the language of poetry had to pass before it could attain to the level of poetic discourse (*sukhan*).

In his masterful study of the medieval Islamic literary imagination, Bürgel identified three strategies for medieval Islamic poets seeking validation for their craft. The first was to rely on the arguments of Ibn Rashiq and ʿAbd al-Qahir al-Jurjani that the Prophet took no issue with poetry's famed untruthfulness and that he employed poets to propagate the Quranic message.[6] The second strategy, most popular with Persian poets and Persian poets writing in Arabic, was to assimilate non-Islamic and even anti-Islamic understandings of magic into Islamic poetics. The result of this process was a celebration of licit magic (*sihr-i halal*). The third strategy was to reconcile poetry with Quranic teachings. As Bürgel notes, this strategy could be sustained only by poets familiar with Persian mysticism or Andalusian Neo-Platonism, and was therefore demographically negligible.[7] These three strategies reinforced each other and often overlapped. Collectively, they cleared a path for medieval Persian poets to cultivate a vision of poetry's discursive authority that contested the power of the sultan.

One of the earliest presentations of licit magic in the Persian tradition occurs in a *qasida* of Masʿud Saʿd wherein the poet elevates poetry's discursive primacy above the material power wielded by his sovereign. The *qasida* begins by celebrating the poet's craft:

If it is right to boast of one's poetry and prose,
today, I claim my poetry and prose.
My poetry and prose will never decline.
My poetry and prose are pearls and my talent is a sea.

به نظم و نثر کسی را گر افتخار سزاست
مرا سزاست که امروز نظم و نثر مراست
به هیچ وقت مرا نظم و نثر کم نشود
که نظم و نثرم در است و طبع من دریاست [8]

This boast concerning poetry and prose (*nazm o nathr*) is followed by the assertion that his poetry may not attain renown in his lifetime. Poetry's temporality, Masʿud Saʿd suggests, is extrinsic to the sultan's worldly power:

Do not be surprised if my poetry is unknown to them.
Their talents are shallow. My poetry is sublime.

شگفت نیست اگر شعر من نمی‌دانند
که طبع ایشان پست است و شعر من والاست

Then, suddenly, we are confronted with an argument for poetry's autonomy from worldly power. After asserting his primacy over his detractors who cannot gauge his genius, the poet declares:

They don't see me with the eyes of solemnity and truth.
They can't see my status and dignity reasonably.

به چشم جد و حقیقت مرا نمی بینند
که نزد عقل مرا رتبت و شرف به کجاست

This declaration is followed by another rhetorical question which takes even more paradoxical form:

Although the spring of the Sun is lucid and high,
it cannot be seen by the one who is blind.

اگرچه چشمه خورشید روشن است و بلند
چگونه بیند آن کش دو چشم نابیناست

The blind eyes that cannot see the sun belong to those who cast judgement on the poet. Meanwhile, the poet equates his literary gifts with the sun (*khurshid*) and implicitly with God, whose location in the world's intellect cannot be assayed, so expansive is his reach. The sun's illumination (*rawshan*), aligned with worldly sovereignty in the political theory discussed in Chapter 6, is connected here to the poet's supernatural genius and contrasted to the worldly – and corruptible – power of the poet's jailers and enemies.

The remainder of this lengthy *qasida* transfers power away from vision and onto language. An array of rhetorical terms enable this shift, including the distinction between poetry and prose (*nazm* and *nathr*), figurative language (*badi'*), example (*mathal*), story (*qissah*) and, most importantly, the licit magic (*sihr-i halal*) in which poetic creation partakes. When Mas'ud Sa'd refers to licit magic, he suggests that its power will not be discerned by his auditors. Instead of recognising the divine sparks emitted by his words, the poet's listeners perceive only children's speech:

If I recite licit magic for them they will say:
his speech was immature and infantile.

اگر برایشان سحر حلال بر خوانم
جز این نگویند آخر که کودک و برناست

Mas'ud Sa'd launches into a defence of poetry on quasi-religious grounds, claiming that he can be judged by God alone and that his poetic creed (*i'tiqad*) will prevail even in a world where the sun grows cold:

No matter if it rains fire on my head from the sky,
I won't change. My creed [*i'tiqad*] is just.

اگرچه بر سرم آتش ببارد از گردون
ز حال خود نشوم، اعتقاد دارم راست [9]

The poet then returns to the patronage matrix, apart from which his *qasida* cannot exist, by dressing incarceration in the raiment of praise. Although his putative task is to praise the ruler, the *qasida*'s opaque language allows for multiple interpretations. Consider the multiple associations of *gawhar* (jewel), each of which conceals an ambivalent valence:

I will give my jewels to the one who deserves them.
I sing the praises of the one who deserves praise.

گهر بر آن کس پاشم که در خور گهر است
ثنا مر او را گویم که او سزای ثناست

The second hemistich alters the political valence of the first and reveals that praise is not automatically bestowed on everyone. Anticipating Khaqani, Mas'ud Sa'd concludes with a paean to his poetry and a citation (*tazmin*) from a little-known poet named Labibi:[10]

His glorious name at the head of my rare poems
is like a dirham's emblem and the designs on fine silk clothes.
In this *qasida* I imitated
My teacher Labibi, who is the poet-king.
I composed it according to his principle:
discourse given poetic form should be true and taut.

خجسته نامش بر شعرهای نادر من
چو مهر بر درم است و چو نقش بر دیباست
بدین قصیده که گفتم من اقتدا کردم
به اوستاد لبیبی که سیدالشعراست
بر آن طریق بنا کردم این قصیده که گفت
سخن که نظم دهند آن درست باید وراست

Mas'ud Sa'd here appropriates the words of Labibi in distinguishing between his own verse and the panegyrics of earlier Ghaznavid court poetry. He continues:

It's a small *qasida*, but big in power and virtues,
concise in words [*lafz*] but rich in meaning [*ma'ni*].
Every expert in poetry knows that
every distich is itself a brilliant *qasida*.
Just ask Mas'ud Sa'd Salman for a *qasida* like this.
Such *qasidas* can be found only with Mas'ud Sa'd Salman.

قصیده خرد ولیکن به قدر و فضل بزرگ
به لفظ موجز و معنیش باز مستوفاست
هر آن که داند داند یقین که هر بیتی
از این قصیده‌ی من یک قصیده‌ی غراست
چنین قصیده ز مسعود سعد سلمان خواه
چنین قصاید مسعود سعد سلمان راست

The very minuteness of the poet's verse demonstrates its discursive advantage over the sultan's grandiose displays. Alien to jewels and other royal pomposities, poetic discourse is manifested in aesthetic minutiae: figures on a cloth and fine silk cloth. These minor tones and muted colours offer an alternative to the gaudy displays of sovereigns and patrons who cannot appreciate the verbal delicacy (*lutf-i alfaz*) that, according to Vatvat, characterises the prison poem.

Masʿud Saʿd's engagement with licit magic is the first stage in the development of the prison poem's political theology. The next phase, which used licit magic to elaborate a political theology of the poet's prophetic body, was activated by the introduction of prison poetry to Shirvan, and its transformation by Khaqani's poetic alchemy.

Kingdoms of Speech

The two major prison poets of Persian literature, Masʿud Saʿd and Khaqani, both wrote from peripheries, far from the traditional centres of Islamic rule in Baghdad, and far from regional centres of power in Ghazna and Nishapur. While Lahore and Shirvan, respectively, were becoming local centres of Persianate culture at the time of their writing, their political roles were marginal. Even more relevant than their respective distance from centres of imperial power is the high proportion of non-Muslim populations found in these borderland regions. Every day these poets came into contact with non-Muslims, and every day they confronted the politics of Islamic rule over non-Muslim peoples. These encounters, along with the Christian and otherwise non-Muslim origins of many prison poets, gave them special insight into the discriminatory structures of the empires under which they lived, and alerted them to the potential that poetry had to productively manoeuvre within these power structures.

As Akimushkina argues in her study of the prison poem, certain poetic dimensions of the genre were activated only after its migration to the Caucasus.[11] Writing in nearby Ganja, Khaqani's contemporary Nizami attests to the revival of poetry's ancient relationship to licit magic:

> It is so difficult to deny
> magic that is so licit.

I'm so perfect in poetry's magic
that my name mirrors the invisible.
The sword of my tongue is so eloquent
that it aims to perform a Christ-like miracle.

سحری که چنین حلال باشد
منکر شدنش وبال باشد
در سحر سخن چنان تمامم
کایینه غیب گشت نامم
شمشیر زبانم از فصیحی
دارد سر معجز مسیحی [12]

With his unique talent for manifesting the transformative capacity of literary language, Khaqani infused the theme of licit magic into verses such as the following, which elevate his stature as a poet over that of his rivals:

Fresh poetry cannot be found in their dry talent.
Who can find a water-lily in their mirage?
Comparing my licit magic to their superstition
is like comparing ʿAli with Abu Lahab.

از طبع خشکشان نتوان یافت شعر تر
نیلوفر آرزو که کند از سرابشان
سحر حلال من چو خرافات خود نهند
آری یکی است بولهب و بوترابشان (Khāqānī, *Dīvān*, 329)

Abu Lahab is the most notorious sceptic of early Islamic history. The uncle of the Prophet, he refused to convert to Islam and was therefore cursed in the Quran (*sura* al-Masad; Q. 111) as someone who would be tortured in hell. Abu Lahab is additionally one of the few non-prophetic personalities referenced by name in the Quran.[13] Khaqani uses the figure of Abu Lahab to contrast his jailer's infidelity to his own putative sanctity, attested by his command of licit magic. In the process, he develops a hierarchy of discourses that places poetry at the top. Far from reproducing the religious genre hierarchy that treated magic as suspect, Khaqani aligns prison poetry favourably with magic. Licit magic is consistently linked to poetry's discursive authority by Khaqani wherever it is deployed. The increased emphasis on the discursive specificity of poetic knowledge results from the emergence of the lyric ode as a site of political critique.

Khaqani's most striking allusion to licit magic occurs not in a *qasida*, but in a fragment (*qit'eh*) commemorating the death of Caliph al-Muqtafi (r. 1136–1160) and the succession of his son, al-Mustanjid (r. 1160–1170), to the throne. In Sajjadi's edition of Khaqani's poems, this fragment is prefaced by a heading, presumably added by a later copyist, stating that it was composed during a journey to Baghdad (*dar al-khilafeh*), from which location the poet sent it elsewhere, probably to his hometown, Shirvan.[14] These details concerning both the poem's provenance and its genre status as a fragment provide clues as to its role in mediating prison poem aesthetics, a point made especially evident in the poem considered in the next chapter, Khaqani's the Aivan Qasida.

The alteration in the fragment's opening (*nasib*) section (vv. 1–2), between al-Muqtafi and al-Mustanjid, the two caliphs who provide the raison d'être for this poem, makes sense when the dual task the author faced is grasped. In the first instance, Khaqani was expected to lament the passing of al-Muqtafi, who had reigned for nearly a quarter of a century. In the second instance, he was expected to celebrate the succession to the throne of his son, al-Mustanjid. These imperatives were mutually exclusive: the 'tragedy' of the first caliph's passing made possible the second caliph's succession. Had Khaqani erred either by grieving too intensely over the passing of the former caliph and thereby neglecting to commemorate the succession of his son or by failing to pay his respects to the deceased caliph through excessive delight at his son's succession, he would have failed to achieve his goal.

The poem treads a narrow path between elegy and panegyric, as seen already in the distich that opens the poem, which invokes the two caliphs simultaneously. Of relevance especially to the transference of sovereignty from the ruler to the poet – and anticipating the crowning of the poet as a kind of sovereign that is a major aim of the prison poem – is the poet's insistence that the reigns of father and son have been divinely ordained, or, as he phrases it, 'inscribed on the sky':

> When the sky signed the order of Muqtafi's reign,
> Mustanjid's sign appeared on the letter as well.

چو آسمان ورق عهد مقتفی بنوشت
برآمد آیت مستنجد از صحیفه‌ی حال

In the above-cited verse, the poet conveys the cosmos' agreement with the transfer of power, without placing the two rulers in competition with each other. In the verse immediately following, the poet alternates metonymically between al-Muqtafi and al-Mustanjid, without naming either ruler:

When the true morning of faith was covered by the eternal shadow,
the morning was followed by the sun that shadows the entire sky.

چو صبح صادق دین را نهفت ظل ابد
برآمد از پس صبح آفتاب عرش ظلال

Although the caliphs are not named, we can infer from context that the 'eternal shadow' refers to the death of al-Muqtafi, and the 'morning of faith' refers to the accession of his son. By the third distich, the poet has ceased lamenting the passing of al-Muqtafi and shifted to celebrating the new reign inaugurated by al-Mustanjid's succession. He compares the new caliph's power with the sun's radiant rays that melt the snow on the mountain, which in turn trickles like sweat along the pock-marked skin of a fever-stricken patient:

What a sun! From its fear feverish sweat flows
from the mountain's pores, like clouds.

چه آفتاب که سهمش چو آفتاب از ابر
روان کند خوی تب لرزه از مسام جبال

Al-Muqtafi has disappeared from the scene, but his regal aura has not. His divine sanction is continuously evoked by the movement of the sun, which sends the caliph into the world and inscribes auspicious messages on the sky. Khaqani delineates the path followed by the sun's light in its journey across al-Mustanjid's kingdom, including the moment when the sun makes an example of the caliph's vizier Nur al-Din. The meaning of the vizier's first name, light (*nur*), is exploited by the poet in the following verses:

When he arrived in the four corners of his kingdom,
he dispatched orders of light in four directions, like the sun.
When the sun turns the air into a silver letter,
it writes on air with light, like a pen.

چو در چهار در ملک شد به چهار جهت
مثال نور فرستاد آفتاب مثال
که آفتاب چو کرد از هوا صحیفه‌ی سیم
مثال نور نویسد بر او قلم تمثال

The narrative is interrupted by a startling image that is the penultimate sign of the prison poem's political theology: the cross. At varying junctures in Persian prison poetry, alongside its Christian association with the crucifixion of Jesus, the cross corresponds to a windowpane, to human physiognomy and to a cartographic representation of the world. In this fragment commemorating the death of one ruler and the succession of his son, the cross is the sign made by the sky when confronted with stars that fade as the sun rises.

The poet then compares the twinkling of the stars with the patient encountered above, now in the throes of an epileptic fit. Mindful of the popular association between epilepsy (*sar'*) and the spirit world, the poet notes how the sun's rays make the sign of the cross to ward off evil spirits:

> The sky wraps an amulet around the stars
> since stars are epileptic at the time of their descent.

فلک چو عود صلیبش بر اختران بندد
که صرع دار بوند اختران به گاه زوال

Without abandoning the panegyric framework, the poet shifts the grounds of *qasida* poetics. Literally translated, *'ud-i salib*, the amulet used by the sky, means 'wood of the cross'. However, this term more directly refers to the root of the peony flower, believed to have medicinal properties, in particular for epilepsy.[15] Although the plant is not directly associated with the cross other than by name, Khaqani's Christological poetics activates this association, making visible the untapped significations intrinsic to language itself. It is not for nothing that this text is marked by scribes as having been composed in a fit of inspiration (*badiheh*).[16]

Although written to honour momentous events in the life of two Abbasid political luminaries, the keynote of this text is not the patron–poet relation. Khaqani uses the passing of one caliph and the succession of another as a pretext for celebrating his poetic genius. The poem's obsession with inscriptions furthers the metapoetic commentary examined in the previous chapter.

Khaqani draws on Mas῾ud Sa῾d's precedent while further turning the lyric ode outwards in his Aivan Qasida (discussed in the next chapter). Like the fragment commemorating al-Mustanjid's succession, the Aivan Qasida presents itself as an occasional poem (*qit῾eh*) improvised on the spur of the moment by a poet travelling through Baghdad. Additionally, it relates licit magic (*sihr-i halal*) to sovereign power:

> Lament! The moment's haste doesn't let me
> praise the caliph with [my] licit magic [*sihr-i halal*].

> دریغ تنگ مجال است و بر نمی‌تابد
> که راندمی به ثنای خلیفه سحر حلال

Although the poet pays lip service to his task of praising the caliph with his licit magic, the fragment commemorating al-Mustanjid's succession concludes in the same introspective register that marks Khaqani's greatest prison poems. It is not ultimately the caliph whom the poet seeks to praise, and glorification of the sovereign is not the ideology driving his poem. As the final two verses of this poem (vv. 11–12) make clear, the burden of Khaqani's poetics is borne by the poet himself:

> Sometimes you rejoice from ignorance. Sometimes you grieve from thinking.
> There is no prudence or profit in either state.
> Khaqani! Leave this two-forked path:
> either live by your intellect or lead a life of ignorance.

> گه خرمی از غفلت و گه غمگنی از عقل
> در هیچ دو رنگت نه درنگ است و نه حاصل
> خاقانی از این راه دو رنگی بکران شو
> یا عاقل عاقل زی، یا غافل غافل

The fragment commemorating the succession of Caliph Mustanjid demonstrates the role of licit magic and the architectonics of the cross with Khaqani's poetics. But Khaqani's most explicit linkage of prophecy to poetry occurs in the context of the literary rivalry between himself and the poet Athir al-Din Akhsikati (d. 1211). Athir al-Din travelled all the way from Turkestan to Shirvan to visit Khaqani, at a time when he had attained fame far beyond his hometown. When he stayed with the Saljuq sultan Arslan b. Tughrul on the way to Shirvan, his host proposed an epistolary dual (*muʿariza*) between the two poets.[17] Khaqani's reply elaborates the prophetic idiom that drove such appropriations:

Wisdom is the servant to my mind and eloquence [*bayan*].
Speech [*sukhan*] is the stable boy to my fingers and my pen.
By Him who makes the times turn,
this turn is mine. This time is mine.
In the drought-year of speech, I am the Joseph of Time,
as my tongue hosts those hungry for speech,
I have nothing to fear from idiots' gibberish.
My equal has yet to appear on earth.
I am the poets' prophet in the revelation of meanings [*vah-yi maʿani*].
The miracle of speech [*sukhan*] today is my eloquence [*bayan*].

خرد خریطه کش خاطر و بیان من است
سخن جنیبه بر خامه و بنان من است
بکردگار که دور زمان پدید آورد
که دور دور منست و زمان زمان منست
منم که یوسف عهدم بقحط سال سخن
که میزبان گرسنه دلان زبان منست
ز ژاژخایی هر ابلهی نترسم از آنک
هنوز در عدم است آنکه همقران منست
منم بوحی معانی پیمبر شعرا
که معجز سخن امروز در بیان منست [18]

So profound was the impact of Khaqani's attempt to mark himself as a prophet that, 600 years later, these verses were cited in a local history of Shirvan and Daghestan by ʿAbbas Quli Agha Bakikhanuf (1794–1847), who also composed his own verses in praise of the poet's prophetic imagination.[19] Khaqani's pride as a poet is oddly congruous with, and even contingent on, his experience of imprisonment. Taking advantage of his deep learning in the Islamic sciences, Khaqani plays on the complex associations inhering within *sukhan* (poetic discourse). While many Persian poets regard poetic discourse as their birthright, few went as far as Khaqani in embracing *bayan*, a term for eloquence with Quranic associations that were put to literary ends by theorists such as ʿAbd al-Qahir al-Jurjani. Khaqani lays claim to the full range of terms for eloquence in this poem. The title that Imam Majd al-Din Khalil conferred on Khaqani – 'sovereign of the kingdom of speech [*tajdar-i mamlikat-i sukhan*]' – corroborates the poet's self-presentation.[20] This title also recalls the terminology of the first recorded prison poem: Masʿud Saʿd's *dubayti* addressed to Sultan Ibrahim, in which the poet refers to the chains (*band*) that wear down the crowned sovereign (*tajdari*).

The political theology that animates this fragment by Khaqani brings into relief the role of prison poetics on eastern Islamic borderlands and reveals the poet's identity becoming increasingly aligned with that of the prophet. In sacralising the poet's vocation – a process enabled by the disintegration of a sacralised caliphate and the proliferation of corrupt sultanates that replaced it – Khaqani elevated the prison poem to a genre for subsequent generations. The concluding chapter of this book shows how the capacity for saintly miracles (*karamat*) was ascribed to the sultan Malikshah, while stopping short of applying the evidentiary miracles performed by prophets (*muʿjizat*) to the political figurehead. Placing religious doctrine in the service of his literary ambitions, Khaqani violates the political norms of his milieu: he ascribes miracles (*muʿjizat*) to himself rather than to the ruler.

When he lays claim to the concept of inimitability that was originally developed in order to establish the miracle of the Quran, Khaqani uses this discourse to undermine the sultan's earthly power. Rashid al-Din Vatvat, encountered in Chapter 2 as the first literary theorist to incorporate aspects of the prison poem into a rhetorical manual, described Khaqani as 'a father of virtues, philosopher, stimulator of religion and crusher of heresy'. Khaqani in turn ascribed life-giving capacities to Vatvat's poetry, as in the following verse:

> The season of spring has balanced the elements of the world.
> This unique spring is the poem of the poet-king [*al-sayyid al-shuʿara*].

بهار عام جهان را ز اعتدال مزاج
بهار خاص مرا شعر سید الشعرا [21]

This verse, composed in response to Vatvat's praise, reveals the mutual admiration between the two poets. The first hemistich emphasises spring in general, as a season that everyone experiences and that is appreciated by everyone. The second hemistich emphasises the unique 'spring' of Vatvat's poem, which Khaqani alone is capable of appreciating. (As often in Khaqani's poems, even when praising another poet, he manages to make the praise reflect his own brilliance.) Both the literal and figurative meanigs of spring are enshrined in this verse, which emphasises – and *enacts*, though double entendre (*iham*) – poetry's ability to create life through language.

More than most Persian poets, Khaqani's poetry was enriched by Quranic inimitability. It is not for nothing that, as noted in the preceding chapter, one of the names by which Khaqani was known is Hassan al-ʿAjam, a Persianisation of Hassan al-ʿArab, and an indirect allusion to Hassan-i bin Thabet, a celebrated early poet of Arabia who was 'unrivalled in the laudatory poems addressed to the Prophet'.[22] In claiming this title for himself, Khaqani suggests that his speech should be praised by the Prophet just as the Prophet had praised the poetry of his beloved poet Hassan.

The critics who canonised the prison poem also portrayed Khaqani, its most notable exponent, as a poet whose verse was pleasing to the Prophet. Consider, for example, ʿAwfi's citation from Khaqani in his influential compendium, in which the poet justifies his illustrious sobriquet by asserting that his poetic genius was recognised by his uncle:

When he realised I am perfect in art [*hunar*],
he named me Hassan al-ʿAjam.

چون دید که در هنر تمامم
حسان عجم نهاد نامم [23]

As if seeking to intensify the analogy embedded in his sobriquet between his Persian verse and the inimitable Arabic of the Quran, Khaqani incorporates Quranic Arabic into his response to Vatvat:[24]

Although all my household is my enemy,
I don't reply except to say they're fools.
Then a sinful tongue in the prison of hell
gives the necessary reply: fools go to hell.

اگرچه هر چه عیال منند خصم منند
جواب ندهم الا انهم هم السفها

که خود زبان زبانی به حبس گاه جحیم
دهد جواب به واجب که اخسئوا فیها

The Quranic citation incorporated into the above verse – 'but they talk nonsense [*al-sofaha*]' – is taken from *sura* al-Baqara (Q. 2:13). In the Persian poem, it is the fools who are in prison, while poets pick fruit from the tree of knowledge (*dirakht-i dana*):

> The arbiters of poetic discourse pick the fruits of this tree
> though they all become little trees of knowledge [*dirakhtak-i dana*].
> May my pure prayer follow your wish.
> I have no prayer better than your remembrance.

محققان سخن زین درخت میوه برند
وگر شوند سراسر درختک دانا
دعای خالص من پس رو مراد تو باد
که به ز یاد توام نیست پیشوای دعا

As usual with Khaqani, the tree that is named in this poem, *dirakht-i dana*, is aptly chosen.[25] Literally 'little tree of knowledge' (the diminutive is signalled by the *-ak* ending), *dirakht-i dana* is a tree that, according to ancient Iranian tradition, serves as an aid to memory. Anyone who puts a leaf of this tree under their pillow will remember what they have forgotten. The tree of knowledge acts as a sorcerer, summoning the spirit of memory, much like the poet. *Dirakht-i dana* is also a specific species of tree, the leaves of which turn towards the sun.

Although Vatvat treated Mas'ud Sa'd as the paradigmatic prison poet in his rhetorical treatise, he did not withhold his praise of Khaqani in his poetry, as his *qasida* on Khaqani attests. Vatvat enjoined Khaqani to imitate Jesus, and to seek contentment from the small pleasures of life:

> Be content in this declivity so that, like Jesus,
> you'll reach the heights by the ladder of contentment.

در این نشیب قناعت گزین که عیسی وار
بنردبان قناعت رسی بدان بالا

Drawing on theological distinctions between extended time (*zaman*) and *vaqt*, the time of the now, roughly analogous to Walter Benajmin's concept of *jetztzeit*,[26] Vatvat contrasts the time (*vaqt*) of the Messiah to the time (*zaman*) of the poet-prophet, thereby reversing the conventional associations of these two terms, and comparing the prison poet with no less than four prophets: Jesus ('Isa), Moses (Musa), Elijah (Khizr in the Islamic tradition) and John the Baptist (Yayha):

Messiah of time, Moses of days: Khaqani.
May he enjoy Khizr's life, and Yayha's innocence.

مسیح وقت و کلیم زمانه خاقانی
که عمر خضرش بادا و عصمت یحیا

Vatvat's association of the time of the now time with prophets and extended time with poets contrasts with historiographic norms, including that of al-Tabari (d. 923), who in narrating the creation of the world describes the time of the now as a subdivision of extended time.[27]

Together with these temporal inflections, the chain of prophets in this verse suggests more than meets the eye on first inspection. The link with Jesus is clear, given Khaqani's Christian parentage. But the invocation of Moses, known to the Islamic tradition as *kalim Allah* ('speaker with God') for the words he exchanged with God on Mt Sinai, requires readers to use their imaginations.[28] By associating the prison poet with the prophet known for his ability to speak to God, Vatvat went beyond simply attesting to Khaqani's eloquence. He fostered the image that Khaqani would also propagate: of a poet whose mastery of poetic discourse gave him a sacred status and authority that rivalled that of kings.

While Khaqani was associated by others with the prophets Jesus ('Isa), Moses (Musa), Elijah (Khizr) and John the Baptist (Yahya), his own self-descriptions supplements this list with a fifth prophet: Abraham (Ibrahim), known to Islamic tradition as *khalil Allah* ('the friend of God'). Comparing himself with Abraham (here called *khalil Allah*), Khaqani asserts that his father was a carpenter. The most potent association evoked by the motif of the father carpenter, however, is with Jesus, whom Khaqani affiliates with his mother.

Khaqani narrates his own birth as a kind of immaculate conception, whereby a spring flew 'into the well of a womb' without the mediation of his father:

I however, like Abraham, was born of a carpenter.
My Christian mother was Jesus' adopted sister.
A spring flowed from my father's loins into the well of a womb.
From that auspicious spring was born this pearly ocean of mine.

وز دگر سو چون خلیل الله دروگر زاده‌ام
بود خواهر گیر عیسی مادر ترسای من
چشمه‌ی صلب پدر چون شد به کاریز رحم
زان مبارک چشمه زاد این گوهرین دریای من (6:51–2)

Moving beyond metaphor while remaining tethered to figurative language, Khaqani figures himself here as both the pearly ocean that received the zygote of his father's sperm and his mother's egg. What has hitherto only been postulated figuratively is here articulated literally. Cleverly inverting the label that was used to insult him by his peers, Khaqani invokes his humble parentage as a badge of pride. He reminds his readers that the lowly vocation of carpenter was shared with the fathers of Abraham and Jesus.

Already in pre-Islamic oral poetry from Central Arabia, *sulb*, translated here as 'loins', was associated with 'rank, quality, power, [and] strength'.[29] It is defined in the Quran as the body part 'between the backbone and the ribs' (*bayna al-sulbi wa al-tara'ib*) (Q. 86:6–7). This verbal re-enactment of the poet's birth is also reminiscent of God's reflection on the Quranic account of the creation of humanity: 'We first created you from dust, then from a living germ, then from a clot of blood . . . We cause to remain in the wombs whatever we please' (Q. 22:5). By embedding the story of his own creation within an inimitable Quranic idiom, Khaqani further consolidates the prison poem's confluence of poetry and prophesy.

Vatvat concludes his lengthy praise poem for Khaqani by attributing charismata (*karamat*) to his friend. Khaqani's verse is so powerful, he suggests, that it violates the laws of nature, causing tongues to open in their throats like violets in bloom:

For anyone who despises the flower of your charismata,
pull their tongue out from the back of his neck like a violet.

هر آن کسی که بنوید گل کرامت تو
بنفشه وار برون کن زبان او ز قفا

These many associations between Khaqani and Moses, Abraham, Elijah and John the Baptist pave the way for the elaborate Christology that develops over the course of Khaqani's work, and which is particularly pronounced in his prison poems. Vatvat's prophetic associations may have inspired his friend to compare himself with Jesus in his monumental Christian Qasida, discussed in the next chapter.

Appropriating Prophecy

Although he developed the prison poem's political theology more thoroughly than any prior poet, Khaqani was building on a foundation that had been laid in South Asia a few decades earlier. As noted in the Introduction, Mas'ud Sa'd compared the poet's pen with Jesus on the cross (*chalipa*):

Be astonished at how the pen
looks like a cross in his fingers.
They intend to kill the pen
as they killed Jesus: by cutting its nib.
But when suspended on the fingers,
the pen's rank and status increase.
The pen ascends to the glorious heavens
where there is no path for the soul.
Why do we detect Manichean traces
in the works of this good Christian?

شگفتی نگه کن که کلکش همه
چلیپا نماید به انگشت بر
چو عیسی به کشتنش دارند قصد
که هر ساعت او را ببرند سر
ولیکن چو بر دار انگشت شد
فزون گرددش قدر و جاه و خطر
بر آن آسمان بزرگی شود
که ره نیست جانرا از آن بیشتر
چو دین مسیح است کردار او
چرا مانوی ماند از وی اثر [30]

These prolific references to prophets by both Mas'ud Sa'd and Khaqani attest to the prison poem's intimate engagement with prophecy across its shifting geographies of sovereignty as well as to the genre's role in sacralising poetry, which accompanied the desacralisation of sultanate power.

In order to unpack these variables, the semantic field under investigation must be reviewed. The theme of Moses (Musa) on Mt Sinai in the valley of Tuwa is a good place to begin. According to the Quran (20:9–20), Tuwa is where Moses received one of the first signs (*ayat*) of God's power. He was ordered by God to throw his walking staff (*ʿasa*) onto the ground, whereupon it was transformed into a serpent (*hayyah*). Moses was afraid, but he obeyed the order to pick it up. The staff reverted into its original form, and Moses, along with his brother Harun, was confirmed in the gift of prophecy. In Ashʿari and Muʿtazili theology, the miracles performed by Moses, and to a lesser extent, Jesus, form the bedrock of Islamic prophetology.[31] Success in the genre of prison poetry was contingent on poets' ability to incorporate these exegetical traditions into their poetry.

Moses' miracles were not confined to the transformation of the staff into a serpent. According to al-Tabari, Moses performed miracles with rods and serpents, deluges, locusts, lice, frogs, blood, darkness, and by separating the waters of the sea.[32] The rod-to-serpent transformation became a regular motif in prison poetry under the Ghaznavids and Shirvanshahs and came to characterise prison poetry as a topical genre. Just as the staff of Moses and his white hand entered the canon of Islamic historiography, animating the works of al-Thaʿalibi and Kisa'i, so too did these motifs shape prison poetry. For medieval Persian readers, these motifs revealed poetry's discursive authority and served as a foil to worldly power.

Masʿud Saʿd refers to Moses' prophetic miracles on many occasions. Frequently, these invocations of Moses and the transformation of his staff into a serpent are accompanied by a comparison with Jesus' miracle of giving life to Lazarus, as in the following verses that parody the story by retelling it as one of the poet's sexual encounters:

I found a girl last night and said lustfully
that I'd make love a lot tonight.

بتی یافتم دوش گفتم بحرص
که امشب جماعی فراوان کنم [33]

The poet continues the satirical narrative, reporting on his inability to ejaculate due to exhaustion. He then asks the girl to restore his virility. Her reply, that such a miracle is beyond her powers, parodies the prophetic tradition by comparing the staff (*ʿasa*) of Moses with a penis:

She said to me: If I were Moses,
I'd make your stick (*ʿasa*) into a moving serpent.
What do you want from me?
I won't become Jesus to bring the dead to life.

مرا گفت اگر زانکه موسی شوم
عصای تو در دست ثعبان کنم
چه خواهی ز من من نه عیسی شوم
که اندر چنین مرده یی جان کنم

These verses parody the two moments in the Quran in which the serpent appears, first, as a sign plain for all to see (*thuʿban mubin*, Q. 7:107), and, second, as a moving snake (*hayya tasʿa*, Q. 20:20); both are compared with an erect penis.

Beyond such parodies, the widespread use of Moses' staff as a trope in prison poetry advances serious claims concerning the link between prophecy and poetry. The serpent (*thuʿban*) associates poetry, and the poet, with a prophetic capacity for lucid experience. The sign (*aya*) that the serpent represents is one that the poet creates in the text. It is therefore significant that the vast majority of references to miracles in Masʿud Saʿd's poems are linked to a serpent (*thuʿban*) rather than a snake (*hayy*). Given its association with miracles, the serpent confounds not only reason, but also, as in poetry, the prosaic discourse pertaining to worldly things.

The most striking reference to Moses' prophetic miracles in Masʿud Saʿd's poems occurs in prison poems in which the Quranic serpent and snake (Q. 7:107 and 20:20, respectively) are rendered by the Persian 'serpent' (*azhdaha*):[34]

Why should I mourn? I must endure.
Why should I hide my face where no one knows me?
Every morning on this sloped mountain
a cloud like Mt Sinai makes a pilgrimage to me.

A light like Moses' hands miraculously,
emerges from the air's luminous collar.
Although goodness guided me like a staff,
the serpent of the skies became a serpent to my soul.

انده چرا برم چو تحمل بایدم؟
روی از که بایدم؟ که کسی نیست آشنا
هر روز بامداد بر این کوهسار تند
ابری بسان طور زیارت کند مرا
برقی چو دست موسی عمران به فعل و نور
آرد همی پدید ز جیب هوا ضیا
گشت اژدهای جان من این اژدهای چرخ
ورچه صلاح، رهبر من بود چون عصا [35]

In another prison poem, Mas'ud Sa'd compares the condition of the poet imprisoned in the fortress of Nay with that of Moses awaiting God's command on Mt Sinai:

Why don't I have my portion of the Almighty's effulgence
when I've spent all my life on Mount Sinai?

از تجلی چرا نصیبم نیست
که همه عمر جای من طور است [36]

Whereas Mas'ud Sa'd distinguished between poet and prophet, Khaqani incorporated the power of the prophet into the prison poem. In prison poem 6, Khaqani fuses the figures of the poet and the prophet. Drawing on the Quranic account of the Golden Calf (Q. 20:83–98; 7:148–54), the poet distinguishes himself from a certain Samiri, who is credited with the construction of the idol.[37] ('Samiri' can be interpreted as a personal name, as I have done here, or as a label reflecting his association with the Samaritans, as in some sources quoted below.) Although Khaqani initially affiliates with Moses, he ends by celebrating the idol, if not the idol-maker:

I resemble Samiri, not Moses if for the rest my life,
my white hand will touch the heel of the Golden Calf.

سامری سیرم نه موسی سیرت ار تا زنده‌ام
در سم گوساله آلاید ید بیضای من (6:35)

The Quran reports that while Moses was speaking to God on Mt Sinai, his fellow Israelites in the valley below had taken to worshipping a golden idol in the likeness of a calf (Q. 20:88). When Moses descended from the mountain and asked what his people had done, they replied that Samiri had advised them to mould a golden calf and throw it into the fire, after which he told the people that the god burning in the fire was the true god of the Israelites. Moses confronted Samiri, who defended himself by explaining that his soul (*nafs*) instructed him to take a handful of dust from the footprint of the messenger (*rasul*) and throw it onto the Golden Calf. According to most subsequent accounts and commentaries, the messenger is the Angel Gabriel, who imparted to the idol-maker a special gift for bringing dead objects to life. Ibn al-ʿArabi famously analysed this event in his *Bezels of Wisdom* (*Fusus al-Hikam*), in which he states that Samiri's divine mandate enabled him to explain to Moses that he was acting in accordance with what he understood to be the will of God.[38]

The Quranic account is fraught with ambivalence towards the mysterious Samiri. Uri Rubin's commentary underscores the latter's ties to a world governed by supernatural forces and even black magic. Rubin notes that 'the manner in which the Samiri creates the calf is a mystery. He sees a "messenger" which others cannot see, and he seizes a handful of dust from the messenger's track . . .when the Calf was made he took a handful of dust from under the foot of the horse of life, and cast it into a Calf. Thus life was infused into it.'[39] Ibn al-ʿArabi likewise stresses the magical knowledge on which Samiri's actions were based. 'Samiri,' Ibn al-ʿArabi writes elliptically, 'had knowledge of this matter. When he realised that [the messenger] was Gabriel, he knew that life would flow into whatever he walked on, so he took a handful of dust from the track of the messenger [*al-rasul*] . . . [and] threw it onto the Calf.'[40] These exegeses help to account for why the story of Samiri and his idol-making activities had such salience for Persian prison poets.

The white hand alluded to by Khaqani in prison poem 6 speaks less to the exegetical traditions pertaining to Samiri than to the traditions concerning Moses. Although the 'white hand' is not mentioned in *sura* Taha, it is found in a related passage of *sura* Aʿraf (Q. 7:107–8). In this *sura*, the Pharaoh challenges Moses to prove that he has come with a sign (*ayatun*; Q. 7:106) and that he tells the truth in claiming to have made a covenant (*ʿahd*) with

God. Moses responds to the challenge by throwing his staff to the ground, whereupon the staff becomes a serpent (*thuʿban*). Moses then withdraws his hand, which has now turned white.

Khaqani's declaration that his white hand will be joined to the heel of the Golden Calf thus merges two distinct and even contradictory prophetic traditions. The first is the tradition concerning the idolatry of the Golden Calf. The second is the white hand of Moses. Although these two traditions were often opposed to each other in poetry, they address related aspects of the prison poem's prophetic poetics.[41] By merging these figures in his verse, Khaqani further developed the prison poem's political theology.

In the prison poem's first phase, Masʿud Saʿd recognised the poet's prophetic gifts but assumed an unbridgeable divide between the two domains. In the genre's second phase, Khaqani portrayed the poet as a literal prophet. From within his confinement, Masʿud Saʿd envisioned an escape. Khaqani by contrast claimed prison as the poet's birthright and immortalised the poet's imprisoned body through a carceral aesthetics. Khaqani drew on Masʿud Saʿd's prophetic motifs, but he used these images in different ways. The prison poem's early phase laid the foundation for the reconfiguration of the poet's body as a sacred vessel. The results of this reconfiguration only became evident, however, during the second phase of the prison poem following its migration from South Asia to the Caucasus, when a new political theology was developed under the Shirvanshah vassals of the Saljuqs.

Masʿud Saʿd lamented the resemblance between his condition and that of Moses. Khaqani by contrast regarded his spiritual kinship to prophets as the logical consequence of prison poem poetics. Far from being an aberration, the resemblance between poet and prophet was represented by Khaqani as his destiny and birthright. Akimushkina registers this difference, noting that Khaqani revels in his shared kinship with the prophet to whom God revealed his voice. Whereas Masʿud Saʿd conceals the similarity between the situations of the incarcerated poet and the prophet, Khaqani, she writes, 'implies that the real affinity is between the imprisoned poet and the prophet'.[42]

Masʿud Saʿd distinguishes the poet's vocation from that of the prophet; Khaqani insists on their affinity. Both poets develop prison poetry as a transgressive genre that destabilises existing norms of form and content. The blurring of boundaries among formal genres – including the quatrain, the ghazal and the *qasida* – that produced the lyric ode introduced in Chapter 2 stimulated an increased emphasis on thematic genre markers. This shift further clarifies the prison poem's discursive uniqueness.

A further provocative use of Quranic Arabic by Khaqani occurs in a fragment exhibiting one of the most frequent rhetorical tropes in prison poem poetics, self-praise (*fakhr*):

> I am Khaqani, beloved of God.
> [God] has called me his dear slave.
> Every time I called God
> he answers me: don't be afraid.

> من که خاقانیم عزیز حقم
> ز آن که عبدی خطاب من رانده است
> هرچه یارب ندای حق راندم
> لاتخف حق جواب من رانده است [43]

God's advice to Khaqani – 'Don't fear' (*la takhaf*) – fortifies the chain that links Khaqani to Jesus, Elijah, Abraham, John the Baptist and particularly Moses, *kalim Allah* ('speaker with God').

On multiple occasions in the Quran, Moses requires reassurance from God to persist in his mission. God's admonition not to fear is addressed to Moses during his struggle against the unjust pharaoh. The following passage from the Quran includes all the elements of the prophetic narrative that informs Khaqani's prophetic poetics, including the white hand and the staff:

> A voice cried from the right of the watercourse, in the sacred hollow, coming from the tree: 'Moses, I am God, the Lord of all Being.' 'Cast down thy staff.' And when he saw it quivering like a serpent, he turned about retreating, and turned not back. 'Moses, come forward, and fear not [*la takhaf*]; for surely thou art in security.' Insert thy hand into thy bosom, and it will come forth white without evil; and press to thee thy arm, that thou be not afraid. So these shall be two proofs from thy Lord to Pharaoh and his Council; for surely they are an ungodly people.' (Q. 28:31)[44]

In both Khaqani's poem and the Quran, the injunction not to fear condenses many political and literary meanings. By addressing God's speech to Moses to himself, Khaqani locates himself within a prophetic lineage. However, the sign of Khaqani's prophecy is unlike that of any other prophet. Instead of being attested by his ability to perform miracles, the poet's prophetic gift is demonstrated by the magic of his verse (here called *sihr-i nab*, a variant on *sihr-i halal*). The movement away from external signs and towards poetry's discursive authority is further attested in a poem that begins 'I am Khaqani, beloved by the True One [*'aziz-i haqqam*].' In this poem, Khaqani claims worldwide fame for his poetry, as in the following verse which insists that his magic has been scattered by God across the 'seven climes', an ancient description for the entire world:

> I am in a corner, but God has scattered
> the effect of my pure magic across the seven climes.
>
> و حق به هفت اقلیم من به کنجی
> مدد سحر ناب من رانده است [45]

The conclusion to prison poem 6 reaffirms Khaqani's lofty spiritual calling by again asserting his mastery of poetic discourse and aligning the sacred and profane. Khaqani achieves this by juxtaposing the second-holiest location in Islam, the Masjid al-Aqsa in Jerusalem, with a brothel, using a term (*al-qamama*), that also – ironically – means church (as well as synagogue). He visits this site as an infidel:

> If someone can recite poems like this in seven climes,
> consider me an infidel whose sacred church is a brothel.
>
> گر به هفت اقلیم کس دانم که گوید زین دو بیت
> کافرم دارالقمامه مسجد اقصای من (6:62–5)

While insisting that his mind is virginal (*'adhra*), Khaqani states that he gives birth to a manly soul (*jan-i mardan*). By the time that Khaqani began to compose prison poems, poetry's elevated status enabled him to set it above religious creeds and to use it to contest political norms.

While Khaqani recreates himself in the image of Moses, he refashions his Shirvanshah patron in the image of Moses' patron and jailer, the Pharaoh. Both rulers were notorious for their abuses of discretionary power, and their reliance on imprisonment as a tool of governance. Prison poem 6 ends with an apostrophe to the poet's genius that recalls the genre's lyric phase.

Like his many successors and imitators, including Lumaki, Mujir and Barandaq, Khaqani relied on avian tropes to sing his prison songs. His lyric *qasida*, sometimes referred to as 'Language of the Birds [*Mantiq al-tayr*]', incorporates the words of King Solomon as recorded in the Quran – 'O people, we have been taught the language of birds, and we have been given from all things' (Q. 27:16) – into the Persian lyric. Farid al-Din 'Attar's narrative *masnavi*, also called 'Language of the Birds' (1177), offered a more extended elaboration on Solomon's words during these same decades, but Khaqani evokes the speech of the birds with the ambitious agenda of elevating the prison poet's voice.[46] The ending of the poem suggests that Khaqani composed this poem while on a journey, perhaps during his famous pilgrimage to Mecca (which occasioned the Aivan Qasida, discussed in the next chapter).

In placing poetry alongside the discourse (*mantiq*) of the birds, Khaqani draws on the tradition that preceded him, while characteristically inflecting it with an idiom all his own. How, Khaqani asks rhetorically, could his eloquence suit anyone other than a prophet? That would mean throwing the pearl (*durr*) of his speech into the mud. Khaqani responds to his rhetorical question in the poem's concluding verses by referring to himself in the third person and calling Shirvan a prison:

Oh Lord, free him from this prison [*habsgah*].
Shirvan is the worst of cities and my enemies are the worst beasts.
Protect [the poet's] soul from these severe difficulties.
You will speedily accept the prayers of the exiled one.

یارب از این حبسگاه، باز رهانش که هست
شروان شرالبلاد خصمان شرّالدواب
زاین گره ناحفاظ حافظ جانش تو باش
کز تو دعای غریب زود شود مستجاب [47]

Khaqani's sense of confinement intensifies his rancour toward his native city. He has travelled far from Shirvan, yet he fears being compelled to return. Shirvan is a prison (*habsgah*), one of Khaqani's favourite ways of describing his hometown.[48] While Mas'ud Sa'd's poems radiate affection and longing for his hometown of Lahore, Khaqani repeatedly declares his hostility to Shirvan.

In labelling Shirvan, a city which was, along with Shemakhi, the centre of Shirvanshah regal glory, a prison (*habsgah*), expanded the terrain of his confinement to his entire hometown. The political and spiritual authority he arrogated to poetry through his adoption of the language of prophecy set the tone for the two monumental poems that occupy the next chapter. Formally, topically and discursively, the Christian Qasida and the Aivan Qasida – both of which belong to a late phase of Khaqani's creative activity – bring the prison poem to a new stage in its evolution. With these poems, we witness the genre grafting the aesthetics of imprisonment onto the politics of prophecy, and thereby creating a new space for poetry – and the poet – in the world. The result was a political theology of the poet's body that usurped the sovereign's role in legislating language and conferred this authority on the poet. This transformation in turn anticipated subsequent realignments of poetry in relation to kingship across medieval Europe, most notably in Dante. The first *qasida* in the monumental dyad that structures the next chapter marks the pinnacle of Khaqani's carceral poetics. The second *qasida* marks its equally dramatic denouement.

Notes

1. *The Divāns of ʿAbīd Ibn Al-Abraṣ, of Asad and ʿAmīr Ibn Aṭ-Ṭufail, of ʿĀmīr Ibn Ṣaʿṣaʿah*, trans. and ed. Charles Lyall, Gibb Memorial Series (London: Luzac, 1913), poem X; vv. 16–17, p. 35 (Arabic text). Lyall's translation has been modernised.
2. Ibn Ḥanbal, i, 190–1. *Hadīth* citations in nn. 2–4 are taken from T. Fahd, 'Siḥr', *EI*[2].
3. Al-Tirmiḍhī, *Ḥudūd*, 27.
4. Abū Muslim, *Imān*, 144; al-Bukhārī, *Waṣāyā*, 23. Also see Jane I. Smith and Yvonne Y. Haddad, *The Islamic Understanding of Death and Resurrection* (Albany, NY: SUNY Press, 1981), 23.
5. J. Christoph Bürgel, *The Feather of Simurgh* (New York: New York University Press, 1988), 54. Also see Emily Selove, 'Magic as Poetry, Poetry as Magic: A Fragment of Arabic Spells', *Magic, Ritual, and Witchcraft* 15(1) (2020): 33–57.

6. J. C. Bürgel, '"Die beste Dichtung ist die lügenreichste". Wesen und Bedeutung eines literarischen Streites des arabischen Mittelalters im Lichte komparatistisher Betrachtung', *Oriens* 23 (1974): 7–102.
7. Bürgel, *Feather of Simurgh*, 56
8. Mas'ūd Sa'd, *Dīvān*, 1:74, *qaṣīda* 26, vv. 12.
9. Mas'ūd Sa'd, *Dīvān*, 1:85.
10. For a brief tabulation of extant sources on this poet, see J. T. P. de Bruijn, 'Labībī', *EI*². The entry on Labībī in Dehkhodā's *Lughatnāmeh* identifies Labībī as Mas'ūd Sa'd's teacher.
11. Akimushkina, *Zhanr Habsiyyat*, 34.
12. Niẓāmī Ganjevī, *Laylā and Majnūn*, ed. Āmīn Bābāyi Panāh, 35.
13. Colin Turner, 'Abū Lahab', *The Qur'an: An Encyclopedia*, ed. Oliver Leaman (London: Routledge, 2006), 9.
14. For this heading and the text of the poem that follows, see Khāqānī, *Dīvān*, 897–8.
15. See Marten Stol, *Epilepsy in Babylonia* (Leiden: Brill, 1993), 124. *'Awd-i ṣalīb* is also important for its intertext with v. 43 of Khāqānī's Christian Qasida (discussed below).
16. In his edition of Khāqānī's *Divān* (p. 897), Sajjadī (p. 897), refers to a manuscript in the *Kitābkhāna-'i Majlis-i Shūrā-yi Millī* that uses the term 'inspiration [*badīheh*]' in the title of this *qiṭ'eh*.
17. *Dīvān of Athīr al-Dīn Akhsikatī. British Museum.* or. 268, 180a-Ie. This conflict is discussed in Rifaqatullah Khan, 'Life of Khaqani', *Indo-iranica* 12(2) (1959): 38.
18. Khāqānī, *Dīvān*, 754–5.
19. 'Abbās Qulī Agha Qudsī Bākīkhānuf, *Gulistān-i Iram* (Tehran: Asnād va Khadamāt-i Pazhuheshi, 1382/2003/4), 260–61. For Bākīkhānuf's own verse on this topos, see *Gulistān-i Iram*, 282.
20. Ṣafā, *Tārīkh-i Adabīyāt dar Īrān*, 2:774.
21. The full text of this *qaṣīda* is in Vaṭvāṭ, *Dīvān*, 30–5.
22. Maulavi Abdul Muqtadir (ed.), *Catalogue of the Arabic and Persian Manuscripts* (Calcutta: Bengal Secretariat Book Depot, 1908), 40 (capitalisation added). The most complete comparison of the poems of Khāqānī and the historical Ḥassān al-'Ajam is Ḥassūkī, 'Madḥ-i nabawī dar shi'r-i Ḥassān-i bin Thābet va Khāqānī-yi Shirwānī'.
23. 'Awfī, *Lubāb*, 405. Khāqānī is listed here by the title Ḥasān al-'Ajam Ḥakīm Khāqānī al-Ḥaqā'iqī.

24. For a tabulation of further allusions to the Quran and *ḥadīth* in prison poetry, see Ẓafarī, *Ḥabsīyyāt*, 255–6.
25. For an overview of the symbolism pertaining to this tree, see Nāzīlā Daryāyī, 'Ustūreh-ye dūzakhī dar qālī-ye īrānī ['Infernal Mytheme in Iranian Carpet']', *Pajuhesh-hā-ye ensānshenāsī-ye irān* 4(2) (2014): 89–104.
26. The relation between *zamān* and *vaqt* is explored in detail in Kayvan Tahmasebian and Rebecca Ruth Gould, 'The Temporality of Interlinear Translation: *Kairos* in the Persian Hölderlin': *Representations* 155 (2021): 1–28.
27. *The History of al-Ṭabarī* [*Tārīkh al-rusul wa al-mulūk*], trans. Franz Rosenthal (Albany, NY: SUNY Press, 1989), 1:171. The root *w-q-t* occurs in the Quran (e.g., 7:187; 15:38; 38:81); *z-m-n* does not.
28. According to Muḥammad Ḥosseīn-i Karamī, there are 229 allusions to Moses in Khāqānī's *divan* ('Negāhī be maḍāmīn-i Musawī o zībāīhāyi ān dar dīwān-i Khāqānī', *Majalleh-yi ʿulūm-i ijtemaʿ-yī o insānī-yi Dānishkadeh-yi Shīrāz* 22(3) (1384): 182).
29. P. M. Kurpershoek, *Oral Poetry and Narratives from Central Arabia: The Poetry of ad-Dindān* (Leiden: Brill, 1994), 293.
30. Masʿūd Saʿd, *Dīvān*, 1:338, *qaṣīda* 137. Parallels between Masʿūd Saʿd's and Khāqānī's Christian *qaṣīda*s are discussed in Muḥammad Muʿīn, 'Khāqānī o āʾīn-i masīḥ: masīḥīyat o nofūḍ-i ān dar Iran', *Dānishnāmah* 2 (1326/1947), 32; Sharma, *Persian Poetry at the Indian Frontier*, 143.
31. A classical Ashʿari source for this discussion is al-Bāqillānī, *Kitāb al-bayān ʿan al-farq bayn al-muʿjizāt waʿl-karāmāt wa'l-ḥiyal wa'l kahāna wa'l siḥr wa' l-nāranjāt*, ed. Richard J. McCarthy (Beirut: Librairie Orientale, 1957), 59–60. See also Sarah Stroumsa, 'The Signs of Prophecy', *Harvard Theological Review* 78(1/2) (1985): 103; Richard J. McCarthy, 'Al-Baqillanī's Notion of the Apologetic Miracle', *Studia Biblica et Orientalia* 3(12) (1959): 247–56.
32. *The History of al-Ṭabarī*, 1:485.
33. Masʿūd Saʿd, *Dīvān*, 2:881–2, *qiṭʿeh* 104.
34. For *azhdahā* in Persian poetry, see M. Omidsalar, 'Aždahā', *EIr*.
35. Masʿūd Saʿd, *Dīvān*, 1:22, *qaṣīda* 8.
36. Masʿūd Saʿd, *Dīvān*, 1:88, *qaṣīda* 31.
37. For background on this story, see Michael Pregill, *The Golden Calf between Bible and Qur'an: Scripture, Polemic, and Exegesis from Late Antiquity to Islam* (Oxford: Oxford University Press, 2020).
38. Ibn al-ʿArabī, *Fuṣūṣ al-Ḥikam*, ed. Abū al-ʿAlāʾ ʿAfīfī (Beirut: Dār al-Kitāb, n.d.), 138.

39. Uri Rubin, 'Traditions in Transformation', *Oriens* 36 (2001): 203.
40. Ibn al-ʿArabī, *Fuṣūṣ al-Ḥikam*, 138.
41. Annemarie Schimmel notes that Sāmirī has 'in poetry often been confronted with Moses as symbol either of outward power and wealth, or of loveless magical science' (*Gabriel's Wing* (Leiden: Brill, 1963), 264).
42. Akimushkina, *Zhanr Habsiyyat*, 53.
43. Khāqānī, *Dīvān*, 832.
44. I use here the Arberry translation. Also see Q. 20:21; 27:10; 51:28.
45. Khāqānī, *Dīvān*, 832.
46. For a discussion of Khāqānī's poem in the context of ʿAṭṭār's ouevre, see Hellmut Ritter, *Das Meer der Seele: Mensch, Welt und Gott in den Geschichten des Farīduddīn ʿAṭṭār* (Leiden: Brill, 1955), 8–33.
47. Khāqānī, *Divān*, 45.
48. See, for example, Khāqānī, *Divān*, 157.

5

Crucifixion as Critique

The preceding chapters have tracked the shift in twelfth-century Persian poetry as the prison poem genre migrated from South Asia to the Caucasus, yielding changing conceptions of the poet's body in relation to the experience of incarceration and the critique of kingship. While Arabic poets such as ʿAdi b. Zayd, Abu Firas, al-Mutanabbi, Ibn Jahm, Ibn Zaydun, Ibn al-Muʿtazz and Muʿtamid b. ʿAbbad created aesthetic frameworks for the poetry written from prison many centuries prior to the advent of the Persian prison poem, Persian poets such as Masʿud Saʿd, together with critics such as ʿAruzi and ʿAwfi, added new dimensions to traditional forms by associating the lyric ode with the topos of imprisonment. Formalising literary innovation as rhetorical norms, rhetoricians like Vatvat distilled the principles of the prison poem while paving the way for its formal transgressions.

The major protagonist in the story of the prison poem – of its astonishing proliferation, its absorption into other literary genres, its reconfiguration of patron–poet relations, and its transfiguration of the poet's body – is Khaqani. Khaqani reimagined the entirety of Persian – and much of Arabic – poetry from the vantage point of his incarcerated imagination.[1] Two of Khaqani's monumental poems, both of which contribute to the ethos of the prison poem, are the subject of this chapter. In probing Khaqani's carceral aesthetics, this chapter also sheds light on how the literary representation of the poet's body shifted in response to the changing status of the sovereign, whereby the king's sacred legitimacy was undermined by his mortal and ethical decay.

The poet who, as he states, nourished himself on the dust (*khak*) and oppression (*zulm*) of Shirvan, conceived of prison as a metonym for the poet's position in the world. As noted in Chapter 1, the Persian prison poem introduced a different metonymic relationship into Persian poetics. In poetic terms, there was little difference for Khaqani between the confinement he experienced from within his prison cell and the world outside. Prison, for Khaqani as for many Persian prison poets, was more than a metaphor: it was a feature of his life. When he compared his creaturely existence with a pair of dice, the sky arching over Khaqani's head was oblivious to the poet's demand for cogent speech. Similarly, the Saljuqs and their Shirvanshah vassals, like rulers past and present, were indifferent to poets' demands for justice.

Khaqani's dice without inscription, and his signless sky, are among the products of post-caliphal sovereignty. From the tension between the sultan's discretionary power and poetry's new-found authority, the prison poem used carceral aesthetics to assert poetry's sovereignty. The engagement with Khaqani that has extended over the preceding chapters will therefore culminate with two readings of the poet's best-known – although still poorly understood – poems, the lengthy Christian Qasida (prison poem 1 in terms of the Appendix) and his briefer elegy on the ruins of the Sasanian palace known as Ctesiphon in antiquity and Mada'in (the Arabic plural of 'cities') after Islam. Khaqani's six prison poems (each of which are listed in the Appendix) are thereby brought into dialogue with the entire trajectory of the poet's literary output.

Khaqani's biography – specifically his mother's origins – illuminates the issues at stake in the Christian Qasida, a poem composed from Shabaran prison in Shirvan. While his father was, according to his own testimony, a carpenter, Khaqani's mother was a Nestorian Christian who converted, possibly by force, to Islam.[2] Named for the bishop whose Christological doctrine was condemned at the council of Ephesus in 431, Nestorian Christianity denied that Jesus Christ suffered in his divine capacity when he was crucified. While acknowledging the consubstantiality of the three persons of the Trinity, Nestorius accounted for this unity by distinguishing God's divine nature from his humanity.[3] He taught that the person who suffered on the cross and who died for humanity's sins was not divine, but human. Although the debates concerning the coexistence of Christ's two natures may appear arcane now, Nestorius' teachings had profoundly political dimensions at the time they were disseminated and for many centuries after. 'Nestorius' different levels appeared to threaten the unity of Christ', notes one scholar commenting on the political risks posed by Nestorian teaching.[4] In undermining the teaching concerning the unity of Christ's two natures, Nestorius threatened the cogency of Christianity as the hegemonic discourse of late antiquity.

Yet another aspect of the Nestorian legacy should inform a reading of Khaqani's Christian Qasida. In denying orthodox Christian doctrine concerning Jesus' co-equivalent divinity and humanity, Nestorianism became a heresy. When, with the spread of Islam across formerly Christian territories, Christianity was itself marginalised, the marginality of Nestorianism was doubly constituted: first, with respect to Christianity, and, secondly, with respect to Islam. Ctesiphon (the Arabic Mada'in), one of the sites from which Khaqani recollects the fallen dynasties of past eras, was a stronghold for Nestorian intellectual and political life. At the same time, Nestorianism's double doctrinal marginality did not prevent its adherents from contributing extensively to the medieval Islamic sciences of logic (at the Iraqi monastery Dayr Kunna), civil administration, medicine (through the school of Gundishapur) and theology, through polemics with Muslims concerning the Trinity and other matters of Christian doctrine.[5] Indeed, Nestorians contributed substantially to the Abbasid translation movement that introduced the learning of Greek antiquity to the Islamic world on an unprecedented scale. Nestorians who converted to Islam while in office rose to positions of power and influence in the Abbasid hierarchy.[6]

Muslim Christology and the Christian Qasida

Khaqani's Christian Qasida builds on Nestorian contributions to the Islamic sciences as well as on Nestorianism's doctrinal commitment to Jesus' humanity. Additionally, the theological provocations that permeate this poem echo those of the Nestorian catholicos Timothy I. Sometime between the years 781 and 794, Timothy engaged in a theological debate with the Caliph al-Mahdi (r. 775–785) concerning the respective merits of Christianity and Islam.[7] Prior to debating the caliph, Timothy I had been commissioned by this same caliph to translate Aristotle's *Topics* into Arabic.[8] This debate between the Catholicos and the caliph, perhaps the most important in the history of Christian–Islamic polemics, touched on Christology, the Trinity, circumcision, the direction of prayer, the corruption (*tahrif*) of the Scriptures and the crucifixion.[9]

The Christian Qasida recreates in verse the theological debate, adapting Nestorian erudite polemic to a critique of twelfth-century sovereignty. Its poetics is informed by the teaching, heretical within orthodox Christianity but more amenable to Islam, that the man who died on the cross was only human, albeit a prophet. Stressing the humanity of Jesus facilitated the prison poem's extended comparisons of the poet with the Christian saviour. Islamic tradition maintains that the person who died on the cross was Judas, not Jesus.[10] And yet Jesus is closely associated with the cross in Persian prison poems, especially but not only those of Khaqani. Such poems depart from both Muslim and Christian traditions by merging them, and also by identifying the imprisoned poet with Jesus as prophet.

The Christian Qasida is not the only attestation to the poet's fascination with this revered Islamic prophet and Christian saviour. Minorsky identified over two hundred references to Jesus in Khaqani's *divan*.[11] In his classic account of representations of Jesus in premodern Persian poetry, Muhammad Muʿin argued that Khaqani's Christology was the most developed of all the classical Persian poets.[12] And it is in the Christian Qasida that the political significance of Khaqani's identification with Jesus Christ – in both his prophetic Muslim and Christian soteriological manifestations – is most fully fleshed out.

Khaqani's most salient Christological allusions are recur throughout his prison poems. The preceding chapter examined how Khaqani linked his genealogy to Jesus, through his father, who, like Jesus' human father Joseph, was a carpenter (*durudgar*, 6:51). Worth adding to this archive is Khaqani's description of his mother's conversion to Islam as a combination of the judgement of the intellect (*ʿaql*) with the inspiration (*ilham*) of the heart:

From Nestorian and Zoroastrian seed,
her customs were Islamic and godly.
Aided by intellect and inspiration,
she preferred Islam to Christianity.

نسطوری و موبدی نژادش
اسلامی و ایزدی نهادش
پس کرده گزین بعقل و الهام
بر کیش کشیش دین اسلام [13]

Just as Masʿud Saʿd's poems are dense with references to his body, Khaqani's poems are suffused with autobiographical elements, which are in turn reshaped for poetic ends. His poems include elegies on the deaths of his sons and his wife, moving recollections of his parents and his uncle, and denunciations of his hometown, Shirvan. To an even greater extent than the prison poets who preceded him, Khaqani crafted poetry from experience. But Khaqani's poetic persona took priority over his empirical experience. His comparisons of himself to Jesus and Moses introduced a new conception of the poet's sovereign authority into the world.

Khaqani invoked Jesus, Mary and other Christian figures in all of his writing, including in many *qasidas*. One notable precursor to the Christian Qasida is a quatrain comparing the lips of Jesus to the face of a boy whose beauty captivates him. In this poem, Khaqani initiates the resignification of the *zunnar*, a belt that signified non-Muslim identity in general, and specifically the persecution that non-Muslim minorities faced:

Dear boy, you have the lip of Jesus and the face of the sun.
A *zunnar* is etched onto your face. Your hair forms a cross.
You crusade and invade in search of captives.
Khaqani became your captive. What, boy, do you say?

عیسی لب و آفتاب روئی پسرا
زنار خط و صلیب موئی پسرا
لشکرکشی و اسیر جوئی پسرا
خاقانی اسیر شد چه گوئی پسرا [14]

Dense with Christological imagery, the images in this poem are reconfigured in the light of the poet's desire. The *zunnar*, discussed in greater detail below, is laden with multi-confessional associations.[15] The Christological lexicon and semiology of many of Khaqani's other poems, though striking, is less intense than that found in the Christian Qasida. Only the Christian Qasida joins carceral aesthetics to the politics of prophecy in terms that actualise the prison poem's status as a transgressive genre.

From among the wide corpus of prison poems that engage with Jesus' life and legacy, Khaqani's Christian Qasida is the most profoundly Christological text: it merges the political with the aesthetic in the service of poetry's discursive autonomy. Like Rumi, Khaqani draws substantially on traditions concerning Jesus not mentioned in the Quran.[16] He demonstrates a profound command of Sufi traditions that remained marginal to Islamic theology, as well as of pre-Islamic Iranian and other non-Muslim traditions, and of Christian traditions situated outside the realm of Christian orthodoxy. The result is a poem that interrupts the *qasida*'s panegyric idiom with a political theology focused on the poet's persecution. Although indebted to the lyric odes of Mas'ud Sa'd, Khaqani's anti-panegyrics reach beyond the prison poems of Lahore through forthrightly political critique.

Parsing the Crooked Sky

The Christian Qasida is divisible into three sections, each of which roughly correlates to the tripartite structure of the polythematic *qasida* that dates back to pre-Islamic Arabic poetry.[17] The first section (vv. 1–26) contains the poet's statement of his predicament, a description of his suffering and incarceration, and multiple comparisons between himself and Jesus, on the one hand, and with Jesus' mother Mary, on the other. The second section (vv. 27–72) lists the poet's plans for proving his fidelity to Islam. These proposed actions are tinged with irony, since they verge on heresy for both Islam and Christianity. Additionally, they demonstrate Khaqani's profound knowledge of non-Islamic traditions and his talent for religious polemic, a skill he gained from his readings in Nestorian Christian polemics.

The second section revolves around the implicit conflict between the poet's explicit statements and the contrary implications of his words. Irony is its discursive keynote. The third section (vv. 73–91) is the most porous of the three sections in terms of its conflicting significations. As if suddenly cognising the gap between his words and their implications, the poet vows to cease uttering infidelity and to return to his renewed faith (*iman tazeh*). Recapitulating the syncretic imagery of sections one and two, the poet reinforces the request that his Christian patron approach the king with a petition for permission to visit Jerusalem, which would, by implication, free him from prison.

The Christian Qasida begins with a comparison between the sky (which is crooked because the poet is in prison) and the Christian script (which appears backwards for Khaqani and his audience, who read in the opposite direction); the first and second sections are sustained by this comparison. A new topos is introduced in the third and final section. The poet recreates in his imagination a journey to the sacred sites of Islamic and Christian history, during the course of which he imagines spreading a new creed forged idiosyncratically from Christian teachings. The imagined journey begins when Khaqani asks what will happen if he seeks the 'threshold of infidelity' (*astan-i kufr*, v. 34). This rhetorical question launches a series of bold proposals during the course of which the poet threatens to abandon Islam and convert to Christianity. Instead of proposing a new religion to replace Islam, Khaqani offers his poetry as a surrogate for all religion. Christianity fulfilled the Jewish dispensation, and Islam fulfilled the Christian dispensation. Analogously, Khaqani proposes his poetry as the fulfilment of all prior creeds, including, besides the monotheistic triad (Judaism, Islam, Christianity), Zoroastrianism, Manichaeism and Nestorianism.

Bearing in mind its overall structure, we can now proceed with a close analysis of a poem that has yet to be recognised for its formative role in global prison literature. The word that opens this poem – *falak* (sky, cosmos) – has been encountered many times in this book before, not least in the name of the first prison poet of the Caucasus, Falaki Shirvani. Chapter 3 showed how *falak* is linked to prison poetry's cosmology. In the Christian Qasida, the word evokes a conflict between the imprisoned poet and the powers that watch over his destiny; the circuit of the sky determines the course of the entire text, just as the poem determines the course of the poet's life.

Khaqani then moves to the old topos of his conflict with the sky (*falak*), which now appears in the guise of 'heavenly fathers [*aba-yi 'ulwi*]'. We have already seen how rivalry between the poet and the cosmos inflects prison poem poetics. This impression is reinforced by the following verses of Nasir Khusraw that draw on the personified version of evil in Zoroastrian cosmology, Ahriman:

Oh oppressive sky, oh sister of Ahriman!
Why don't you say what you want from me?
You've made me soft and jaundiced like an apricot.
You're also aiming to devour me.

ای ستمگر فلک ای خواهر آهرمن
چون نگویی که چه افتاد ترا با من

نرم کردستیم و زرد چو زرد آلو
قصد کردی که بخواهیم همی خوردن [18]

Mas'ud Sa'd also emphasises this topos by metonymically associating the act of fastening chains with the expression of the poet's resolve:

I am in chains [*dar bandam*]. Who will free my feet from these chains
while the heavenly sky [*falak*] has resolved to keep me in chains?

در بندم و این بند ز پایم که گشاید
تا چرخ فلک بند مرا بسته میانست [19]

The same poet's comparison between the sky (*falak*) and the mirror (*ayineh*) reflects another's face alongside that of the viewer. In the above-quoted poem, *falak* is aligned with hypocrisy and duplicity. In another poem by Mas'ud Sa'd, the cosmos is compared with a rusty mirror that only dimly reflects reality:

Let me cry at this sky [*falak*] that acts like a mirror.
It rusts the mirror of my fate.

فریاد مرا زین فلکِ آینه کردار
کایینهٔ بخت من ازو دارد زنگار [20]

In prison poem 2, Khaqani poignantly registers the hostility of fate. 'The sky,' he declares, 'draws a bow aiming for my heart / the arrow's trembling strikes my bones' (2:7). The comparison in prison poem 3 of the sky to a signless Ka'ba (3:3–5) is also worth recalling here. In contrast to prison poems 2 and 3, the poet's hostility towards the sky in the Christian Qasida (prison poem 1) is fleshed out through prophecy. Jesus' renunciation of his heavenly father here motivates the prison poet's rebellion. The 'star of knowledge [*akhtar-i danish*]' – a metonym for Jupiter and Mercury as well as the entire cosmos – is rendered useless by the ascription of divinity to the poet himself.[21] The description of the sky as more broken than the Christian script (*khatt-i tarsa*) culminates this Christological cosmology.

The comparison of the poet with a monk (*rahib*) in chains (vv. 1 and 6) further deepens the poem's entanglement within a heterodox political theology. Although Khaqani vigorously insists on his Muslim identity by the end, he uses Christology here to undermine the ruler's legitimacy. The term used here for monk, *rahib*, is also the active participle of the Arabic root ر ه ب, denoting 'fear'. This usage mirrors the Persian *tarsa* (Christian), used in the first hemistich of the same verse, for *tarsidan* is the Persian infinitive form of 'to fear'.[22] Ironically for a poem that relies on a comparison between the poet and Jesus, Khaqani's first figural impulse is to deny the presence of Jesus (*ruh Allah*) in his prison cell. There are many monks, and the imprisoned poet is among them, even when God's spirit is absent. The contrast between the multitude of monks and the absence of God recalls prison poem 3's signless Ka'ba. It also sets the stage for the imagery noted in the Introduction: the poet's body is compared with Mary's folded thread with the statement that 'My heart is one [*yikta*] like the needle of Jesus' (v. 4).

Nestorianism's paradoxical position within medieval Islamic society yields a second reading. Born to a Nestorian woman, Khaqani inevitably identified with the Christian tradition. The autobiographical dimension is reinforced by the poet's statement in his *Gift from Two Iraqs* that his grandmother was, like Jesus' mother Mary, a weaver. At the same time, Khaqani's success as a court poet was premised on his Muslim identity. Later commentators have even suggested that Khaqani was imprisoned not, as might be expected, due to his distance from Islamic orthodoxy, but because he refused to convert to Christianity. The Qajar-era commentator Muhammad 'Ali Mudarris offered some speculations: 'In the last years of his life, he was inclined to solitude. Because the Khaqan did not permit him [to be away from the court], he escaped. At the Khaqan's order, he was arrested and imprisoned in Shadarvan. Or, on return from Mecca pilgrimage, he was imprisoned because he was forced to convert to Christianity, which he refused.'[23]

In any case, the real threat posed by the Christian Qasida was the poet's refusal to internalise political subordination in the legal realm within his poem. Khaqani preserved his affiliation with Islam while poetically aligning himself with the so-called *ahl al-dhimma*. The term *ahl al-dhimma* (or simply *dhimmi*) was used to refer to non-Muslim minorities whose religions predated Islam, and who were understood to be 'people of the book': Jews, Zoroastrians and Christians. While *dhimmi* were second-class citizens within most Islamic empires, they were also – nominally at least – protected by the state, and guaranteed the right to freely practise their beliefs, provided that they observed certain restrictions. As will be seen below, the belt (*zunnar*) that they were mandated to wear in many contexts shaped prison poem poetics.

Although the Shirvanshahs were a Muslim dynasty, their iconology suggests that many non-Islamic – especially pre-Islamic and Iranian – traditions were active at this court. Barthold and Bosworth have noted that the 'progressive Persianisation of [the] originally Arab' Shirvanshah dynasty that occurred during the eleventh and twelfth centuries paralleled the Kurdisation of the contemporary Rawwadid dynasty in northwestern Persia.[24] Similarly, Iranian names such as Akhsitan I (r. 1120–60), Khaqani's patron, and his predecessor Faridun proliferated among the Shirvanshah rulers, in lieu of the formerly Arabo-Islamic names for rulers in this region. The Iranian iconology and naming practices both attest to the Persianisation of twelfth-century Azerbaijan that accompanied the Shirvanshahs' rise to power.

Beyond his genealogy, Khaqani's Christology is at once metaphysical and political. During the period when prison poetry flourished in the vicinity of Azerbaijan, the Shirvanshahs were closely tied through intermarriage to Georgia's Christian Empire, ruled by Queen Tamar (r. 1184–1212) and her successors.[25] The proximity of the Shirvanshah court to Christian Georgia is reflected in the poetry of the first prison poet of Shirvan, Falaki, who composed Persian panegyrics for Georgian Christian rulers as readily as for the Muslim kings of Shirvan. This *qasida*'s panegyric style soon became commonplace in Georgian poetry from this period, especially in the courtly panegyrics of Grigol Chakhrukhadze and Ioane Shavt'eli.[26] In a poem commemorating the union of the Georgian Bagrationi and Shirvanshah dynasty through the marriage of a daughter of Queen Tamar to a Shirvanshah prince, Falaki describes the members of Queen Tamar's family using the same panegyric register he applied to Muslim lineages:

> Through four auspicious stars and two auspicious jewels,
> God has decorated and beautified the world.
> Although her father withdrew his kindly shadow,
> fortune brought three hundred sons as good news.

فرخنده چهار اختر و فرخنده دو گوهر
کایزد ز بقاشان بجهان زیب و فر آورد

گر برد پدر سایهٔ شفقت ز سر او
اقبال بدو مژدهٔ سیصد پسر آورد [27]

The four stars mentioned above correspond to Tamar's four sons, each of whom bore Persian names: Akhsitan, Faridun, Shahinshah, Farrukhzud. The two jewels reference her unnamed daughters. Such poems reveal how the poets of Shirvan blended praise for Christian Georgia with praise for the Muslim Shirvanshah regime.

The ambiguities intrinsic to Islamic laws for dealing with non-Muslims living in Islamic territories have been extensively examined alongside pre-Islamic Sassanian and Byzantine strategies for dealing with religious minorities. These studies have more frequently been carried out with respect to the Arabic-speaking regions of the Islamic world than from the Persian peripheries. However, to quote C. E. Bosworth, 'it was on the fringes of the Islamic world . . . that discriminatory measures lasted longest'.[28] Maryam Shenoda has demonstrated that a major topos in Coptic Christian literature dealing with the status of non-Muslims was to portray 'Coptic wonder-working victors who, through faith and miracles, are heroes, not *dhimmi*.'[29]

Congruently with its celebration of religious difference, the Christian Qasida portrays Nestorian Christians as cosmopolitan intellectuals whose scholarly achievements earned them a respected place in Islamic history and theology. Coptic texts align Christian identity with victimisation and persecution; similarly, the prison poem associates Christianity with political marginality. Yet while Coptic narratives erased their protagonists' *dhimmi* status, the Persian prison poem turned the *dhimmi*'s marginalised identity into a basis for political critique.

Dhimmi norms underwent significant variation across Umayyad, Abbasid, Ayyubid, Saljuq and Shirvanshah domains. The relation between literary representations of *dhimmi* experience and official *dhimmi* policies was always shaped by political pressures. Yet certain conclusions can be drawn about the past, even from literary sources. In contrast to the earliest days of Islam, when many major Arabic poets identified as Christian, a Christian poet pursuing a career at a twelfth-century Saljuq (or Shirvanshah) court would have faced considerable challenges. Extant records make no mention of any non-Muslim poets at Saljuq, Shirvanshah or Ghaznavid courts. The politics of Islamic governance in these regions would have motivated any poet to avoid marking himself as Christian, given that such marking could have could have harmed his career.

The identity that was supressed in Khaqani's family history was one he adopted in his poetry. The poet's ambivalent identity is manifested in v. 28, where Khaqani states, 'After these forty days of mourning finishes in thirty years / Do I publicly practise fifty days?' Whereas the first hemistich implies a lifelong adherence to Islam, the second suggests and then immediately, if implicitly, denies that the renunciation of Islam will ever occur in public view. Even while insisting that he will never convert to Christianity publicly, the poem leaves open a possibility of secret conversion, as well as of conversion in the purely figurative sense. While such proclamations are literary conceits, their figural meanings, imaginary threats and declarations of poetic power shaped the discursive sovereignty of Persian prison poetry.

The verses preceding this declaration stress the poet's commitment to Islam. Although Muslims have denied him justice (*dad*), the poet insists that he will never turn away from Islam. Khaqani then relates his extensive study of seven Quranic *suras* after having received revelation (*wahy*) from experts in the seven ways of reading the Quran, performed the *hajj* and the actions associated with this pilgrimage: circling the Kaʿba (*tawaf-i Kaʿba*), throwing stones at Satan, and reciting the prayers required of the pious pilgrim to Mecca.

In section two (according to the tripartite typology outlined above), the poet begins to express his frustration, as his piety has not resulted in any promise of his release from prison. He threatens to change the orientation of the 'house of God' (*bayt Allah*), meaning that he will reverse the direction of his prayers towards Jerusalem. Whereas the Prophet Muhammad instructed Muslims in the Quran to face Mecca in their prayers, Khaqani proposes, after recounting in triumphant detail his successful completion of the *hajj*, to reverse the Quranic injunction of praying towards the Kaʿba. After declaring his plans to pray in the direction of Jerusalem (*bayt al-maqdis*), the poet complains that, after fifty years of being a pious Muslim, his feet are weighed down by chains (*band*).

Khaqani also includes in this hemistich a comparison between his chains and the cross (*salib*). The comparison is interesting for, among other reasons, complicating the anti-Jewish stereotypes discernible in v. 32, and which are also in evidence in Khaqani's invective against Abu'l ʿAla' Ganjavi, discussed in Chapter 3. On the one hand, Khaqani declares that, like Jesus, he is oppressed by a group of Jews (*mushti yahudi*), who are his enemies, perhaps the very same ones who hang the poet from the ceiling in imitation of a candelabrum (v. 19). Yet, no less than four lines later, the poet proposes to reverse the *qiblah* – the direction of Islamic prayer – away from Mecca and towards Jerusalem.

These unexpected and paradoxical reversals suggest that there is more to the contradictory representation of non-Muslim peoples than a cursory reading suggests, as is made fully manifest by the paradoxical request that closes the poem, petitioning his patron for permission to visit Jerusalem (*bayt al-muqaddas*, v. 89), rather than, as might be expected from a Muslim poet, to visit Mecca. Is the poet making another surreptitious allusion to Christianity, given that Jerusalem is the location from where Jesus ascended to heaven? Or is he conveying his desire to follow the path of Jesus, in his capacity as Muslim prophet (ʿIsa), liberated from captivity? Perhaps, adapting the chancery petition (*ʿarz-i hal*) genre to his own ends, Khaqani simply decided to conclude his poem with a request of some kind, and considered a demand for pilgrimage to another holy city more appropriate.[30]

The proposal to do away with Mecca as the *qiblah* sets a pattern for the catalogue that follows. Immediately after abolishing prayers in the direction of Mecca, Khaqani declares that he will kiss the Christian church bell (*naqus*, also referring to the wooden clappers used to summon the faithful to worship) in response to an unspecified punishment (*tahakkum*). Then, even more boldly, he declares that he will make himself captive by wearing the *zunnar*, the belt referenced at the beginning of this chapter, worn in medieval Islamic societies by Christians, Zoroastrians and Jews to distinguish them from Muslims (as shown in Figure 5.1). The *zunnar* belonged to a sartorial repertoire for non-Muslims that included head coverings and cloaks such as the *qalansuwa* and *burnus*, the *ruqʿa* (badge placed over the shoulder), and *shiʿar*, a general term for any mark that identified the *dhimmi* as non-Muslims.[31] Together, these sartorial items comprised the code of *ghiyar*, 'the compulsory distinctive mark in the garb of *dhimmi* subjects under Muslim rule'.[32] While *ghiyar* codes were not uniformly applied, the late medieval

Figure 5.1 The *zunnar* worn by non-Muslims.

Persianate world is considered to be a context in which *ghiyar* regulations were strictly implemented.[33]

An Arabic verse by thirteenth-century Iraqi poet Ibn Abi al-Yusr reveals the political charge associated with this garment, and the blame that was cast on those who wore it:

> The cross is raised over [Baghdad's] highest pulpits.
> The *zunnar* wearers are responsible for this.

علا الصليب على أعلى منابرها
وقام بالأمر من يحويه زنار [34]

Like the *naqus*, the *zunnar* is deeply embedded in histories of discrimination against non-Muslim minorities, as well as in their literary representations. Since these histories are intrinsic to the prison poem's political theology, it is worth dwelling on its trajectory in Persian poetry. In the process of such an investigation, the resemblances among the many different kinds of chains (*band*), belts and threads (including the thread of Mary referenced by Khaqani) discussed in the preceding chapters begin to coalesce.

Dressing in Chains: The *Zunnar's* Trajectories

Translated from the Greek *zonarion* (ζωνάριον), the *zunnar* was originally associated by medieval Islamic authors with the reign of ʿUmar b. al-Khattab (r. 634–644), the second Islamic caliph.[35] In Khaqani's time, the *zunnar* was featured in a pseudepigraphic composite text that came to be known as ʿUmar's Covenant (*ʿahd ʿumar*), or, alternately, as ʿUmar's Stipulations (*al-shurut al-ʿumariyya*). Modern historians associate the institutionalisation of discriminatory practices with a later period, specifically with the reign of another ʿUmar, ʿUmar b. ʿAbd al-ʿAziz (r. 717–720). When the Hungarian Orientalist Ignaz Goldziher called ʿUmar b. ʿAbd al-ʿAziz the 'Hezekiah of the house of the Umayyads', referencing the purist defender of the Hebrews from Assyrian paganism, he was alluding to the lengths to which ʿUmar went to defend Islam from those he regarded as idolaters.[36]

The text of this pseudepigraphic covenant, widely believed to stem from a later period in Islamic history, is preserved in the form of a putative letter from the Christians of Syria to the Umayyad governor and general of ʿUmar b. al-Khattab, Abu ʿUbayda. One of the most counter-intuitive features of this text is that its discriminatory proposals are said to have been requested by the Christians in order to ensure their safety (*aman*). According to Albrecht Noth, this feature connects this genre to conquest (*futuh*) treatises, 'according to which non-Muslims asked for agreements in the form of contracts'.[37] 'When you came against us,' begins a standard version written in the voice of Syrian Christians, 'we asked you for a guarantee of protection [*al-aman*].' Here we see a façade of justice fabricated from the fiction of Christians' willing consent to the terms of their discrimination.[38]

Light is shed on the relationship between the fiction of Christians' consent to the terms of their persecution and historical reality by two Syriac sources that cite an early version of the text that ultimately became ʿUmar's Covenant: the anonymous Nestorian *Chronicle of Seert* and Bar Hebraeus' *Ecclesiastical Chronicle*.[39] Both sources regard the discriminatory regulations as a guarantee of protection. This same document was in the possession of many Christian monasteries across the Islamic world, and it was further consecrated with allusions to historical figures such as the Caliph Muʿawiya (r. 661–680) and the Nestorian Catholicos Ish'oyahb II.[40] Khaqani's

Christian Qasida demonstrates an awareness of the fictitious foundations of Christians' consent to the terms of their own discrimination, while also suggesting how exposing this story as a fiction can undermine the legitimacy of the sovereign's authority.

This pseudo-covenant has the Christian community promise to only 'beat the *naqus* gently'. Moreover, they promise to abide by a long series of negative restrictions to 'not display a cross, not raise our voices in prayer or chanting in our churches; not carry in procession our cross or our book,[41] not raise our voices over our dead; not light fires in Muslim markets, nor bring our funerals near them'. Finally, the Syrian Christians promise:

> *to keep our religion wherever we are*; not to resemble the Muslims or to wear their hat, their turban, their shoes, nor the parting of the hair, nor [to copy] their way of riding, nor to use their language, nor be called by their names; to cut our hair in front and divide our forelocks; to tie the *zunnar* round our waists; not to engrave Arabic on our seals, not to ride on saddles . . . not to make our homes higher than theirs; not to teach our children the Quran; not to be partner with a Muslim except in business.[42]

This covenant was quoted across the eastern Islamic world in the legal manuals that comprised the local *madrasa* curriculum during the prison poem's efflorescence. *Kitab al-Umm* (*Mother Book*), the legal compendium of Shafi'i (d. 820) contains the most comprehensive version of this covenant. Shafi'i's inclusion of the covenant, minus the fictional premise of an epistolary exchange between the Syrian Christian community and their Muslim conqueror, indicates that the stipulations in 'Umar's Covenant had 'achieved legal force already by the beginning of the ninth century'.[43] Shafi'i's rehearsal of *dhimmi* regulations illustrates how 'Umar's Covenant originated as 'an exercise in the schools of law to draw upon pattern treatises'.[44] References to 'Umar's Covenant also permeate the legal writings of Ibn Hanbal (d. 855) and the Hanbali jurist Ibn Qudama (d. 1223).[45]

Although influenced by Hanafi rite in later stages of its history, Shirvan was most closely affiliated with the Shafi'i rite during the period under discussion here. For this as well as other reasons, the version of the covenant in *Kitab al-Umm* is a likely source for Khaqani's knowledge of *dhimmi* regulations.[46] Thus, we have every reason to assume the poet's familiarity with 'Umar's

Covenant, and to read the references to oppression (*tahakkum* and *taʿadda*) in the Christian Qasida as allusions to the stipulated moratorium on the loud ringing of the *naqus* and obliging non-Muslims to wear the *zunnar*. To my knowledge, the deep connection between the Christian Qasida and ʿUmar's Covenant has not been recognised previously in scholarship.[47] Ignorance of this link has obscured our understanding of Khaqani's poetics, and muted the political implications of his prison poems. Grasping the *intertextuality* of Khaqani's literary refashioning is crucial to perceiving its status as a transgressive genre, both with respect to its formal components and to its content. Khaqani's literary rewriting of canonical *dhimmi* texts marks a significant turning point in prison poem poetics.

ʿUmar's Covenant, which specifically forbids non-Muslims from raising their voices in prayer or chanting, also elucidates verse 7 of this poem: the poet proposes to 'split the cross panes' of his window with his morning horn (*sur-i subhgahi*), and thereby to break the silence imposed by the terms of the covenant. Aware that Christians are forbidden from mourning loudly according to the terms of ʿUmar's Covenant, the poet polemically projects his voice until it is loud enough to break the cross that confines him to his cell.

Many of the injunctions in ʿUmar's Covenant are more concerned with fabricating and consolidating religious, and thus social, distinctions, than in implementing Islamic teachings. Scholars have argued that the primary purpose of *dhimmi* regulations was less to oppress than to erect boundaries between the conquerors and the conquered. According to Noth, this explains their formal resemblance to treatises 'between conquering Muslims and conquered non-Muslims'.[48] The Christians whose voice the covenant purports to represent promise to pray away from public view, to remove all external paraphernalia of Christian worship, especially the cross, from their churches, to avoid public processions, not to publicly mourn their dead, to dress differently than their Muslim neighbours, not to use Arabic in their public records, and not to build homes taller than the homes of Arabs. Most significantly, Christians were forbidden from converting *out* of their religion and from teaching their children the Quran. These last points bear most directly on the Christian Qasida.

By encouraging segregation along religious lines, ʿUmar's covenant ensured the usefulness of a minority religion from the point of view of the state. The popularity of ʿUmar's Covenant with later Abbasid, Ayyubid and Saljuq rulers suggests that, far from posing a threat to Islam, minority populations strengthened the position of Muslim rulers. Prison poetry was one of the few literary genres available to premodern Persian poets to contest the terms of this discrimination.

A century after the period assigned to ʿUmar's Covenant in Islamic historiography, the Abbasid Caliph al-Mutawakkil (r. 821–861) endeavoured to erase the influence that heretical Mu'tazilis had gained under his predecessor al-Maʿmun (r. 813–833). This controversial caliph undertook drastic measures to persecute *dhimmi* peoples. As recorded by historian Ibn al-Athir, in the year 850, al-Mutawakkil issued an order that imposed a number harsh regulations on all non-Muslims (*ahl al-dhimma*):

> And in this year al-Mutawakkil ordered the *ahl al-dhimma* to wear honey-coloured capes with *zunnars* . . . and on the backs of their saddles they put circles made of wood. *Dhimmi* women had to wear a yellow hood while leaving the house while men had to wear another. [Al-Mutawakkil] then ordered the destruction of all new churches and synagogues . . . He also ordered that on their doors would be placed pictures of demons [*shayatin*] made of wood . . . Also, no Muslim was allowed to teach them. They were not allowed to uses crosses [*saliban*] . . . and they were forced to build roads. Mutawakkil ordered the gravestones of all *dhimmis* to be made level with the earth. These proclamations were inscribed everywhere in his domains [*al-afaq*].[49]

The extent to which al-Mutawakkil's stipulations were enacted is unclear. It has been noted that 'there is no evidence of any violent persecution of non-Muslims under al-Mutawakkil, nor is it clear how far, how wide, or how far these restrictions were enforced'.[50] As always when dealing with the influence of historical documents on literary texts and cultural memory, what counts most are the narratives such representations generate in the memories of those who repeat them. Of particular interest here are the sartorial aspects of al-Mutawakkil's persecution policies, which were incorporated in a critical spirit into the Christian Qasida.

That the details of al-Mutawakkil's persecution were reported in a twelfth-century anonymous Persian text, exactly contemporary with the Christian

Qasida, demonstrates just how alive was the memory of these actions, even among Muslims, three centuries later.[51] The economic benefits that Muslim rulers extracted from Christian minorities – in the form of *jizya*, the poll tax paid by *dhimmi*s – may help to explain why the Shirvanshah ruler Akhsitan I is said to have pressured Khaqani to officially convert to Christianity. It also explains why Khaqani would have resisted this demand, notwithstanding his Christian background. Whereas in its original context *dhimmi* stipulations may simply have served the goal of protecting a Muslim minority from assimilation by a Christian majority, by the time of al-Mutawakkil's reign, these regulations, operative perhaps more in the domain of discursive representations than in everyday life, had come to serve a more insidious – as well as more complicated – goal: to prevent equality through the putative preservation of difference. These two pillars of *dhimmi* regulations were to become the prison poem's central object of critique during the genre's migration to the Caucasus and further development in the hands of Khaqani.

ʿUmar's covenant suggests that the obligations attached to the *dhimmi* community were financially beneficial for Muslim rulers. *Dhimmi*s were obliged to pay a poll tax, to serve Muslims in particular ways, and to host any Muslim traveller who passed through the area as a guest for up to three days. Even if zealous Muslim leaders wished for their non-Muslim subjects to convert to Islam, such conversions would have been detrimental to the financial interests of the state, and were therefore discouraged in subsequent centuries. Economically, Muslim rulers benefitted more from *dhimmi*s who refused to accept Islam than from eager converts.

The details enumerated in ʿUmar's Covenant and later (reportedly) implemented by al-Mutawakkil also indicate why a poet like Khaqani, with an identity rooted in both the Islamic and Nestorian Christian traditions, might prefer to publicly affiliate with Islam. Being Christian in medieval Islamic society meant more than simply adhering to a set of doctrines and performing certain rituals. It meant systematically acknowledging one's otherness vis-à-vis mainstream society, and making one's dress, hair style, linguistic habits, mode of transport, education and even mourning rituals conform to this difference. All such adaptations were incorporated into the prison poem. Nestorian Christians faced the double stigma of being Christian in a Muslim society and of being perceived as heretics by orthodox Christians. Poets with borderline identities such as Khaqani inevitably preferred to pass as Muslim. More surprising is how, in passing as Muslim, these poets activated the subversive potential of their marginalised identities to make poetry into an instrument of political critique.

ʿUmar's Covenant is not attested in its complete form before the eleventh century, a period which witnessed a resurgence in legislation against non-Muslim communities.[52] The prison poem's political-theological trajectory should be situated within such developments, particularly given the formative role played in the genre's trajectory by Christological motifs. Contemporaneously with the prison poetry of Shirvan, ʿUmar's Covenant was systematised into a body of regulations governing the social status of non-Muslims. Within a few years of Khaqani's birth, the Saljuq Sultan Mahmud promoted a new set of regulations requiring non-Muslims to wear garments (*ghiyar*) that further distinguished them from the Muslim majority. The new sartorial regulations were legitimated through ʿUmar's Covenant, a text that, as we can now appreciate, reveals more about the status of non-Muslim minorities during the twelfth century than in the seventh century.

Further reflecting the impact of ʿUmar's Covenant as a tool of segregation, jurist Abu Yusuf (d. 789), one of the major codifiers of *dhimmi* regulations, advised against beating but supported imprisonment for non-Muslims who were unable to pay the poll tax (*jizya*) to their Muslim overlords. *Dhimmis* who fail to pay the *jizya* 'should not be beaten', advised the Hanafi jurist: 'Instead, they should be imprisoned until they pay it.'[53] Abu Yusuf attests to the use of prisons under Abbasid rule, and suggests that imprisonment was used by rulers for the purposes of punishment as well as coercion. Preferable to beating and other forms of torture, imprisonment was useful for extracting payment from disobedient subjects. As in modernity, punishment by imprisonment could be presented as a benefaction bestowed in lieu of a crueller punishment, such as execution.

While stipulations regulating the conduct of non-Muslims proliferated, images of the *zunnar* circulated across the Muslim world, shaping its disciplines and lexicons, and impinging on jurisprudence as well as on poetry. Most pertinent for the prison poem, the *zunnar* became a politically loaded sartorial artefact. While it acquired specifically Sufi connotations in the poetry of Sanaʾi Ghaznavi and Farid al-Din ʿAttar,[54] outside poetry, the *zunnar* evoked the binary divisions that legitimated discrimination against minorities. The price for not wearing the prescribed *zunnar* in public was forfeiture of all one's property, as a document from the Geniza archives referencing a crackdown in 1249 against those who violated *dhimmi* regulations attests. 'On that day,' writes the anonymous observer, 'a herald of the Sultan announced both morning and evening that the property and life of any Jew or Christian walking in the streets by day or night without a distinguishing badge [*ʿalama*] or *zunnar* would be forfeit.'[55] When Khaqani made the *dhimmi* dress code a point of departure for his carceral poetics, he was cognisant of these political implications.

Bearing such contexts in mind, section three of the Christian Qasida, in which the poet declares that he will kiss the *naqus* and fasten a *zunnar* around himself in response to the oppression he faces (v. 38), takes on new dimensions:

> I'll kiss the church bell [*naqus*] from this tyranny.
> I'll fasten myself in the belt [*zunnar*] from this oppression.

روم ناقوس بوسم زین تحکم
شوم زنار بندم زین تعدا

The verb in the second hemistich – *bandam* – recalls the many prison poems by Masʿud Saʿd, that similarly play with variations on this word.[56] As noted in the Introduction, *band* is arguably the most frequently encountered term in the prison poem lexicon; it is more prominent even than the word for prison (*zindan*) or the condition of confinement that names the genre (*habs*). Here, *bandam* affects the meaning of the entire poem, adding a layer of uncertainty to the poet's plans. In Persian, the verse can be read as either a question or as a threat; the use of the subjunctive in the translation ('I shall' in abbreviated form as 'I'll') aims to approximate this semantic duality. Do we understand the poet's promise to fasten the *zunnar* of oppression around his waist as a genuine threat or merely as a rhetorical flourish? The grammar and placement of this verse – amid many questions – situates the utterance in the realm of probability rather than certainty, thereby protecting the poet from accusations of blasphemy, while leaving perpetually open the possibility of subversion.

The poetic force of the Christian Qasida derives in large measure from the ambivalence of the poet's statements as he enumerates a sequence of powerful action verbs that reveal his resolve to seek release from prison, even when his actions bring him to the threshold of infidelity: kiss (*busam*), go (*ravam*), become (*shavam*) and fasten (*bandam*). That the poet rebels against his imprisonment by proposing to wear a *zunnar* acquires significance when we recall that Christians, Jews and Zoroastrians were required by law to follow these sartorial regulations to make their minority status visible. For Persian prison poets, the dress code imposed on non-Muslim minorities was a mark of their confinement. Yet no amount of historical context can wholly establish what Khaqani achieved with such imagery: the verses are deliberately ambiguous; their meaning and implications must be read within the framework of the literary genre to which they belong.

The verses that follow further develop the lexicon of discrimination against non-Muslims. The poet proposes to exchange two items of clothing worn by Muslims (*rida* and the *taylasan*) for clothing worn by *dhimmi*s (*zunnar* and *burnus*), like the Muslim shaykh and folk hero Pur Saqa (whose name literally means 'son of a water-carrier') who fell in love with a Christian girl and converted to Christianity for her sake:[57]

> I'll exchange the *rida* and the *taylasan*
> for a *zunnar* and *burnus*, like [the shaykh] Pur Saqa.

بدل سازم به زنار و به برنس
ردا و طیلسان چون پور سقا

'Umar's Covenant forbade non-Muslims from wearing the close-fitting hat – later a lengthy hooded cloak – called the *qalansuwa* or the *burnus*. Like the *zunnar*, the *burnus* was a marker of Christian identity, and specifically of Christian piety, as evidenced by the definition offered by the Indian scholar Murtada al-Zabidi: 'The *burnus* is a long *qalansuwa*. It is a long garment with stitching and a coat of mail or hat for beauty. Monks dressed in the *burnus*.'[58]

In his commentary on the Christian Qasida, Zarrinkub cites a satire (*hija'*) through which the Muslim Umayyad poet Jarir (*c.* 650–728) mocked the Christian poet Akhtal:

God curses the god of the cross worshippers
and everyone who dresses in a monk's cloak [*burnus*].

لعن الإله من الصليب إلهه
واللابسين برانس الرهبان [59]

Such literary intertexts clarify the political dimensions of the proposed clothing exchange in the Christian Qasida, which uses sartorial details to identify with non-Muslim peoples persecuted by Muslim rulers.

With respect to the Islamic legal regulations governing the behaviour and apparel of non-Muslims, there is a salient gap between theory and practice. The discriminatory rhetoric in ʿUmar's Covenant has not prevented scholars from arguing that the position of Jews in the medieval Islamic world was intellectually, economically and socially far superior to their position in medieval Europe.[60] Religious minorities in general fared better under Islamic law than in contemporaneous Byzantium until the thirteenth century.[61] Although the protests in prison poetry against the discrimination faced by non-Muslims in Muslim lands remain constant over time, this does not mean that the injunction to wear the *zunnar* was enforced with equal rigour in all times and places.

As shown in Chapter 3's discussion of dice and the cosmos, gambling metaphors suffuse many prison poems. Similarly, wearing a *zunnar* in a Muslim-majority society involved a perpetual gamble with the state. Hence, the attraction of this most dangerous of sartorial accoutrements for the prison poem. As a topos of infidelity and the marker of true spiritual attainment, the *zunnar* is deployed with even greater dexterity in Indo-Persian poetry, as if marking a third stage in the evolution of the prison poem. To cite only one of the more striking examples from this tradition, the following verse by Amir Khusraw presents the *zunnar* in vernacular terms, incorporating it into an Indo-Persian context as a Brahmanical thread (*yajñopavīta*). In this guise, the belt worn by religious minorities becomes a metaphor for a faith that looks beyond all narrow orthodoxies:

I am an infidel who worships love. Being Muslim has no use for me.
Each and every vein of me has become a thread. A *zunnar* has no use for me.

کافر عشقم مسلمانی مرا در کار نیست
هر رگ من تار گشت حاجت زنار نیست

Far from signifying imprisonment or persecution, the *zunnar* here conveys the poet's ecstatic embrace of a religion based on love. Amir Khusraw refers to himself as a lover and as an infidel (*kafir*) while dispensing with any pretence of orthodoxy.

Muhammad Iqbal of Lahore (d. 1938) contributed perhaps more than any other modern Persian poet to keeping alive the polysemy of *zunnar*. Iqbal follows the conclusion of Khaqani's Christian Qasida (v. 91) that proclaims the poet's intention to make a rosary (*tasbih*) of his 'brilliant verses' when joining the *zunnar* to a syncretic rosary:

> The shaykh has gambled Islam away for love of idols.
> From the *zunnar*, he has created a rosary [*tasbih*].

شیخ در عشق بتان اسلام باخت
رشته ی تسبیح از زنار ساخت [62]

Inasmuch as *tasbih* refers to the rosary or prayer beads used by Hindus, Buddhists, Christians and Muslims, it is a particularly ecumenical symbol that correlates with the heterodox orientation of poetry in this tradition. Not all poetry that invokes the *zunnar* is directly linked to imprisonment. Nor do all such poems belong to the formal genre of the prison poem. But many of the verses cited above were authored by poets who had composed prison poems, or who had imbibed deeply from the prison poem genre.

Further accentuating the beauty of Iqbal's verse is a mixed metaphor that associates the thread (*rishteh*) not with the *zunnar*, as might be expected given the term's association in Indo-Persian contexts as the Brahmanical thread, but with the Muslim–Christian rosary (*tasbih*). The comparison in the Christian Qasida between the *zunnar* and the rosary in the following verse is a likely subtext for Iqbal's imagery in the following verse:

> The cupbearer's body has become an idol. The wine has become a cross-bearer.
> The candelabrum has become a wine cup. The *zunnar* has now become a rosary.

ساقی صنم پیکر شده باده صلیب آور شده
قندیل ازو ساغر شده تسبیح زنار آمده

Iqbal and Amir Khusraw reinvent the *zunnar* as a symbol not of a non-Muslim identity or even of discrimination, as in Middle Eastern contexts marked by Muslim–Christian and Muslim–Jewish tensions, but rather of a syncretism that transcends religious identities. As one of the earliest representatives of a composite Hindu–Muslim culture, Amir Khusraw makes new and innovative use of the prison poem aesthetics developed on Central Asian and Caucasus borderlands.[63] In this way, the *zunnar* came to be associated in Indo-Persian texts with poetry's political theology rather than with the sovereign's discriminatory tools of governance once it migrated from the Caucasus back to South Asia. Along with a broadly Christological repertoire, this garment served as a tool in the development of the prison poem's political theology and strengthened its contribution to world literature.

In Mughal India, the ecstatic celebration of the *zunnar* that marks Indo-Persian poetry was countered by the hostility to this marker of non-Muslim identity in other textual genres, particularly in conquest narratives that aimed to legitimate Muslim rulers. The attitude of Padishah Babur (r. 1526–1530) to the *zunnar* is typical of those rulers who opposed merging Islam and Hinduism. Eager to use the image of the *zunnar* to generate a binary opposition between Muslim and infidel, Babur in his autobiography represents the *zunnar* as a marker of divine disfavour and associates it with apostasy. Babur refers to a group of his enemies as the 'cavalry of the damned', and says that they wore 'the accursed band of the *zunnar* around their necks', and 'were sullied with the brambles of apostasy'.[64] Contextualised within these widespread depictions of the *zunnar* as a marker of evil, the Christian Qasida's incorporation of *dhimmi* garments into its poetics offers yet another instance of how the prison poem's carceral poetics was used to critique oppressive governance.

The process through which the *zunnar* became a tool for the critique of injustice recapitulates the broader history of the prison poem. Prior to Khaqani, Masʿud Saʿd took the first step in aligning the *zunnar* to the condition of imprisonment, writing of his sovereign:

If I don't open my mouth in his praise,
he binds my waist with a *zunnar*.

گر نه به ثنای او گشایم لب
بسته است میان به بند زنارم [65]

The binding here occurs with the same word repeatedly encountered in relation to the prison: *band*. As with the Christian Qasida, the *zunnar* was incorporated into the prison poem in its first phase in order to expose the poet's wrongful persecution. While this early usage broke new ground, Mas'ud Sa'd's intervention had to await the genre's migration to the Caucasus for its political potential to be actualised.

As a Muslim of Christian origins, Khaqani located himself in the subaltern space of a religious minority oppressed by discriminatory laws. Refusing to renounce Islam, Khaqani honoured his mother's persecuted faith by creating a space in his poetry in which the Islamic legal regulations pertaining to non-Muslims could be subjected to systematic critique. Speaking in the first person, across Perso-Turkic empires that were cosmopolitan in their geography and oppressive in their modes of punishment, prison poets from South Asia to the Caucasus clothed their bodies and their poems in subaltern chains of oppression. Mas'ud Sa'd developed the lyric ode to memorialise the poet's captive body; Khaqani suffused his *qasida*s with self-praise, cosmic doubt and prophecy. Together, these and other prison poets from South Asia to the Caucasus developed a political theology for the prison poem.

The *zunnar* was not the only means through which the Christian Qasida fabricated a subaltern status to serve the aesthetics of incarceration. Khaqani's fragment (*qit'eh*) discussed in the preceding chapter commemorating the death of Caliph al-Muqtafi referenced an amulet (*'ud al-salib*), which 'Christians hang on children's breasts' (v. 44); this verse too engages with *dhimmi* regulations. As noted above, the 'wood of the cross [*'ud al-salib*]' amulet is primarily used to heal epilepsy. In Khaqani's fragment, however, the etymology of the amulet's evocative name becomes relevant. From the autobiography of the Norman proselyte Johannes-Obadiah, preserved in the Geniza documents, we learn of the local impact of the injunction delivered in 1121 by the Saljuq Sultan Mahmud (r. 1105–1131) regarding a renewal of old legal regulations enjoining specific clothing on non-Muslims. 'Every Jew,' writes Johannes-Obadiah, was required to 'hang on his neck a piece of lead weighing one dirham, on which the word *dhimmi* was engraved.'[66] On the year this observation was made, Khaqani was born to a Christian mother who had been forcibly converted to Islam. Incorporating this amulet into his text was his way of offering a surreptitious critique of Muslim rulers' persecution of religious minorities. This verse also evokes the moment in the gospels of Luke (23:26–49) when Jesus carried his cross along the Via Dolorosa in Jerusalem.

Even without accepting the implausible hypothesis that Khaqani was pressured to convert to Christianity, we can still see how the Christian Qasida was a vehicle through which the poet called into question multiple religious identities. World literature offers few examples of a poem – or of a genre – that offered such a visceral engagement with the poet's lyric and prophetic body as that found in the Persian prison poem. Writing of the literature of exile in European literatures, Northrop Frye perceived that, though rarely formalised as a genre within European literatures, this body of work was characterised by 'the individual demanding attention, speak[ing] for himself, and . . . represented as the poet himself'.[67] In charting the evolution of the poet's self, Frye's account of exile literature as a genre suggests parallels with the Persian prison poem. As with the prison poem, the subject of exile literature is often an oppositional self, full of complaints against the agent responsible for the poet's banishment.

At the same time, prison poetry has a corporeal dimension missing from the literature of exile. The parallels that that have been suggested between Ovid and the first phase of the prison poem do not, for example, extend beyond this stage.[68] Much early Arabic prison poetry, including the captivity poems of Abu Firas al-Hamdani that appears to have influenced the Persian prison poem in its earliest phases, begins in a lyric lament against captivity.[69] Among the poets of Shirvan, in particular Khaqani, the prison poem developed a political meaning premised on the proximity of the poet's body – now arrayed in the garments of persecution – to the sources of power. In his self-appointed capacity as a poet-prophet, and no doubt to advance his stature as a poet, Khaqani caused the genre's lyric idiom to yield to a cosmopolitan critique of Muslim rulers' persecution of religious minorities.

By reconstituting the prison poem, the Christian Qasida fulfils Samuel Johnson's insight that 'every new genius produces some innovation, which, when invented and approved, subverts the rules which the practice of foregoing authors had established'.[70] With greater proximity to the Persian prison poem, we can turn to the words of Vatvat, who, in his *Magic Gardens* parts ways with his predecessors by arguing that innovation (*ibda'*) is more than a mere literary device (*badi'*). For Vatvat's poetics, originality is the substance of literary discourse and the origin of literary meaning. As he writes: 'The device [*ibda'*] is considered by masters of literary discourse [*arbab-i bayan*] to comprise innovative meanings [*ma'ani*] ordered in pleasant words [*alfaz*] without complication [*takalluf*].' Vatvat insists that 'innovation [*ibda'*] is not to be considered as a device because the discourse of the wise and the learned in verse or in prose must be innovative'.[71] Indirectly, yet significantly, Vatvat clears with these words a space for a new way of thinking about literature that enabled genres like the prison poem to shape the Persian literary system. The binary between the formal and thematic genres that constrains the modern study of premodern literatures in the Islamic world is hereby overcome.

Having discussed the legacy of the Christian Qasida – the poem that shaped the later trajectory of the prison poem more than any other – it is now time to turn, in this chapter's concluding section, to a shorter poem that has often been regarded as the crowning achievement of the final phase of Khaqani's literary career. Just as often, it has been misunderstood. The pages that follow contest the nationalist misreadings of the poem and establish it as a work that shifts the focus from the king's mortal body to the poet's prophetic body, who reveals truths suppressed by rulers.

The Sovereign's Temporality versus the Temporality of Poetry

The Aivan Qasida is a product of Khaqani's late style in multiple senses.[72] First, as we know from the chronogram that concludes this poem, it was composed in 1166, when Khaqani was in his mid-forties, after he had composed his most notable works, and at a juncture in his life when he had little to lose by criticising his sovereign.[73] By 1166, Khaqani had already composed the six poems that belong to the core corpus of the prison poem genre. He had refashioned his poetic persona within a prophetic lineage and presented in his verse his argument for poetry's discursive authority. Second, and following from the placement of the poem within the overall chronology of his work, the Aivan Qasida attests to a mature stage in the poet's reflections on poetry. Third, the poem is 'late' in Edward Said's sense that it renders 'disenchantment and pleasure without resolving the contradiction between them'.[74]

At the point in Khaqani's poetic journey when he wrote the Aivan Qasida, the prison poem had made great strides in undermining the sovereign's authority. Khaqani's poem is a thrillingly incautious attempt by a court poet to cognise the full extent of his entanglement with his patron's corruption and of the poet's dependency on the sovereign's corrupt power. It outlines a political theology of the poet's prophetic body that opposes the material power of the sovereign. Explicitly and implicitly, through sophisticated deployment of multiple poetic devices, the Aivan Qasida suggests that the poet, acting in the guise of a mad prophet, will inherit the kingdom the sultan has forsaken. This poem makes the poet's authority sovereign.

A few words are in order concerning the historical site that gave rise to this elegy. Built during the reign of the Sasanian king Khusraw Anushirvan (r. 531–579), the *aivan* (palace) of Ctesiphon, a mud brick vault 'thirty-five meters high covering an audience hall eleven hundred square meters in area' 35 km southeast of present-day Baghdad, is still regarded as a 'crowning achievement of ancient architecture'.[75] Still standing, albeit in ruins (as in Figure 5.2), the original parameters of this structure are known primarily through the recollections of poets and other travellers who made their way to Baghdad's environs. For many Persephone travellers, such as the eighteenth-century Qajar author Mir ʿAbd al-Latif Khan Shushtari, the encounter with Sasanian ruins was mediated by Khaqani's poem.[76]

Figure 5.2 'Ancient Ctesiphon', in John Philip Newman, *The Thrones and Palaces of Babylon and Nineveh from Sea to Sea: A Thousand Miles on Horseback* (Harper & Brothers, 1876), 90.

Mada'in, the Arabic word by which Ctesiphon is known, refers to the two Sasanian cities – it is the plural form of the Arabic word for city, *madina* – on the banks of the Tigris: Ctesiphon and Seleucia. Together, these cities comprised a bishopric within the Nestorian Church. Ctesiphon itself dates back to the Arsacid dynasty (247 BCE–228 CE), during which period it became the major administrative centre of Semitic Mesopotamia.[77] The capital of the Parthian and Sasanian empires for a total of 800 years, Ctesiphon was considered by Edward Gibbon as the successor to Babylon and 'one of the great capitals of the East'.[78] Although Anushirvan did not found Ctesiphon, with which he is forever associated through his palace, he augmented the city architecturally, most notably through the iconography of royal sovereignty. This in turn set the stage for the city's post-Sasanian appropriation under Saljuq rule and its new Muslim identity as Mada'in.

One striking evocation of these ruins occurs in a book-length collection of poems and reflections on Khaqani's poem published in 1924 by the Berlin-based publisher Iranshahr (Figure 5.3), best known for the eponymous journal that it published from 1922 to 1927. This book includes three poems received in response to the magazine's call for nationalist reconstructions of the Aivan Qasida in the form of six-line stanzas (*tasdis*). These versions were intended to introduce young readers to Khaqani's poem. The creators of these reconstructions are, respectively, the Turkish-born Persian writer Hosseinkhan Danish, the famed constitutionalist Yahya Dowlatabadi, and the newspaper editor Golshan.[79] The book appears to have modelled its form, parts of its content and its nationalist orientation on a Turkish translation of Khaqani's Aivan Qasida by the poet Hüseyin Daniş, best known in Turkish literature as the translator of Omar Khayyam, that had been published in Istanbul a decade earlier.[80] In particular, the Turkish introduction by Rıza Tevfik Bölükbaşı (d. 1949), a Turkish philosopher who impressed British Orientalist Edward Browne with his 'attainments in the learning of both East and West', is translated into Persian for the Iranshahr edition.[81] Giving visual form to its poetic vision, the book includes images of the ruins of the Ctesiphon Arch (Figure 5.4).[82]

The preface to this volume, signed by the publisher Hussein Kazimzada Iranshahr, inaugurates the nationalist interpretation of the Aivan Qasida that was to frame many modern renderings of the text. Locating the poem

Figure 5.3 Cover of *Aiwan-i Mada'in: tasdis-i qaṣida-i Khaqani, bi qalam-i chand nafar az fuḍala' wa shu'ara'-i Iran* (Berlin-Wilmersdorf: Iranschähr, 1343).

within an extended genealogy of appeals to pre-Islamic Iranian sovereignty, the editor begins by programmatically declaring that 'love for one's people [*millat*] is greater than love for one's mother and children'.[83] According to the volume's nationalist interpretation, Khaqani is a poet who, like Ferdowsi, stands among the ruins that frame his poem and gazes with tearful eyes at the little that has remained from the days of Iran's glory (*sar bolandi-yi iran*).[84] A poem by one 'Abd al-Rahim Hindi, published the following year in the journal *Iranshahr*, continues the tradition of poetic imitations of the Aivan Qasida and develops an even more conclusively nationalist reading of Khaqani's poem.[85] Appealing to a concept of Iranian ethnic identity that transcended national borders while also enshrining them in the past, these Berlin-based publications were part of an effort by émigré Iranian intellectuals to revive traces of Iran's pre-Islamic glory for modern nationalist ends. New poetic possibilities were born with this modernist and nationalist reconfiguration, but many aspects of Khaqani's political theology, particularly his opposition to worldly power, were lost amid the temporal translation.

Figure 5.4 Depiction of Mada'in-Ctesiphon in *Aiwan-i Mada'in* (Berlin-Wilmersdorf: Iranschähr, 1343), 40.

The proto-nationalist reading adopted by *Iranshahr* (both the publisher and the journal) has dominated the poem's reception for more than a century. Meanwhile, many other aspects of the Aivan Qasida – in particular its exposure of the corruption of the ruler's body and of the poet as a transcendental prophet who speaks the truth as if from another realm – remain underexplored.

More even than as a result of its own glory, poets including al-Buhturi and Omar Khayyam, and historian-chroniclers including al-Masʿudi and al-Tabari, inscribed the ruins of Anushirvan's palace on Muslim cultural memory both before and after Khaqani set himself to the task.[86] Khaqani's elegy is in many respects continuous with its predecessors. Al-Buhturi anticipated Khaqani when he glorified the 'generals and troops, / as far as the eye can see' in his homage to the ruins.[87] Al-Buhturi had already noted on gazing at the palace and imagining its inhabitants that 'It was built up for joy forever, but / their domain is for commiseration and consolation now.' Khayyam went even further in locating this chain of references within world literature. Along with its intertextual links to the Arabic tradition of urban elegy (*ritha' al-mudun*) and laments on ruins, the Aivan Qasida participates in the global medieval literary genre of the *ubi sunt.* During the Latinate Middle Ages as well as globally, *ubi sunt* poems contrasted the transience of life to the permanence of mortality.[88] Named for their association with the refrain that occurs in poems belonging to this genre – *ubi sunt qui ante nos in mundo fuere*, meaning 'where are they who have gone before us' – *ubi sunt* poems offered much material for reflection on the contingency of creaturely existence.[89] This Latinate genre elaborated a poetics of the mortal body before the bifurcation of the king's two bodies conferred a new prominence on the poet. In their revelation of the speakers' mortality amid a vision of ruins, both the early Arabic and the medieval European *ubi sunt* poems converge with Khaqani's prison poems on the cosmos and the dual Kaʿba.

A quatrain by Khayyam in the *ubi sunt* mode plays on the multivalent meanings of the name of the king Bahram Gur, whose sobriquet (*gur*) alludes to his fondness for hunting the wild ass. More precisely it is the onager (*gur*) whom Bahram Gur hunted, and *gur* in Persian also means 'grave':

> The palace where Bahram raised his cup,
> became a place for lions' rest and foxes' propagation.
> Bahram, who constantly hunted onagers [*gur*],
> today hunted by the grave [*gur*].

آن قصر که بهرام درو جام گرفت
روبه بچه کرد و شیر آرام گرفت
بهرام که گور می‌گرفتی دایم
امروز نگر که گور بهرام گرفت[90]

In the poet's present, the palace where Bahram raised his goblet (*jam*), a symbol of Iranian sovereignty associated with the mythical Iranian ruler Jamshid, has now become a grave for the much-revered king. Khayyam's *ubi sunt* extends across three temporalities: first, the temporality of Bahram's reign, when the Sasanian king excelled in capturing onagers and displaying his sovereign power; second, the intermediate temporality when the palace was reduced to ruins, and became a resting ground for lions and of procreation for foxes; third, the temporality of the poet who gazes on the past as a traveller gazes on a foreign country.

This third temporality has done the poet's work by burying the great king Bahram Gur, slayer of onagers (*gur*), now taken captive by a very different kind of *gur*, a grave. Khayyam's *ubi sunt* is but one of many texts in this genre that relies for its meaning on an interplay of homonyms, a poetic device known in Arabo-Persian rhetoric as *jinas*. The frequent recurrence of this mode of verbal juxtaposition in so many *ubi sunt* poems indicates how the genre's poetics is premised on a linguistic antinomy that is both temporal and spatial.

Even before poets turned their mind to the task of representing the ruins of Ctesiphon, early Muslim orators such as the famous Muʿtazili leader Wasil b. ʿAta' (d. 748) had already engaged with this image to suggest the fleetingness of worldly power. 'Where are the kings,' asked Wasil b. ʿAta', 'who built Mada'in?' He then enumerates their royal deeds: after the kings 'strengthened palaces and fortified gates . . . trained purebred horses . . . and possessed all the lands' the world 'crushed them with its breast' and 'chomped on them with its canines. It gave them in exchange for vast space, narrow confines; for might, humility; for life, perishing.' The kings 'went to reside in graves. Maggots ate them.' Now, the orator says, 'you see only their abodes, and you find only their signposts [*maʿalimahum*] . . . You do not hear a single sound from them.'[91] Typically for the *ubi sunt*, Wasil b. ʿAta' contrasts the king's body, which is subject to physical corruption, to the orator's words, which will outlast the body of the king. His oration on the sovereign's demise resonates with Ferdowsi's declaration during the inauguration of Ardashir (r. 379–383) as the next Sasanian king:

Where are the mighty ones with their throne and crown?
Where are the horsemen elated with victory?
Where are the wise ones?
Where are the proud warriors?
Where are our exalted ancestors?
Where are our valiant servants?
All have dust and brick for their pillows.
Happy are those who didn't sow except the seed of goodness.

کجا آن بزرگان با تاج و تخت
کجا آن سواران پیروزبخت
کجا آن خردمند کندآوران
کجا آن سرافراز و جنگی سران
کجا آن گزیده نیاکان ما
کجا آن دلیران و پاکان ما
همه خاک دارند بالین و خشت
خنک آنک جز تخم نیکی نکشت [92]

As with the Latin genre, Ferdowsi offers a parallel, at the opening of each hemistich, to the *ubi sunt* refrain: *kuja* ('where?'). Ferdowsi deploys anaphora (repetition at the beginning of successive phrases) rather than epistrophe (repetition at the end of successive phrases), but the effect is the same. From the reflections of Wasil b. ʿAta' to al-Buhturi to Khayyam and Ferdowsi, Persian and Arabic poets used ruins to depict the king's corrupted body. They contrasted this physical corruption to poetry, a discourse marked by perpetuity and impermeable to corruption. Uniting the polarities of perpetuity and contingency, the poet's body became the vehicle for this emergent opposition to earthly sovereignty.

Just as the prison poem rearranges space to bring into relief the tension between the power of poetry and the power of kingship, the *ubi sunt* rearranges time. The contrast between the power of the king and the authority of the poet inspired al-Buhturi to insist on the equality of races and peoples, thereby challenging hierarchical discourses of cultural difference, including those that structured Sasanian ideologies of kingship and ʿUmar's Covenant. He declares: 'I find myself thereafter in love with noble / men of every race [*sinkhin*] and origin [*issi*]' (v. 56). Al-Buhturi's oppositional poetics was absorbed into the Persian prison poem. Drawing on centuries of poetry concerned with exile and displacement in Arabic and Persian, Khaqani brought a world literary genre concerned with the poetics of ruins into conversation with the prison poem. The result was the further contestation of the sovereign's legitimacy, the exposure of his corrupted and decaying body, and the revelation of the poet's prophetic authority.

From medieval Europe to the Middle East, the *ubi sunt* is inflected by the 'ever present theme of death' characteristic of global medieval literature, which reaches well beyond any specific national tradition.[93] The Aivan Qasida pays homage to the temporal contrasts intrinsic to the genre when Khaqani asks in v. 13 'What is there to be surprised about [*chi ʿajab dari*]? In the world's garden / the owl follows the nightingale [*bulbul*] just as lament [*awheh*] follows a sweet song [*al han*].' In the poem's second section (vv. 26–35), the focus shifts. Khaqani introduces a political theological dimension to the *ubi sunt*'s revelation of the fleetingness of worldly existence and the eternal repetition of birth and death, anticipating and indeed superseding the genre's later practitioners. Turning to ekphrasis, the poet evokes a panorama of ruins, onto which is projected a tableau comprising images from Iran's past.[94]

Instead of surveying a panorama of ruins, the poet evokes the past. As with his prison poems, the evocation of the past is not done in response to a royal mandate. Instead of chronicling the achievements of Sasanian kings, but in keeping with the prison poem's political theology, Khaqani exposes the king's body as corrupted. Here and elsewhere, the conceptual severance of power and authority follows from the poet's carceral aesthetics. The opening hemistich of the Aivan Qasida further develops the rhetorical shift initiated in his prison poems. Readers are asked to receive an admonition (*ʿibrat*) from the ruins, which is the text of the poem itself, a mirror (*ayineh*) to the passage of time:

Beware, oh my lesson-taking heart, gaze with your eyes, beware!
See the *aivan* of Mada'in (Ctesiphon) as a mirror of lessons.

هان ای دل عبرت بین از دیده نظر کن هان
ایوان مدائن را آیینه‌ی عبرت دان [95]

This verse simultaneously addresses the poet and the regime that determines the horizons of the poet's vocation. This duality of address is a hallmark of the prison poem, which developed its mode of political critique through a poetics of indirection.

We have witnessed this duality of address – and its consequent bifurcation of political and poetic meaning – in the first recorded Persian prison poem, by Masʿud Saʿd addressed to Sultan Ibrahim, concerning the poet's attempted betrayal of his king. As shown in Chapter 2, this quatrain was introduced by ʿAruzi as the inaugural prison poem. While ʿAruzi presented a formal account of the genre in the poetry of Masʿud Saʿd, Falaki of Shirvan, in greater geographic proximity to Khaqani, situated his contribution to the prison poem within an ambiguous duality of address crystallised by the Persian term for admonition, *ʿibrat*. Similarly, in opening the Aivan Qasida, Khaqani instructs himself and his readers to make an *ʿibrat* from the ruins of Ctesiphon. A few decades earlier, Falaki had described his poetic discourse as an *ʿibrat*, counterposed to the ruler's sword:

If I get no respect in your court,
I'll be worthy of no lesson [*ʿibrat*] but the sword.

بار عبرت نمای من تیغ است
گر ازین بار اعتبارم نیست

On the one hand, the poet suggests that his legitimacy as a poet is dependent on respect from the court. On the other hand, he demeans the insignia of courtly legitimacy: the sword. Khaqani and Falaki's intersecting prison poems show how the renunciation of the sovereign's aura of legitimacy is written into the genre.

'Umar's Covenant offered a quasi-legal legitimation for discrimination against religious minorities; the prison poem pioneered a political theology of religious difference. While Khaqani protested the *dhimmi* covenant, the prison poem conferred discursive sovereignty on the poet, by virtue of his imprisoned body and his chains. Dual address – whether through apostrophe, double entendre or other rhetorical devices – offered a range of strategies for achieving the prison poem's contract with the reader, ruler and patron. The concept of *'ibrat* was one of many means through which Persian prison poets developed the genre's political theology.

From the hemistich 'The earth is drunk. It has drunken deep' (v. 26) onwards, the poem's otherworldly idiom becomes inflected by this-worldly critique. This poem, a masterpiece of Khaqani's late style, is less concerned with the fleetingness of time than with the corruption of earthly power, as epitomised by the corrupted corpse of a celebrated Sasanian king. Rather than invoke a generalised human mortality, the poem evokes an earth drunk (*mast*) with the blood of Anushirvan that flows from his son's cup (*kas*). Goblets typically symbolise regal power, but this poem makes them vessels for the king's blood. The image that follows shocks the reader with its double entendre (*iham*) on *pand*, a word meaning counsel and also referring to the bird (specifically a kite), that feeds on carrion:[96]

So many hawks [*pand*] shined on his crown.
Now one hundred precepts [*pand*] are hidden in his brain.

بس پند که بود آنگه بر تاج سرش پیدا
صد پند نوست اکنون در مغز سرش پنهان

Parallelisms (many hawks, one hundred precepts) and contrasts (shining on a crown versus hiding in a brain) make manifest the conlicts embedded in the prison poem. Just as the crown is a metonym for the king's sovereignty, so is his brain a metonym for his corrupted body. This tableau of bodily decay reflects the ruinous state of the Ctesiphon Arch after its conquest by Arab armies.

Khaqani's imagery reveals how power breeds corruption in its most grotesque form: a spectre of birds feasting on the brains of Anushirvan. As indicated in the translation above, *pand* is used both in the sense of counsel and to refer to birds who feast on human flesh. Khaqani's double entendre on *pand* – meaning both royal counsel and the bird that feeds on rotting flesh – calls into question the social order on which medieval kingship is founded. Sacralised across medieval literature, especially in the *qasida*, the king's sacred body is reduced in this late example to rotting carrion. The Aivan Qasida can be read as a challenge in this respect to more than medieval Persian concepts of kingship; broadly it undermines the entire ideological infrastructure of the sovereign's sacralised body, and the ways in which it has shaped global medieval literature.[97]

Following the semiotically exhilarating pun on *pand*, the critique moves even further. The poem's rhetorical question 'where have they gone (*kuja raftand*)?' (v. 30) briefly returns to the *ubi sunt* genre. Unusually, the poet answers his rhetorical question. When the Sasanian king departed, it was not to heaven: the earth's belly, the poet says, is pregnant (*abistan*) with the kings' rotting flesh. The verses that follow are a case study in how, as Walter Benjamin pointed out, genres are most fully realised in the act of their transgression. While the most significant literary works violate existing genre boundaries, every text that transcends its genre continues to be accountable to it. 'A major work either establishes a genre [*Gattung*] or abolishes it,' argued Benjamin. 'A perfect work does both.'[98] As simultaneously an exemplar of the global *ubi sunt* and as this genre's antithesis, written long after the poet's release from prison, the Aivan Qasida seals the prison poem genre by centring its political theology around the poet's prophetic body rather than the sovereign's corrupted body.

'Giving birth [*zayidan*] is difficult,' the poet continues, 'but sowing seed [*nutfeh sitadan*] is easy.' Alongside their destruction of the ideal of the king's sacralised body, these words at once extend the thematic focus of the *ubi sunt*, as exemplified by al-Buhturi, Ferdowsi and Khayyam, and sharpen its political agenda, contrasting it to the sovereign's power. Suddenly, the poet's subject is less the fleetingness of earthly existence than the corruption of the king and poetry's discursive sovereignty. Anushirvan and Hormuz, the deceased kings whose bodies are interred in the earth, perform the masculine labour of sowing seeds (*nutfeh sitadan*), an activity that is here configured as fruitless and weak. While kings who sow their sperm indiscriminately are corrupted by the cycle of decay, the Aivan Qasida aligns poetic creation – and thus the poet – with the feminine work of giving birth.

The poem's fertility imagery recalls the river of sperm in Khaqani's prison poem 6 that 'floods the womb' and 'births a pearl in the sea of me' (6:52). Rather than feed his body to the earth by lusting after worldly glory, Khaqani vows with his verse to generate discursive sovereignty from poetry. Fashioned in the idiom of the medieval *ubi sunt*, the Aivan Qasida's final apostrophe – 'How many tyrants' bodies [*tan-i jabbaran*] has the earth eaten so far?' (v. 34) – signals the apotheosis of a certain kind of literary form. It also reveals the perpetuity of poetry, for the cycle of violence that cannibalises the king's power knows no end. The voracious earth will never be sated (*sir nashud*) by human blood.

Other poets who contributed to the *ubi sunt* genre place a cosmic valuation on the fleetingness of worldly power. Whereas prior (and future) poets would use the genre's refrain (*Ubi sunt qui ante nos in mundo fuere?*) to suggest that nothing on earth is permanent and to present worldly existence as a shadow among shadows, Khaqani offers a counterweight to the sovereign's corrupted body. Inaugurating section three (vv. 36–42) with an apostrophe to himself, the poet instructs himself to learn the lesson (*ʿibrat*) of Anushirvan's court, in the expectation that the balance of power between poet and ruler will be reversed. The hemistich that follows uses a chiasmus to reverse the balance of power between poet and ruler:

> If today the beggar seeks food from the sultan,
> tomorrow the sultan will be seeking food at a rogue's door.

امروز گر از سلطان رندی طلبد توشه
فردا ز در رندی توشه طلبد سلطان

This prophecy of an inversion in the social order is immediately followed by a verse that arguably links the *Gift from Two Iraqs* with the Aivan Qasida, composed much later. The repeated use of the word gift (*tuhfeh*) in the verse below suggests the connection with the *Gift from Two Iraqs* (known as *Tuhfat*):

> Since viaticum from Mecca is a gift [*tuhfeh*] for other cities,
> take this viaticum from Mada'in as a gift [*tuhfeh*], for Shirvan.
>
> گر زاد ره مکه تحفه است به هر شهری
> تو زاد مدائن بر تحفه ز پی شروان [99]

Perhaps more significantly, this verse draws a parallel between the pious pilgrim who brings food from Mecca – translated here as *viaticum*, the Latin term for provisions for those undertaking long journeys – to share as a gift (*tuhfeh*) with the cities he passes through on his journey home, and the poet who shares his poems with the inhabitants of Shirvan. Like the Christian Qasida, the parallel verges on apostasy, since it involves a comparison between the poet who creates poetry on the Ctesiphon Arch and the Prophet (this time Muhammad rather than Jesus), whose activities in the region of Mecca made it into a site of pilgrimage. Khaqani's creation of poetry is analogised to a pilgrimage to Mecca. In the Islamic tradition, pilgrimage to Mecca is considered the highest achievement for a Muslim. In the above-quoted line, poetry creation is equated with that lofty goal. Both acts have purifying effects, that remove the taint of sovereign power.

Khaqani's verses are neither an offering nor an homage. In the best tradition of the prison poem's critique of sovereignty, they are an admonition (*ʿibrat*) to the sultan to follow the path of justice. The above-cited verse from the Aivan Qasida relates pilgrimage to poetry creation, thereby configuring both acts as potential types of political insubordination. Like the pilgrim, the poet's body is suffused with a spirituality that prevails over the carrion-infested and mortal body of the king.

In words that are simultaneously self-effacing and self-aggrandising, Khaqani calls his poem a fragment (*qitʿeh*) – although it is in fact a finished work – while figuring himself as a miracle-worker who wields licit magic (*sihr-i halal*) through his verse:

> Observe in this fragment, how the licit magic [*sihr-i halal*] moves:
> a dead man with the heart of Christ, a madman with a wise mind.

بنگر که در این قطعه چه سحر همی راند
مهتوک مسیحا دل، دیوانه‌ی عاقل خوان

This poem marks the end of the second phase of the prison poem's trajectory: it transmutes political resistance into spiritual authority. Whereas in the Christian Qasida, as in Khaqani's five other prison poems, the poet seeks the patron's material support and the patron requires the poet's eloquence, the Aivan Qasida treats this dependency as obsolete. Born from within the patronage nexus, the prison poem here transcends its political genesis by envisioning a world in which the king's corrupted body cannot compete with poetry's prophetic authority. At the moment of its apotheosis, Khaqani brings about prison poetry's obsolescence, for a ruler cannot imprison a poet whose power exceeds his own.

Having studied prison poetry's appropriation of prophecy, its polemical reworking of ʿUmar's Covenant and, finally, its apotheosis into a poetics of ruins that exposes the corruption of the king's body, we are in a position to conclude our account of Khaqani's role in shaping the prison poem. The Aivan Qasida merges the ethos of the lyric ode introduced in Chapter 2 with the anti-panegyric idiom of the Christian Qasida encountered earlier in this chapter. Analogously, licit magic merges here with the prison poem's Christology. In this late verse, the itinerate poet figures himself as a dead man with the heart of Christ who is uniquely endowed with the ability to speak the truth to power. In the Aivan Qasida's concluding verse, which also gives the date of the poem as 1166 in the form of a chronogram, the poet, driven mad by the king's corruption, suddenly discovers that his own words are a source of prophetic power.

While the Christian Qasida developed the prison poem's political theology by drawing on the discourse of prophecy, the Aivan Qasida developed a poetics of ruins that performed a similar political role by undermining worldly power. Like Khaqani's earlier poems, the Aivan Qasida sets forth a conception of poetry's sovereignty. Poetry is the court from which the sultan must seek the nourishment (*tusheh*) and counsel (*daryuzeh*) of those he is mandated to protect (vv. 37–38). The legitimacy of the sultan's sovereignty depends on his willingness to heed the admonitions of the poets at his court. Political treatises composed in Persian courts, including by ʿAruzi, the first theorist of the prison poem, instructed princes to heed poetry's lessons; here the poet instructs himself to learn from the ruler's flaws. In the world of Khaqani's poems, the poet *always* triumphs. The political theology sustained by his bifurcated body, which belongs to both the spiritual and material realm, prevails over competing forms of power.

The Aivan Qasida rewrites tales of kingly glory, including Persian epics such as the *Shahnama*, in the service of an aesthetics that treats poetry, rather than kingship, as the most exalted form of sovereignty. Khaqani was keenly aware of his dependency on the court. But he also perceived that the path to worldly power was paved with bloodshed and hypocrisy. The poet's twilight vision of a rapacious earth bloated with the blood gushing from the corpses of Sasanian kings exposes the fraught dialectic between the sovereign and the poet that underwrites the prison poem's political theology. Rather than simply turn away from worldly power, the poet critiques the material grandeur of royal kingship, and the splendour of the ruins of the Ctesiphon Arch, through his verse. The sacralised idiom of the sovereign's body is undermined by the image of his carrion-infested corpse, which has neither posterity nor perpetuity. The sultan's corrupted power is replaced with the vatic capacity of poetry, and the poet's prophetic body replaces the king's mortal flesh.

By the end of Khaqani's poem, al-Buhturi's nostalgic *ubi sunt* has been superseded. Al-Buhturi excused the travesties promulgated at the Ctesiphon Arch by invading Arab armies in 637 CE with reference to human fallibility. He shed 'tears of affection for the cycles of history' while turning a blind eye to the destruction wrought by his own people on Persian civilisation.[100] Khaqani by contrast sheds no tears for anyone, including himself and his fellow poets. Notwithstanding the still prevalent nationalist reading of this text, the Aivan Qasida does not weep for the Sasanian kings. Nor does it weep for the poet's self. The Aivan Qasida's poetics of ruins simultaneously celebrates and overcomes the condition of the imprisoned poet.

Over the course of his work and especially through his engagement with the topoi of imprisonment, Khaqani demonstrated poetry's authority over other discourses of power. He turned Masʿud Saʿd's lyric ode into a discourse on poetry-as-prophecy that could challenge the sultan's abuses of power. As a reader conversant with Arabic versions of the Christian gospels, Khaqani would likely have been aware of the statement that Jesus appropriated from the Psalms in establishing his new discursive order: 'The stone that the builders rejected will become the chief cornerstone' (Psalms 118:22; Luke 20:17). When we substitute – as Khaqani did – Jesus' prophetic authority for the poet's vision, we recapitulate the trajectory of the political theology of the prison poem under Khaqani's tutelage.

As he went about crafting his political theology, Khaqani conjured a time-space of the ruin, where poetry prevailed over the power of rulers, jailers and patron. He thereby intervened in a long tradition within world literature of using the temporality of ruins to enhance the power of poetry.[101] From the battlements of the Ctesiphon Arch, rendered through the same toothless mouths and mouthless teeth that spoke from hollowed-out skulls of prison poem 2, Khaqani predicted that rulers who wielded their power without regard for justice and with diminishing claims to its sacred justification would ultimately be judged by poets, acting in the capacity of prophets. 'You are dust,' the poet states from this otherworldly realm, following the destruction of the king's body, 'We are now your earth' (v. 11).

Notes

1. On Khāqānī's innovative style, see Karamī, 'Negāhī be maḍāmīn-i Musawī o zībāīhāyī ān dar dīvān-i Khāqānī', 182, who connects the poet's new design (*ṭarḥī nū*) to his appropriation of the metonyms sovereignty.
2. The most comprehensive account of Khāqānī's life is Kandli's *Khāqāni-ye Shirvānī*. Khanikof's two-part study is still useful as a biographical source ('Mémoire sur Khâcâni, poëte persan du XIIe siècle', *Journal Asiatique* 6(4) (1864): 137–200; 6(5) (1865): 296–367), as is the preface to Karl Zaleman's (alt. sp. Salemann) study of Khāqānī's *rubāʿīyyāt*: *Chetverostishiia Khakani* (St Petersburg: Tipografiia Imperatorskoi akademii nauk, 1875).
3. Michael Whitby, *The Ecclesiastical History of Evagrius Scholasticus* (Liverpool: Liverpool University Press, 2000), xxxiv–xxxviii, esp. xxxv.
4. Whitby, *The Ecclesiastical History of Evagrius Scholasticus*, xxxvi.
5. Muḥammad Muʿīn surveys Nestorian contributions to medieval Arabic civilisation from the vantage point of Khāqānī's poetry in 'Khāqānī o āʾīn-i masīḥ', *Majmūʿah-ʾi maqālāt*, ed. Mahdukht Muʿīn (Tehrān: Mu'assasah-'i Intishārāt-i Muʿīn, 1985), 201–16.
6. Dimitri Gutas, *Greek Thought, Arabic Culture: The Graeco-Arabic Translation*

Movement in Baghdad and Early ʿAbbāsid Society (2nd–4th/8th–10th Centuries) (New York: Routledge, 1998), 131.

7. A. Mingana argues for the year 781–782 in *The Apology of Timothy the Patriarch before the Caliph Mahdi* (Cambridge: W. Heffer, 1928), 11. Hans Putnam argues for 786–794 in *L'Église et l'Islam sous Timothée I (780–823)* (Beirut: Dar el-Machreq, 1975), 185. Although debate took place in Arabic, the earliest written version is in Syriac, from which language it was soon afterwards translated into Arabic.
8. On this translation, see Erica C. D. Hunter, 'Interfaith Dialogues', in Karl Hoheisel and Wassilios Klein (eds), *Der Christliche Orient und seine Umwelt* (Wiesbaden: Harrassowitz, 2007), 291; Gutas, *Greek Thought, Arabic Culture*, 61 and 137. The translation into Arabic was done with the help of an earlier Syriac translation and after consultation with the Christian secretary of the governor of Mosul, Abū Nūḥ.
9. These points are tabulated and discussed in Putnam, *L'Église et l'Islam sous Timothée I*, 189–200.
10. The range of different Muslim traditions covering Jesus' death is discussed in Todd Lawson, *The Crucifixion and The Qur'an: A Study in the History of Muslim Thought* (London: One World, 2009).
11. Minorsky, 'Khāqānī and Andronicus Comnenus', 554.
12. Muhammad Muʿīn, 'Khāqānī o ā'īn i massīh', 33.
13. Khāqānī, *Tuḥfat*, 215–16.
14. Khāqānī, *Dīvān*, 802.
15. Dehkhodā defines *zunnār* first as 'any thread in general [*har rishteh rā gūyand ʿumūmān*]', notes that the word derives from ancient Greek, and only later specifies its meaning in the context of *dhimmī* regulations. Although associated with Christianity, the *zunnār* can signify much more than a Christian affiliation.
16. Lloyd Ridgeon, 'Christianity as Portrayed by Jalal al-Din Rumi', Lloyd Ridgeon (ed.), *Islamic Interpretations of Christianity* (London: Palgrave Macmillan, 2001), 101–2.
17. Major scholarly commentaries that inform my reading of this poem include Mīrza Muḥammad Qazwīnī, 'Qaṣīdeh-i ḥabsiyye-i Khāqānī', in Jamshīd ʿAlī Zādah (ed.), *Sāgharī dar miyān-i sangistān* (Tehran: Nashr-i Markaz, 1999), 185–226; ʿAbd al-Ḥosseīn Zarrīnkūb, *Didār ba kaʿbah-i jān: dar'bārah-'i zindagī, āthār va andīshah-'i Khāqānī* (Tehran: Sukhan, 1378/1999–2000), 70–120; Minorsky, 'Khāqānī and Andronicus Comnenus'; Mīr Jalāl

al-Dīn Kazzāzī, *Sūzan-i ʿĪsā* (Tehran: Dānishgāh-i ʿAllāmeh Ṭabāṭabāyi, 1997); ʿAbbās Māhīyar, *Sharḥ-i mushkilat-i Khāqānī* (Tehran: Jām-i Gul, 1382/2001).

18. Nāṣir-i Khusraw, *Dīvān-i ashʿār-i Ḥakīm-i Nāṣir-i Khusraw Qubādiyānī*, 35.,
19. Masʿūd Saʿd, *Dīvān* 1:97, *qaṣīda* 35, v. 36.
20. Masʿūd Saʿd, *Dīvān* 1:208, *qaṣīda* 95, v. 1.
21. For the scholarly debate around the semantic implications of *akhtar-i dānish* in this context, see Sa'īd Mahdavīfar, '"Akhtar-i dānish" dar shiʿr-i Khāqānī', *Kārnāmeh Mīrās Maktūb* 5(49) (1390/2012–3): 32–6.
22. According to Kazzāzī (*Suzan*, 4), *tarsā* derives from the Pahlavi *tarsāk*, and thus the calque is less from Arabic to Persian as from Middle Persian to Arabic.
23. Muḥammad ʿAlī Mudarris, *Rayḥānatu al-ʿadab* (Tehran: Chāpkhānah-'i Shirkat-i Sihāmī, 1948–1955), 3:110–11. Mudarris' account is disputed in Ẓafarī, *Ḥabsīyyah dar adab-i fārsī*, 85.
24. W. Barthold and C. E. Bosworth, 'Shirwānshah', *EI*². Both the Rawwādid and the Shirvānshahs were originally of Arab descent, although this origin was displaced by Persian by Khāqānī's time.
25. Hādī Ḥasān, *Falakī-i Shirwānī*; also see Sara Ashurbeli, *Gosudarstvo shirvanshakhov: VI–XVI vv* (Baku: ELM, 1983).
26. See Grigol Chakhrukhadze, *Tamariani* (Tbilisi: Tbilisskogo gosudarstvennogo universiteta, 1943) and Ioane Shavt'eli, *Abdul-messiia* (Tbilisi: Zaria Vostoka, 1942).
27. Hādī Ḥasān, 'The Poetry of Muḥammad Falakī', in *Researches in Persian Literature* (Hyderabad: Government Press, 1958), 66–7. This poem is missing from Ṭāhirī Shahāb's edition of Falakī's *divan*.
28. C. E. Bosworth, 'The Concept of Dhimma in Early Islam', in Benjamin Braude and Bernard Lewis (eds), *Christians and Jews in the Ottoman Empire* (New York: Holmes & Meier, 1982), 1:48. For rare examples of scholarship on *dhimmī*s under non-Arab Muslim rule, see O. Turan, 'Les souverains Seldjoukides et leurs sujets non-musulmans', *Studia Islamica* 1 (1953): 65–100; F. W. Hasluck, *Christianity and Islam under the Sultans* (Oxford: Oxford University Press, 1929). Two excellent discussions of Coptic Christians in medieval Islamic are Tamar el-Leithy, 'Coptic Culture and Conversion in Medieval Cairo 1293–1524', PhD dissertation, Princeton University, 2005) and Maryam Shenoda, 'Lamenting Islam: Copto-Arabic Opposition to Islamicization and Arabization in Fatamid Egypt (969–1171 CE)', PhD dissertation, Harvard University, 2010).

29. Maryam Shenoda, 'Displacing Dhimmī, Maintaining Hope', *IJMES* 39 (2007): 589.
30. Geoffrey Khan's seven-part typology of medieval Arabic petitions corresponds in certain respects to the Christian Qasida, suggesting yet another genre affiliation for this text: 1. Invocation; 2. Address; 3. Initial Blessing on addressee; 4. Exposition; 5. Request; 6. Motivation; 7. Final Blessing on addressee (Khan, 'The Historical Development of the Structure of Medieval Arabic Petitions', *BSOAS* 53(1) (1990): 8). ʿUmar's Covenant, the text discussed below that came to dominate representations of *dhimmī* regulations, also fits the structure of a petition.
31. See Y. K. Stillman and N. A. Stillman, *Arab Dress: A Short History: From the Dawn of Islam to Modern Times* (Leiden: Brill, 2000), 101–19.
32. M. Perlman, '*Ghiyār*', *EI*^{2}. More recently on the *ghiyār*, see Luke Yarbrough, 'Origins of the *ghiyār*', *JAOS* 134(1) (2014): 113–21; Milka Levy-Rubin, *Non-Muslims in the Early Islamic Empire: From Surrender to Coexistence* (Cambridge: Cambridge University Press, 2011), 88–98. Like most who have researched this topic, these scholars do not discuss *ghiyār* in the eastern Islamic world, nor do they mention the *zunnār*.
33. Hadas Hirsch, '*Ghiyār*', in Norman A. Stillman (ed.), *Encyclopedia of Jews in the Islamic World* (Leiden: Brill, 2010).
34. Cited in ʿAbd al-Karīm Tawfīq ʿAbbūd, *al-Shiʿr al-ʿArabī fī al-ʿIrāq: min suqūṭ al-Salājiqah ḥattā suqūṭ Baghdād (547–656 H)* (Baghdad: Wizārat al-Iʿlām, 1976), 185.
35. Wilhelm Pape, *Handwörterbuch der griechischen Sprache*^{3}, ed. Maximilian Sengebusch (Braunschweig, F. Vieweg und Sohn, 1884–94), s.v.; Antoine Fattal, *Le statut légal des non-Musulmans en Pays d'Islam* (Beirut: Dar El-Machreq Sari, 1958), 62, n. 101.
36. Ignáz Goldziher, *Muhammedanische Studien* (Halle an der Saale: Max Niemeyer, 1889/1890), 2:34.
37. Albrecht Noth, 'Abgrenzungsprobleme zwischen Muslimen und Nicht Muslimen', *JSAI* 9 (1987): 295.
38. Al-Muttaqī al-Hindī, *Kanz al-ʿummāl,* ed. Ḥ. Razzaq and S. al-Saqqā (Aleppo: Maktabat al-Turāth al-Islāmī, 1969), 4:503.
39. Anton Baumstark, *Geschichte der syrischen Literatur* (Bonn: Marcus Webers Verlag, 1922), 2:312; Georg Graf, *Geschichte der christlichen arabischen Literatur* (Vatican City: Bibliotheca Apostolica Vaticana, 1944–1953), 2:195–6.
40. Fattal, *Le statut légal de non-musulmans en pays d'Islam*, 27.

41. Contrary to the pseudepigraphic covenant, Cahen notes that the prohibitions concerning ringing the church bell and public processions 'were never general in the earlier centuries of Islam' ('Dhimma', *EI*²).
42. Abī ʿAbd Allāh Muḥammad ibn Idrīs al-Shāfiʿī, *Kitāb al-ʿUmm* (Cairo: al-Maṭbaʿah Kubrā, 1903–1907), 4:118; emphasis added. I have drawn on, but in many instances modified, the translation in A. S. Tritton, *The Caliphs and their non-Muslim Subjects: A Critical Study of the Covenant of ʿUmar* (London: Frank Cass, 1930), 6–8.
43. Mark Cohen, 'What Was the Pact of ʿUmar? A Literary-Historical Study', *JSAI* 23 (1999): 119.
44. Tritton, *The Caliphs and Their Non-Muslim Subjects*, 12.
45. Aḥmad ibn Muḥammad al-Khallāl, *Aḥkām ahl al-milal min al-jāmiʿ li-masāʾil al-Īmām Aḥmad ibn Ḥanbal* (Beirut: Dār al-Kutub al-ʿIlmīyah, 1994), 357–59; Ibn Qudāma, *Al-Mughnī*, ed. Muḥammad Rashīd Riḍā (n.p., 1367/1947–48), 10:606–7. Prior to these legal texts, the pact is included in Abū Yūsuf's (d. 798) *Kitāb al-Kharāj* (Cairo: al-Maṭbaʿah al-Salafiyah wa-Maktabatuhā), one of the first texts to ascribe *dhimmī* regulations to ʿUmar b. al-Khaṭṭāb (72 ff). Because these texts lack 'the distinctive literary frame of the pact proper', Mark Cohen insists, they do not constitute 'a true version of the pact' ('What Was the Pact of ʿUmar?' 104).
46. For *madhāhib* arrangements in the medieval Caucasus, see A. K. Alikberov, *Epokha klassicheskogo islama na Kavkaze* (Moscow: RAN, 2003).
47. I first introduced these connections in Rebecca Ruth Gould, 'Wearing the Belt of Oppression: Khāqānī's Christian Qaṣīda and the Prison Poetry of Medieval Shirvān', *JPS* 9(1) (2016): 19–44.
48. Noth, 'Abgrenzungsprobleme zwischen Muslimen und Nicht Muslimen', 303.
49. Ibn al-Athīr, *Al-Kāmil fi al-Tārīkh*, ed. Moḥammad ʿAbd al-Salām Tadmorī (Cairo: Dār al-Kitāb al-ʿArabi, 1997), 6:126–7.
50. Bernard Lewis, *Jews of Islam* (Princeton, NJ: Princeton University Press, 1984), 49. According to J. M. Fiey (*Chretiens syriaques sous les Abbassides: 749–1258* (Louvain: Corpus Scriptorum Christianorum Orientalium, 1980), 93–4), Christian sources connect al-Mutawakkil's reported persecutions to the removal from office of the caliph's Christian court doctor, Buktīshūʿ.
51. *Mujmal al-Tawārīkh wa al-Qaṣṣas* [*c*. 1126], ed. Malik al-Shuʿarāʾ Bahār (Tehran: Chāpkhāneh-yi Khāvar, 1318/1939), 361.
52. Majid Khadduri, *War and Peace in the Law of Islam* (Baltimore, MD: Johns Hopkins University Press, 1955), 193–4; Claude Cahen, 'Dhimma', *EI*²,

2:228, column 2; Turan, 'Les souverains Seldjoukides et leurs sujets non-musulmans', 65–100.

53. Abū Yūsuf, *Kitāb al-Kharāj*, 122.
54. Hellmut Ritter, 'Philologika. XV. Farīduddīn ʿAṭṭār. III', *Oriens*, 12(1/2) (1959): 19, 31, 34, 49, 64, 66.
55. University Library Cambridge, TS6J7 f 3, recto 1, 18 verso, II, 1–3, ed. in S. D. Goitein, 'Mikhtav el ha – Rambam be-ʿInyanê Heqdashōt v-Idyōt ʿal ṣaʿṣaʿāv ha-Negīdīm', *Tarbiz* 34 (1962): 241. Cited in Stillman and Stillman, *Arab Dress*, 110.
56. Masʿūd Saʿd, *Dīvān* 1:97, *qaṣīda* 35, v. 36; also see 1:208, *qaṣīda* 95, v. 1.
57. This story is retold by the Persian poet ʿAṭṭār in his *Conference of the Birds* (*Manṭiq al-Ṭayr*, 1177), in which context the Muslim shaykh Khaqani refers to as Pūr Saqā is called Sanʿān.
58. Murtaẓā al-Husaynī al-Zabīdī, *Tāj al-ʿArūs*, cited in Zarrīnkūb, *Didār ba kaʿbah-i jān*, 94.
59. Abū ʿUbaydah Maʿmar ibn al-Muthanná al-Taymī al-Baṣrī, *Kitāb al-Naqāʾiḍ: naqāʾiḍ Jarīr wa-al-Farazdaq* (Beirut: Dār al-Kutub al-ʿIlmīyah, 1998), 208.
60. See, for example, Bertold Spuler, 'The Disintegration of the Caliphate in the East', in P. M. Holt, Ann K. S. Lambton and Bernard Lewis (eds), *The Cambridge History of Islam: IA* (Cambridge: Cambridge University Press, 1970), 144.
61. Claude Cahen, 'Ḍhimma', *EI*², 2:228, column 1. While Cahen maintains that 'nothing in mediaeval Islam which could specifically be called anti-semitism' (229, column 2), Goitein argues that 'scrutiny of the Geniza material has proved the existence of "anti-Semitism" . . . but it appears to have been local and sporadic, rather than general and endemic' (S. D. Goitein, *A Mediterranean Society: The Jewish Communities of the Arab World as Portrayed in the Documents of the Cairo Geniza* (Berkeley: University of California Press, 1971), 2:283).
62. Muḥammad Iqbāl, *Kulliyāt-i ashʿār-i fārsī-yi Mawlānā Iqbāl Lāhorī*, ed. Aḥmad-i Sorūsh (Tehran: Kitābkhān-yi Sana'i, 1343), 48. This verse originally occurs in Iqbāl's *Asrār-i khūdī* (*Secrets of the Self*, 1915).
63. For Amir Khusraw's contribution to Indo-Persian syncretism see Khan, *Some Important Persian Prose Writings*, 46.
64. *Bâburnâma* (Cambridge, MA: Department of Near Eastern Languages and Civilizations, Harvard University, 1993), 3:380 (translation of Wheeler Thackston, slightly modified).

65. Mas'ūd Sa'd, *Dīvān*, 1:473, *qaṣīda* 189, v. 28.
66. Text translated in Goitein, *A Mediterranean Society*, 2:287.
67. Northrop Frye, *Anatomy of Criticism* (Princeton, NJ: Princeton University Press, 1957), 297.
68. Sharma, *Persian Poetry at the Indian Frontier*, 65, n. 70 and 118.
69. Jaroslav Stetkevych, *The Hunt in Arabic Poetry: From Heroic to Lyric to Metapoetic* (Notre Dame: University of Notre Dame Press, 2016), 131.
70. *The Rambler*, May 28, 1751, No. 125, *The Works of Samuel Johnson* (Oxford: Talboys & Wheeler, 1824), 3:93.
71. Vaṭvāṭ, *Ḥadā'iq al-siḥr*, 83.
72. The poem is called in Persian *Aivān-i Madā'in* after the Arabic name for Ctesiphon. 'Aivan Qasida' is used here for the sake of English readers.
73. See Vil'chevskii, 'Khronogrammy Khakani'.
74. Edward Said, *On Late Style: Music and Literature Against the Grain* (New York: Knopf, 2008), 148.
75. Scott John McDonough, 'Power by Negotiation', PhD dissertation, University of California Los Angeles, 2005, 3.
76. Mīr 'Abd al-Laṭīf Khan Shūshtarī, *Tuḥfah al-'ālam va zayl al-tuḥfa* [*c.* 1799], ed. S. Muvaḥid (Tehran: Ṭahūrī, 1984), 76–81. For discussions of Shūshtarī and other Qajar-era travellers, see Abbas Amanat, 'Through the Persian Eye: Anglophilia and Anglophobia in Modern Iranian History', in Abbas Amanat and Farzin Vejdani (eds), *Iran Facing Others: Identity Boundaries in a Historical Perspective* (New York: Palgrave, 2011), 136–7, and Mana Kia, *Persianate Selves: Memories of Place and Origin Before Nationalism* (Stanford: Stanford University Press, 2020), 73–5.
77. V. Minorsky, 'Geographical Factors in Persian Art', *BSOAS* 9(3) (1938): 624.
78. Edward Gibbon, *The History of the Decline and Fall of the Roman Empire* (Philadelphia. PA: B. F. French, 1830), 4: 78.
79. *Aivān-i Madā'in: tasdīs-i qaṣīda-i Khāqānī, bi qalam-i chand nafar az fuḍalā' wa shu'arā'-i Īrān=Aïwan-i-Medâin: un poème de Khâgâni (1606), adapté et augmanté par quelques poêtes contemporains* (Berlin-Wilmersdorf: Iranschähr, 1343), 45–64.
80. *Medayin haraberleri* (Istanbul: Cem'i Kütüphanesi, 1330/1912); the text is unpaginated, but it is 6–19 of the version available at http://hdl.handle.net/2027/uc1.l0104594429; translated into Persian in *Aiwān-i Madā'in*, 33–44.

81. Edward G. Browne, *A History of Persian Literature under Tartar Dominion* (Cambridge: Cambridge University Press, 1920), 375.
82. Not all editions of this book are illustrated, but the one I accessed in the Columbia University Libraries and from which Figure 5.3 is taken, is.
83. *Aivān-i Madā'in*, 4.
84. *Aivān-i Madā'in*, 11.
85. ʿAbd al-Rahīm Hindī and Mīrzā Ismāʿīl Aṣaf, 'Dū shāhkār-i ṣinʿat', *Irānshāhr* 2(3) (1925): 282–92.
86. Persian and Arabic poets elegies on Madā'in are cited in Sayyid Aḥmad Pārsā, 'Dirangī bar Īwān-i Madā'in-i Khāqānī', *MDAT* 41(54/5) (1385): 5–18. For comparisons of Buḥturī and Khāqānī's poems on Madā'in, see Amīr Maḥmūd Anvār, *Aiwān-i Madā'in* (Tehran: Dānishgāh-i Tehrān, 1383/2004); Jerome W. Clinton, 'The *Madā'en Qaṣida* of Xāqāni Sharvāni, II: Xāqāni and al-Buhturī', *Edebiyât* 2(1) (1977): 191–206.
87. *Dīwān al-Buḥturī*, ed. Ḥasan Kāmil Ṣayrafī (Cairo: Dār al-Maʿārif, 1963), 2:1152–62. On al-Buḥturī's sympathetic representation of the Sāsānians, see Samer M. Ali, 'Reinterpreting Al-Buḥturī's Īwān Kisrā Ode', *JAL* 37(2) (2006): 58.
88. For links with Arabic literature, see Muhjah Amīn Bāshā, *Rithā' al-mudun wa-al-mamālik fī al-shiʿr al-Andalusī: ittijāhātuh, khaṣā'iṣuhu al-fannīyah: dirāsa* (Damascus: Shirāʿ lil-Dirāsāt wa-al-Nashr wa-al-Tawzīʿ, 2003); Ibrahim Musa Al-Sinjilawi, *The 'atlal-nasib in Early Arabic Poetry: A Study of the Development of the Elegiac Genre in Classical Arabic Poetry* (Irbid, Jordan: Yarmouk University Publication, Deanship of Research and Graduate Studies, 1999). For a comparable, if under-theorised, Persian genre, see Maḥmūd Haydarī and Fātemeh Taqīzadeh, 'Marsiya-yi shahr dar shiʿrī fārsī va ʿarabī', *Majalleh-yi būstān-i adab dānishgāhi Shirāz* 14 (1391): 22–42.
89. The most comprehensive study is Mary Ellen Becker, 'The Ubi Sunt: Form, Theme, and Tradition', PhD dissertation, Arizona State University, 1981. For the Arabic *ubi sunt*, see Carl Becker, '*Ubi sunt qui ante nos in mundo fuere*', in *Aufsätze zur Kultur- und Sprachgeschichte vornehmlich des Orients* (Breslau: Marcus, 1916), 87–105.
90. *Tarānehayi Khayyām*, ed. Ṣādeq Hedāyat (Tehrān: Jāvīdān, 1352), 71, *rubāʿī* 74.
91. Aḥmad Zakī Ṣafwat, *Jamharat khuṭab al-ʿarab fī l-ʿuṣūr al-ʿarabiyya al-zāhira* (Beirut: Dar al-Matbuʿat al-ʿArabiyah, 1933), 2:501–3, No. 475 (following, with minor modifications, the translation of Tahera Qutbuddin, 'Khutba:

The Evolution of Early Arabic Oration', in Beatrice Gruendler and Michael Cooperson (eds), *Classical Arabic Humanities in Their Own Terms: Festschrift for Wolfhart Heinrichs* (Leiden: Brill, 2008), 267).

92. *Shāhnāma*, eds Djalal Khaleghi-Motlagh and Mahmoud Omidsalar (New York: Bibliotheca Persica, 2005), 6:230.
93. J. Huizinga, *The Waning of the Middle Ages* (Garden City: Anchor-Doubleday, 1954), 139.
94. As Clinton notes, most readings of Khāqānī's Aivan Qasida end here, neglecting the exposure of the sovereign's corrupted body that transpires over the rest of the poem. For another example of how the Aivan Qasida is treated in modern Iranian historiography as a proto-nationalist appeal to lost Sāsānian glory, see Mehdī Ma'khūzī, *Ātash andar chang* (Tehran: Sukhan, 1388).
95. Khāqānī, *Dīvān*, 358.
96. The *īhām* on pand is noted by Julie Scott Meisami in her insightful annotations to her translation of this poem, 'Poetic Microcosms: The Persian Qasida to the End of the Twelfth Century', in Stefan Sperl and Christopher Shackle (eds), *Qasida Poetry in Islamic Asia and Africa* (Leiden: Brill, 1996), 1: 137–82.
97. See Azfar Moin, *The Millennial Sovereign: Sacred Kingship and Sainthood in Islam* (New York: Columbia University Press, 2012), for this concept in a Persianate context.
98. Benjamin, *Ursprung des deutschen Trauerspiels*, 27.
99. Khāqānī, *Dīvān*, 360, following here the variant offered by Sajjadi: تحفه instead of توشه in the first *miṣrā'*.
100. 'Tears of affection' features as a leitmotif in Ali, 'Reinterpreting Al-Buḥturī's Īwān Kisrā Ode', 46–67.
101. See Andrew Hui, *The Poetics of Ruins in Renaissance Literature* (New York: Fordham University Press, 2017); Anne F. Janowitz, *England's Ruins: Poetic Purpose and the National Landscape* (London: Blackwell, 1990); Leo Mellor, *Reading the Ruins: Modernism, Bombsites and British Culture* (Cambridge: Cambridge University Press, 2011).

6

The Sovereign and the Poet's Body

Sovereignty entails the ability not only to issue laws, but also to enforce obedience to them.[1] Authority is the key to such obedience: it makes power efficacious, giving it elasticity and the capacity to govern. If, to paraphrase postcolonial theorist Ranajit Guha, power is dominance without hegemony, authority is what makes power hegemonic.[2] Raw power needs authority in order to govern with legitimacy. When legitimacy is added to power, the result is sovereignty. Yet scholars of non-European and non-modern cultures have challenged modern conflations of power and authority. In this concluding chapter, I reconsider the relations between these two concepts in order to arrive at a better understanding of the prison poem's political theology.

In his study of popular sovereignty in the modern Islamic world, Andrew March argues that 'to the extent that we can speak about sovereignty in premodern Islamic theory and practice, it was largely a matter of a kind of power sharing between various elites or experts' rather than the exclusive possession of the ruling regime.[3] In accounting for the development and circulation of premodern South Asian literatures, Sheldon Pollock develops a concept of 'power without a center' to describe what he terms the 'Sanskrit cosmopolis'.[4] For Pollock, 'Sanskrit cosmopolitanism was not about absorbing the periphery into the center but turning the periphery itself into a center.'[5] By way of demonstrating the process through which Sanskrit culture circulated non-coercively, Pollock argues that 'Sanskrit cosmopolitanism duplicated locations everywhere; it was a world of all centers and no circumferences.'[6]

Meanwhile, anthropologists of Africa have argued that power and authority are fundamentally opposed to each other. As Skalnik explains on the basis of his fieldwork in Ghana, 'power means that decisions are taken on behalf of the whole society by specific state agencies that rely on the state's monopoly of organised violence. Authority, in contrast, is legitimate without the backing of power, and is voluntarily recognised by all people.'[7] Writing on the basis of his fieldwork among the Guayaki in Paraguay, anthropologist Pierre Clastres describes what he considers to be 'stateless societies' that organise themselves in the absence of centralised power, and without relying on coercion.[8] These accounts of premodern and non-European societies collectively demonstrate the inadequacy of theories of governance that focus exclusively on the state. Their shared critique of the modern tendency to overvalue the role of the state highlights the need for a political theology of poetry's power.

Although based on entirely different and incommensurable material from worlds distant from the prison poem, these examples outline ways of delineating the relationship between power and authority that contest their treatment in much of contemporary social theory. Collectively, they conceptualise authority as more than the instrument or handmaiden of power. They also indicate authority's potential to undermine the power of the ruling regime. This chapter develops this conception of authority as the subversion of the sovereign's power by situating prison poetry within the political theory that accompanied the genre's genesis and shaped its reception across Ghaznavid and Saljuq domains, from South Asia to the Caucasus. Having focused in Chapter 1 on the prison poem within the Persian genre system, in Chapter 2 on the prison poem as a nascent lyric ode, in Chapter 3 on prison poets' conflictual relations, in Chapter 4 on the poet's prophetic body, and in Chapter 5 on the imprisoned poet's body clothed in the garments of persecution, this final chapter focuses on the poet's sovereign body, and its reconfiguration in specific contrast to the decaying body of the sovereign.

From Caliph to Sovereign (Padishah)

'It was in response to the discrepancy between the ideal and the real in the Islamic state,' writes Fawzi Najjar of medieval Islamic political theory, 'that the jurists developed their constitutional theories, articulating a model of the *siyasa shar'iyya,* which reflected the form, if not the substance, of the ideal community.'[9] Measured against this bifurcation between the ideal and the real, Baber Johansen's assertion that the twelfth century marks the moment when Islamic legal theorists first began to use *siyasat*, the Islamic term for governance, as a synonym for discretionary punishment (*ta'zir*), elucidates the political theology of Persian prison poetry, in particular the paradox of the genre's rapid and geographically expansive dissemination.[10] This chapter examines the relation between twelfth-century Persian political theory's articulation of discretionary power and the discursive elevation of the poet as prophet in these same texts.

Najjar demonstrated that *siyasa* was refashioned during the eleventh and twelfth centuries to address what Spuler calls the 'disintegration' of caliphal power, whereby the caliph functioned less as a locus of power than as a sign of imperial decay.[11] The ways in which these political transformations were registered aesthetically, in poetry, has yet to be taken up in sustained fashion. Recognising that politics (*siyasa*) became more closely associated with punishment (*ta'zir*) during the twelfth century, this chapter examines the implications of this development for the prison poem's transmutation of imprisonment into literary form.

The caliphal system was premised on the ruler having the direct imprimatur of God, as well as a link to the first four caliphs of Islam, known as the Rashidun.[12] To prevent the interruption of caliphal continuity from undermining the entire system of Islamic governance, a political ethic based on secular power (*siyasa*) was developed, and the vacuum of authority generated by a declining caliphate was filled by a form of power that lacked divine imprimatur. In response to this shift in authority and the increased use of discretionary punishment, the prison poem brought into relief the gap between the theorisation of sovereignty (in mirrors-for-princes works such as 'Aruzi's *Four Discourses*) and its practical implementation.

As a result of the distance between the office of the sovereign and the caliphate, political life under the Ghaznavids and Saljuqs was increasingly alienated from Islamic concepts of justice. Multiple scholars have referred to the 'succession crisis' that marks the advent of both the Ghaznavid and Saljuq regimes. The efforts of these dynasties to maintain their power, and to legitimate their modes of punishment, came under ever-greater scrutiny while prison poems proliferated across the eastern Islamic world.[13] Although Ghaznavid, Saljuq and Shirvanshah sovereigns were haunted by the need to claim the mantel of divine legitimacy, their claims were increasingly difficult to sustain in light of their reliance on discretionary punishment. From within these conditions, and as a means of shifting authority from the sultan to the poet, the prison poem was born.

Drawing on the scholarship of H. K. Sherwani, Aziz al-Azmeh and Omid Safi, each of whom has, together with Najjar and Johansen, illuminated medieval Islamic political theory's conceptualisations of sovereignty, this chapter studies two Persian political treatises that were composed in the same milieu that fostered the prison poem. The first text, known as *Conduct of Kings* (*Siyyar al-muluk*) or, alternately, as the *Book of Governance* (*Siyasatnama*), is the first political treatise in New Persian.[14] Composed in the late eleventh century, this work has been subjected to extensive debate concerning its authorship.[15] It has recently been suggested that part of this work was composed by Muʿizzi (1028–1125), one of the most important panegyric poets of the eleventh and twelfth centuries.[16] The second work, ʿAruzi's *Four Discourses*, was discussed in Chapter 1 for its reflections on the power of literary form and in Chapter 2 as the first work to critically reflect on the prison poem. *Four Discourses* is examined here in tandem with *Conduct of Kings* as a work that mediates between worldly power and discursive authority while situating the prison poem within the social–political landscape of twelfth-century eastern Islamic sultanates.

Discursive Authority and Worldly Power

The Saljuqs were to western Asia what the Ghaznavids were to the eastern Islamic world: a political force that introduced a mode of governance that was to undo the forms of governance crafted in the preceding centuries by the Abbasids and Buyids. In tracking the transformation of these changing political structures, scholars such as Sherwani emphasise the actions of Alp Arslan (r. 1063–1072), a Saljuq ruler who astonished his contemporaries through his conquests of Armenia and Georgia and his victory over Byzantine forces at the battle of Melazgird (Manzikert) in 1071.[17] The driving force behind the Saljuq (and Shirvanshah) separation of worldly power from discursive authority is Alp Arslan's son Malikshah (r. 1074–1092), at the request of whom *Conduct of Kings* was written. Malikshah is described by British historian Edward Gibbon as a 'barbarian' who 'by his personal merit, and the extent of his empire, was the greatest prince of his age'.[18]

After completing a work in thirty-nine chapters on the conduct of kings for Malikshah, Nizam al-Mulk embarked on a journey to Baghdad. He entrusted the manuscript of his work to a scribe named Muhummad Meghrebi. Nizam al-Mulk ended up being assassinated during his journey, and it was left to the scribe to present this text to the world. The extant text of *Conduct of Kings* includes chapters that appear to have been added later, in part because they refer to Malekshah's son Ghiyath al-Din rather than to Malekshah as sovereign. Ghiyath al-Din Muhammad b. Malikshah (r. 1104–1117) was stepbrother of Barkiyaruq (r. 1094–1104), whom he succeeded after the latter's death. This same Ghiyath al-Din was the addressee of al-Ghazali's manual *Molten Gold* (*Tibr al-masbuk*, also known as *Nasihat al-muluk*, and dated between 1105 and 1111), a work in the tradition of Persian ethics (*akhlaq*).[19]

Scholars have long debated the possible authorship of these later chapters. As noted above, Khismatulin has proposed, based on textological analysis, that Meghrebi is in fact the court poet Muʿizzi, and that he fabricated the entirety of *Conduct of Kings* for his own purposes. The vast majority of Muʿizzi's output is devoted to panegyrics praising Alp Arslan, Malikshah and Sanjar.[20] Muʿizzi additionally wrote a small number of *qasida*s addressed to Malikshah's vizier Nizam al-Mulk, and one memorable elegy addressed to Masʿud Saʿd, discussed below. According to Khismatulin, Muʿizzi did not intend to conceal his identity; he signed his actual name on the manuscript, but it was transcribed by a copyist as Maghrebi (meaning 'Westerner').[21] As a result of this scribal error, Muʿizzi's contribution to the work was erased from the historical record, argues Khismatulin. Iranian scholars who have contested Khismatulin's argument nonetheless accept that certain parts of *Conduct of Kings* (specifically chapters 40–47) were written by someone other than Nizam al-Mulk.[22] Khismatulin's argument is controversial, but Nizam al-Mulk's authorship for parts of *Conduct of Kings* has been disputed by scholars for decades.[23] Whatever its authorial genesis, the text is a rich source for insights into the relation between poetry and power during the period of the prison poem's genesis. Since this debate is unlikely to be resolved in the near future, the analysis that follows refers to an anonymous author using the generic third person; while this third person was likely Nizam al-Mulk in many instances, it is also possible that it was not him in all instances.

Conduct of Kings differs from the canonical Arabic text that, by many accounts, marks the apex of its genre – al-Mawardi's *Precepts of Sovereignty* (*Ahkam al-Sultaniyya*, 1030) – in at least one crucial respect: whereas al-Mawardi invokes no patron, *Conduct of Kings* is written explicitly in response to a patron's request. In beginning and ending with praise for the ruler – variously termed padishah, sultan, *malik* and *khodawand* – the Persian text is inflected by patronage with an intensity unmatched by al-Mawardi. This has implications for its political theology. The author begins by conflating the orders of the padishah with his deepest desires, and declares his readiness to make them his own. 'These chapters [*fasl'-ha*] are written according to the desires of my heart,' we read, 'There is nothing to add. I will make these writings my own, and act on that basis.'[24] As might be expected from a writer at the Saljuq court, this statement suggests support for the sultanate mode of governance. By conjoining the terms *saltanat*, *siyasat* and *ta'zir* the author consolidates the sultan's power.

The author appears to accept without reservation the ascription of the title sultan to his patron, an ascription that the caliph al-Mustazhir (r. 1094–1118) was at that time contesting. Moreover, the poet elevates *padishahi* – the most common Persian term for sovereignty in texts ranging from *Qabusnama* (1082) to *Four Discourses* (1155) – into a concept of the divine right of kingship that reaches back to pre-Islamic Persian and ancient Mesopotamian concepts of governance.[25] Indeed, the foreword, epilogue, the concluding *qasida* and many of the text's chapters attest to a concept of political sovereignty unlike any found in the normative writings of the jurists (typically called *ahkam*).

Let us begin by considering the language of chapter (*fasl*) one, which opens by asking for the ruler of the world [*khudawand-i 'alam*] to be blessed in the afterlife (5). Khismatulin suggests that the elated tone of this section was stimulated by the recent ascension of Ghiyath al-Din to the throne and his recognition by the Baghdad caliph as the head of the Saljuq Empire.[26] Elated by this victory, the author conflates *padishah* and *sultan* and invokes the ruler's suppression of rebellion in terms more strident than any yet seen in the genre of legal precepts (*ahkam*). 'In every age,' we read, 'glorious God appoints someone from among creation and endows him with the attributes of grace and sovereignty [*padishahani*]. [God] entrusts this person with the world's welfare [*masalih-i jahan*] and with ensuring the tranquillity of God's servants.'[27]

Most important among the ruler's responsibilities is the task of guarding against corruption (*fasad*), insurgency (*ashub*) and rebellion (*fitneh*). Throughout the history of Islamic political thought, this triad of concepts – corruption, insurgency and especially rebellion – have been seen to present the deepest challenge to the stability of Islamic states. The most effective means of keeping the peace has been by vesting in God's chosen representative the ability to evoke awe (*haybat*) and majesty (*hishmat*). The political theology of *Conduct of Kings* assumes that the best way to prevent *fitna* is to propagate fear. A further injunction follows to resort to whatever means necessary to suppress potential rebels. Anyone who rebels against the ruler of the world will face *'uqubat*, a term ranging in meaning from torture to authorised punishment. As for those who are insufficiently obedient to the ruler's commands, God will inflict on them the punishment (*'uqubat*) that is *shari'a*'s recompense.[28]

Failing political regimes, the text continues, are marked by the withdrawal of beneficent sovereignty (*padishahi-yi nik*), the pursuit of war through the drawing of swords and the shedding of blood, and the temporary victory of raw power. Such violence is treated in this text as a purification ritual necessary to re-establish justice. A fascinating analogy is proposed: a forest fire's conflagration spreads through contact and burns everything moist, due to its proximity to what is dry. During a rebellion, death spreads like this fire, causing the guilty (*gunahkaran*) to die. Far from requiring ethical justification, political suffering is inflicted through an arbitrary system that fosters guilt by association. Politics is divorced from ethics through the same process by which discretionary power (*saltanat*) comes to replace sacred kingship (*khalafat*).

A political catastrophe facilitates the rise to prominence of an individual whom God has chosen to rule the Islamic world. Laconically referred to as 'the one' (*yiki*, 6). God has granted this individual singular powers of discernment (*'aql*) and erudition (*'ilm*) – a stipulation that incidentally jars against what is known regarding the illiteracy that prevailed at the highest levels of the Saljuq dynasty.[29] The ascription of learning to a ruler reputed for illiteracy shows how the author – whether Mu'izzi or someone else – used the panegyric idiom to inscribe his actual sovereign in the image of a learned author, perhaps a poet. Relying on his discernment and erudition, this chosen individual selects ministers and functionaries within his administration to help the worldly ruler conduct the spiritual (*dini*) and worldly (*dunyavi*) affairs of the state.

The stipulations that follow concerning the ideal sovereign jar against the normative strictures of legal precepts. Not only does the padishah – as the text most commonly refers to the sovereign – possess God-given powers of discernment (*ʿaql*) and erudition (*ʿilm*); he also possesses sacred powers that al-Mawardi's *imam* lacks. The padishah's uniqueness is indicated through a series of comparisons linking kingship to various synecdoches for light – including fire (*atash*) and a candle (*shamʿ*) – and the capacity for giving light. The first analogy to a rebellion that spreads death like fire has already been introduced. The majority of the comparisons between sovereignty and light are reserved for the final paragraphs of this discourse on power. The patron is informed that the ministers who serve in his administration dwell in the shadow of the king's justice (*sayeh-i ʿadl*). Repeating a phrase that also occurs in a parallel section on power in *Qabusnama*, the author asserts that deserving ministers in his administration will awaken from the 'sleep of ignorance' (*khwab-i ghaflat*, 6). Otherwise they will merit punishment commensurate with their crimes (*be miqdar-i jurm-i ishan*).

According to what authority is this punishment adjudicated? Ancient associations between light, justice, divinity and power in Persian culture shed light on this question. The key locus is the Old Persian *farrah* (*farnah*; Avestan *khwarenah*), which entered New Persian as *farr*. *Farr* figures heavily in, among other New Persian texts, Ferdowsi's *Shahnama*. As with all medieval Persian appropriations of ancient Persian culture, pre-Islamic Persian religious systems are reformulated for contemporary purposes. Typically of medieval literature, the recounting of pre-Islamic stories is characterised by a certain vagueness. Yet there is striking continuity between the multiple semantic equations between sovereignty and light in this text and *farrah* in its original meaning, even as scholars have emphasised the break between Sasanian concepts of kingship and medieval Persian political ideals.[30] The latter has been glossed as divine fortune, cosmic munificence, fame and glory, and, finally, as the 'luminous nimbus surrounding the heads of heroes, especially kings'.[31]

As early as the *Avesta* (committed to writing circa 500 CE), *farrah* was regarded as an 'indispensable qualification for kingship'.[32] Five kinds of fire are distinguished in the *Avesta* and later commentaries: the fire of the temple, which is used daily; the fire in human bodies and animals; the fire in plants; the fire in clouds' and the fire that burns in paradise in front of the Zoroastrian God, Ahura Mazda. As Christensen explains in his classic account of the Sasanian social order, this last type of fire is equivalent to *farrah*, 'la Gloire qui accompagne les rois aryens légitimes'.[33]

While the literal sense of *farr* as a luminous nimbus is lost in *Conduct of Kings*, traces of the concept linger in the remarkable genealogy for the Saljuq sultan, which derives from the lineage of the Turanian king Afrasiyab, as narrated in the *Shahnama*, as well as in a host of earlier, no longer extant, Pahlavi texts. As one of the earliest such presentations on record, this genealogy marks a moment in the history of Islamicate political thought when the caliph's sovereign body was split. Henceforth, a form of bifurcated sovereignty – with power and authority maximally divided against each other – would stimulate the development of the prison poem. Testifying to its severance from authority and its dependence on emergent technologies of power, the new mode of Saljuq governance was attended by systems of 'surveillance and reconnaissance'.[34] While surveillance was still in its infancy under the Ghaznavids, by the time Shirvanshah domains became incorporated into the Saljuq Empire, the carceral system was fully in effect, as reflected in the literary output of the prison poets of Shirvan.

In *Conduct of Kings*, the caliph exists only as a relic from the past. When the caliph (*khalifa*) is explicitly contrasted to the sovereign (*padishah*) and his dominion (*mulk*), it is to an institution evoking an era before Islam was infrastructurally absorbed by the state. By the time *Conduct of Kings* was written, the caliphate had long been reduced to a purely symbolic institution, lacking political authority. With this text, as under Ghaznavid and Saljuq rule generally, power was separated from the divinely sanctioned authority bestowed on the caliph via the Prophet (Q. 38:26). Buyids, Saljuq and Ghaznavids all ruled amid tenuous claims to authority. Even under Abbasid rule 'caliphal authority was . . . the product of an evolving historical relationship between center and periphery, between the existence of authority and the exercise of power'.[35] Whereas, under the early Abbasids, the caliph combined power and authority in himself, Ghaznavid and Saljuq transformations in the practice of governance and the conceptualisation of sovereignty turned the body of the king into a vehicle for discretionary power. Ebrahim Moosa uses a bodily metaphor to render the delicate entelechy entailed in the concept of the caliph: 'Just as the sovereignty of an earthly monarch requires the optimum functioning of all organs of government to secure justice and order, similarly, all the bodily organs must be disciplined so that the monarch of the body, namely, the spirit, may reign supreme and turn the person into a true vicegerent (*khalīfa*) of God on Earth.'[36] The caliphal mode of political theology was yielding to one in which the links between kingship and divine mandate were more mediated and opaque. This transformation in kingship was reflected in the proliferation of modes of punishment linked to imprisonment. Sovereignty was internally bifurcated, and power became increasingly discretionary.

The old concepts derived from legal manuals, which advised on methods of governance for rulers with a divine mandate, were increasingly unable to capture the complexities of political life under Saljuq rule, and it became necessary to turn to pre-Islamic systems to glorify the sultan's sovereignty. Old and Middle Persian royal genealogies served as a rich repository of concepts for authors and courtiers who endeared themselves to their patrons even as they appropriated for their vocation the authority that the new rulers could no longer command. Such strategic moves correlated well with efforts to realign the relation between power and authority, which included giving poets a greater role in shaping political sovereignty. The description of the ideal padishah as one who combines discernment (*ʿaql*) and erudition (*ʿilm*) is a case in point: in order to wield power effectively – to combine authority and power – the king had to strive to resemble a poet.

Court poets rose to the challenge of reconceiving the relation between power and authority in the determination of sovereignty in terms that better accommodated their literary ambitions. During the same years that this prose panegyric to the sultan was written – perhaps by Muʿizzi – Masʿud Saʿd languished in Maranj due to the arbitrary wiles of his Ghaznavid patron, Masʿud III (r. 1096–1115). Muʿizzi and Masʿud Saʿd participated in a common endeavour to shift the discursive authority that the sultan could not claim as his own onto the institution of poetry. While Muʿizzi pursued this goal through his panegyrics, Mas'ud Sa'd shifted discursive authority through his prison poems.

Several steps remain to be traversed before the transition from caliph to padishah was complete. After the patron is informed that, having been weakened by rebellion and sectarian conflict, the caliphate is no longer viable, the author undertakes to ensure a place for the poet within this new hierarchy. The first task is achieved by conferring on the new ruler the marks of the sultan's charisma. Rather than positing the old genealogy leading from Muhammad and his companions (*ashab*) and helpers (*ansar*), this genealogy originates in pre-Islamic Persia; its past is so ancient that it has no place in the historiographic record. There is however an unexpected twist. The pre-Islamic ruler who is linked to the Saljuq sultan through a fictive bloodline is not an Iranian king, as might be expected. He is Turanian, and thus a rival to Persian dynasties such as the Kayanids and Pishdadis.[37]

The major source for our knowledge of the myths surrounding Afrasiyab is the Avesta, *yasht* 19.[38] Here we are told of Frangrasyan the 'Turanian villain' who sought glory (*khwarna*) 'in all the seven continents (*kishwar*)' (19:82). Frangrasyan is an archetype for Ferdowsi's Afrasiyab. He is an enemy of Kawi Haosrawa (Ferdowsi's Kay Khusraw), who murdered Kawi Haosrawa's father, Siyawarshan (Ferdowsi's Siyavush). Frangrasyan was motivated by the desire to secure for himself *khwarna*, the fortune that according to the Avesta 'belongs to the Aryan lands, / to the born and unborn, / and to the orderly Zarathustra' (19:57, 59, 62). Frangrasyan promises to 'mingle together all things, dry and wet / in greatness and goodness and beauty', so that the cosmos is inverted and the Zoroastrian God Ahura Mazda becomes disturbed (19:58). After seeking refuge from his enemy in Azerbaijan, Frangrasyan is caught and killed by Kay Khusraw. In the Avesta, he seeks a divine bounty that is not rightfully his.

For a medieval readership, the most accessible sources for Frangrasyan/Afrasiyab were, in addition to Ferdowsi, al-Tabari and al-Tha'alibi's chronicles of Persian kings.[39] Given that the representation of Frangrasyan is pejorative in all of these sources, the decision to furnish the sultan with a genealogy leading back to Frangrasyan invites deeper inquiry. Could the author perhaps have known that Frangrasyan's rivals are all referred to in the Avesta as poets (*kawi*)?[40] Allowing for the possibility that this association persisted in medieval Persian memory, perhaps the sultan was given a Turanian genealogy in order to emphasise the discursive authority of the poet, a figure who in the Avesta is comparable to a king. While it is not easy to discern the purpose of this Turanian genealogy, we can be sure that this lineage helped to separate earthly power from discursive authority. The author may have expected that the sultan would not catch every reference and would therefore miss the moments when this prose panegyric crossed the line from legitimating the patron's power to constituting the poet's discursive authority.

While determining that the Saljuq sultan would descend from the Turanian king, in *Conduct of Kings*, God bestows on the sultan what the poet, drawing on the theological distinction between the miracles of prophets and the miracles of saints (discussed in Chapter 4), calls *karamat*, a term derivative of the Greek *charisma* (χάρισμα).[41] Unlike evidentiary miracles (*muʿjizat*), reserved for prophets, and demonstrative of the inimitability of the Quran, *karamat* are performed by saints (*awliyaʾ*). Unlike prophetic miracles, saintly miracles are invisible to those not directly implicated in the miraculous act. One possible source for the distinction between these types of miracles in *Conduct of Kings* is the early Persian mystical treatise, *Uncovering of the Covered for People of the Heart* (*Kashf al-mahjub li arbab al-qulub*) by al-Hujwiri of Lahore (d. 1077). In this first Persian treatise on mysticism, al-Hujwiri explained the difference between the two categories of divine intervention through a series of antitheses that clarify the significance of the later appropriation of saintly miracles (*karamat*) for the padishah. Whether or not the author of *Conduct of Kings* knew al-Hujwiri's work directly, both works abound in similar theological distinctions.[42]

In al-Hujwiri's account, the prophet who performs evidentiary miracles (*muʿjizat*) fully understands the nature of this act, whereas the performer of saintly miracles (*karamat*) cannot fully grasp the validity of this miracle. Whereas the performer of evidentiary miracles (*sahib-i muʿjiz*) has authority over the law (*sharʿ*), the performer of saintly miracles (*sahib-i karamat*) must accept the precepts (*ahkam*) imputed to him.[43] *A fortiori*, saintly miracles cannot conflict with *shariʿa*; by contrast, evidentiary miracles can and do violate legal norms. Beyond being above *shariʿa*, the performer of evidentiary miracles possesses a divinely given right to intervene in the law when guided by God, whereas saintly performers of *karamat* must permit all their actions to be adjudicated by the law. It is not accidental that the padishah who performs saintly miracles is entrusted with patronising scholars (*ahl-i ʿilm*) and philosophers (*hukamaʾ*), for the author of *Conduct of Kings* (whether Nizam al-Mulk, Muʿizzi or an anonymous scribe) belonged to these groups.

Although the elevation of padishah above the caliph increases the ruler's distance from temporal authority, the author refrains from assimilating the padishah to the prophet. Muʿizzi's elegy commemorating the death of Masʿud Saʿd speaks directly to the arguments advanced in the preface to *Conduct of Kings*. The poem opens with a series of grammatically incomplete clauses which imply that, temporally gauged, the beauty of the prison poet's verse exceeds that of all worldly creations:

> As long as there are thorns amid the lightning and thunder of discord
> [*nisan*]
> as long as there are hearts burning on the beloved's locks,
> as long as decay accompanies being in this world,
> as long as the promise of God is intermixed with His threat [*vaʿid*].

تا هست تیغ گلها در برق و رعدِ نیسان
تا هست سوزِ دلها در زلف جعد جانان
تا با فساد باشد همواره کون عالم
تا با وعید باشد پیوسته وعد یزدان [44]

There are at least two striking instances of double entendre (*iham*) in these verses, each of which pay tribute to the semiotic richness of Masʿud Saʿd's poetics. First, *nisan*, which refers both to the month of April and to discord. Second, the verbal noun *vaʿid*, which means threat, but can be slightly modified to signify good tidings. That in both double entendres the connotations are opposed in meaning underscores the semiotic richness of these verses. The everyday world, subject to decay, is populated with objects that evoke pathos through their transience: roses (*gulha*), spring showers (*barq o raʿd-i nisan*, also glossable as 'showers of discord'), and locks of the beloved's hair (*jaʿd-i janan*). This world, the poet declares, is subject to decay (*fasad*).

Although they inspire awe, these decaying objects cannot compete with Masʿud Saʿd's verse. Anticipating ʿAruzi's anatomy of prison poem poetics, specifically his deployment of *fasad* as the temporal framework within which poetry transpires, Muʿizzi here creates a geography for the prison poem's genre transgressions. Because these verses occur in an elegy commemorating death, the temporal contrast between *fasad* and poetry's permanence is brought into even clearer relief. The focus then shifts from worldly decay (*fasad*) to the poet's authority. This lays the groundwork for the next comparison, between the prison poem and the Quran. In the following verses, the most revered text in the Islamic world, the eloquence of which exceeds human attainment, retains its superior position:

> May the assembly of great men never be empty from
> the ornament of greatness, Masʿud Saʿd Salman.
> That eloquent [*sukhanvar*] poet whose verse [*nazm*] exceeds
> all that anyone has heard, except the Quran.

در مجلس بزرگان خالی مباد هرگز
پیرایهٔ بزرگی مسعود سعد سلمان
آن شاعر سخنور کز نظمِ او نکوتر
کس در جهان کلامی نشنید بعد قرآن

While in Muʿizzi's rendition the padishah lacks evidentiary miracles (*muʿjizat*), the same cannot be said for the first prison poet. Although Muʿizzi had earlier exercised restraint in praising his patron, in his elegy for Masʿud Saʿd, he collapses the distance between *kalam*, an everyday Arabic word that is here implicitly applied to the Quran, and *sukhan*, a term that can be rendered as 'discourse' or as 'poetry'. Here, *sukhan* is applied to the eloquent poet (*shaʿir-i sukhanvar*), Masʿud Saʿd. Masʿud Saʿd's poetry is subordinated to the Quran in terms of its eloquence, and it also takes precedence over all other Persian genres.

Read literally, Muʿizzi's framing of Masʿud Saʿd's verse as purer (*nikutar*) than any text after the Quran yields political-theological implications. This verse reflects how the concept of Quranic inimitability that developed within the Arabic rhetorical tradition during the height of Abbasid rule contributed to a bifurcated mode of exegesis. Bringing the lyric and prophetic dimensions of the poet's body into new alignment, the prison poem pushed the boundaries of the Arabo-Persian genre system across the the eastern Islamic world. Although Masʿud Saʿd's poetry was said to be second to the Quran in terms of eloquence, Muʿizzi's comparison suggests proximity. By elevating the poet in this poem as he elevated the padishah in other panegyrics, Muʿizzi brought the poet's authority into competition with the sovereign's power. The lyric and prophetic dimensions of the poet's body produced a new kind of discursive sovereignty, based on the discursive authority of poetic discourse. Whether through Masʿud Saʿd's elegiac lyrics or Khaqani's political allegories that exposed the fragility of worldly power, the affective, political, and aesthetic terms of the transformation were dictated by the prison poem's transgressions of existing genres.

Although the distinction between poet and prophet was carefully preserved within Islamic hermeneutics, as early as the *sura* on the poets (Q. 26), the form of knowledge specific to poetic creativity, intuition (*shuʿur*), was also considered to be dangerously proximate to soothsaying and other kinds of supernatural knowing. Like his Arabic counterparts, Muʿizzi perceived that an eloquent work of poetry approached to the condition of inimitability (*iʿjaz*), which was the exclusive property of the Quran. When his eloquence in verse surpassed that of his peers, the poet's verse merged with miracle-working abilities of prophets, whose special abilities licensed them to violate the laws governing worldly affairs. Transcending the law was beyond the reach of the padishah, even according to medieval Persian political theory, which significantly enhanced the ruler's discretionary power. As a result of the wide dissemination of the Persian prison poem, the evidentiary miracles (*muʿjizat*) forbidden to even the most exalted ruler were available to poets who sang incarceration's song.

The distinction between evidentiary and saintly miracles reveals the ways in which Islamic norms were reconfigured when saintly miracles (*karamat*) were attributed to the sultan; it also illuminates the transposition of caliphal authority outside the caliphal domain in *Conduct of Kings*. Although the caliph still wielded nominal sacral authority from his seat in Baghdad during the Saljuq ascendency, *Conduct of Kings* excludes him entirely from the distribution of power. The poet's interest lies wholly with the sultan, said to be endowed by God with qualities formerly reserved for saints. The attribution of saintly miracles (*karamat*) to the sultan attests to how the institution of the caliphate yielded to a new understanding of the locus of sovereignty. By 1106, when the preface to *Conduct of Kings* was composed, poetry had yet to be galvanised by the prophetic orientation of Khaqani's prison poems. The attribution of charismata (*karamat*) to a ruler sets a precedent for the later ascription of prophetic capacities (*muʿjizat*) to prison poets tracked in Chapter 4.

As *Conduct of Kings* progresses, the endeavour to elevate the patron and consequently the poet become ever more subtle and persistent. We move from a comparison between rebellion and a forest conflagration to a comparison between the ruler and a burning candle. People find their path with the candle's light and emerge from darkness into the world outside (8). The ruler himself does not require light, for he stands in need of no guide. After the ruler is cleared of any imputation of imperfection, we turn to speculation concerning the poet's location in the cosmic hierarchy leading from God (variously named *izadi taʿala, haqq taʿala, khuda*) to the ruler (variously named *padishah, shah, khudawand-i ʿalam, khalifa*) to his servants. The self-denominated servant (*bandeh*) who decided to compose, or edit, a text on the principles of good governance fulfils the sacred command. Here a new term is introduced to describe his style of governance: illuminated (*rawshan*). This illuminated style of governance replaces an Arabised lexicon with a Persian register.

When this description of style is juxtaposed to the pre-Islamic Persian concept of *farr*, the effect of the disquisition on the prerogatives of post-caliphal sovereignty is further intensified. In *Conduct of Kings*' political theology, the padishah attains sovereignty by appropriating or emulating the attributes of divinity. By the same token, when the poet approximates his patron, he threatens to overtake the ruler in his own endeavours. While material power is a prerogative for governance, discursive authority can be acquired by any poet gifted with eloquence. The prison poets of South, Central and West Asia claimed this authority through their poetry. To situate their contributions within the political and philosophical contexts that formed their literary sensibilities, we now turn to a second work of prose, that, even more conclusively than Vatvat's rhetorical manual and *Conduct of Kings*, canonised the prison poem: ʿAruzi's *Four Discourses*.

Discursive Authority and Decentralised Power

By way of tracing the textual and historical itineraries that culminated in the reversal in power relations described above, this book concludes by returning to the most influential critical document in the genesis of the prison poem, by ʿAruzi. Chapter 2 examined how *Four Discourses* canonised the lyric ode written from prison by describing its impact on the reader's body, for example, by making the reader's hair stand on end and paralysing the reader's lips. This concluding chapter focuses on ʿAruzi's theorisation of cosmic and political sovereignty in the context of the caliphate's demise and the increasing power of regional sultans who could not legitimate their power through divine imprimatur. Since *Four Discourses* contains the first extant discussion of the Persian prison poem, it is appropriate to conclude this book's account of the emergence of the poet's sovereign body with the cosmological vision that informs ʿAruzi's work.

In addition to being the first text to provide a critical exegesis of the prison poem genre, *Four Discourses* is also the first extant attempt to clarify poetry's location within the sultan's court and in relation to other disciplines. This work consists of four discourses (*maqaleh*), on the scribe (*dabir*), poet (*sha ʿir*), astrologist (*munajjim*) and doctor (*tabib*), respectively. ʿAruzi explains his intentions in an Introduction (*dibacheh*) that breaks with the norms that had hitherto governed Arabic legal (*ahkam*) literature while laying the foundations for a parallel but distinctive Persianate ethical (*akhlaq*) tradition. 'It is an old custom,' ʿAruzi writes, 'for the writer and composer [*mu ʾallif o musannif*] to praise his patron and to pray for him in the opening to his discourse [*tashbib-i sukhan*] and in his introduction. Instead of praising the padishah, I . . . record all that the Almighty has bestowed on him so that he will be filled with gratitude [towards God]' (*CM*, 33).

Tashbib-i sukhan, the term ʿAruzi uses to characterise his prose discourse, evokes the tripartite *qasida* structure recorded most famously by Ibn Qutayba (d. 889) in his *Book on Poetry and Poets* (*Kitab al-shiʿr wa-l-shuʿaraʾ*).[45] The tripartite *qasida* structure consists of the *nasib* (equivalent to *tashbib*), *rahil* (journey section), and *madih* (praise section). Poets varied this typology by adding the *du ʿa* (address to God), and *takhallus* (here in the meaning of a closing signature verse rather than a pen name). Modern scholars have argued that Ibn Qutayba's tripartite structure is a formalised abstraction with only tenuous bearing on poetic composition even for the Arabic poetic tradition within which it was forged.[46] Nonetheless, his account elucidates the *qasida's* canonical status, and concomitantly explains the importance of *tashbib*, whether encountered in poetry or prose. At all stages in its morphology, the *qasida* is constituted by its relationship to praise. Following the example of the poets whose verses he had committed to memory, ʿAruzi recapitulates in prose the *qasida*'s structure of praise. It is relevant to recall here that ʿAruzi, best known to posterity as a literary critic, was also a poet.[47]

Not wishing to lavish praise on a single ruler, ʿAruzi avoids the praise section (*madih*) conventionally suffused with flattery for the patron. His real goal, he states, explicitly addressing his ruler-patron, is to inspire his Ghurid sovereign to praise God. Praise of the patron never becomes an end in itself in this work. Already in these opening words, a cosmic theogony unfolds through the systematic recalibration of causal relations. Whereas, according to convention, the purpose of an introduction, be it a prose *dibache* or a poetic *tashbib*, is to praise the ruler, ʿAruzi explains that praise for a sovereign must be subordinated to the glorification of that which the sovereign at best palely reflects: God in relation to His creation.

In making the poet's praise of the ruler conditional on the ruler's praise for God, ʿAruzi vindicates the political efficacy of praise addressed to the sovereign. Readers – including the sovereign himself – are reminded that the panegyric can bring about ethical, political, and indeed metaphysical transformation. The writer who dispenses praise judiciously brings their readers into closer proximity to God by illuminating the virtues of creation. This capacity assumes the freedom of the poet to defer praise when his conscience conflicts with the mandate to praise his patron. This disquisition is followed by a catalogue of the many reasons why the Ghurid sovereign should be thankful. He is young, his parents are alive, he is surrounded by brothers. These blessings are not merit-based. Rather, they are gifts, bestowed by a power over which the sovereign has no authority. It is not the ruler who is remarkable, ʿAruzi insists, but God, who generously bestows his blessings on those who can never merit such grace.

As part of its broader commentary on the politics and poetics of patronage, *Four Discourses* registers the moment when power (*saltanat*) became alienated from authority (*khilafa*) in Persianate kingship. The treatise activates distinctions among prophet, imam, and padishah that resulted, inter alia, in the prison poem. Further, the presentation in this treatise of cosmic interdependency – among minerals (*ma'adin*), plants and animals (*nabat va haywan*), among prophets, imams and rulers, and the various occupations that collectively undergird the efficacious state – surpasses in subtlety any other contemporaneous treaty in the Islamic world. Sovereignty in 'Aruzi's conception is vertically organised according to a cosmic hierarchy. Constructed cosmically rather than territorially, and moving from the human to the divine via the intermediary stages of creation – minerals, plants and animals – this hierarchy encompasses the entire created world. The territorialised power that underpins medieval Persianate sovereignty is here juxtaposed to the cosmic chain of being that leads vertically from God to creation. This vertical nexus structures sovereignty's territoriality according to multiple nodes of power.

The text moves from an ambivalent appraisal of the sovereign to a greater concentration on the location of sovereignty within a threefold cosmology. This cosmology extends from the prophet, who occupies the highest position in the hierarchy, and is followed, in order of importance, by the imam and padishah. Even in this encomium, praise for the sovereign (*padishah*) is subordinated to praise for the prophet: 'in the degrees of beings [*madarij-i mawjudat*] and the ranks of comprehension [*ma'arij-i ma'qulat*], aside from prophecy [*nubuvvat*], which represents the apex of human capacities, there is no higher rank than that of the sovereign' (35). The fact that 'Aruzi discusses prophecy (*nubuwwat*) as a vocation without citing specific prophets suggests that his overriding interest is in the *concept* of prophecy rather than in the elevation of a specific prophet.

This cosmic theogony is followed by an exegesis on the chain of being (*silsileh-i asbab*) that reverberates with metaphysical and poetic implications. Its ontology derives first and foremost from Ibn Sina's *Book of Healing* (*Kitab al-Shifa'*, *c.* 1020), an encyclopaedic compendium that applied Neo-Platonic cosmologies to medieval Islamic conditions. 'Aruzi develops a basic distinction between the necessarily existent (*wajib al-wujud*) and the contingently possible (*al-wujud al-mumkin*). Humans and all of creation belongs to the second order of being. The necessarily existent has its being (*wujud*) for itself (*be khud*) and is both eternally existent and completely independent of any intermediate entity. The contingently possible, most accessible to mortals, depends on the causal nexus of the chain of being for its survival. Its seed (*mani*) derives from blood; its blood derives from food; its food derives from water, earth, and heat (*aftab*, meaning 'sun'), and so on. In short, the created things on which the necessarily existent depend are perpetually generating other created things (35).

The universe consists of four subservient forces (*khadim*), in parallel to the text's four discourses on four basic professions (on the scribe, poet, astrologer and doctor), the four humours in the Hippocratic–Galenic system, and the four elements: wind (*bad*), water (*ab*), earth (*khak*), fire (*atash*) within Ptolemaic cosmology. In addition to the four subservient forces, there are three faculties (*quvvat*), with no immediately apparent Ptolemaic parallel. The four subservient forces are defined by their function in the world: attracting (*jazibeh*), maintaining (*masikeh*), assimilating (*hazimeh*) and exorcising (*dafi'eh*). The attracting force performs the greatest labour by ensuring that the sun warms all things through its reflection (*'aks*), and thereby sustains the world. Recapitulating in brief the story of creation, 'Aruzi reports that, when the waters received the warmth of the sun, they dried up. On this desiccated base, the terrestrial world was created. This dynamic of attraction, from sun to water to earth, is the attracting force, the Islamic counterpart to the Platonic *harmonia*.[48] The attracting force unites all creation in the countenance of the cosmos (*mizaj-i 'alam*), assuring their mutual cooperation and indebtedness.

Along with the other three subservient forces, the attracting force relies on the three faculties for its activation. 'Aruzi characterises these faculties in terms of their functional interdependencies. The first ensures an equal distribution of the sustenance (*ghaza*) on which life depends. The second accompanies this sustenance on its journey through the universe, insuring its perpetual availability until those entities depending on it are ready to face extinction (*fana'*). The third faculty, the reproductive (*quvvat-i muvallida*), is responsible for the perpetuation of the species (*naw'*). While the attracting force occupies a preeminent position in the hierarchy of subservient forces, the reproductive faculty occupies a corresponding position among the faculties. 'When an organism has attained completeness [*be kamal rasid*],' writes 'Aruzi, 'and tends towards defect, then this third faculty appears and produces a seed [*tukhm*], so that, when the organism passes from this world, it will have a representative [*na'ib*], the order of the world will not decay, and the species will not be extinguished [*naw' munqati' nashavad*]. This is called the reproductive faculty' (*CM*, 37–8).

Before abandoning the world, 'Aruzi notes, prophets disseminate a legal code (*dastur*). This sacred text is inscribed with their insights as well as divinely inspired instructions. This text bequeaths law and customs (*shar' va sunnat*, 43). But no sacred text can make provisions for every given situation. A living mediator is required to negotiate among humans, prophets and God. Driven by the mediating logics that structure the cosmic as well as the terrestrial order, the prophet finds a replacement (*na'ib*) for his physical presence. This replacement puts into circulation within a desacralised world power that was sacred in origin.

'Aruzi's concept of sovereignty as the circulation of power among various forces resonates with Aziz al-Azmeh's use of the paradigm of mimetic representation to account for the circulation of power within medieval Arabic political theory.[49] According to the mimetic model, neither authority nor power are localised within any single entity. Rather, sovereignty is constituted through ideological persuasion. The consolidation of sovereignty in 'Aruzi's cosmology is an ontological – and therefore relational – process. As with Khaqani's cosmological prison poems which emphasise the prophetic dimensions of the poet's lyric self (especially prison poem number 3), 'Aruzi's account of sovereign power is a mimesis of the cosmos itself.

'Aruzi's political theology also aligns with that of Max Weber, best known for his definition of the state as a 'monopoly on the legitimate use of violence'.[50] For Weber, as recognised by Skalnik, 'authority does not have a rational base'; 'commands are obeyed because they possess authority', and not solely or primarily due to their monopoly on violence.[51] Like Weber, theorists of kingship and sovereignty across the medieval world understood that, for a political system to be sustainable, it had to rely on a great deal more than force. According to both 'Aruzi and al-Azmeh, the discursive dimension of governance is vital to its efficacy. Sovereignty is not reducible to raw power alone. Particularly in 'Aruzi's cosmology, specific classes of individuals, including poets and philosophers (*hukama*), are assigned the task of using their authority to transmute power into sovereignty. As this book has shown, the rapid advent and dissemination of the prison poem were facilitated by the emergence of a new ideology that increased the state's monopoly on violence while transferring authority to the poet.

After explicating the chain of being leading from the mineral world to humans, ʿAruzi stipulates that not only is the cosmos structured hierarchically; so is humanity. There are three classes of humans, corresponding to the mineral, plant, and animal worlds. The first and lowest group inhabit deserts and mountains, and think only of themselves. This group is closest to the animal kingdom. The second group consists of city-dwellers (*ahl-i bilad o madaʾin*). Members from this group enter into partnership (*shirkat*) with each other. The second group is richer in civilisation (*tamaddun*) than the desert and mountain dwellers. The major limitation of this second group is that their crafts (*sinaʿat*), their technical labour, are the goal (*maqsud*) of their existences. Their vision is constrained by their vocations. As with the second faculty (*quvva*) in the natural world, the function of this intermediary category of humans is to enable the third and highest class to prosper. Although civilised, members of the second category lack an autonomous existence.

The third and highest category of humans is paradoxically although perhaps not accidentally nameless. It comprises two demographics: wise men, including philosophers (*hukama*), and prophets (*anbiya*). By philosophers (*hukama*) ʿAruzi means the four classes of state functionaries whose vocations *Four Discourses* delineates: scribes, poets, astrologers and doctors. *Hukama* are not solely philosophers in the Greco-Arabic tradition, or even practitioners of dialectical theology (*kalam*), although the term encompasses both those groups; they are intellectuals who consecrate their lives to the welfare of the state. In terms of the prison poem's political theology, *hukama* generate the discursive authority on which worldly power – namely, the sultans who imprison poets – depends, but which can also undermine it. They are the 'elite' who lead Andrew March to describe sovereignty in the premodern Islamic world as 'a matter of a kind of power sharing between various elites or experts'.[52] The agency of these intellectuals – poets, critics, and rhetoricians – in exposing the contingency of the king's mortal body and in substituting it with the body of the prophetic poet comprises the basic framework for understanding the prison poem.

As we saw above, *hukama* refers in *Conduct of Kings* to the intellectual class whom the ruler must defend with the same tenacity that he brings to his care for the poor (8). For ʿAruzi, as for the author of *Conduct of Kings*, *hukama* does not refer solely to the mystics who have dispensed with the cares of the world and require nothing from the state; nor does it refer primarily to the practitioners of dialectical theology (*mutakallimun*), as it did in earlier periods. Under eastern Islamic empires, the term was broadened to include the intellectuals – poets such as Muʿizzi, critics such as ʿAruzi, rhetoricians such as Vatvat – whose writings helped to canonise the prison poem. In devising a political theology suited for the empires of the eastern Persianate world, ʿAruzi canonised poetry within a political world that was adjusting to new modes of governance, and to new relations between power and authority. During the second phase of the prison poem, the decay of the king's mortal body so agonisingly chronicled in Khaqani's Aivan Qasida was gradually yielding to a new perception of sovereignty devoid of divine authority. Amid this transformation, poets claimed the mantle that the king could no longer claim as his birthright.

Thoroughly institutionalising his new inflection of an old word, ʿAruzi defines the role of the philosophers in terms that convey their moral commitments before assimilating their them to a concrete sociology. Philosophers (*hukama*) debate the essence of things (*haqa'iq-i ashiya'*). They reflect how we arrived in this world (*chiguneh amadim*) and where we are headed (*kuja khwahim raftan*) (42). It is the vocation of these philosophers, according to ʿAruzi, to engage in reflection. The term he uses for reflection (*tafkir*) is morphologically related to *mutafakkira*, the cognitive faculty that is the human counterpart to the animal's *mutakhayyala*, the third internal sense among the ten components of the perceptive faculty, *mudrika*. Through their reflection, intellectuals imagine into being the discursive authority that constitutes poetic discourse (*sukhan*), and which augments the authority of poets.

The place of the poet within this new political cosmology has yet to be specified in ʿAruzi's epistemology. As a precursor to the Persian ethical treatises (*akhlaq*) that proliferated across the eastern Islamic world in subsequent centuries, *Four Discourses* devotes as much attention to the medicinal arts, astrology, and the chancellery as to poetry's shifting claims to political authority. These vocations developed an alternative language for power in the age of the caliphate's disintegration and the proliferation of sultanates. ʿAruzi's quick transition to the prophet as the second category in the third and most exalted human group underscores the weight of discursive authority, as does his manner of dealing with this authority, newly severed from worldly power.

Three qualities (*khasiyyat*) mark the prophet off from other orders of created beings. First, unlike the *hukama*, and as Ibn Sina has already argued in the section of his *Book of Healing* – itself a commentary on Aristotle's *De anima* – prophet have knowledge of the sciences (*'ulum*) without having studied formally.[53] Second, prophets have been given information (*khabar*) concerning past and future (*di u farda*) without having received this knowledge from a parable (*mathal*) or from the syllogistic reasoning (*qiyas*) that features in Islamic jurisprudence. Third, prophets' souls (*nafs*) possess such power (*quvva*) that they can assume whatever form (*surat*) they wish (43).[54] Although 'Aruzi adds that this latter capacity is reserved primarily for angels (*mala'ikeh*), the poet is a figure whose body, as shown in Chapters 4 and 5, resembles the bodies of prophets. Not only was poetry's authority regarded as prophetic by other poets; so too did numerous classical Persian literary theorists, from 'Awfi to Shams-i Qays, connect poetic knowledge to the form of intuitive knowledge possessed by prophets, *shu'ur*.[55]

The textual trail for the discursive linkage between poetry and prophecy begins a few decades after *Four Discourses*, but this may be merely an effect of the state of our sources, as well as of the fact that poetic knowledge was theorised primarily in Arabic at the time of 'Aruzi's writing.[56] Or perhaps there is another explanation: although the link between poetry (*shi'r*) and intuition (*shu'ur*) was clear even in the age of the caliphate, it took the atrophy of the caliphate – and illegitimate claims of a rapid succession of regional Turkic and Persianate sultanates from South Asia to the Caucasus – to make this link explicit. In the early centuries of Abbasid rule, the caliphate maintained a tenuous continuity with charismatic authority of Muhammad and his successors, who combined authority and power. In the age of the declining caliphate and amid changes that were initiated during the Abbasid period with the institution of the vizierate, power was transferred to the regional sultanates, particularly the Ghaznavids and Saljuqs, and from there to their vassal dynasties such as the Ghurids and Shirvanshahs.

The task faced by medieval Persian political and literary theorists, including 'Aruzi and Nizam al-Mulk, was to disambiguate power from authority, and thereby to legitimate the desacralised sovereignty of the sultan while providing a new – and separate – foundation for poetry. As a literary genre that entered this world at a time when the caliphate was unable to provide a solid foundation for governance, the prison poem came to function as the panegyric's antithesis, first, in the pen of Masʿud Saʿd as a lyric ode, and subsequently, in the pen of Khaqani as an anti-panegyric challenge to the sovereign. From the prison poet's point of view, the genre usefully exposed the sultan's desacralised power. Khaqani's poetics of ruins attests that the panegyric *qasida* that had previously conferred authority on the caliph, granting him sovereignty, had become an instrument of irony as well as of critique. As he predicted in his Aivan Qasida, no longer would the banks of the Tigris or the battlements of Sasanian palaces whisper the melodies of royal sovereignty. Khaqani's carceral poetics exposed the king's carrion-infested corpse while replacing it with the poet's prophetic body.

Regional sultanates developed military strategies for reconciling power with authority, most of which lasted no longer than a few decades. The literary-critical explorations of prison poetry by leading Persian critics of the age were driven by the impulse to make sense of the changing political norms within this milieu. Among its many intertexts, ʿAruzi's delineation of the intellectual's role in society resonates with the first extant prison poem in the Caucasus, authored by Falaki, in which the poet declares to the ruler:

My fear of your punishment [*siyasat*]
is no scandal among the intelligent [*ahl-i ʿaql*].

گر بترسیدم از سیاست تو
ببر اهل عقل عارم نیست

In these verses, as in *Conduct of Kings*, *siyasat* has the dual meaning of politics and punishment. In juxtaposing the two meanings, and in distinguishing between a carceral regime and the intellectuals who expose that regime's injustices, Falaki and ʿAruzi revealed the widening gap between power and authority that influenced the circulation of the prison poem.

Midway through *Four Discourses*, the cosmic typology evaporates. After the three categories ʿAruzi specifies for the human realm have been exhausted, it would seem that any further enumerations would need to fit within the fourfold typology already explicated. The next example adduced by ʿAruzi challenges that view, for the imam, whose sacred body presides over a sovereign state, does not belong to any of the demographics earlier elucidated: (1) wild men and desert-dwellers; (2) civilised and urbanised artisans; (3) intellectuals (*hukama*ʾ) and prophets (*anbiya*ʾ). No further categories are placed at the reader's disposal, perhaps because the imam was seen to exhaust all conceivable taxonomies, or because, by the time of ʿAruzi, the imam had disappeared. The panegyric idiom that underwrote his power with authority had similarly fallen into decline.

ʿAruzi inverts the Farabian ideal of the ruler who combines in himself two other kinds of authority, distinctive from poetry: philosophy (*hikma*) and prophecy (*nubuvvat*). Al-Farabi (d. 950) wrote his *Inhabitants of the Virtuous City* (*Mabadi' ara' ahl al-madina al-fadila*), an Arabic work that shaped ʿAruzi's political theology, in order to assimilate prophecy and kingship to philosophy. Merging Platonic metaphysics and Aristotelian political philosophy, al-Farabi claims that 'a man becomes wise [*hakiman*], philosophical, and intelligent' by virtue of what is poured into his passive intellect (*ʿaql al-monfaʿil*). By contrast, a prophet (*al-nabi*) is made from what is poured into the imaginative faculty (*quvva al-mutakhayyila*). 'The prophet,' al-Farabi continues, 'warns of what will be, and announces the particulars that are now.' A few sentences later, al-Farabi states that the person who attains to prophecy has arrived at the highest 'condition for humanity and enters into the most advanced stage of bliss'.[57]

For al-Farabi, the prophet and the philosopher are assigned the same function; the differences between them are matters of degree rather than kind. Al-Kindi (d. 873), al-Farabi's predecessor in the field of Arabic Neo-Platonism, held a similar position with an important difference: he was willing to subordinate reason to revelation because he believed, as Fawzi Najjar puts it, that 'revelation unlocks the door to a domain of reality which pure thought cannot enter'.[58] For al-Kindi as for al-Farabi, prophetic knowledge was superior to philosophical knowledge 'in degree, not in kind' and the prophet was regarded as a sub-species of the philosopher.[59] Echoing both thinkers, the Jewish-Arabic philosopher Moses Maimonides (d. 1204) argues that 'most prophecies are given in images, for this is the characteristic of the imaginative faculty; the organ of prophecy'.[60] While the merger of philosophy and prophecy effected by these Arabic thinkers considerably shifts the terrain away from Plato's *Phaedrus*, a work that examined artistic creation (mimesis) in light of prophetic knowledge (*phantasia*), it is also a signpost in the evolution of the prison poem.[61] Al-Farabi tied the imaginative faculty (*quvva al-mutakhayyila*) to the active intellect (*ʿaql al-faʿʿal*) with a depth and explicitness no extant Greek philosophical treatise had done. With al-Farabi, the active intellect is the sun that gives light to the eyes and in the absence of which no one can see.[62] Writing in Persian, ʿAruzi developed this Farabian precedent in the process of generating a political theology for poetry.

The merger of philosophy and prophecy effected by al-Kindi and al-Farabi within medieval Arabic Neoplatonism stimulated the later convergence of prophecy and poetry in twelfth-century Persian poetry and prose. Alongside *Conduct of Kings*, *Four Discourses* played a major role in effecting this transference. Two moments in *Four Discourses* attest to the transformation. The first is the subtle semantic shift as the text moves from *nabi*, the Arabic term for prophet, to *payghambar*, its Persian equivalent. Such Persianisations of prophecy shaped the perception of the poet as prophet in the case of Khaqani and other prison poets during these same decades.

While, as seen above, philosophers ask probing questions (42), and prophets impart knowledge unattainable through reason (43), the new class of poet-philosophers does both. Hence, ʿAruzi's statement at the end of his introduction that poetry, along with prose, belongs to the branch of science called logic (*mantiq*). ʿAruzi calls to mind two occurrences of the *n-t-q* root in the Quran, both of which link the concept commonly, if imprecisely, translated by 'logic', with the miraculous inimitability (*iʿjaz*) of the sacred text. Both occurrences are presented as the unmediated statements of God: 'Before us is a book which tells the truth' (*yantiqu bi 'l-haqq*; Q. 22:62) and 'This is our book; it pronounces against you in all truth' (*yantiqu ʿalaykum bi 'l-haqq*; Q. 45:29).[63] While Quranic hermeneutics associates logic (*mantiq*) with prophecy, the term is most closely associated with philosophy. The coalescence of these two disciplines in *Four Discourses* brings into relief the prophetic body of the poet that is acutely represented in the prison poem.

Many agents are needed to administer the imam's mandate in the political realm. The highest-ranking among these agents, called the padishah by ʿAruzi, is inferior not only to the prophets who mediate between God and humans, but also to the imam. The padishah may even be inferior to the poet-philosophers (*hukama*), a group to which the critic himself belonged. The sovereign's ability to command obedience derives from his position within this hierarchy. As with the poet, the sovereign's claim to power is linked to his ability to represent. In himself he signifies nothing, but his mediating role justifies his place of pre-eminence within the social order.

Refusing to conflate the imam's or the sovereign's power with the authority of prophecy, ʿAruzi upholds the Mawardian distinction between absolute power and delegated authority (*tafwid*). While the *shariʿa* that the sovereign is tasked to administer is seen to have a sacred origin, the ruler's own power is decidedly secular. His power is a consequence of his relations to others, to the imam, not of any virtue intrinsic to himself. In spite of the elevated associations that the padishah evoked for Ferdowsi and other chroniclers of Persian kingship, and even for Khaqani who chronicled the king's carrion-infested body, the ruler in this context negates the classical idealisation of kingship. Concretely, the padishah is a metonym for power in its crudest, most brutal form. ʿAruzi's sovereign is the Ghurid Sultan Jahansuz, the ruler whom Bertold Spuler called 'one of the worst monsters the Islamic world has ever seen'.[64] Jahansuz's brutal attack on Ghazna in 1150, which included the slaughter of the city's entire population after they were lured from their hiding places by the call to prayer, illustrates the cruelty and corruption that characterised sultanate governance during this period. For court poets trained in the art of praising their king, such regimes posed a representational challenge: how to legitimate the sultan's sovereignty while critiquing his abuse of power? This same representational challenge was faced, in a different way, by the king: how to bring the representation of his power into conformity with his will to power?

The courtly panegyrics of Muʿizzi and his contemporaries are shot through with these contradictions of sultanate sovereignty. The terms through which ʿAruzi and Muʿizzi register the bifurcation between power and authority distinguishes their political theology from the earlier Ghaznavid poetry of ʿUnsuri and Farrukhi. This bifurcation brings late panegyrics into an even closer relationship with the prison poem genre. For the courtly panegyric, legitimating power was the primary goal. The prison poem by contrast transferred the sacred authority of the ruler onto the poet's body. The two goals

– and the two genres – were intimately intertwined. First, the poet had to establish the superiority of the sovereign, who was often also his jailer and patron, and legitimate his power. For prison poets, this meant crafting an aesthetic from within their imprisonment, that was simultaneously in support of and opposed to their ruler.

Several shifts confront the reader in moving from early Ghaznavid panegyrics of ʿUnsuri and Farrukhi (among others) to the prison poem. First, and most obviously, we witness the emergence of the lyric ode with Masʿud Saʿd and the emasculated body with which it was associated, and which later becomes the emboldened body of the poet-as-prophet. Whereas court poets such as ʿUnsuri and Farrukhi provide little direct information about their selves, let alone their bodies, Masʿud Saʿd confronts the reader time and again with his corporeal deterioration, as in the following complaint:

> Misfortune makes my life crooked.
> Why should I move the tongue in my mouth?
> The wheel [of fortune] does not spin according to my wish.
> Why should I speak to one who does not understand?

کارم همه بخت بد بپیچاند
در کام زبان همی چه پیچانم
این چرخ بکام من نمی گردد
بر خیره سخن همی چه گردانم[65]

This litany of complaints identifies the poet's imprisonment with his crooked fate and suggests the futility of resistance:

> Sometimes the plague of Lahore wears me down.
> Sometimes the slander of Khurasan enchains me.
> How strange! I am captive since my birth.
> Perhaps I'm bound to prison until my death.

گه خستهٔ آفت لهاوورم
گه بسته تهمت خراسانم
تا زاده ام ای شگفت محبوسم
تا مرگ مگر که وقف زندانم

The intensity of the poet's identification with his physical surroundings is underscored by the end rhyme *anam* that grammatically denotes the first-person voice. Thus, the endings to the final two hemstitches – *mahbusam* ('I am captive') and *vaqf-i zindanam* ('I am bound to prison', or more literally, 'I am donated to prison') – merge the poet's prison cell with his vatic self. Beyond simply *being* in prison, the poet's body *becomes* a prison cell. The final distich in this citation follows an apostrophe – 'How strange [*ay shigift*]' – with the statement that he was born captive and the prediction that he will be in prison until the end of his life. With these declarations, the poet's imprisoned body becomes a metaphor for his metaphysical condition. His question to himself, suggesting that complaint is futile – 'Why should I move the tongue in my mouth?' – calls to mind Awfi's description of the effect of the prison poem on the movement of the lips, discussed in Chapter 2.

Like the author of *Conduct of Kings*, ʿAruzi responded to his sovereign's request for new idioms of governance with cosmologies that elevated the role of the poet. In ʿAruzi's schema, the sovereign's access to God is heavily mediated. The first agent after the Prophet entrusted to represent God's will is the imam. The imam is the true sovereign according to ʿAruzi's schema. Across the medieval world, the ideal state was abstracted from the conditions of material power. Dante, for example, proposed world governance in his *De Monarchia* (1312) as the only legitimate form of governance, although he could not cite a monarch who could fulfil his mandate.[66] A century and a half earlier, ʿAruzi was unable to nominate an actual imam to fulfil the role outlined in his cosmology. He made no effort to connect his notional imam to the Baghdad caliph. Long after the Mongol conquest of 1258 ended with the wholesale destruction of Baghdad and the caliphate, rulers of the Delhi-based Tughluq dynasty (1320–1412), situated on the outer peripheries of the Islamic world, sought legitimation from the caliphate. However, blessing from an eviscerated caliphate could not legitimate the sovereign's claims to power.[67]

Although the imam is postulated by ʿAruzi as a logical necessity, he remains a hypothesis. The historical correspondence between the text's padishah and ʿAruzi's ruler-patron Jahansuz is evident. By contrast, there is little in the way of historical correspondence between the imam in the text and its immediate political environment. Clearly, ʿAruzi could not anchor his cosmic theogony in his own political world. The imamate presented here is a premise designed to set the stage for the reconstitution of sovereignty through poetry's discursive authority. ʿAruzi doubts that any regime could command obedience throughout the world. As with Dante, the imam whose mandate is to rule the world is an ever-recurring potentiality, not an actuality. In the absence of the legitimacy conferred by authority, the ruler's earthly power cannot compete with the prophetic awareness that constitutes the poet's authority. Hence the need to sharply distinguish between imam and padishah in this domain of Persian political theology.

More easily identifiable than the poet-philosophers is the class of rulers falling under the direct jurisdiction of the imam. These are the administrators (*sa'is*) who exist only as collectivities. Although most political theorists assign kingship to the highest level on the chain of being, ʿAruzi is of a different disposition. The rulers in his cosmology are subordinate not only to God, but also to prophets and the imam. Thrice-removed from divinity, they are arguably even lower on the ladder of being than the poet-philosophers (*hukama*) who lack political power and spend their time debating life's meaning. ʿAruzi concludes his disquisition on the relation between sovereign power and biological existence with a concise formula that reveals much about the political hierarchies that shaped his world: 'The *padishah* is the representative [*na'ib*] of the imam; the imam is the representative of the prophet [*payghambar*]; the prophet is the representative of God [*khuda*]' (*CM*, 43). The mimetic circulation of power among these various nodes of governance can be schematised as in Diagram 6.1.

Although ʿAruzi does not specify this here, this threefold typology paves the way for a fourth mimesis, of the poet as sovereign. A comparison of this typology with that found in al-Mawardi reveals that the Persian theorist has introduced a radical change into Islamic political theory's mimetic hierarchy.[68] The Persian text has added the padishah. Just as imam for al-Mawardi corresponds to the vice-regent (*khalifa*), so does padishah for ʿAruzi correspond to the sultan. In both instances, an abstract and universalising referent is preferred over a concrete historical one. As a result of this preference, al-Mawardi's readers encounter the imam more frequently than the caliph, and ʿAruzi's readers encounter the padishah more frequently than the sultan. Far from demonstrating their irrelevance, the absence of the caliph and sultan from normative Islamic political theory (both Arabic *ahkam* and Persian *akhlaq*) suggests their ubiquity, along with the ease with which these figures were grafted onto more general political cosmologies.

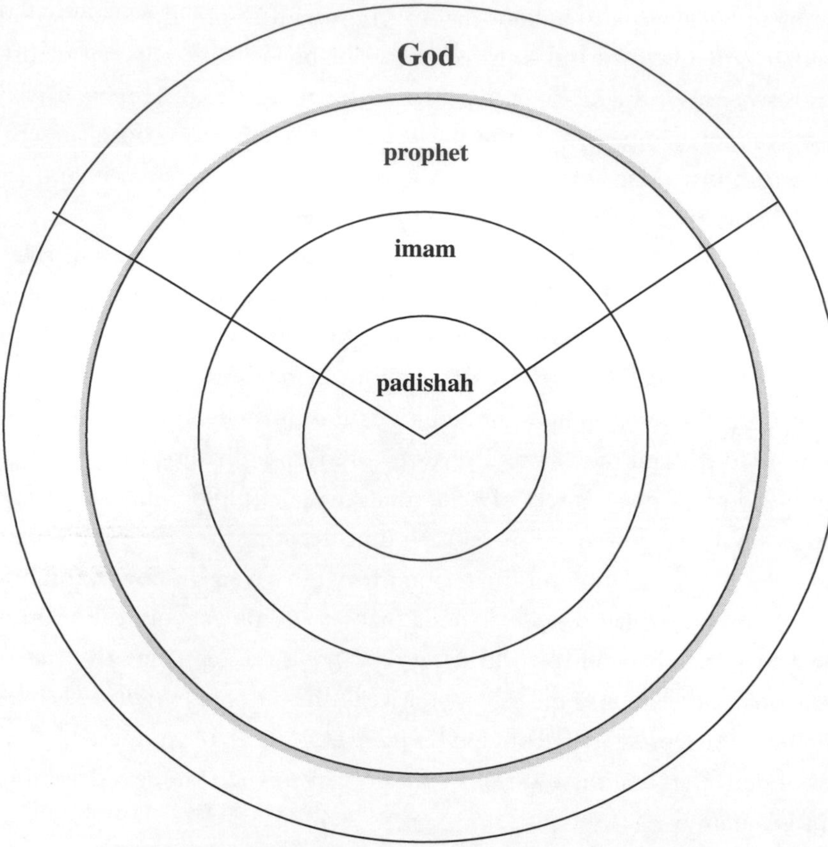

Diagram 6.1 Power as representation (designed by Nila Namsechi).

Conduct of Kings and *Four Discourses* are as permeated by the sultanate as al-Mawardi's treatise is by the caliphate. Although these texts rarely name their focal points, their omissions reveal more than their inclusions. Rather than undermine the institution of the caliph in the age of its decline, the prison poem channels the authority of the poet's body to expose the contingency of king's body. By temporalising the ruler's power, prison poets used their imprisoned, captive and eviscerated bodies to shine a light on the corruption of worldly power.

ʿAruzi's chain of being is circumscribed by mortality. It moves beings and non-beings from one moment in time to the next: the knowledge that they participate in a cycle of birth and death (*kawn u fasad*; *CM*, 32, 36), the regime of generation and corruption, of that which is mortal because it is created. ʿAruzi sees this realm, which is necessarily collective and intrinsically political, as more monumental than anything an individual could achieve alone. By invoking the world of generation and corruption repeatedly at strategic junctures in his work, ʿAruzi inserts himself into an Arabic philosophical tradition heavily dominated by the Farabian legacy. As pertinent as al-Farabi to ʿAruzi's New Persian cosmology is a little-studied work of al-Kindi, *On the Explanation of the Active Proximate Cause of Generation and Corruption*. In articulating for the first time in Arabic the contingency of the political, this work introduced an awareness of time as a philosophical category that shaped subsequent Arabic political theory.[69] ʿAruzi supplemented al-Kindi's insight into the contingency of the political by systematically distinguishing between authority and power.

ʿAruzi's account of sovereignty under post-caliphal rule calls to mind George Makdisi's description of the relation between caliphal authority and sultanate power during this same period. Makdisi understands authority in this context to refer to the 'right to command and direct'. A right freely exercised entails freedom for those who command as much as for those who are commanded. By contrast, Makdisi's concept of power harkens back to European political thought, in which context authority often refers to the capacity to compel 'obedience by others'. Coercion assumes the absence of agency on the part of those who administer the law as well as those to whom the law is administered. While the exercise of authority entails agency, power rules through coercion.[70]

ʿAruzi concludes his disquisition on the logic of sovereignty and political representation with a telling citation from the *Shahnama*, a text Masʿud Saʿd is said to have anthologised for Masʿud of Ghazna.[71] Written a century and a half earlier, at a time when the Ghaznavids were still ascendant, the *Shahnama* was becoming the major source for representations of pre-Islamic kingship in the eastern Islamic world. As the only explicitly poetic citation in ʿAruzi's introduction, Ferdowsi's dictum concerning the interdependency of the prophet and the sovereign is likely to attract the reader's attention:

> Know that kingship and prophethood
> are two jewels in one ring.

چنان دان که شاهی و پیغمبری
دو گوهر بود در یک انگشتری (*CM*, 42)

Towards the close of the second discourse (*maqaleh*) on 'the essence of the poetic art, and the task of the poet' we find an equally fortuitous invocation of the *Shahnama* and an even more nuanced presentation of the relation between the poet and the sovereign. The citation from Ferdowsi is uttered by Mahmud of Ghazna's vizier. Having just returned from a campaign spent wreaking destruction in India, the sultan does not grasp its import until the meaning is expounded to him. On the road home, Mahmud sends a robe as a gift to a rebellious Indian ruler who commands a powerful fortress in the hopes of quelling his seditious Indian subjects with luxury. When Mahmud expresses anxiety over the Indian ruler's reply to his vizier, the latter replies with a verse from the *Shahnama* that recalls the martial psychology of Rostom, who fought the enemy of the Iranians, Afrasiyab:

> If the answer goes against my wishes,
> I will [go with] the mace into the battlefield with Afrasiyab.

اگر جز بکام من آید جواب
من و گرز و میدان و افراسیاب (*CM*, 88)

Mahmud does not recognise the quote, so he asks his vizier to tell him its source. The speaker, the sultan adds, 'must have been rich in humanity'. The vizier explains that the poem was composed by poor (*bichareh*) Ferdowsi, who 'laboured for thirty years to finish the *Shahnama* and yet never saw a reward for his labours'. Mahmud expresses regret for his callous treatment of the poet who brought him the earliest complete version of the epic (an event the text narrates in detail) and orders his vizier to remind him to send a gift to Ferdowsi. When he returns to Ghazna, the vizier reminds the sultan of the gift. Mahmud is generous: he sends 60,000 dinars' worth of indigo to Tus, the poet's ancestral home. Fittingly, the gift arrives on the very day of Ferdowsi's funeral. Even more fittingly, Ferdowsi's daughter proudly rejects the sultan's bounty.

One would be hard-pressed to find a more moving evocation of the multifaceted dialectic between poetry and power than this incident, here accompanied by a detailed account of its oral transmission. 'Aruzi reports that the anecdote was told to him by Muʿizzi. This was just one year before Masʿud Saʿd's death, four years before Muʿizzi's own death, and four years after the critic visited Ferdowsi's grave. Mahmud's diminished and corrupted sovereignty thereby enters Persian literary history in (at least) three iterations: through Ferdowsi as an epic poem; through Muʿizzi as an oral anecdote; and ʿAruzi as a memory in literary-critical prose. The role played in the anecdote's transmission by Mahmud of Ghazna and his vizier is less evident than the role that the sultan's regret had for poets, his putative propagandisers, in undermining his authority while elevating poetry's discursive sovereignty.

With his account of the events surrounding Ferdowsi's death, ʿAruzi instructs his readers that the sovereignty of poetry is not always, or even usually, discernible in contexts contemporaneous with itself. No straightforward historical analysis can yield the ways of its mattering, or elucidate the channels of its fertility. When W. H. Auden famously argued that poetry 'survives / In the valley of its making,' he intended this clause restrictively, for poetry, he added, survives merely as a 'way of happening, a mouth'.[72] Auden's gloss offers a framework for understanding ʿAruzi's use of the *Shahnama*: the critic who memorialised the prison poet's lyric body was inspired by Ferdowsi's epic critique of Ghaznavid sovereignty.

ʿAruzi reads Muʿizzi's account of Mahmud's inadequate and belated recognition of Ferdowsi as testimony to poetry's untimeliness, which confers on it a special – and specifically political – power. Much like Ferdowsi's epic, if driven by different aesthetic mandates, Masʿud Saʿd's prison's poetry reconfigured power dynamics between patron and poet. By shifting authority onto poetry, the prison poet cultivated a new conception of poetry's discursive sovereignty. Although Masʿud Saʿd introduced the prison poet's lyric body to Persian poetics, it was in the prophetic body introduced to the prison poem by Khaqani that the genre achieved political salience.

The prison poem's conception of poetry's discursive sovereignty was also shaped by a growing awareness of the distinctiveness of Persian poetic discourse in the post-caliphal age. ʿAruzi was among the most discerning chroniclers of the transformations in sovereignty, rhetoric, and poetry that shaped the eastern Islamic world. His work has been closely examined here because his treatise inspired subsequent prison poets to produce their own prison poems, thereby extending the genre's parameters. Without his critical intervention, the prison poem could not have circulated as widely as it did across West, South and Central Asia, nor could it so boldly have reconfigured relations between poets and their sovereigns.

To return to ʿAruzi's initial reference to the *Shahnama*, comparing prophetic authority and sovereign power: 'Know that prophet and king [*payghambari o shahi*] / are two jewels on one ring.' This verse can be read at multiple levels. 'Two jewels in one ring' would seem to suggest complementarity, but, as shown in the analysis of the prison poet's prophetic body, *gawhar* (jewel) has many ambivalent valences. These tensions become apparent while probing into its subtextual associations. Might a ring with two jewels become a burden? Wouldn't two jewels weigh too much, like two bodies trying to fit on a throne intended for one ruler? The poem's syntax underscores the awkwardness: 'two jewels on one ring' violates logic and aesthetic harmony, and is hardly sustainable over the long term. A ring loaded with two jewels is as gaudy and excessive as Mahmud's dynasty, sustained through violent raids on Indian territory.

Contemporaneous authors such as al-Biruni wrote contemptuously of Mahmud's raids, the very same conquests celebrated by his court poets ʿUnsuri and Farrukhi.[73] Revisiting ʿAruzi's representation of Ghaznavid sovereignty in this context reveals the impact of the prison poem in reframing the discourse around power and authority. ʿAruzi perceived that sovereignty under Ghaznavid rule resembled a ring, like the ring in the *Shahnama*, overburdened with too many demographics vying for power. Far from being a perfect fit, the effort to fit too many jewels into a tightly circumscribed space is a prescription for disaster.

According to ʿAruzi's reading of this epic, penned a century earlier, Ferdowsi brings sovereignty (*padishahi*) and prophecy (*payghambari*) into close relation. Although the sovereign and the prophet (*payghambar*) – by this point in ʿAruzi's text the Persian term has entirely replaced the Arabic *nabi* – are indeed located in a single ring, they are situated at three degrees of separation from each other, with the imam intervening. Rather than concentrating power in a single entity, ʿAruzi and his contemporaries separated power from authority, just as they separated the king's sacred from his worldly body. This bifurcation in turn brought earthly power and poetry's authority into conflict. At this juncture, the prison poem transferred the internal contradictions of the king's bifurcated body onto the poet. Uniting the emasculated lyric self with the virile poet-as-prophet into a single body, the prison poem crowned the poet with otherworldly sovereignty.

ʿAruzi's attachment to the institution of poetry leads us to read the critic's assertion that after prophecy, 'no office is more powerful (*qavitar*) than that of the king (*malik*)' (*CM*, 44) with close attention to what goes unsaid: however powerful the sovereign may be, he cannot compete with the prophet. Further desacralising kingship by describing the king uncharacteristically as *malik* rather than as padishah, ʿAruzi registers the point clearly. Because ʿAruzi perceived that the prophet could potentially advance the poet's claim to discursive authority, he institutionalised poetic knowledge (*ʿilm-i shiʿr*), along with the arts of the chancellery (*ʿilm-i dabiri*), astronomy (*ʿilm-i nujum*) and medicine (*ʿilm-i tibb*). This reformulation of the status of poetry in relation to other disciplines, forms of knowledge, speech genres, and modes of power accompanied the development of the prison poem and its migration across the eastern Islamic world.

Guided by the new role accorded the poet in the age of sultanate power, twelfth-century literary and political theory subordinated philosophy to poetry. While Abbasid rule generated its own brand of theoretical speculation – as evidenced by the flourishing of dialectical theology (*kalam*) under the caliphs al-Maʾmun and al-Muʿtasim – the rise of the Ghaznavid and Saljuq sultanates was accompanied by political-theoretical speculation that enshrined the prison poem into the Persian literary system. Perceiving that a complete merger between the poet-philosopher-prophet and sovereign was unthinkable, ʿAruzi revived the concept of the imam, protector of the Islamic state and representative (*naʾib*) of the Prophet, as an agent who required the four elements of Persian statecraft – poetry, chancellery, astronomy and medicine – to secure his sovereignty.

This explains why many prison poets discussed in this book, most notably Khaqani, mobilised the semiotics of Sasanian kingship to evoke a world that medieval Persian polities never achieved: a society wherein the ruler was vested not only with the power to punish, but also with the sovereign authority to command. Whereas the caliph could compel consent as well as obedience, in the era of the prison poem, the authority to pronounce on the duties of the ruler was ceded to the poet. The ruler meanwhile closed his ears and shut his eyes to the injustices taking place around him. 'Authority,' Danish philosopher Søren Kierkegaard has reasoned, 'is that specific quality that enters from somewhere else and qualitatively asserts itself precisely when the content of the statement or act is made a matter of indifference.'[74] With respect to the light it sheds on how authority only comes into being through its performance in language, though not with respect to the relation between form and content, Kierkegaard could have been describing the Persian prison poem.

Notes

1. Daniel Philpott, 'Sovereignty', in Edward N. Zalta (ed.), *The Stanford Encyclopedia of Philosophy* (Summer 2016), available at: https://plato.stanford.edu/archives/sum2016/entries/sovereignty.
2. Ranajit Guha, *Dominance without Hegemony: History and Power in Colonial India* (Cambridge, MA: Harvard University Press, 1998).
3. March, *The Caliphate of Man*, xix.
4. Pollock's argument is introduced in Rebecca Ruth Gould, 'How Newness Enters the World: The Methodology of Sheldon Pollock', *Comparative Studies of South Asia, Africa and the Middle East* 28(3) (2008): 533–57.
5. Sheldon Pollock, *The Language of the Gods in the World of Men: Sanskrit, Culture, and Power in Premodern India* (Berkeley: University of California Press, 2006), 572.
6. Pollock, *The Language of the Gods in the World of Men*, 572.
7. Peter Skalnik, 'Authority versus Power: A View from Social Anthropology', in Angela Cheater (ed.), *The Anthropology of Power: Empowerment and Disempowerment in Changing Structures* (London: Routledge 1999), 162.
8. Pierre Clastres, *Society Against the State: Essays in Political Anthropology*, trans. Robert Hurley (New York: Zone Books, [1974] 1989).
9. Fawzi Najjar, 'Siyāsa in Islamic Political Thought', in Michael E. Marmura (ed.), *Islamic Theology and Philosophy* (Albany, NY: SUNY Press, 1984), 92–110; Bernard Lewis, '*Siyāsa*', in A. H. Green (ed.), *In Quest of an Islamic Humanism* (Cairo: American University of Cairo Press, 1984), 95.
10. Johansen, 'Eigentum, Familie und Obrigkeit', 54. Johansen cites Burhān al-Dīn Farghānī al-Marghīnānī's (d. 1197) *Al-Hidāya* as offering the first instance of this merger in the history of Islamic jurisprudence.
11. Spuler, 'Disintegration of the Caliphate in the East'.
12. For this early period in the formation of the caliphate, see Tayeb El-Hibri,

Parable and Politics in Early Islamic History: The Rashidun Caliphs (New York: Columbia University Press, 2010); Hugh Kennedy, *The Armies of the Caliphs: Military and Society in the Early Islamic State* (London: Routledge, 2001).

13. Farhad Daftary relates the succession crisis in the medieval Islamic world to the proliferation of sectarian differences in *Ismailis in Medieval Muslim Societies* (London: I. B. Tauris, 2005), 5.
14. For the claim to the inaugural status of this text for New Persian, see A. Khismatulin, 'Two Mirrors for Princes Fabricated at the Seljuq Court: Nizām al-Mulk's *Siyar al-mulūk* and al-Ghazālī's *Nasīhat al mulūk*', in Edmund Herzig and Sarah Stewart (eds), *The Age of the Great Saljūqs: The Idea of Iran* (London: I. B. Tauris, 2015), 95.
15. Morteză Dānishyār, 'Siyar al-mulūk -i Nizām al-mulk: aghlāt, maju'lāt va 'āmil-i ānhā', *Journal for the History of Islamic Civilization* 52(1) (2019): 27–57, criticises Khismatulin's thesis that the poet Mu'izzī was the author of the treatise. Khismatulin's argument is also criticised by Neguin Yavari, 'Siar al-Moluk', *Encyclopædia Iranica*, available at: http://www.iranicaonline.org/articles/siar-al-moluk, whose study of the genre, *Advice for the Sultan: Prophetic Voices and Secular Politics in Medieval Islam* (London: Hurst, 2014), remains a valuable resource.
16. Alexey Khismatulin, 'To Forge a Book in the Middle Ages', *JPS* 1 (2008): 30–66; Alexey Khismatulin, 'The Art of Medieval Counterfeiting', *Manuscripta Orientalia* 14(1) (2008): 3–29. Khismatulin reiterates his view concerning Mu'izzī's authorship in 'The Persian Mirrors for Princes Written in the Saljuq Period: the Book Series', *Vestnik of Saint Petersburg University, Asian and African Studies* 11(3) (2019): 321–44.
17. Haroon Khan Sherwani, *Studies in Muslim Political Thought and Administration*[2] (Lahore: Muḥammad Ashraf, 1945), 98; Spuler, 'Disintegration of the Caliphate in the East', 150.
18. Gibbon, *The History of the Decline and Fall of the Roman Empire*, 4:85.
19. This tradition includes works such as Kaykāwūs Ibn Iskandar's *Qābūsnāma* (1083), Naṣīr al-Dīn Muḥammad ibn Muḥammad Ṭūsī's *Akhlāq-i Nāṣirī* (1232), and Ḥusayn Vā'iẓ Kāshifī's *Akhlāq-i Muḥsinī* (1516). For the dating of *Naṣīḥat al-Mulūk*, see Patricia Crone, 'Did al-Ghazali Write a Mirror for Princes?' *JSAI* 10 (1987): 167–97. Sherwani (p. 149) notes that the authenticity of the attribution to al-Ghazālī has been questioned.
20. See Khismatulin, 'To Forge a Book', 46–52.
21. Khismatulin, 'To Forge a Book', 53–4. According to this account, the confusion

was caused by the omission of a single concluding dot that caused *bī* to be read in place of *zī*: معزي (Muʿizzī) became (Maghrebī) مغربی.

22. Dānishyār, 'Siyar al-mulūk', 54.
23. Before Khismatulin, see Murtaẕā Mudarrisī Chahārdahī, 'Muqaddimeh: Az Murtaẕā Mudarrisī Chahārdahī', *Siyāsat'nāmah*, ed. Muḥammad Qazvīnī, revised M. M. Chahārdahī (Tehran: Ṭuhūrī, 1334/1955/6), 7–8.
24. *Sīyāsatnāma*, ed. Charles Schefer (Paris: Ernest Leroux, 1891), 2.
25. Montgomery Watt examines the forms of pre-Islamic kingship inherited by the ʿAbbāsids from local Mesopotamian culture in two of his major studies on Islamic theology: *The Formative Period of Islamic Thought* (Edinburgh: Edinburgh University Press, 1973), esp. 46, 54, 170, and *Islamic Philosophy and Theology* (Edinburgh: Edinburgh University Press, 1985). In the latter work, Watt notes the 'long tradition of divine kingship' (21) in pre-Islamic Iraq which he associates with Semitic and Persianised Aramaens.
26. Khismatulin, 'To Forge a Book', 40.
27. *Sīyāsatnāma*, 5.
28. *Sīyāsatnāma*, 5–6.
29. Julie Scott Meisami, *Persian Historiography to the End of the Twelfth Century* (Edinburgh: Edinburgh University Press, 1999), 143.
30. See Amir H. Siddiqi, *Caliphate and Kingship in Medieval Persia* (Philadelphia, PA: Porcupine Press, 1977), who notes that pre-Islamic Persian kings such as Khusrow II called themselves gods and considered themselves above the law, while the sultan was bound to follow *sharīʿa* (p. 85).
31. Oktor Skjærvø, 'Introduction to Zoroastrianism', unpublished reader for 'Early Iranian Civilizations' course, Harvard University, 2006, 25.
32. Skjærvø, 'Introduction to Zoroastrianism', 25. For the relevant chapter from the *Avesta* dealing with *khwarnah*, see Yasht 19, 'To the Earth and the Divine Fortune' (Skjærvø trans., 112–19). The dating of the *Avesta* used here follows Skjærvø, 2.
33. For an explication of the five types of fire, based on Yasht 17.11, and the *Bundahishn* commentary, see A. L. Christensen, *L'Iran sous les Sassanides*[2] (Copenhagen: Ejnar Munksgaard, 1944), 141–78, esp. 146.
34. Safi, *The Politics of Knowledge in Premodern Islam*, 85.
35. Auer, *Symbols of Authority in Medieval Islam*, 105.
36. Ebrahim Moosa, *Ghazālī and the Poetics of Imagination* (Chapel Hill: University of North Carolina Press, 2005), 215.
37. Ferdowsī describes Tūrānians in terms that reference nomadic Turks in 3:7,

24 (Bertel's edn, Moscow). In the earlier sections of the *Shāhnāma* (e.g., 3:75, 1159–60), he seems to include China (*chīn*) within Tūrānian domains, thus complicating the ethnic equation. Contrary to the representations of Ferdowsī, Tūrānians are largely thought now to have been themselves an Iranian tribe (S. M. Stern, 'Afrāsiyāb', *EI*²).

38. 19:55–64; 19:77. The Avesta is cited from the translation in Skjærvø, 'Introduction to Zoroastrianism'.
39. Ferdowsī, *Shāhnāma*, ed. Vullers and Landauer (Leiden: Brill, 1977–84), 2:764, 3, v. 1444. al-Ṭabarī, *Tārīkh al-Rusul wa al-Mulūk*, 1:605 ff; al-Tha'ālibī, *Histoire des rois des Perses*, texte arabe publié et traduit par H. Zotenberg (Paris: Imprimerie Nationale, 1900), 222 ff.
40. The Kayanid kings listed in 19:71 include Kawi Kawâta, Kawi Aipivohu, Kawi Usadhan, Kawi Arshna, Kawi Pisina, Kawi Biyarshan, Kawi Siyāwarshan. They are contrasted to the Turanian villain Frangrasyān, and, without necessarily being deified, are declared to be 'beyond other living beings' (19:81).
41. L. Gardet ('*karāma*', *EI*²) argues that *karāma* was adopted as a synonym of the the verb *karuma*, 'to be generous', through the phonetic assimilation of χάρισμα. The difference between the early Christian χαρισματα and the Islamic *karāma* is registered, though not explored, in McCarthy, 'Al-Baqillani's Notion of the Apologetic Miracle', 248, n. 2.
42. As Arabic sources al-Hujwīrī cites *Book of Illumination* (*Kitāb al-Luma'*) of Abū Nasr al-Sarrāj (d. 987), which anticipates the structure of the Persian text, and *Acts of the Saints* (*Ṣirāṭ al-awliyā'*) by the mystic al-Ḥakīm al-Tirmiḍhī (d. 905–910).
43. al-Hujwīrī, *Kashf al-Maḥjūb*, ed. F. A. 'A. Zanjānī, 135–6.
44. Mu'izzī, *Divān*, ed. 'Abbās Iqbāl (Tehran: Kitābfurūshi-yi Islāmiyah, 1318/1938), 894.
45. On the *tashbīb* as a constituent element of the *qaṣīda*, see Alam, 'Persian in Precolonial Hindustan', 153, n. 68. For the tripartite *qaṣīda* structure generally, see Suzanne Pinckney Stetkevych (ed.), 'Introduction', in *Early Islamic Poetry and Poetics*, vol. 6, The Formation of the Classical Islamic World (Burlington, VA: Ashgate, 2009), xiii–xxxviii.
46. Greet Jan van Gelder, *Beyond the Line: Classical Arabic Literary Critics on the Coherence and Unity of the Poem* (Leiden: Brill, 1982), 43; Julie Scott Meisami, 'The Uses of the *Qaṣīda*: Thematic and Structural Patterns in a Poem of Bashshar', *JAL* 16 (1985) 58; Renate Jacobi, 'The Camel Section', of the Panegyrical Ode', *JAL* 13 (1982): 1–22.

47. For the little that has survived of Niẓāmī ʿAruẓī's poetry, see ʿAwfī's *Lubāb*, 246, 395–7.
48. See, for example, *Plato: The Symposium*, ed. Frisbee C. C. Sheffield (Cambridge: Cambridge University Press, 2008), 19 (187A–187B).
49. Al-Azmeh translates *mushākala* as 'mimesis' (*Muslim Kingship: Power and the Sacred in Muslim, Christian, and Pagan Polities* (London: I. B. Tauris, 2001), 155, 160, esp. 175 on the mimetic relation between prophets and kings). Niẓāmī ʿAruẓī's concept of mimetic representation derives from terms like *nā'ib* (representative) and *khalifa* (vice-regent).
50. See Max Weber, 'Politik als Beruf', *Gesammelte Politische Schriften*, ed. Johannes Winckelmann (Tübingen: Mohr, 1988), 505–60, later elaborated on in *Wirtschaft und Gesellschaft. Grundriss der verstehenden Soziologie* (1922), §17. I discuss Weber's account of the state use of violence in the epilogue to *Writers and Rebels*, 232–3.
51. Skalnik, 'Authority versus Power', 171. For an application of Weberian conceptions of power and authority to Islamic history, see Hamid Dabashi, *Authority in Islam: From the Rise of Muhammad to the Establishment of the Umayyads* (Piscataway, NJ: Transaction Publishers, 1989).
52. March, *The Caliphate of Man*, xix.
53. Compare Ibn Sīnā, *De anima*, Arabic text, ed. Fazlur Rahman (London: Oxford University Press, 1959), 248–50.
54. Compare Ibn Sīnā, *De anima*, 199–201, where prophets are said to have the capacity to induce natural disasters, including earthquakes and storms. Ibn Sīnā calls this capacity 'the practical faculty of the soul [*quwwā nafsiyya ʿamaliyya*]'.
55. See Shams-i Qays al-Rāzī, *Kitāb al-muʿjam fī maʿayīr ashʿār al-ʿajam*, ed. Mudarris-i Raḍawī, 148.
56. An early singular exception is Rādūyānī's Persian-language *Tarjumān al-balāgha*, which is the subject of Rebecca Ruth Gould, 'The Persian Translation of Arabic Aesthetics: Rādūyānī's Rhetorical Renaissance', *Rhetorica: A Journal of the History of Rhetoric* 33(4) (2016): 339–71, and is translated in full by Michelle Quay in *Balaghas Compared.*
57. Al-Fārābī, *Mabādi' ārā' ahl al-madina al-faḍila*, ed. Freidrich Dieterici (Leiden: Brill, 1895), 58–9.
58. Fauzi M. Najjar, 'Fārābī's Political Philosophy and Shīʿism', *Studia Islamica* 16 (1961), 66, n.1.
59. A. L. Ivry, *Al-Kindi's Metaphysics* (Albany, NY: SUNY Press, 1974), 29. Al-Kindī

and al-Fārābī's views on prophecy demonstrate the necessity of distinguishing among the many divergent intellectual traditions that fall under the heading 'Islamic'. Max Horten argued a century ago that in Islam prophecy coincides with philosophy at certain junctures and battles with it at other moments (*Texte zu dem Streite zwischen Glauben und Wissen in Islam* (Bonn: Marcus & Weber, 1913), 12). Oliver Leaman argues that Ibn Sīnā's theory of prophecy was 'strenuously opposed in the Islamic intellectual world' due to its questioning of the Quranic account (*The Quran*. ed. Leaman, 511).

60. Moses Maimonides, *The Guide to the Perplexed* [*Dalālat al-ḥā'irīn*], trans. M. Friedländer (London: Trübner, 1885), 2:221.
61. R. Walzer, 'Al-Fārābī's Theory of Prophecy and Divination', *Journal of Hellenic Studies* 77(1) 1957: 142–8, esp. 146.
62. As Sherwani notes (*Muslim Political Thought*, 74), al-Fārābī reproduces al-Kindī's distinction between the active intellect (*'aql al-fa''āl*) and the acquired intellect (*'aql al-mustafād*); the former realises itself in the latter.
63. A third Quranic reference to *manṭīq* (Q. 28:16) also anticipates prison poem poetics. The semantic field of *manṭīq* is alluded to in the discussion of Khāqānī's *qaṣīda* called 'Manṭīq al-ṭayr' ('Language of the Birds').
64. Spuler, 'Disintegration of the Caliphate in the East', 158.
65. Mas'ūd Sa'd, *Divān*, 1:493.
66. For Dante's political theology, see Kantorowicz, *The King's Two Bodies*, 451–95. Like 'Aruẓī, Dante argued for poetry's discursive authority, and like his Persian counterpart he did so in order to displace the ruler's power. The attribution of sovereignty to a poet is encountered '*Omero poeta sovrano* [Homer sovereign poet]', in the fourth canto of the *Inferno* (line 88).
67. R. Pande, *Succession in the Delhi Sultanate* (New Delhi: Commonwealth Publishers, 1990), 41.
68. Al-Māwardī, *Al-Aḥkām al-Sulṭānīyya*, ed. Maximiliam Enger (Bonn: Adolphum Marcum, 1249/1853), 3–33.
69. This work is published in *Rasā'il al-Kindī al-Falsafiyyah*, ed. Muḥammad 'Abd al-Hādī Abū Rīda (Cairo: Yuṭlabu min Dār al-Fikr al-'Arabī, 1950–3), 1:226–37. Al-Kindī may have taken his title [*al-Ibāna 'an al-'illa al-fā'ila al-qariba li al-kawn wa-l-fasād*] from Aristotle's *On Generation and Corruption*.
70. George Makdisi, 'Les rapports entre calife et sultan a l'epoque saljuqide', *IJMES* 6.2 (1975): 228–36. In this stimulating attempt to show that the continual hostility between the caliph and the sultan co-existed with 'une attraction magnetique entre pouvoir et autorite', Makdisi argues that 'The advent of the sultans

is explained by the fact that the caliph no longer had sufficient coercive force to maintain power [*pouvoir*]' (228, my translation).

71. Mahmud Omidsalar, 'Masʿūd Saʿd Salmān o Shāhnāma-yi Ferdowsī', *Gulistān* 3 (1999): 99–112; E. E. Bertels, *Istoriia persidsko-tadzhikskoi literatury* (Moscow: Vostochnoi Literatury, 1960), 386. Bertels says that Masʿūd Saʿd's patron Abū Naṣr Fārsī asked the poet to summarise one-third of Ferdowsī's poem. The result was *Ikhtiyaratī-yi Shāhnāma*, the first rewriting of Ferdowsī's poem. Omidsalar disputes the attribution of this lost work to Masʿūd Saʿd.
72. W. H. Auden, 'In Memory of W. B. Yeats', *Collected Poems*, ed. Edward Mendelson (New York: Vintage, 1979), 80–3.
73. Muḥammad ibn Aḥmad al-Bīrūnī, *Kitāb al-Bīrūnī fī taḥqīq mā lil-Hind min maqūlah maqbūlah fī al-ʿaql aw mardhūlah*, ed. Edward Sachau (London: Trubner, 1887), 11.
74. Søren Kierkegaard, 'The Difference Between a Genius and an Apostle', in *Without Authority*, trans. Howard Hong and Edna Hong (Princeton, NJ: Princeton University Press, 1997), 98.

Epilogue

Incarceration, Metonymy, Modernity

In this book, I have argued that the prison poem developed from existing conceptions of kingship a new concept of the poet's body – and a new role for the poet – to elaborate what was to become among the most nuanced dialectics between material power and poetic authority within Persian literature. The prison poem genre merged the prison poet's lyric and prophetic self to produce a literary language for discursive sovereignty, that gave poetry a political valence. In celebrating poetry's sovereignty, the prison poem shifted the authority that used to be attached to the ruler's body to the poet, a process facilitated by the decline of caliphal power. Stimulated by a new perception of the fragility and contingency of worldly power, this genre introduced a new political aesthetic into the twelfth-century eastern Islamic world.

As a genre that developed analogously with other topical genres such as the wine poem, the prison poem compellingly attests to the force of the 'new agendas' that characterise minor genres, which are often initiated by particular historical and political circumstances.[1] This case study of the Persian prison poem therefore provides a means of plotting genre's three overlapping dimensions. The formal dimension of the prison poem genre shaped the emergence of the lyric ode (as shown in Chapter 2), and of satirical and narrative poetic forms (as shown in Chapter 3). The topical and thematic content of the prison poem associated imprisonment with prophetic traditions relating to Muslim prophets (as shown in Chapter 4) and to Jesus (as shown in Chapter 5). Both developments consolidated the poet's discursive authority. The genre's discursive dimension – the content of its form, to adapt a phrase from Hayden White[2] – is further manifested in its use of discourses of governance to assert the poet's spiritual authority (as shown in Chapter 6). As these chapters show, the tensions generated by the clash between the constraints of the prison poem's form and the theme of imprisonment uniquely realign the dialectic between literature and experience.

Although it was inspired by the premodern prison poem tradition, *Prison Feats* (*Karnameh-yi zindan*, 1933) by modern Iranian poet Muhammad Taqi Bahar breaks with this classical Persian genre in several important respects.[3] First, and most obviously, Bahar's lexicon diverges from that of his predecessors. Whereas Khaqani interpolated Arabic into his Persian verse, Bahar uses Russian and French lexicons to generate similar forms of estrangement, albeit in a different historical context and for a different readership. A second divergence between modern and premodern prison poetry pertains to the formal dimension of genre. As seen throughout this study, the majority of classical prison poems are *qasida*s, even when the *qasida* takes the unconventional form of a lyric ode, as in the prison poetry of Masʿud Saʿd. The special relationship between the aesthetics of imprisonment and the panegyric have been documented throughout this book. But what about other literary forms? How did the prison poem relate to the narrative *masnavi*, a poetic form that occurs in rhymed couplets and which is used when the poet has a story to tell? And, moving into the contemporary period, how does the aesthetics of imprisonment operate in the medium of prose?[4]

The sources introduced in this book reveal a sharp distinction between poetry and prose for the classical prison poem.[5] This distinction becomes more fluid in modernity, with the advent of modern Iranian prison literature, which is overwhelmingly narrated in prose, especially in memoirs.[6] Although in verse, *Prison Feats* introduces a narrative dimension into a genre that until this point had been most at home in the lyric and panegyric modes. In the classical prison poem, the poet's lyric and prophetic body is external to space and time. With his prison narrative, Bahar introduces an element of contingency to the poet's body that earlier prison poets had projected onto the sovereign. As such, Bahar's verse narrative anticipates the prose memoirs that were to become a staple of the modern Iranian literature of incarceration, in Persian and later in English.[7]

As he moved away from the lyric ode that had hitherto dominated the genre of the prison poem, Bahar adapts another classical Persian verse form, the *masnavi*. In so doing, he further developed the transgressive potential of the prison poem, which is central to the logic of its existence as a genre.

Although the *masnavi* had long been a staple of classical Persian literature, *Prison Feats* is the first text to narrate a sustained experience of imprisonment using this form. Even Khaqani did not attempt this feat in his *Gift from Two Iraqs*, which was also a *masnavi*. Adapting the *masnavi* enabled Bahar to construct a narrative of imprisonment that engages with the historical record – and with the contingency of everyday political existence – in ways that eluded Mas'ud Sa'd and Khaqani. Historical consciousness is a constitutive feature of Bahar's literary modernity. Bahar's section headings are wholly consistent with the tradition of classical Persian narrative verse. They include such staples as 'on the reason for the composition of the book [*dar sabab-i nazm-i kitab*]'; 'description of prison [*sharh-i zindan*]'; 'reason for the construction of prison [cell] number two [*sabab bana-yi zindan*]'; and anecdotes (*hikayat*) of specific individuals, both fictional and literary-historical, including Sana'i and Shahid Balkhi.[8] *Prison Feats*' debt to the premodern prison poem tradition is further indicated lexically, by Bahar's use of terms such as *habsgah* (place of imprisonment), also used by Khaqani to signal his physical location (669, 681).

Bahar's debt to the classical tradition notwithstanding, many aspects of *Prison Feats* mark a sharp break with tradition. Terms such as *palto* (from the Russian *pal'to*, meaning coat) and *zhaket* (from the Russian *zhaket*, meaning jacket) and *ashkaf* (from the Russian *shkaf*, shelf) are reflective of Iran's contact with modern empires. Alongside these material accoutrements borrowed from the Russian lexicon, Bahar also uses more abstract and ideological French terms, such as *coup d'état* (681). With respect to the poem's appearance on the page, there are also major differences. Bahar's punctuation signals a clear departure from the manuscript tradition. More importantly, it registers a different medium by operating in a world of prose.

Punctuation has a specific function in modern narrative, as can be seen from Bahar's use of self-references within parentheses. When he says to himself 'Don't say that' (666), the statement is clearly marked as part of an internal monologue; it is enclosed within parentheses. He then follows with a sarcastic response couched between parentheses ('They were guests!') – which means the opposite of what it says – and ends in an exclamation mark. Through such modern punctuation, the poet evokes a dialogue, either between himself and an unnamed interlocutor, or within himself. Both are well-suited to the irony of this exchange. Equally, while many of the section headings could have been taken straight from the classical *masnavis* of Nizami and his imitators, other headings bear more in common with chapter headings of a modern novel or a Chekhovian short story. Among the latter category are 'Prison Row Number Two' (670) and 'Prison Row Number One' (672). What makes this second category of headings modern is that they denote specific historical locations that cannot be incorporated into a recurring narrative or an allegory. Their aesthetic is that of the realist short story, not of the medieval romance suffused with archetypes and symbols.

When Bahar deploys the techniques of literary modernism, he imagines the world in prose, albeit from within the confines of a classical verse. When he deploys the language of modernity, Bahar also adopts techniques, specifically the privileging of metonymy to metaphor that Roman Jakobson has shown to be characteristic of prose.[9] Another mark of Bahar's modernist aesthetic is an entanglement within an historicist sensibility that conceives of temporal progress as a succession of monumental individuals. The particularising aesthetics of Bahar's catalogue of famous men – Shah ʿAbbas, Peter the Great and Napoleon (697) – resonates with this modern sense of history, and stands in tension with the classical aesthetics that inform other parts of the poem. Catalogues featured widely in premodern literature, of course, notably in Homer's famous catalogue of ships in the *Iliad*, but their function was to generate a sense of epic grandeur rather than to mark a specific historical moment. Rather than evoking awe in the reader, the function of Bahar's catalogue is to capture a specific moment in place and time. *Prison Feats* situates the poet as an historical being in a way no classical prison poem had ever done. The paradigmatic untimeliness of the premodern Persian prison poem stands in contrast to the historicising orientation of the modern Iranian literature of incarceration, which stake their political legitimacy precisely on the evidence they bring forward of torture, forced confession and interrogation, summary execution, rape and other abuses of sovereign power.

While Khaqani's prison poetry is densely intertextual, *Prison Feats* is intertextual in specifically modernist ways. Like T. S. Eliot's 'The Wasteland' (1922), *Prison Feats* flaunts its learning. Bahar brandishes his debts to his predecessors by naming them at multiple junctures in his narrative. An entire section of the poem is devoted to the poet's dreamtime encounter with Sana'i (687–689), author of *Feats of Balkh* (*Karnameh-yi Balkh*), a *masnavi* invoked in the title of Bahar's poem (*Karnameh-yi zindan*). Similarly, Bahar closes with an encounter with the tenth-century Central Asian poet Shahid Balkhi (778). Such encounters are not unheard of in premodern Persian poetry. In a *masnavi* that he called the '*Shahnama* of Hindustan', the fourteenth-century south Indian poet ʿIsami incorporated a lengthy dream narrative of an encounter with Nizami, for example.[10] Bahar's classical allusions co-exist with a modernist intertextuality that ruptures past from present.

The migration of the carceral aesthetic to a prosaic and historicising orientation can be observed across world literature, not only in Persian. A prose poem by Borges, entitled simply 'A Dream', offers a striking intertext with the Persian prison poem.[11] Borges describes a medieval Iranian setting that strikingly evokes, intentionally or not, the prison poem in its early phase, as developed by Masʿud Saʿd. 'In a deserted place in Iran there is a not very tall stone tower that has neither door nor window,' Borges writes, tracing in his imagination the outlines of a prison cell. Borges then characteristically develops the referential thread of his narrative, inserting himself as narrator into the action: 'In that circular cell, a man who looks like me is writing in letters I cannot understand a long poem about a man who in another circular cell is writing a poem about a man who in another circular cell . . .'[12] We may never know the source of Borges' knowledge of Persian prison poetry, but this sentence magically reproduces the genre's core feature: the perpetual deferral of empirical experience onto the otherworldly temporality of poetry, only to bring it back, with even greater force, to the present. Borges concludes his prose poem on a circular note: 'The process never ends and no one will be able to read what the prisoners write.' It is as if Borges stopped with the first phase of the Persian prison poem and chose not to narrate its apotheosis in the political-theological poems of Khaqani. He perceives what the prison poem was in its beginning but does not refer to what it had become by its end. While it is indeed true that the process of writing prison poetry never ends, it was not the case – certainly not after Khaqani – that no one could ever read what prisoners wrote. Across the centuries of Persian literature, up to and including the moment in which I write, the prison poem genre has amplified the voices of prisoners and other victims of injustice.[13] It has been able to marry aesthetics and politics so effectively thanks to the transhistorical, transnational and transgressive force of genre.

Nergis Ertürk has argued in her account of modern Turkish aesthetics that 'under modernity, this debt economy of poetic language yields to the logic of general equivalence, the tulip returning to its random formal being as the arbitrary representation of a flower'.[14] Such is the impact of capitalist aesthetics on the prison poem. The classical rhetoric of the twelfth-century prison poem yielded to the prosaic logic of general equivalence, informed by the prose of the world, even when poetry remained the medium of composition, as it did in the poems of Bahar discussed above. These literary transformations were accompanied by political shifts, from a state ruled by a single sovereign, to a polity, to the agitations for a constitutional mode of governance that would make Parliament sovereign during Iran's Constitutional Revolution (1906–1911). Viewed from this angle, the political history of the Persian prison poem is a microcosm of the role that literary genres play in shaping political resistance. In this way, the Persian prison poem entered world literature, constructing a framework for poetry's mobility across continents and across genres, before the geography of world literature was reconfigured by the nation-state.

Notes

1. Mark Phillips, 'Histories, Micro- and Literary', *NLH* 34(2) (2003): 213.
2. Hayden White, *The Content of the Form: Narrative Discourse and Historical Representation* (Baltimore, MD: Johns Hopkins University Press, 1987).
3. For this text, see Malik al-Shuʿarāʾ Bahār, *Dīwān-i ashʾār-i shadravan Muḥammad Taqī Bahār 'Malik al- Shuʿarā'* (Tehran: Intishārāt-i Ṭūs, 1368/1989), 661–778. Page references are to this edition.
4. This question is beyond this scope of this study, but it is the focus of works such as Rebecca Ruth Gould, 'Literature as a Tribunal: The Modern Iranian Prose of Incarceration', *Prose Studies* 39(1) (2017): 19–38.
5. The only classical prison poet who was primarily known for his prose is Naṣrullāh Munshī, translator of *Kalīla wa Dimna*. Two of his prison poems are included in *Zindān, nāmah'hā-yi Fārsī*, 151.
6. One of the first such memoirs is by Ali Dashti, and is the subject of J. E. Knörzer's study, *Ali Dashti's Prison Days: Life under Reza Shah* (Costa Mesa, CA: Mazda, 1994)

7. A few recent titles include Shahrnush Parsipur, *Kissing the Sword: A Prison Memoir*, trans. Sara Khalili (New York: The Feminist Press, 2013); Jason Rezaian, *Prisoner* (New York: Ecco Books, 2019).
8. These influences are discussed in Matthew Chaffee Smith, 'Literary Courage: Language, Land and the Nation in the Works of Malik al-Shuʿara Bahar', PhD dissertation, Harvard University, 2006, 28, 95.
9. Roman Jakobson, 'Two Aspects of Language and Two Types of Aphasic Disturbances', *On Language* (Cambridge, MA: Harvard University Press, 1990), 115–33, esp. 111.
10. ʿAbd al-Malik ʿIṣāmī, *Futūḫu's salāṭīn: or, Shāh nāmah-i Hind of ʿIṣāmī*; Translation and Commentary by Agha Mahdi Husain (Bombay: Aligarh Muslim University, 1967–1977). The Persian text is published as *Futuhus-Salatin*, ed. A. S. Usha (Madras: University of Madras, 1948).
11. Jorge Luis Borges, *Poesía completa* (New York: Knopf, 2012), 558 (for all citations on this page). Borges was an avid reader of Persian literature; see Borges, *This Craft of Verse* (Cambridge, MA: Harvard University Press, 2000), 35, 69–71, 73.
12. Ellipses in the original.
13. For the most recent iteration of the genre by the contemporary Baha'i poet Mahvash Sabet, see *Prison Poems*, trans. Bahiyyih Nakhjavani (London: George Ronald, 2020), and the single poem by her: 'Name of the Poem: The Word', trans. Rebecca Ruth Gould, *Index on Censorship* 47(1) (2017): 117.
14. Nergis Ertürk, 'Modernity and Its Fallen Languages: Tanpınar's "Hasret", Benjamin's Melancholy', *PMLA* 123(1) (2008): 50.

Appendix

Khaqani's Six Prison Poems

The six poems identified in this work as Khaqani's prison poems are listed below. As noted above, the list could be expanded depending on one's definition of 'prison poem'. This particular list aims to help the reader follow the discussion, not to identify every potential prison poem. In keeping with the conventions for organising poetry in Persian, the order of the poems is given in alphabetical order according to their rhyme. Page numbers listed below refer to *Dīvān-i Afẓal al-Dīn Bedīl b. ʿAlī Najjār Khāqānī Shirvānī*, ed. Ziyā' al-Dīn Sajjādī (Tehran: Zuvvār, 1388).

Prison Poem No. 1 (Christian Qasida) (pp. 23–8)

فلک کژروتر است از خط ترسا
مرا دارد مسلسل راهب آسا

The sky goes astray more than the Christian script.
It holds me in chains like a monk.

Prison Poem No. 2 (pp. 60–2)

راحت از راه دل چنان برخاست
که دل اکنون ز بند جان برخاست

Comfort left the path to my heart,
as the heart rose from the shackles of life.

Prison Poem No. 3 (pp. 173–4)

غصه بر هر دلی که کار کند
آب چشم آتشین نثار کند

When grief strikes a heart,
it brings fiery water to the eyes.

Prison Poem No. 4 (pp. 279–83)

روزم فرو شد از غم و هم غمخواری ندارم
رازم برآمد از دل و هم دلبری ندارم

My day set in sorrow. I have no one to share my grief.
My heart has revealed its secret. No one takes my heart.

Prison Poem No. 5 (pp. 239–43)

هر صبح پای صبر به دامن درآورم
پرگار عجز، گرد سر و تن درآورم

Every morning, I fold the legs of patience under my robe.
I wrap a compass of helplessness round my head and body.

Prison Poem No. 6 (pp. 320–4)

صبح‌دم چون کله بندد آه دود آسای من
چون شفق در خون نشیند چشم شب پیمای من

In the morning when my smoke-like sigh hovers in the air,
my night-treading eyes drown like the dawn in blood.

Abbreviations

Prose Texts

CM	Niẓāmī al-ʿAruẓī Samarqandī, *Chahār maqāleh* (=*Majmaʿ al-nawāder*; *Four Discourses*)
HS	Rashīd al-Dīn Vaṭvāṭ, *Ḥadāʾiq al-siḥr fī daqāʾiq al-shiʿr* (*Magic Gardens: On the Nuances of Poetry*)
SM	Niẓām al-Mulk [and Muʿizzī Nishāpurī], *Sīyāsatnāma* (=*Siyyar al-Mulūk*; *Conduct of Kings*)

Journals

BSOAS	*Bulletin of the School of Oriental and African Studies*
DWI	*Die Welt des Islams*
IJMES	*International Journal of Middle Eastern Studies*
JAL	*Journal of Arabic Literature*
JAOS	*Journal of the American Oriental Society*
JNES	*Journal of Near Eastern Studies*
JPS	*Journal of Persianate Studies*
JRAS	*Journal of the Royal Asiatic Society of Great Britain and Ireland*
JSAI	*Jerusalem Studies in Arabic and Islam*
MDAT	*Majallah-yi Dānishkada-yi Adabīyāt-i Tehrān*
MLQ	*Modern Language Quarterly*
NLH	*New Literary History*
PMLA	*Proceedings of the Modern Language Association*
TSLL	*Texas Studies in Literature and Language*
YCLG	*Yearbook of Comparative Literature and General Literature*
ZDMG	*Zeitschrift der Deutschen Morgenländischen Gesellschaft*

Reference Works

Dehkhodā	ʿA.-A. Dehkhodā, *Lughatnāma-yi Dehkhodā*[2] (Tehran: University Printing and Publishing, 1994), available at: https://dehkhoda.ut.ac.ir/fa/dictionary.
EI[2]	*The Encyclopaedia of Islam*[2], eds C. E. Bosworth, E. van Donzel, W. P. Heinrichs and G. Lecomte (Leiden: Brill, 1961–2004).
EIr	*Encyclopedia Iranica*, ed. Ehsan Yarshater, *Encyclopaedia Iranica* (London and Costa Mesa, CA: Encyclopaedia Iranica Foundation, 1982–), available at: www.iranica.com.

Bibliography

Manuscript Catalogues

Catalogus Codicum Orientalium Bibliothecae Academiae Regiae Scientiarum, ed. P. de Jong (Leiden: Rijksuniversiteit, 1862).

Maulavi Abdul Muqtadir (ed.). *Catalogue of the Arabic and Persian Manuscripts* (Calcutta: Bengal Secretariat Book Depot, 1908).

Ahlwardt, Wilhelm. *Verzeichniss der arabischen Handschriften der Königlichen Bibliothek zu Berlin* (Berlin: Schade, 1894).

Primary Sources

Abjadī, Muḥammad Ismā'il Khān. *Sharḥ-i Tuḥfat al-ʿIraqayn*, ed. Muḥammad Ḥusayn Maḥvī (Madras: University of Madras, 1954). [Volume 4 of *Kullīyāt-i Abjadī*].

Abū Yūsuf, *Kitāb al-Kharāj* (Cairo: al-Maṭbaʿah al-Salafiyah wa-Maktabatuhā, 1962–1963).

al-Abraṣ, ʿAbīd Ibn. *The Divāns of ʿAbīd Ibn Al-Abraṣ, of Asad and ʿAmīr Ibn Aṭ-Ṭufail, of ʿĀmīr Ibn Ṣaʿṣaʿah*, trans. and ed. Charles Lyall, Gibb Memorial Series (London: Luzac, 1913).

al-ʿArabī, Ibn. *Fuṣūṣ al-Ḥikam*, ed. Abū al-ʿAlā' ʿAfīfī (Beirut: Dār al-Kitāb, n.d.).

al-ʿAruẕī, Niẕāmī Samarqandī. *Chahār maqāleh* (=*Majmaʿ al-nawāder*), ed. Muḥammad Qazwīnī (Berlin: Irānshahr, 1927).

al-Bāqillānī, Abū Bakr. *Kitāb al-bayān ʿan al-farq bayn al-muʿjizāt wa'l-karāmāt wa'l-ḥiyal wa'l kahāna wa'l siḥr wa' l-nāranjāt*, ed. Richard J. McCarthy (Beirut: Librairie Orientale, 1957).

al-Bīrūnī, Muḥammad ibn Aḥmad. *Kitāb al-Bīrūnī fī taḥqīq mā lil-Hind min maqūlah maqbūlah fī al-ʿaql aw mardhūlah*, ed. Edward Sachau (London: Trubner, 1887).

al-Buḥturī, al-Walīd ibn 'Ubayd. *Dīwān al-Buḥturī*, ed. Ḥasan Kāmil Ṣayrafī (Cairo: Dār al-Ma'ārif, 1963).

al-Farabi, Abū Naṣr Muḥammad ibn Muḥammad. *Mabādi' ārā' ahl al-madina al-faḍila*, ed. Freidrich Dieterici (Leiden: Brill, 1895).

al-Kindī, Ya'qūb Ibn Ishaq. *Fī al-Falsafah al-Ūlā* [=A. L. Ivry (trans.), *Al-Kindi's Metaphysics: A Translation of Ya'qub ibn Ishaq al-Kindi's Treatise 'On First Philosophy'*] (Albany, NY: SUNY Press, 1974).

al-Kindī, Ya'qūb Ibn Ishaq. *Rasā'il al-Kindī al-Falsafiyyah*, ed. M. A. H. Abū Ridāh (Cairo: Yuṭlabu min Dār al-Fikr al-'Arabi, 1950–3).

al-Ma'arrī, Abū'l 'Alā'. *Dīwān luzūm mā lā yalzam*, ed. Kamāl al-Yāzjī (Beirut: Dār al-Jamīl, 1992).

al-Māwardī, *Al-Aḥkām al-Sulṭānīyya*, ed. Maximiliam Enger (Bonn: Adolphum Marcum, 1249/1853).

al-Mulk, Niẓām. *Sīyāsatnāma* (=*Siyyar al-Mulūk*), ed. Charles Schefer (Paris: Ernest Leroux, 1891).

al-Mu'tamid bin 'Abbād, *Dīwān al-Mu'tamid b. 'Abbād*, Reẓā al-Ḥabīb al-Suwaysī (Tunis: Dār al-Tūnesiah, 1975).

al-Rāzī, Shams-i Qays. *Kitāb al-mu'jam fī ma'ayīr ash'ār al-'ajam*, ed. Mudarris-i Raḍawī (Tehran: Kitābfurūshī-yi Tehrān, 1338/1959).

al-Shāfi'ī, Abī 'Abd Allāh Muḥammad ibn Idrīs, *Kitāb al-'Umm* (Cairo: al-Maṭba'ah Kubrā, 1903–1907).

al-Tha'ālibī, Abd al-Malik ibn Muḥammad. *Thimār al-qulūb fī al-muḍāf wa-al-mansūb* (Cairo: Maṭba'at al-Ẓāhir, 1326/1908).

al-'Ulamā-yi Garakanī, Muḥammad Ḥusayn Shams. *Quṭūf al-rabī' fī ṣunūf al-badī'*, ed. Murtaẓā Qāsimī, Aṣghar Dādbih and Badr al-Zamān Qarīb (Tehran: Farhangistān-i Zabān va Adab-i Fārsī, [1843] 2010).

'Aṭṭār, Farīd al-Dīn. *Dīvān*, ed. Badī' al-Zamān Fūrūzānfar (Tehran: Negah, 1994).

'Awfī, Muḥammad. *Lubāb al-Albāb*, ed. Sa'īd Nafīsī (Tehran: Fakhr-i Rāzī, 1333/1954/5)

Bābur [Ẓahīr al-Dīn Muḥammad]. *Bâburnâma: Chaghatay Turkish Text with Abdul-Rahim Khankhanan's Persian Translation*, ed. and trans. Wheeler Thackston (Cambridge, MA: Harvard University Press, 1993).

Bahār, Malik al-Shu'arā' (ed.). *Mujmal al-Tawārīkh* (Tehran: Chāpkhāneh-yi Khāvar, 1318/1939).

Bahār, Malik al-Shu'arā'. *Dīvān-i ash'ār-i shadravan Muḥammad Taqī Bahār 'Malik al- Shu'arā"* (Tehran: Intishārāt-i Ṭūs, 1368/1989).

Bākīkhānuf, ʿAbbās Qulī Agha Qudsī. *Gulistān-i Iram* (Tehran: Asnād va Khadamāt-i Pazhuheshi, 1382/2003/4).

Baranī, Ẓiyāʿ al-Dīn. *Fatāwā-yi jahāndārī*, ed. Afsar Salīm Khān (Lahore: Idāre-i Taḥqīqāt-i Pākistān, Dānishgāh-i Panjāb, 1972).

Baylaqānī, Mujīr al-Dīn. *Dīvān-i Mujīr al-Dīn Baylaqānī*, ed. Muḥammad Abādī (Tabriz: Mu'assassah-'i Tārīkh va Farhang-i Irān, 1358).

Chakhrukhadze, Grigol. *Tamariani*, trans. Shalva Nutsubidze (Tbilisi: Tbilisskogo gosudarstvennogo universiteta, 1943).

Dawlatshāh Samarqandī. *Taḏhkira al Shuʿarā'*, ed. Edward Granville Browne (London: Luzac, 1901).

Falakī Shirvānī, *Dīwān-i Falakī*, ed. Ṭāherī Shahāb (Tehran: Ibn Sīnā, 1345).

Ferdowsī, *Shāhnāma*, eds Djalal Khaleghi-Motlagh, Mahmoud Omidsalar and Abū al-Faẓl Khaṭībī (New York: Bibliotheca Persica, 1987–2008).

Ferdowsī, ʿAbd al-Qāsim. *Shāhnāmeh-ye Ferdowsi*, ed. Jules Mohl (Tehran: Sherkat-e sahāmī-ye ketāb-hā-ye jībī, 1974).

Ḥāfiẓ Shīrāzī, *Ghazalhā-yi Khvājah Ḥāfiẓ Shīrāzī bih taṣḥīḥ va muqābalah-'i Parvīz Nātil Khānlarī*, ed. Parvīz Nātil Khānlarī (Tehran: Intishāt-i Sukhan, 1337/1958).

Ḥassān ibn Thābit, *Diwan of Hassan ibn Thabit*, ed. Walid ʿArafat, Gibb Memorial Series (London: Luzac, 1971).

Hedāyat, Reẓā Qūlī Khān, *Majmaʿ al-Fuṣāḥa'*, ed. Maẓāhir Muṣaffā (Tehran: Chāp-i Mūsawī, 1960).

Ibn al-Athīr, *Al-Kāmil fī al-Tārīkh*, ed. Moḥammad ʿAbd al-Salām Tadmorī (Cairo: Dār al-Kitāb al-ʿArabi, 1997).

Ibn Hishām, *The Life of Muhammad: A Translation of Ishāq's Sīrat Rasūl Allāh*, trans. A. Guillaume (London: Oxford University Press, 1955).

Ibn Jubayr al-Andalusī, Muḥammad ibn Aḥmad. *Taḏhkira bi-al-akhbar ʿan ittifāqāt al-asfār* (Abu Dhabi: Dar al-Suwaydi, 2001).

Ibn Qudāma, *Al-Mughnī*, ed. Muḥammad Rashīd Ridā (n.p., 1367/1947–48).

Ibn Qutayba, *Kitāb ash shiʿr wa shuʿarā'*, ed. Gaudefroy-Demombynes (Paris: Les Belles Lettres, 1947).

Ibn Rashīq al-Qayrawānī, *al-ʿUmda fī ṣināʿat al-shiʿr wa naqdih* (Cairo: Maṭbaʿat al-Saʿādah, 1907)

Ibn Sīnā, *De anima*, Arabic text, ed. Fazlur Rahman (London: Oxford University Press, 1959).

Iqbāl, Muḥammad. *Kulliyāt-i Ashʿār-i Fārsī-yi Mawlānā Iqbāl Lāhorī*, ed. Aḥmad-i Sorūsh (Tehran: Kitābkhān-yi Sana'i, 1343).

ʿAbd al-Malik ʿIṣāmī. *Futuhus-Salatin*, ed. A. S. Usha (Madras: University of Madras, 1948).

ʿAbd al-Malik ʿIṣāmī. *Futūḫu's salāṭīn : or, Shāh nāmah-i Hind of ʿIṣāmī*; translation and commentary by Agha Mahdi Husain (Bombay: Aligarh Muslim University, 1967–1977).

Jāmī, ʿAbd al-Raḥmān. *Nafaḥātu'l uns min khaḍarāt al-quds*, ed. Gholām ʿIsa ʿAbd al-Ḥamīd and Kabīr al-Dīn Aḥmad (Calcutta: W. Nassau Lees, 1859).

Khāqānī Shirvānī, *Dīwān-i Afẓal al-Dīn Bedīl b. ʿAlī Najjār Khāqānī Shirvānī*, ed. Ziyā' al-Dīn Sajjādī (Tehran: Zuvvār, 1388).

Khāqānī Shirvānī. *Tuḥfat al-ʿIraqayn*, ed. Yaḥyā Qarīb (Tehran: Amīr Kabīr, 1978).

Khāqānī Shirvānī. *Aiwān-i Madā'in: tasdīs-i qaṣīda-i Khāqānī, bi qalam-i chand nafar az fuḍalā' wa shuʿarā'-i Īrān=Aïwan-i-Medâin: un poème de Khâgâni (1606), adapté et augmanté par quelques poêtes contemporains* (Berlin-Wilmersdorf: Iranschähr, 1343).

Khusraw, Amīr. *Dībācha-yi ghurrat al-kamāl*, ed. Sayyid Vazīr al-Ḥasan al-ʿAbīdī (Lahore: Nīshnul Kumītī Barāyī Sāt-i Sū Sālah Taqrībāt-i Amīr Khusraw, 1975).

Maimonides, Moses. *The Guide to the Perplexed* [*Dalalat al-ḥāʾirīn*], trans. M. Friedländer (London: Trübner, 1885).

Masʿūd Saʿd Salmān. *Dīvān-i Masʿūd Saʿd Salmān*, ed. Rashid Yāsemi (Tehran: Tabʿ-i Kitāb: 1318/1939).

Masʿūd Saʿd Salmān, *Dīvān-i ashʿār-i Masʿūd Saʿd Salmān*, ed. Mahdī Nūriyān (Isfahan: Inteshārāt-i Kamāl, 1985).

Mudarris, Muḥammad ʿAlī. *Rayḥānatu al-ʿadab: dar tarājim-i aḥvāl-i maʿrūfīn bi-kunyah aw-laqab yā kunan va-alqāb* (Tehran: Chāpkhānah-'i Shirkat-i Sihāmī, 1948–1955).

Muʿizzī, Amīr ʿAbdollah Muḥammad. *Divān*, ed. ʿAbbās Iqbāl (Tehran: Kitābfurūshi-yi Islāmiyah, 1318/1939).

Nāṣir Khusraw. *Dīvān-i ashʿār-i Ḥakīm-i Nāṣir-i Khusraw Qubādiyānī*, eds Mujtabā Mīnuvī and Mahdī Muḥaqqiq (Tehran: Mu'assasah-'i Muṭālaʿāt-i Islāmī, 1978).

Rūdakī. *Dīvān-i Rūdakī*, ed. Manūchihr Dānish'pazhūh (Tehran: Tus, 1995).

Rūmī, Jalāl al-Dīn. *Kuliyat-i Shams-i Tabrīzī*, ed. Badīʿ al-Zamān Fūrūzānfar (Tehran: Sana'i & Sales, 2002).

Sabet, Mahvash. 'Name of the Poem: The Word', trans. Rebecca Ruth Gould, *Index on Censorship* 47(1) (2017): 117.

Sabet, Mahvash. *Prison Poems*, trans. Bahiyyih Nakhjavani (London: George Ronald Publisher, 2020).

Shavt'eli, Ioane. *Abdul-messiia*, trans. Shalva Nutsubidze (Tbilisi: Zaria Vostoka, 1942).

Shūshtarī, Mīr ʿAbd al-Laṭīf Khan. *Tuḥfah al-ʿālam va zayl al-tuḥfa*, ed. S. Muvaḥid (Tehran: Ṭahūrī, 1984).

Turkī, M. R. *Naqd-i Ṣiyrafiyān* (Tehran: Sukhan, 1394/2015).

Vaṭvāṭ, Rashīd al-Dīn. *Ḥadā'iq al-siḥr fī daqā'iq al-shiʿr*, ed. ʿAbbās Iqbāl (Tehran: Kitābkhānah-i Sanā'ī; Kitābkhānah-i Ṭahūrī, 1362/1984).

Vaṭvāṭ, Rashīd al-Dīn. *Sady volshebstva i tonkostiakh poezii*, ed. and trans. Natalya Chalisova (Moscow: Nauka, 1985).

Vaṭvāṭ, Rashīd al-Dīn. *Dīvān-i Rashīd al-Dīn Vaṭvāṭ*, ed. Saʿīd Nafīsī (Tehran: Kitābkhānah-'i Baranī, 1339/1920).

Secondary Sources

Ābād, Marẓīyah. *Ḥabsīyyah ʿsarāyī dar adab-i ʿArabī: az āghāz tā ʿaṣr-i ḥāẓr* (Mashhad: Dānishgāh-i Firdawsī, 2001).

ʿAbd al-Karīm Tawfīq ʿAbbūd, *al-Shiʿr al-ʿArabī fī al-ʿIrāq: min suqūṭ al-Salājiqah ḥattá suqūṭ Baghdād (547–656 H)* (Baghdad: Wizārat al-Iʿlām, 1976).

ʿAbd Allah, ʿAmr. 'Tajroba al-sijn: fī shiʿr Abī Firās al-Ḥamdānī wa al-Muʿtamid b. ʿAbbād', MA thesis, Al-Najah University, Nablus, Palestine, 2004.

Abrams, M. H. *Correspondent Breeze: Essays on English Romanticism* (New York: W. W. Norton, 1986).

Abulafia, David. 'Kantorowicz and Frederick II', *History* 62(205) (1977): 193–210.

Adorno, Theodor. 'Commitment', in Terry Eagleton and Drew Milne (eds), *Marxist Literary Theory: A Reader* (New York: Wiley-Blackwell, 1996).

Ahmad, Nazir. 'Amīd Loiki: A Seventh Century Poet', in Fathulla Mujtabi (ed.), *Indo-Iranian Studies* (Delhi: Indo-Iran Society, 1977).

Ahmad, Nazir. 'Sirajuddin Khurasani', *Islamic Culture* 38 (1964): 107–40.

Aḥmadgulī, Kāmrān and Sajjād Suleimānī Yazdī, 'Sabk-i āzarbāijān va shiʿr-i mitāfīzīk: Shatranj dar shiʿr-i Khāqānī Shirvāni va Abrāhām Kowlī', *Naqd-i zabān va adabiyāt khārijī* 14(19) (1996): 13–32.

Aḥmadī, Bābak. *Sākhtār va ta'vīl-i matn*, 2 vols (Tehran: Markaz, 1992).

Ahnert, Ruth. *The Rise of Prison Literature in the Sixteenth Century* (Cambridge: Cambridge University Press, 2013).

Ajami, Mansour. *The Neckveins of Winter: The Controversy over Natural and Artificial Poetry in Medieval Arabic Literary Criticism* (Leiden: Brill, 1984).

Akimushkina, Ekaterina. *Zhanr Habsiyyat v persoiazychnyi poezii XI–XIV vv* (Moscow: Natalis, 2006).

Alam, Muzaffar. 'Persian in Precolonial Hindustan', in Sheldon Pollock (ed.), *Literary Cultures in History: Reconstructions from South Asia* (Berkeley: University of California Press, 2003).

Alam, Muzaffar. *The Languages of Political Islam: India 1200–1800* (London: Hurst, 2004).

Al-Azmeh, Aziz. *Muslim Kingship: Power and the Sacred in Muslim, Christian, and Pagan Polities* (London: I. B. Tauris, 2001).

al-Baṣrī, Abū ʿUbaydah Maʿmar ibn al-Muthanná al-Taymī. *Kitāb al-Naqā'iḍ: naqā'iḍ Jarīr wa-al-Farazdaq* (Beirut: Dār al-Kutub al-ʿIlmīyah, 1998).

al-Hindī, Al-Muttaqī. *Kanz al-ʿummāl fī sunan al-aqwāl wa-al-afʿāl*, ed. Ḥ. Razzaq and S. al-Saqqā (Aleppo: Maktabat al-Turāth al-Islāmī, 1969).

ʿAlī Karīmī, Ghulām. 'Masʿūd Saʿd va Abū Firās al-Ḥamdānī', *Maʿārif-i Islāmī* 23 (1354/1975): 111–38.

Ali Khan, Mumtaz. *Some Important Persian Prose Writings of the Thirteenth Century AD in India* (Aligarh: Aligarh Muslim University, 1970).

Ali, Samer M. 'Reinterpreting Al-Buḥturī's Īwān Kisrā Ode: Tears of Affection for the Cycles of History', *JAL* 37(2) (2006): 46–67.

Aliev, Gazanfar Iu. *Persoiazychnia literatura Indii. Kratkii ocherk* (Moscow: Nauka, 1968).

Alieva, G. A. *Nizami i gruzinskaia literatura* (Baku: ELM, 1989).

Alikberov, A. K. *Epokha klassicheskogo islama na Kavkaze: Abu Bakr ad-Darbandi i ego sufiskaia entsiklopediia 'Rayhan al-haqa'iq'* (Moscow: RAN, 2003)

al-Khallāl, Aḥmad ibn Muḥammad. *Aḥkām ahl al-milal min al-jāmiʿ li-masā'il al-Īmām Aḥmad ibn Ḥanbal* (Beirut: Dār al-Kutub al-ʿIlmīyah, 1994).

al-Sinjilawi, Ibrahim. 'The Lament for Fallen Cities: A Study in the Development of the Elegiac Genre in Classical Arabic Poetry', PhD dissertation, University of Chicago, 1983.

al-Sinjilawi, Ibrahim Musa. *The 'atlal-nasib in Early Arabic Poetry: A Study of the Development of the Elegiac Genre in Classical Arabic Poetry* (Irbid, Jordan: Yarmouk University Publication, Deanship of Research and Graduate Studies, 1999).

al-Zabidī, A. A. *Zuhdīyyāt Abī Nūwās* (Cairo: Maṭbaʿat Kūstātsūmās, 1959).

Amanat, Abbas. 'Through the Persian Eye: Anglophilia and Anglophobia in Modern Iranian History', in Abbas Amanat and Farzin Vejdani (eds), *Iran Facing Others: Identity Boundaries in a Historical Perspective* (New York: Palgrave, 2011), 136–7.

Amir-Moezzi, Mohammad Ali. 'An Absense Filled with Presences. Shaykhiyya Hermeneutics of the Occultation', in Rainer Brunner and Werner Ende (eds), *The Twelver Shia in Modern Times: Religious Culture & Political* (Leiden: Brill, 2001), 38–58.

Anthony, S. W. 'The Domestic Origins of Imprisonment: An Enquiry into an Early Islamic Institution', *Journal of the American Oriental Society* 129 (2009): 571–96.

Anthony, S. W. 'The Meccan Prison of ʿAbdallāh b. al-Zubayr and the Imprisonment of Muḥammad b. al-Ḥanafiyya', in Maurice A. Pomerantz and Aram Shahin (eds), *The Heritage of Arabo-Islamic Learning* (Leiden: Brill, 2016), 2–27.

Anvār, Amīr Maḥmūd. *Aiwān-i Madā'in: Az Didgāh-i Shāʿir-i Nāmī Tazī o Parsī Buḥturī o Khāqānī* (Tehran: Dānishgāh-i Tehrān, 1383/2004).

Ascoli, Albert Russell. *Dante and the Making of a Modern Author* (Cambridge: Cambridge University Press, 2008).

Ashurbeli, Sara. *Gosudarstvo shirvanshakhov: VI–XVI vv* (Baku: ELM, 1983).

Asif, Manan Ahmed. *A Book of Conquest: the Chachnama and Muslim Origins in South Asia* (Cambridge, MA: Harvard University Press, 2016).

Asín Palacios, Miguel. *La escatologia musulmana en la Divina Comedia*[4] (Madrid: Hiperion, 1984).

Askari Sayed, Hasan. 'Awfi's Jawami-ul-Hikayat', *Patna University Journal* (1966): 9–69.

Auden, W. H. *Collected Poems*, ed. Edward Mendelson (New York: Vintage, 1979).

Auer, Blain Howard. *Symbols of Authority in Medieval Islam: History, Religion and Muslim Legitimacy in the Delhi Sultanate* (London: I. B. Tauris, 2012).

Auerbach, Erich. *Dante als Dichter der irdischen Welt* (Berlin: de Gruyter, 1929).

Bakhtin, M. M. *Russian Formalist Criticism: Four Essays*, trans. and Intro. Lee T. Lemon and Marion J. Reis (Omaha: University of Nebraska Press, 1965).

Bakhtin, M. M. *The Dialogic Imagination: Four Essays* (Austin: University of Texas Press, 1981).

Bakhtin, M. M. *Speech Genres and Other Late Essays*, trans. Vern McGee (Austin: University of Texas Press, 1986).

Bakhtin, M. M. *Rabelais and His World* (Bloomington: Indiana University Press, 1984).

Bakhtin, M. M. 'Problema rechevykh zhanrov', in *Sobranie sochinenii v semi tomakh*, ed. S. G. Bocharov and L. A. Gogotishvili (Moscow: Russkie slovari, 1996), 5:159–206.

Bakhtin, M. M. *Problems of Dostoevsky's Poetics*, trans. Caryl Emerson (Minneapolis: University of Minnesota Press, 2013).

Bakhtin, M. M. and P. N. Medvedev. *Formal'nyi metod v literaturovedenii: kriticheskoe vvedenie v sotsiologicheskuiu poetiku* (New York: Hildesheim, 1974).

Bāshā, Muhja Amīn. *Rithā' al-mudun wa-al-mamālik fī al-shi'r al-Andalusī: ittijāhātuh, khaṣā'iṣuhu al-fannīyah: dirāsa* (Damascus: Shirā' lil-Dirāsāt wa-al-Nashr wa-al-Tawzī', 2003).

Bāshā, Muhja Amīn. *Miḥnat shi'r al-sujūn wa al-'aṣr fī al-Andalus* (Damascus: Dār al-Sa'd al-Dīn, 2005).

Bastānīrād, Ḥossein. 'Ḥabsiyyeh-ye Mujīr al-Dīn Baylaqānī', *Majalleh Yādgār* 6 (1324/1946): 54–8.

Bauer, Thomas and Angelika Neuwirth (eds), *Ghazal as World Literature I: Transformations of a Literary Genre* (Beirut: Orient-Institut Beirut, 2005).

Baumstark, Anton. *Geschichte der syrischen Literatur* (Bonn: Marcus Weber Verlag, 1922).

Becker, Carl. '*Ubi sunt qui ante nos in mundo fuere*', *Aufsätze zur Kultur- und Sprachgeschichte vornehmlich des Orients: Ernst Kuhn zum 70. Geburtstag am 7. Februar 1916 gewidmet von Freunden und Schülern* (Breslau: Marcus, 1916), 87–105.

Becker, Mary Ellen. 'The Ubi Sunt: Form, Theme, and Tradition', PhD dissertation, Arizona State University, 1981.

Beelaert, A. L. F. A. *A Cure for the Grieving: Studies on the Poetry of the 12th Century Persian Court Poet Khāqānī Širwānī* (Leiden: Nederlands Instituut voor het Nabije Oosten, 1996).

Beelaert, A. L. F. A. 'The Ka'ba as a Woman: a Topos in Classical Persian Literature', *Persica* 13 (1988/9): 107–23.

Benjamin, Walter. 'On the Image of Proust', *Walter Benjamin: Selected Writings, vol. 2. Part 1: 1927–1930*, eds Michael W. Jennings, Howard Eiland and Gary Smith (Cambridge, MA: Harvard University Press, 1999), 237–47.

Benjamin, Walter. *Ursprung des deutschen Trauerspiels*, ed. Rolf Tiedemann (Berlin: Suhrkamp, 2000).

Bertels, E. E. *Istoriia persidsko-tadzhikskoi literatury* (Moscow: Vostochnoi Literatury, 1960).

Bertels, E. E. *Nizami i Fuzuli* (Moscow: Nauka, 1962).

Biran, Michal. 'The Mongol Transformation: From the Steppe to Eurasian Empire', *Medieval Encounters* 10(1–3) (2004): 341.

Bloom, Harold. *The Anxiety of Influence: A Theory of Poetry* (Oxford: Oxford University Press, [1973] 1997).

Borges, Jorge Luis. *This Craft of Verse* (Cambridge, MA: Harvard University Press, 2000).

Borges, Jorge Luis. *Poesía completa* (New York: Knopf, 2012).

Bosworth, C. E. *The Later Ghaznavids: Splendour and Decay* (New York, Columbia University Press, 1977).

Bosworth, C. E. 'The Concept of Dhimma in Early Islam', in Benjamin Braude and Bernard Lewis (eds), *Christians and Jews in the Ottoman Empire: The Functioning of a Plural Society* (New York: Holmes & Meier, 1982), 37–51.

Boutz, Jennifer Hill. 'Hassan ibn Thabit, a True Mukhadram: A Study of the Ghassanid Odes of Hassan ibn Thabit', PhD dissertation, Georgetown University, 2009.

Branham, Robert Bracht (ed.). *The Bakhtin Circle and Ancient Narrative* (Groningen: Groningen University Press, 2005).

Browne, Edward. 'Biographies of Persian Poets contained in Ch. V, §6, of the Tárikh-i-Guzída, or "Select History" of Ḥamdu'lláh Mustawfí of Qazwín', *JRAS* 32(4) (1901): 721–62.

Browne, Edward G. *A History of Persian Literature under Tartar Dominion* (Cambridge: Cambridge University Press, 1920).

Bürgel, J. Christoph. '"Die beste Dichtung ist die lügenreichste". Wesen und Bedeutung eines literarischen Streites des arabischen Mittelalters im Lichte komparatistisher Betrachtung', *Oriens* 23 (1974): 7–102.

Bürgel, J. Christoph. *The Feather of Simurgh: The 'Licit Magic' of the Arts in Medieval Islam* (New York: New York University Press, 1988).

Busse, H. *Chalif und Grosskönig, Die Buyiden im Iraq* (Beirut: Steiner, 1969).

Bynum, Carol Walker. 'Did the Twelfth Century Discover the Individual?' *Journal of Ecclesiastical History* 31 (1980): 1–17.

Capinha, Graça. 'Robert Duncan and the Question of Law: Ernst Kantorowicz and the Poet's Two Bodies', in Albert Gelpi and Robert Bertholf (eds), *Robert Duncan and Denise Levertov: The Poetry of Politics, the Politics of Poetry* (Stanford, CA: Stanford University Press, 2006), 18–31.

Cheah, Pheng. *What Is a World? On Postcolonial Literature as World Literature* (Durham, NC: Duke University Press, 2016).

Christensen, A. L. *L'Iran sous les Sassanides*[2] (Copenhagen: Ejnar Munksgaard, 1944).

Clastres, Pierre. *Society Against the State: Essays in Political Anthropology*, trans. Robert Hurley (New York: Zone Books, [1974] 1989).

Clinton, Jerome W. 'The Chronograms of Khaqani', *Iranian Studies* 2(2/3) (1969): 97–105.

Clinton, Jerome W. 'The *Madāen Qaṣida* of Xāqāni Sharvāni, II: Xāqāni and al-Buhturī', *Edebiyât* 2(1) (1977): 191–206.

Cohen, Mark. 'What Was the Pact of ʿUmar? A Literary-Historical Study', *JSAI* (1999): 100–57.

Cohen, Ralph. 'Genre Theory, Literary History, and Historical Change', in David Perkins (ed.), *Theoretical Issues in Literary History* (Cambridge, MA: Harvard University Press, 1991), 85–113.

Cohen, Ralph. 'Introduction: Notes toward a Generic Reconstitution of Literary Study', *NLH* 34(3) (2003): v–xvi.

Colby, Frederick S. *Narrating Muhammad's Night Journey: Tracing the Development of the Ibn ʿAbbas Ascension Discourse* (Albany, NY: SUNY Press, 2008).

Colie, Rosalie Littell. *The Resources of Kind: Genre-theory in the Renaissance* (Berkeley: University of California Press, 1973).

Correale, Daniela Meneghini. *Studies on the Poetry of Anvari* (Venice: Libreria Editrice Cafoscarina, 2006).

Croce, Benedetto. *La poesia di Dante* (Bari: Laterza, 1921).

Crone, Patricia. 'Did al-Ghazali Write a Mirror for Princes? On the Authorship of *Naṣīḥat al-Mulūk*', *JSAI* 10 (1987): 167–97.

Culler, Jonathan. 'Lyric, History, and Genre', *NLH* 40(4) (2009): 879–99.

Culler, Jonathan. *Theory of the Lyric* (Cambridge, MA: Harvard University Press, 2015).

Dabashi, Hamid. *Authority in Islam: From the Rise of Muhammad to the Establishment of the Umayyads* (Piscataway, NJ: Transaction Publishers, 1989).

Daftary, Farhad. *Ismailis in Medieval Muslim Societies* (London: I. B. Tauris, 2005).

Dānishyār, Morteẓā. 'Siyar al-mulūk -i Niẓām al-mulk: aghlāt, majuʿlāt va ʿāmil-i ānhā', *Journal for the History of Islamic Civilization* 52(1) (2019): 27–57.

Dante, *Divine Comedy*, ed. and trans. Charles Singleton (Princeton, NJ: Princeton University Press, 1980).

Daryāyī, Nāzīlā. 'Ustūreh-ye dūzakhī dar qālī-ye īrānī ['Infernal Mytheme in Iranian Carpet']', *Pajuhesh-ha-ye ensanshenasi-ye iran* 4(2) (2014): 89–104.

Davidson, Olga. 'Genre and Occasion in the *Rubāʿīyyāt* of ʿUmar Khayyām: The *Rubāʿī*, Literary History, and Courtly Literature', in Beatrice Gruendler and Louise Marlow (eds), *Writers and Rulers: Perspectives on Their Relationships from Abbasid to Safavid Times* (Wiesbaden: Reichert Verlag, 2004).

de Bruijn, J. T. P. *Of Piety and Poetry: The Interaction of Religion and Literature in the Life and Works of Ḥakīm Sanāʾī of Ghazna* (Leiden: Brill, 1983).

de Bruijn, J. T. P. *Persian Sufi Poetry: An Introduction to the Mystical Use of Classical Persian Poems* (London: Routledge, 1997).

de Man, Paul. 'Lyric and Modernity', *Blindness and Insight: Essays in the Rhetoric of Contemporary Criticism* (London: Routledge, 1983).

Evangelatou, Maria. 'The Purple Thread of the Flesh: The Theological Connotations of a Narrative Iconographic Element in Byzantine Images of the Annunciation', in Antony Eastmond and Liz James (eds), *From Icon and Word: The Power of Images in Byzantium. Studies Presented to Robin Cormack* (Aldershot: Ashgate, 2003), 269–85.

Dickins, Frederick Victor. *Hyak Nin Is'shu Or Stanzas by a Century of Poets, Being Japanese Lyrical Odes Translated Into English, with Explanat. Notes, the Text in Japanese and Roman Characters* (London: Smith, Elder, 1866).

Donoghue, Denis. *Metaphor* (Cambridge, MA: Harvard University Press, 2014).

Eksell, Kerstin. 'Genre in Early Arabic Poetry', in Anders Pettersson (ed.), *Literary History: Towards a Global Perspective* (Berlin: Walter de Gruyter, 2006), 2:156–98.

El-Hibri, Tayeb. *Parable and Politics in Early Islamic History: The Rashidun Caliphs* (New York: Columbia University Press, 2010).

el-Leithy, Tamar. 'Coptic Culture and Conversion in Medieval Cairo 1293–1524', PhD dissertation, Princeton University, 2005.

Elsky, Stephanie. 'Ernst Kantorowicz, Shakespeare, and the Humanities' Two Bodies', *Law, Culture and the Humanities* 13(1) (2017): 6–23.

Ertürk, Nergis. 'Modernity and Its Fallen Languages: Tanpınar's "Hasret", Benjamin's Melancholy', *PMLA* 123(1) (2008): 41–56.

Ethé, Hermann, *Avicenna als persischer Lyriker*, in *Nachrichten von der K. Gesellschaft der Wiss. und der Georg-Augusts-Universität* (Göttingen, 1875).

Farūzānfar, Badīʿ al-Zamān. *Sukhan va sukhanvarān* (Tehran: Intishārāt-i Khwārizmī, 1350).

Fattal, Antoine. *Le Statut légal de non-musulmans en pays d'Islam* (Beirut: Dar El-Machreq Sari, 1958).

Fiey, J. M. *Chretiens syriaques sous les Abbassides: 749–1258* (Louvain: Corpus Scriptorum Christianorum Orientalium, 1980).

Fludernik, Monika. *Metaphors of Confinement: The Prison in Fact, Fiction, and Fantasy* (Oxford: Oxford University Press, 2019).

Foucault, Michel, 'The Orders of Discourse', *Social Science Information* 10(2) (1971): 7–30.

Fowler, Alastair. *Kinds of Literature: An Introduction to the Theory of Genres and Modes* (Oxford and Cambridge, MA: Clarendon Press and Harvard University Press, 1982).

Fowler, Alastair. 'The Future of Genre Theory: Functions and Constructional Types', in Ralph Cohen (ed.), *The Future of Literary Theory* (London: Routledge, 1989), 291–303.

Frolov, D. V. *Klassicheskii arabskii stikh: Istoriia i teoriia aruḍa* (Moscow: Nauka, 1991).

Frye, Northrop. *Anatomy of Criticism* (Princeton, NJ: Princeton University Press, 1957).

Geltner, Guy. *The Medieval Prison: A Social History* (Princeton, NJ: Princeton University Press, 2008).

Ghanim, Ramlah Maḥmud. *Fann al-ḥabsiyat bayna Abī Firās al-Ḥamdānī wa-al-Khāqānī* (Cairo: Dār al-Zahra lil-Nashr, 1991).

Ghiyāth al-Dīn, Muḥammad b. Jalāl al-Dīn. *Ghiyāth al-Lughat* (Bombay: n.d., n.p).

Gibbon, Edward. *The History of the Decline and Fall of the Roman Empire* (Philadelphia, PA: B. F. French, 1830).

Giesey, Ralph E. 'Ernst H. Kantorowicz: Scholarly Triumphs and Academic Travails in Weimar Germany and the United States', *Leo Baeck Institute Year Book* 30 (1985): 196.

GlobalLIT Project. 'Balaghas Compared: Comparative Poetics in the Islamic World', a collaborative anthology, in preparation (EU's Horizon 2020 Research and Innovation Programme under ERC-2017-STG Grant Agreement No. 750346).

Goitein, S. D. *A Mediterranean Society: The Jewish Communities of the Arab World as Portrayed in the Documents of the Cairo Geniza* (Berkeley: University of California Press, 1971).

Goldziher, Ignáz. *Muhammedanische Studien* (Halle an der Saale: Max Niemeyer, 1889/1890).

Gould, Rebecca Ruth. 'How Newness Enters the World: The Methodology of Sheldon Pollock', *Comparative Studies of South Asia, Africa and the Middle East* 28(3) (2008): 533–57.

Gould, Rebecca Ruth. *The Timurid Book of Ascension (Mi'rajnama): A Study of Text and Image in a Pan-Asian Context* (Valencia: Patrimonio, 2009).

Gould, Rebecca Ruth. 'Prisons Before Modernity: Incarceration in the Medieval Indo-Mediterranean', *Al-Masāq: Islam and the Medieval Mediterranean* 24(2) (2012): 179–97.

Gould, Rebecca Ruth. 'Inimitability versus Translatability: The Structure of Literary Meaning in Arabo-Persian Poetics', *The Translator* 19(1) (2013): 81–104.

Gould, Rebecca Ruth. 'The Geographies of *'Ajam*: The Circulation of Persian Poetry from South Asia to the Caucasus', *Medieval History Journal* 18(1) (2015): 87–119.

Gould, Rebecca Ruth. 'The Much-Maligned Panegyric: Towards a Political Poetics of Premodern Literary Form', *Comparative Literature Studies* 52(2) (2015): 254–88.

Gould, Rebecca Ruth. 'The Persian Translation of Arabic Aesthetics: Rādūyānī's Rhetorical Renaissance', *Rhetorica: A Journal of the History of Rhetoric* 33(4) (2016): 339–71.

Gould, Rebecca Ruth. 'Wearing the Belt of Oppression: Khāqānī's Christian Qaṣīda and the Prison Poetry of Medieval Shirvān', *JPS* 9(1) (2016): 19–44.

Gould, Rebecca Ruth. *Writers and Rebels: The Literature of Insurgency in the Caucasus* (New Haven, CT: Yale University Press, 2016).

Gould, Rebecca Ruth. 'Literature as a Tribunal: The Modern Iranian Prose of Incarceration', *Prose Studies: History, Theory, Criticism* 39(1) (2017): 19–38.

Gould, Rebecca Ruth. 'From Pious Journeys to the Critique of Sovereignty: Khaqani Shirvani's Persianate Poetics of Pilgrimage', in Montserrat Piera (ed.), *Remapping Travel Narratives in the Early Modern World: to the East and Back Again* (Amsterdam: Amsterdam University Press and ARC Humanities Press, 2018), 25–47.

Gould, Rebecca Ruth. *Cityscapes* (Monee, IL: Alien Buddha Press, 2019).

Gould, Rebecca Ruth. 'The Persianate Cosmology of Historical Inquiry in the Caucasus: 'Abbās Qulī Āghā Bākīkhānuf's Cosmological Cosmopolitanism', *Comparative Literature* 71(3) (2019): 272–97.

Gould, Rebecca Ruth. 'Constellations', *Chiron Review* 118 (2020): 48

Gould, Rebecca Ruth. 'Russifying the *Radif*: Lyric Translatability and the Russo-Persian Ghazal', *Comparative Critical Studies* 17(2) (2020): 263–84.

Graf, Georg. *Geschichte der christlichen arabischen Literatur* (Vatican City, Bibliotheca Apostolica Vaticana, 1944–1953).

Gruber, Christiane. *The Timurid Book of Ascension (Mi'rajnama)* (Valencia: Patrimonio, 2009).

Gruber, Christiane. *The Ilkhanid Book of Ascension: A Persian-Sunni Devotional Tale* (London: I. B. Tauris, 2010).

Guha, Ranajit. *Dominance without Hegemony: History and Power in Colonial India* (Cambridge, MA: Harvard University Press, 1998).

Guillén, Claudio. *Literature as System: Essays towards the Theory of Literary History* (Princeton, NJ: Princeton University Press, 1971).

Gutas, Dimitri. *Greek Thought, Arabic Culture: The Graeco-Arabic Translation Movement in Baghdad and Early ʿAbbāsid Society (2nd–4th/8th–10th Centuries)* (London: Routledge, 1998).

Hanne, Eric J. *Putting the Caliph in His Place: Power, Authority, and the Late Abbasid Caliphate* (Madison, NJ: Fairleigh Dickinson University Press, 2007).

Hanning, Robert W. *The Individual in the Twelfth-Century Romance* (New Haven, CT: Yale University Press, 1977).

Ḥaqiqat, ʿAbdul Rafiʿ. *Tārīkh-i ʿIrfān va ʿarifān-i īranī: āz Bāyazīd Basṭāmī tā Nūr ʿAlī Shāh Gunābādi* (Tehran: Intishārāt-i Kumish, 1370).

Harb, Lara. *Arabic Poetics: Aesthetic Experience in Classical Arabic Literature* (Cambridge:

Cambridge University Press, 2020).

Ḥasān, Hādī. *Falakī-i Shirvānī: His Times, Life, and Works* (London: Royal Asiatic Society, 1929).

Ḥasān, Hādī. 'The Poetry of Muḥammad Falakī', *Researches in Persian Literature* (Hyderabad: Government Press, 1958).

Haskins, Charles Homer. *Renaissance of the Twelfth Century* (Cambridge, MA: Harvard University Press, 1927).

Hasluck, F. W. *Christianity and Islam under the Sultans* (Oxford: Oxford University Press, 1929).

Ḥassūkī, Naʿimah. 'Madḥ-i nabawī dar shiʿr-i Ḥassān-i bin Thābet va Khāqānī-yi Shirwānī', MA thesis, Tarbiat Modares University, 1385.

Haydarī, Maḥmūd and Fāṭemeh Taqīzadeh, 'Marsiya-yi shahr dar shiʿrī fārsī va ʿarabī', *Majalleh-yi būstān-i adab dānishgāhi Shirāz* 14 (1391): 22–42.

Hayot, Eric. 'Against Periodization; or, On Institutional Time', *New Literary History* 42(4) (2011): 739–56.

Hayot, Eric. *On Literary Worlds* (Oxford: Oxford University Press, 2012).

Hedāyat, Ṣādeq. *Tarānehayi Khayyām* (Tehran: Jāvīdān, 1352).

Hegel, G. W. F. *Aesthetics: Lecture on Fine Arts*, trans. T. M. Knox (Oxford: Oxford University Press, 1975).

Heinrichs, Wolfhart. *The Hand of the Northwind: Opinions on Metaphor and the Early Meaning of Istiʿāra in Arabic Poetics* (Wiesbaden: F. Steiner, 1977).

Heiserman, Arthur. *The Novel Before the Novel: Essays and Discussions About the Beginning of Prose Fiction in the West* (Chicago, IL: University of Chicago Press, 1977).

Hindī, ʿAbd al-Rahīm and Mīrzā Ismāʿīl Aṣaf, 'Dū shāhkār-i ṣinʿat', *Irānshāhr* 2(3) (1925): 282–92.

Hirsch, E. D. *Validity in Interpretation* (New Haven, CT: Yale University Press, 1967).

Hirsch, Hadas. '*Ghiyār*', in Norman A. Stillman (ed.), *Encyclopedia of Jews in the Islamic World* (Leiden: Brill, 2010).

Holt, Kelly. '"In the Sense of a Lasting Doctrine": Ernst Kantorowicz's Historiography and the Serial Poetics of the Berkeley Renaissance', PhD dissertation, University of California, Santa Cruz, 2009.

Horten, Max. *Texte zu dem Streite zwischen Glauben und Wissen in Islam. Die Lehre vom Propheten und der Offenbarung bei den islamischen Philosophen Farabi, Avicenna und Averroes* (Bonn: Marcus & Weber, 1913).

Hui, Andrew. *The Poetics of Ruins in Renaissance Literature* (New York: Fordham University Press, 2017).

Huizinga, Johan. *The Waning of the Middle Ages* (Garden City: Anchor-Doubleday, 1954).

Hunter, Erica C. D. 'Interfaith Dialogues: The Church of the East and the 'Abbāsids', in Karl Hoheisel and Wassilios Klein (eds), *Der Christliche Orient und seine Umwelt: Gesammelte Studien zu Ehren Jürgen Tubachs anlässlich seines 60 Geburtstags. Studies in Oriental Religions* (Wiesbaden: Harrassowitz, 2007), 56:289–303.

Hunter, Lynette (ed.). *Towards a Definition of Topos: Approaches to Analogical Reasoning* (London: Springer, 1991).

Hutson, Lorna. 'Imagining Justice: Kantorowicz and Shakespeare', *Representations* 106(1) (2009): 118–42.

Jacobi, Renate. 'The Camel Section of the Panegyrical Ode', *JAL* 13 (1982): 1–22.

Jakobson, Roman. 'Two Aspects of Language and Two Types of Aphasic Disturbances', *On Language* (Cambridge, MA: Harvard University Press, 1990), 115–33.

Jameson, Fredric. *The Prison-house of Language: A Critical Account of Structuralism and Russian Formalism* (Princeton, NJ: Princeton University Press, 1974).

Jameson, Fredric. 'The Ideology of Form: Partial Systems in "La Vieille Fille"', *SubStance* 5(15) (1976): 29–49.

Jameson, Fredric. *The Ideologies of Theory* (London: Verso, 2008).

Janowitz, Anne F. *England's Ruins: Poetic Purpose and the National Landscape* (London: Blackwell, 1990).

Johansen, Baber. 'Eigentum, Familie und Obrigkeit im hanafitischen Strafrecht: Das Verhaltnis der privaten Rechte zu den Forderungen der Allgemeinheit in hanafitischen Rechtskommentaren', *DWI* 19(1/4) (1979): 1–73.

Kahn, Victoria Ann. *Wayward Contracts: The Crisis of Political Obligation in England, 1640–1674* (Princeton, NJ: Princeton University Press, 2004).

Kahn, Victoria. 'Political Theology and Fiction in *The King's Two Bodies*', *Representations* 106(1) (2009): 77–101.

Kantorowicz, Ernst H. 'The Sovereignty of the Artist: A Note on Legal Maxims and Renaissance Theories of Art', *Essays in Honor of Erwin Panofsky* (New York: New York University Press, 1961).

Kantorowicz, Ernst H. *The King's Two Bodies: A Study in Mediaeval Political Theology* (Princeton, NJ: Princeton University Press, 1997).

Karamī, Muḥammad, 'Negāhī be maḍāmīn-i Musawī o zībāīhāyi ān dar dīwān-i Khāqānī', *Majalleh-yi 'Ulūm-i Ijtema'-yī o Insānī-yi Dānishkadeh-yi Shīrāz* 22(3) (1384).

Kazzāzī, Mīr Jalāl al-Dīn. *Sūzan-i 'Īsā: Khāqānī Shirwānī* (Tehran: Dānishgāh-i 'Allāmeh Ṭabāṭabāyi, 1997).

Kendlī-Harīschī, Ghaffār. *Khāqāni-ye Shirwānī, ḥayāt, zamān o moḥīṭ-i ū*, trans. Mir Hedāyat Ḥeṣāri (Tehran: Markaz Nashr-i Dānishgāhī, 1995; orig. in Azeri Turkish, Baku, 1972).

Kennedy, Hugh. *The Armies of the Caliphs: Military and Society in the Early Islamic State* (London: Routledge, 2001).

Kennedy, Philip. *The Wine Song in Classical Arabic Poetry: Abu Nūwās and the Literary Tradition* (Oxford: Clarendon Press, 1997).

Key, Alexander. *Language between God and the Poets: Ma'nā in the Eleventh Century* (Berkeley: University of California Press, 2018).

Khadduri, Majid. *War and Peace in the Law of Islam* (Baltimore, MD: Johns Hopkins University Press, 1955).

Khan, Geoffrey. 'The Historical Development of the Structure of Medieval Arabic Petitions', *BSOAS* 53(1) (1990): 8–30.

Khan, Rifaqatullah. 'Life of Khaqani', *Indo-iranica* 12(2) (1959): 24–44.

Khanikof, N. 'Mémoire sur Khâcâni, poëte persan du XIIe siècle', *Journal Asiatique* 6(4) (1864): 137–200; 6(5) (1865): 296–367.

Khismatulin, Alexey. 'The Art of Medieval Counterfeiting: the *Siyar al-moluk* (*Sīyāsat-nāma*) by Nizām al-Molk and the "Full" Version of the *Nasihat al-moluk* by al-Ghazāli', *Manuscripta Orientalia* 14(1) (2008): 3–29.

Khismatulin, Alexey. 'To Forge a Book in the Middle Ages: Nezām al-Molk's *Siyar al-Moluk* (*Sīyāsat-Nāma*)', *JPS* 1 (2008): 30–66.

Khismatulin, Alexey. 'Two Mirrors for Princes Fabricated at the Seljuq Court: Nizām al-Mulk's *Siyar al-mulūk* and al-Ghazālī's *Nasīhat al mulūk*', in Edmund Herzig and Sarah Stewart (eds), *The Age of the Great Saljūqs: The Idea of Iran* (London: I. B. Tauris, 2015), 94–130.

Khismatulin, Alexey. 'The Persian Mirrors for Princes Written in the Saljuq Period: the Book Series', *Vestnik of Saint Petersburg University, Asian and African Studies* 11(3) (2019): 321–44.

Knörzer, J. E. *Ali Dashti's Prison Days: Life under Reza Shah* (Costa Mesa, CA: Mazda, 1994).

Korangy, Alireza. 'Development of the Ghazal and Khāqānī's Contribution', PhD dissertation, Harvard University, 2007.

Korangy, Alireza. *Development of the Ghazal and Khāqānī's Contribution: A Study of the Development of Ghazal and a Literary Exegesis of a 12th c. Poetic Harbinger* (Wiesbaden: Harrassowitz Verlag, 2013).

Kraemer, Joel L. *Humanism in the Renaissance of Islam: The Cultural Revival During the Buyid Age* (Leiden: Brill, 1992).

Kurpershoek, P. M. *Oral Poetry and Narratives from Central Arabia: The Poetry of ad-Dindān* (Leiden: Brill, 1994).

Landau, Justine. 2013. *De rythme et de raison. Lecture croisée de deux traités de poétique persans du XIIIe siècle* (Paris: Presses de la Sorbonne Nouvelle/IFRI).

Lange, Christian. *Justice, Punishment, and the Medieval Muslim Imagination* (Cambridge: Cambridge University Press, 2008).

Larkin, Margaret, 'Al-Jurjani's Theory of Discourse', *Alif: Journal of Comparative Poetics* 2 (1982): 76–86.

Larkin, Margaret. *The Theology of Meaning: 'Abd al-Qāhir al-Jurjānī's Theory of Discourse* (New Haven, CT: American Oriental Society, 1995).

Lawson, Todd. *The Crucifixion and The Qur'an: A Study in the History of Muslim Thought* (London: One World, 2009).

Lewis, Bernard. '*Siyāsa*', in A. H. Green (ed.), *In Quest of an Islamic Humanism: Arabic and Islamic Studies in Memory of Mohamed al-Nowaihi* (Cairo: American University of Cairo Press, 1984), 3–14.

Lewis, Bernard. *Jews of Islam* (Princeton, NJ: Princeton University Press, 1984).

Lewis, D. 'The Rise and Fall of a Persian Refrain: The Radif 'Ātash u Āb', in Suzanne Pinckney Stetkevych (ed.), *Reorientations: Arabic and Persian Poetry* (Bloomington: Indiana University Press, 1994), 199–226.

Levy-Rubin, Milka. *Non-Muslims in the Early Islamic Empire: From Surrender to Coexistence* (Cambridge: Cambridge University Press, 2011).

Losensky, Paul. 'The Equal of Heaven's Vault: The Design, Ceremony, and Poetry of the Ḥasanābād Bridge', in Beatrice Gruendler and Louise Marlow (eds),

Writers and Rulers: Perspective on Their Relationship from Abbasid to Safavid Times (Wiesbaden: Ludwig Reichert Verlag, 2004), 195–216.

Losensky, Paul. 'Coordinates in Time and Space: Architectural Chronograms in Safavid Iran', in Colin P. Mitchell (ed.), *New Perspectives on Safavid Iran: Empire and Society* (London: Routledge, 2011), 198–219.

Lukács, Georg. *The Theory of the Novel: A Historico-Philosophical Essay on the Forms of Great Epic Literature* (London: Merlin Press, 1978).

Mahdavīfar, Sa'īd. '"Akhtar-i dānish" dar shiʿr-i Khāqānī', *Kārnāmeh Mīrās Maktūb* 5(49) (1390/2012–13): 32–6.

Māhīyar, ʿAbbās. *Sharḥ-i mushkilat-i Khāqānī: khār khār band o zindān* (Tehran: Jām-i Gul, 1382/2001).

Makdisi, George. 'Les Rapports Entre Calife et Sultan a l'epoque Saljuqide', *IJMES* 6(2) (1975): 228–36.

Ma'khūzī, Mehdī. *Ātash andar chang* (Tehran: Sukhan, 1388).

March, Andrew F. *The Caliphate of Man: Popular Sovereignty in Modern Islamic Thought* (Cambridge, MA: Harvard University Press, 2019).

Masani, Rustom Pestonji. *Court Poets of Iran and India* (Bombay: New Book Company, 1938).

Massé, Henri. 'Aspects du pélerinage à la Mecque dans la poésie persane', *Melanges Franz Cumont* (Brussels: Annuaire of the Institut de Philosophie, 1936), 859–65.

McCarthy, Richard J. 'Al-Baqillanī's Notion of the Apologetic Miracle', *Studia Biblica et Orientalia* 3(12) (1959): 247–256.

McDonough, Scott John. 'Power by Negotiation: Institutional Reform in the Fifth Century Sasanian Empire', PhD dissertation, University of California Los Angeles, 2005.

Meisami, Julie Scott. 'The Uses of the *Qaṣīda*: Thematic and Structural Patterns in a Poem of Bashshar', *JAL* 16 (1985) 40–60.

Meisami, Julie Scott. 'Poetic Microcosms: The Persian Qasida to the End of the Twelfth Century', in Stefan Sperl and Christopher Shackle (eds), *Qasida Poetry in Islamic Asia and Africa* (Leiden: Brill, 1996), 1:137–82.

Meisami, Julie Scott. *Persian Historiography to the End of the Twelfth Century* (Edinburgh: Edinburgh University Press, 1999).

Mellor, Leo. *Reading the Ruins: Modernism, Bombsites and British Culture* (Cambridge: Cambridge University Press, 2011).

Miller, David Lee. *The Poem's Two Bodies: The Poetics of the 1590 Faerie Queene* (Princeton, NJ: Princeton University Press, 2014).

Miner, Earl. *Comparative Poetics: An Intercultural Essay on Theories of Literature* (Princeton: Princeton University Press, 1999).

Miner, Earl. 'Why Lyric?' in Earl Miner and Amiya Dev (eds), *The Renewal of Song: Renovation in Lyric Conception and Practice* (Calcutta: Seagull Books, 2000).

Mingana, A. *The Apology of Timothy the Patriarch before the Caliph Mahdi* (Cambridge: W. Heffer, 1928).

Minorsky, Vladimir. *La domination des Daylamites* (Paris: Leroux, 1932).

Minorsky, Vladimir. 'Geographical Factors in Persian Art', *BSOAS* 9(3) (1938): 621–52.

Minorsky, Vladimir. 'Khāqānī and Andronicus Comnenus', *BSOAS* 11(3) (1945): 550–78.

Minorsky, Vladimir. *A History of Sharvān and Darband in the 10th–11th Centuries* (Cambridge: Heffer, 1958).

Mīnovī, Mujtabā. 'Shiʿr-i Ḥarīrī dar bāre-ye Masʿūd Saʿd', *MDAT* 5(4) (1338/1958): 10–11.

Moin, Azfar. *The Millennial Sovereign: Sacred Kingship and Sainthood in Islam* (New York: Columbia University Press, 2012).

Monroe, James T. and Mark F. Pettigrew, 'The Decline of Courtly Patronage and the Appearance of New Genres in Arabic Literature: The Case of the *Zajal*, the *Maqāma*, and the Shadow Play', *Journal of Arabic Literature* 34(1) (2003): 138–177.

Mooney, Linne R. and Mary-Jo Arn (eds). *The Kingis Quair and Other Prison Poems* (TEAMS Consortium for the Teaching of the Middle Ages, 2005).

Moosa, Ebrahim. *Ghazālī and the Poetics of Imagination* (Chapel Hill: University of North Carolina Press, 2005).

Morris, Colin. *The Discovery of the Individual 1050–1200* (New York: Harper & Row, 1972).

Muʿīn, Muḥammad. 'Khāqānī o ā'īn-i masīḥ: masīḥīyat o nofūḍ-i ān dar Iran', *Dānishnāmah* 2 (1326/1947), 32.

Muʿīn, Muḥammad. 'Khāqānī o ā'īn-i massīh: massīhīyat o nafūz-i ān dar īrān', *Majmūʿah-'i maqālāt*, ed. Mahdukht Muʿīn (Tehran: Mu'assasah-'i Intishārāt-i Muʿīn, 1985), 201–16.

Muʿīn, Muḥammad. 'Tarjuma-yi aḥvāl-i ʿAwfī', *Jawāmīʿ al-Ḥikāyāt* (Tehran: Ibn Sīnā, 1340).

Najjar, Fauzi M. 'Fārābī's Political Philosophy and Shīʿism', *Studia Islamica* 16 (1961): 57–72.

Najjar, Fauzi M. 'Siyāsa in Islamic Political Thought', in Michael E. Marmura (ed.),

Islamic Theology and Philosophy: Studies in Honor of George F. Hourani (Albany, NY: SUNY Press, 1984), 92–110.

Norbrook, David. 'The Emperor's New Body? Richard II, Ernst Kantorowicz, and the Politics of Shakespeare Criticism', *Textual Practice* 10 (1996): 329–57.

Noth, Albrecht. 'Abgrenzungsprobleme zwischen Muslimen und Nicht Muslimen', *JSAI* 9 (1987): 290–315.

Nuc'ubidze, Shalva. *Rustaveli i vostochni Renessans* (Tbilisi: literature da khelovneba, 1967).

Omidsalar, Maḥmūd. 'Mas'ūd Sa'd Salmān o Shāhnāma-yi Ferdowsī', *Gulistān* 3 (1999): 99–112.

Pande, R. *Succession in the Delhi Sultanate* (New Delhi: Commonwealth Publishers, 1990).

Pape, Wilhelm. *Handwörterbuch der griechischen Sprache*[3], ed. Maximilian Sengebusch (Braunschweig, F. Vieweg und sohn, 1884–94).

Papoutsakis, Georgia-Nepheli. *Desert Travel as a Form of Boasting: A Study of Dū r-Rūmma's Poetry* (Wiesbaden: Harrassowitz, 2009).

Pārsā, Sayyid Aḥmad. 'Dirangī bar Īwān-i Madā'in-i Khāqānī', *MDAT* 41(54/5) (1385): 5–18.

Parsipur, Shahrnush. *Kissing the Sword: A Prison Memoir*, trans. Sara Khalili (New York: The Feminist Press, 2013).

Phillips, Mark. 'Histories, Micro- and Literary: Problems of Genre and Distance', *NLH* 34(2) (2003): 211–29.

Philpott, Daniel. 'Sovereignty', in Edward N. Zalta (ed.), *The Stanford Encyclopedia of Philosophy* (Summer 2016), available at: https://plato.stanford.edu/archives/sum2016/entries/sovereignty.

Plato, *The Symposium*, ed. Frisbee C. C. Sheffield (Cambridge: Cambridge University Press, 2008).

Pollock, Sheldon. *The Language of the Gods in the World of Men: Sanskrit, Culture, and Power in Premodern India* (Berkeley: University of California Press, 2006).

Pregill, Michael. *The Golden Calf between Bible and Qur'an: Scripture, Polemic, and Exegesis from Late Antiquity to Islam* (Oxford: Oxford University Press, 2020).

Putnam, Hans. *L'Église et l'Islam sous Timothée I (780–823): étude sur l'église nestorienne au temps des premiers 'Abbāsides avec nouvelle édition et édition et traduction du dialogue entre Timothée et al-Mahdi* (Beirut: Dar el-Machreq, 1975).

Qazwīnī, Mīrza Muḥammad. 'Qaṣīdeh-i ḥabsiyye-i Khāqānī', in Jamshīd 'Alī Zādah (ed.), *Sāgharī dar miyān-i sangistān: zendegī, andīshah va shi'r-i Khāqānī* (Tehran: Nashr-i Markaz, 1999), 185–226

Qazwīnī, Mīrza Muḥammad. 'Mas'ūd Sa'd-i Salmān', *JRAS* (1905): 693–740; (1906): 11–51.

Qutbuddin, Tahera. 'Khutba: The Evolution of Early Arabic Oration', in Beatrice Gruendler and Michael Cooperson (eds), *Classical Arabic Humanities in Their Own Terms: Festschrift for Wolfhart Heinrichs* (Leiden: Brill, 2008).

Rādfar, Abū al-Qāsim. 'Khāqānī o Hind', *Dānishkadeh-yi Adabīyāt va 'Ulūm-i Insānī-yi Dānishgah-yi Tabrīz* 178/179 (1380): 95–117.

Reichert, John. 'More than Kin and Less than Kind: The Limits of Genre Theory', in Joseph P. Strelka (ed.), *Theories of Literary Genre* (University Park, PA: Pennsylvania State University Press, 1978), 57–79.

Reinert, Benedikt. *Haqani als Dichter. Poetische Logik und Phantasie* (Berlin: Walter de Gruyter, 1972).

Rezaian, Jason. *Prisoner* (New York: Ecco Books, 2019).

Ridgeon, Lloyd. 'Christianity as Portrayed by Jalal al-Din Rumi', Lloyd Ridgeon (ed.), *Islamic Interpretations of Christianity* (London: Palgrave Macmillan, 2001).

Ritter, Hellmut. *Das Meer der Seele: Mensch, Welt und Gott in den Geschichten des Farīduddīn 'Aṭṭār* (Leiden: Brill, 1955).

Ritter, Hellmut. 'Philologika. XV. Farīduddīn 'Aṭṭār. III. 7. Der Dīwān (Mit vergleich einiger verse von Sanā'ī und Ḥāfiẓ)', *Oriens* 12(1/2) (1959): 1–88.

Rosenthal, Franz. *The Muslim Concept of Freedom Prior to the Nineteenth Century* (Leiden: Brill, 1960).

Rosenthal, Franz. *Gambling in Islam* (Leiden: Brill, 1975).

Rosenthal, Franz (trans.). *The History of al-Ṭabarī* [*Tārīkh al-rusul wa al-mulūk*] (Albany, NY: SUNY Press, 1989).

Rubin, Uri. 'Traditions in Transformation: The Ark of the Covenant and the Golden Calf in Biblical and Islamic Historiography', *Oriens* 36 (2001): 196–214.

Ṣafā, Ẓabīḥallāh. *Tārīkh-i Adabīyāt dar Īrān*, 5 vols (Tehran: Ferdows, 1371/1992).

Safi, Omid. *The Politics of Knowledge in Premodern Islam: Negotiating Ideology and Religious Inquiry* (Durham, NC: University of North Carolina Press, 2006).

Ṣafwat, Aḥmad Zakī. *Jamharat khuṭab al-'arab fī l-'uṣūr al-'arabiyya al-zāhira* (Beirut: Dar al-Matbu'at al-'Arabiyah, 1933).

Said, Edward. *On Late Style: Music and Literature Against the Grain* (New York: Knopf, 2008).

Sajjādī, Ziyā' al-Dīn. *Farhang-i lughāt va ta'birāt bā sharḥ-i a'lām va mushkilāt-i Dīvān-i Khāqānī Shirvānī* (Tehran: Zuvvār, 1374).

Saussure, Ferdinand de. *Course in General Linguistics*, ed. Roy Harris (London: A. & C. Black, 2013)

Sayyādī, Aḥmad Reẓā and Nūrī, ʿAlī Reẓā. 'Gham-i ghurbat dar ashʿar-i Nāṣir Khusraw, Sanā'ī o Khāqānī', *Majalle-i Keyhāneh Farhangī* 468 (1387): 46–51.

Schiller, Kay E. 'Dante and Kantorowicz: Medieval History as Art and Autobiography', *Annali d'Italianistica* 8 (1990): 406.

Schimmel, Annemarie. *Gabriel's Wing: A Study into the Religious Ideas of Sir Muḥammad Iqbāl* (Leiden: Brill, 1963).

Schmitt, Carl, *Political Theology: Four Chapters on the Concept of Sovereignty*, trans. George Schwab (Chicago, IL: University of Chicago Press, 2005).

Schoeler, Gregor. 'Die Einteilung der Dichtung bei den Arabern', *ZDMG* 123 (1973): 9–55.

Schoeler, Gregor. 'The Genres of Classical Arabic Poetry: Classifications of Poetic Themes and Poems by Pre-Modern Critics and Redactors of Dīwāns', *Quaderni di studi arabi* 7 (2012): 241–6.

Sells, Michael. '"Bānat Suʿād": Translation and Introduction', *Journal of Arabic Literature* 21(2) (1990): 140–54.

Sells, Michael. 'Guises of the Ghuk: Dissembling Simile and Semantic Overflow in the Early Arabic Nasib', in Suzanne Pinckney Stetkevych (ed.), *Reorientations: Arabic and Persian Poetry* (Bloomington: Indiana University Press, 1994), 130–64.

Shafīʿī Kadkanī, Muḥammad Reẓā. *Shāʿir-i āʾīnah'hā: barrasī-i sabk-i Hindī va shiʿr-i Bīdil* (Tehran: Mu'assasah-'i Intishārāt-i Agah, 1987).

Shamīsā, Sīrūs. *Anvāʿ-i adabī* (Tehran: Bāgh-i Āyīnah, 1370/1992).Shamīsā, Sīrūs. *Zindān-i Nāy* (Tehran: Sukhan, 1375/1996).

Shamīsā, Sīrūs. *Sayr-i rubāʿī dar shiʿr-i Fārsī* (Tehran: Ferdows, 1375/1996).

Sharlet, Jocelyn. *Patronage and Poetry in the Islamic World: Social Mobility and Status in the Medieval Middle East and Central Asia* (London: I. B. Tauris, 2011).

Sharma, Sunil. *Persian Poetry at the Indian Frontier: Masʿūd Saʿd Salmān of Lahore* (Delhi: Permanent Black, 2000).

Shenoda, Maryam. 'Displacing Dhimmī, Maintaining Hope: Unthinkable Coptic Representations of Fatimid Egypt', *IJMES* 39 (2007): 587–606.

Shenoda, Maryam. 'Lamenting Islam: Imagining Persecution: Copto-Arabic Opposition to Islamicization and Arabization in Fatamid Egypt (969–1171 CE)', PhD dissertation, Harvard University, 2010).

Sherwani, Haroon Khan. *Studies in Muslim Political Thought and Administration*[2] (Lahore: Muḥammad Ashraf, 1945).

Siddiqi, Amir H. *Caliphate and Kingship in Medieval Persia* (Philadelphia, PA: Porcupine Press, 1977).

Siddiqui, Iqtidar Hussein. '*Lubab-ul-Albab* and *lawami-'ul-Hikayat* of Sadid-ud-din Muḥammad Awfi', in *Perso-Arabic Sources of the Sultanate of Delhi* (New Delhi: Munshiram Manoharlal Publishers, 1992), 1–43.

Siddiqui, Iqtidar Hussein. 'Life and Poetry of Siraji Khurasani (a Thirteenth-century Indo-Persian poet)', *Indo-Iranica* 26 (1973): 1–16.

Sijpesteijn, Petra. 'Policing, Punishing and Prisons in the Early Islamic Egyptian Countryside (640–850 CE)', in Alain Delattre, Marie Legendre and Petra Sijpesteijn (eds), *Authority and Control in the Countryside: From Antiquity to Islam in the Mediterranean and Near East (6th–10th Century)* (Leiden: Brill, 2018), 547–88.

Skalnik, Peter. 'Authority versus Power: A View from Social Anthropology', in Angela Cheater (ed.), *The Anthropology of Power: Empowerment and Disempowerment in Changing Structures* (London: Routledge 1999), 161–72.

Skjærvø, Oktor. 'Introduction to Zoroastrianism', unpublished reader for 'Early Iranian Civilizations' course, Harvard University, 2006.

Smith, Jane I. and Yvonne Y. Haddad. *The Islamic Understanding of Death and Resurrection* (Albany, NY: SUNY Press, 1981).

Smith, Mark J. 'Apostrophe, or the Lyric Art of Turning Away', *TSLL* 49(4) (2007): 411–37.

Smith, Matthew Chaffee. 'Literary Courage: Language, Land and the Nation in the Works of Malik al-Shu'ara Bahar', PhD dissertation, Harvard University, 2006.

Spuler, Bertold. 'The Disintegration of the Caliphate in the East', in P. M. Holt, Ann K. S. Lambton and Bernard Lewis (eds), *The Cambridge History of Islam: IA* (Cambridge: Cambridge University Press, 1970).

Stetkevych, Jaroslav. 'Some Observations on Arabic Poetry', *JNES* 26(1) (1967): 1–12.

Stetkevych, Jaroslav. 'The Arabic Lyrical Phenomenon', *JAL* 6 (1975): 57–77.

Stetkevych, Jaroslav. *The Hunt in Arabic Poetry: From Heroic to Lyric to Metapoetic* (Notre Dame, IN: University of Notre Dame Press, 2016).

Stetkevych, Suzanne Pinckney (ed.). *Early Islamic Poetry and Poetics, vol. 6: The Formation of the Classical Islamic World* (Burlington, VA: Ashgate, 2009).

Stillman, Yedida Kalfon and Norman A. Stillman. *Arab Dress: A Short History: From the Dawn of Islam to Modern Times* (Leiden: Brill, 2003).

Stol, Marten. *Epilepsy in Babylonia* (Leiden: Brill, 1993).

Stroumsa, Sarah. 'The Signs of Prophecy: The Emergence and Early Development of a Theme in Arabic Theological Literature', *Harvard Theological Review* 78(1/2) (1985): 101–14.

Summers, Joanna. *Late Medieval Prison Writing and the Politics of Autobiography* (Oxford: Oxford University Press, 2004).

Szondi, Peter. 'Schlegel's Theory of Poetic Genres', in *On Textual Understanding and Other Essays* (Manchester: Manchester University Press, 1986).

Tabatabai, Sassan. *Father of Persian Verse Rudaki and His Poetry* (Leiden: Leiden University Press, 2010).

Tahmasebian, Kayvan. 'Comparison Beyond Similarity and Difference', unpublished manuscript.

Tahmasebian, Kayvan and Rebecca Ruth Gould. 'The Temporality of Interlinear Translation: *Kairos* in the Persian Hölderlin', *Representations* 155 (2021): 1–28.

Tawfiq, Reḍa. *Medayin haraberleri* (Istanbul: Cemʿi Kütüphanesi, 1330).

Tottoli, Roberto. 'Tours of Hell and Punishments of Sinners in Miʿraj Narratives: Use and Meaning of Eschatology in Muhammad's Ascension', in Christiane J. Gruber and Frederick Stephen Colby (eds), *The Prophet's Ascension: Cross-cultural Encounters with the Islamic Miʿrāj Tales* (Bloomington: Indiana University Press, 2010), 11–26.

Trabulsi, Amjad. *La critique poétique des arabes jusqu'au Ve siècle de l'Hégire* (Damascus: Institut français de Damas, 1958).

Tritton, A. S. *The Caliphs and Their Non-Muslim Subjects: A Critical Study of the Covenant of ʿUmar* (London: Frank Cass, 1930).

Turan, O. 'Les souverains Seldjoukides et leurs sujets non-musulmans', *Studia Islamica* 1 (1953): 65–100.

Turner, Colin. 'Abū Lahab', *The Qur'an: An Encyclopedia*, ed. Oliver Leaman (London: Routledge, 2006).

Utas, Bo. '"Genres" in Persian Literature 900–1900', in Anders Pettersson (ed.), *Literary History: Towards a Global Perspective* (Berlin: Walter de Gruyter, 2006), 2:199–240.

Vacca, Alison. *Non-Muslim Provinces Under Early Islam: Islamic Rule and Iranian Legitimacy in Armenia and Caucasian Albania* (Cambridge: Cambridge University Press, 2017).

van Gelder, Geert Jan. *Beyond the Line: Classical Arabic Literary Critics on the Coherence and Unity of the Poem* (Leiden: Brill, 1982).

van Gelder, Geert Jan. 'Some Brave Attempts at Generic Classification in Premodern Arabic Literature', in Bert Roest and Herman Vanstipout (eds), *Aspects of Genre and Type in Pre-modern Literary Cultures* (Groningen: STYX Publications, 1999), 15–33.

Vil'chevskii, O. L. 'Khronogrammy Khakani', *Epigrafika Vostoka* 13 (1960): 59–68.

Walzer, R. 'Al-Fārābī's Theory of Prophecy and Divination', *Journal of Hellenic Studies* 77(1) 1957: 142–8.

Watt, Ian. *The Rise of the Novel* (Berkeley: University of California Press, 1957).

Watt, Montgomery. *The Formative Period of Islamic Thought* (Edinburgh: Edinburgh University Press, 1973).

Watt, Montgomery. *Islamic Philosophy and Theology* (Edinburgh: Edinburgh University Press, 1985).

Weber, Max. *Wirtschaft und Gesellschaft. Grundriss der verstehenden Soziologie* (1922).

Weber, Max. 'Politik als Beruf', *Gesammelte Politische Schriften*, ed. Johannes Winckelmann (Tübingen: Mohr, 1988), 505–60.

Whitby, Michael. *The Ecclesiastical History of Evagrius Scholasticus* (Liverpool: Liverpool University Press, 2000).

White, Hayden. *The Content of the Form: Narrative Discourse and Historical Representation* (Baltimore, MD: Johns Hopkins University Press, 1987).

Yarbrough, Luke. 'Origins of the *ghiyār*', *JAOS* 134(1) (2014): 113–21.

Yavari, Neguin. *Advice for the Sultan: Prophetic Voices and Secular Politics in Medieval Islam* (London: Hurst, 2014).

Yavari, Neguin. 'Siar al-Moluk', *Encyclopædia Iranica*, available at: http://www.iranicaonline.org/articles/siar-al-moluk (17 September 2015).

Yūsufī, Muḥammad Riẕā and Ṭāhirah Sayyid Riẕāyī (eds). *Zindān-nāma-hā-yi Fārsī az qarn-i panjum tā pānzdahum* (Qum: Dānishgāh-i Qum, 1391/2012–13).

Ẓafarī, Valī Allāh. *Ḥabsīyyah dar adab-i fārsī: az āghāz-i shiʿr-i fārsī tā pāyān-i zandīyah* (Tehran: Amīr Kabīr, 1364/1985).

Ẓafarī, Valī Allāh. *Ḥabsīyyah dar adab-i Fārsī: Az āghāz-i dawrah-'i Qājārīyah tā inqilāb-i Islāmī* (Tehran: Amīr Kabīr, 2001/2).

Zaleman, Karl. *Chetverostishiia Khakani* (St Petersburg: Tipografiia Imperatorskoi akademii nauk, 1875).

Zarrīnkūb, ʿAbd al-Ḥosseīn. *Didār ba kaʿbah-i jān: darbareh-i zendegī, āthār va andīsheh-i Khāqānī* (Tehran: Sukhan, 1378/1999–2000).

Zipoli, Riccardo. 'Il Khāqāni polemico', in Giovanna Pagani-Cesa and Ol'ga Obuchova (eds), *Studi e scritti in memoria di Marzio Marzaduri* (Venice: Quaderni del Dipartimento di Studi Eurasiatici–Universita Ca'foscari, 2002), 457–82.

Index

Abbasids, 48, 104–5, 158, 243
caliphal system, 215–16, 230
dhimmi regulations, 173, 175
Abraham (Ibrahim), 141–2
Abrams, M. H., 62
Abu Firas, 73
Abu Hasan ʿAli b. Masʿud, 65, 70
Abu Lahab, 132
Abu Muslim, 127
Abu Yusuf, 175
Abu'l ʿAlaʾ al-Maʿarri, 106
Abu'l ʿAlaʾ Ganjavi, 96, 97–9, 119*n*15, 168
Adib-i Sabir, 91–2
Adorno, Theodor, 33, 44, 50
ahl al-dhimma see dhimmi regulations
ahl-i ʿaql ('people of Intelligence'), 94–5, 231
Ahlwardt, Wilhelm, 46
Aivan Qasida (Khaqani), 111, 136, 183–4, 185–8, 190–8, 231
akhlaq (Persian ethics), 211, 223, 229, 237
Akimushkina, Ekaterina, 51, 131, 148
Ali Khan, Mumtaz, 85*n*29
Alp Arslan, 210, 211
Amir Khusraw, 95, 111, 178–9, 180
animal imagery, 113–14
birds, 13, 14, 18, 81, 82, 113, 151, 193–4
dogs, 98, 99, 113–14, 116
serpents/dragons, 14, *15*, 113–16, 144–6
Anushirvan, Khusraw, 184, 185, 193–4
Anvari of Balkh, 94
anxieties of influence, 89, 90, 98
apostrophe, 61–2, 63, 151, 194, 236
Arabic philosophy, 232–3, 239
Arabic poetics
dhimma and, 166–7, 169
genre and, 45–6
Khaqani and, 139–40, 156, 187–8
literature of captivity, 42–3, 182
Mujir Baylaqani and, 104
non-religious character of, 127
petition genre, 201*n*30
qasida structure, 223–4
Quranic, 139–40, 142, 149–50
Arberry, A. J., 45
ʿAruzi, Nizami, 51–2, 60, 94, 111, 191
Four Discourses, 40, 64, 65, 67–74, 210, 223–44
ascetic poems (*zuhdiyyat*), 33, 46, 50
Athir al-Din Akhsikati, 136–7
ʿAttar Nishapuri, 106
Auden, W. H., 241
Auerbach, Erich, 6
authorial fluidity, 93–4
authority
of the imam, 225, 232, 233–4, 236–7, 242, 243
of the poet, 8, 118, 125; ʿAruzi on, 227–34; discursive, 52, 127, 132, 144, 150, 183, 192, 210–44; Khaqani on, 12, 20, 132, 141, 160, 193–4, 195–8; and licit magic, 132, 150; prophetic miracles and, 144, 218–19, 230; transfer of the ruler's power to, 2, 49, 52, 104–5, 107, 170–1, 184, 210, 241; *see also* prophet, poet as
relation of to power, 207–8, 215, 216, 224–5, 227–8, 230–1, 239, 242–4
Avesta, 215, 217

avian imagery, 13, 14, 18, 81, 82, 113, 151, 193–4
ʿAwfi, Muhammad, 60, 116
on Masʿud Saʿd, 71–4, 76
on Nasrullah Munshi, 74–5, 76–7, 78–9
Pith of Essences, 64, 72–9, 139
al-Azmeh, Aziz, 210, 227

Babur, Padishah, 180
backgammon (*nard*), 103, 108, 109
Bahar, Muhammad Taqi, *Prison Feats*, 252–5
Bahram Gur, 188
Bakhtin, Mikhail M., 33, 37, 38–40, 43, 45, 49, 52
Bakikhanuf, ʿAbbas Quli Agha, 137
Balkhi, Shahid, 255
band (chain), 14, 47–8, 74, 169
ʿAwfi's use of, 73
Falaki's use of, 93
Khaqani's use of, 13, 113–14, 167–8, 176
Lumaki's use of, 35–6, 82
Masʿud Saʿd's use of, 62–3, 66, 73, 163
Mujir Baylaqani's use of, 100–2
Nasrullah Munshi's use of, 77
Rumi's use of, 106
zunnar and, 170, 176, 181
Barandaq Khujandi, 18
Barthold, W., 165
Bastanirad, Hossein, 100
bayan (eloquence), 137–8
Benjamin, Walter, 30–1, 36–7, 140–1, 193
Bertels, Evgenii Eduardovich, 250*n*71
Bidil, 82
Bijan, 14, 15, 22, 23, 62
biographical compendium (*tazkira*), 64, 91
birds *see* avian imagery
al-Biruni, 242
bodies
poets': in the Aivan Qasida, 184, 193, 195; in the Christian Qasida, 164, 182; embodied prison poetry, 2, 79, 95, 235–6; Lumaki on, 82; mapped onto sovereign's, 5–6, 7, 9; in Masʿud Saʿd's elegy for Lahore, 61–4; as nexus of conflict between worldly and poetic power, 5, 241–3; before the prison poem, 9–17; related to animal imagery, 113–14; sacralisation of, 4, 5, 118, 138, 148, 195, 231; suffering of as political critique, 2, 4, 9, 106, 113–17; symbolising the sultan's oppression, 52, 238
readers', 71, 73–4, 116, 223
rulers': corruption of, 105, 187, 189–90, 191, 192–4, 197, 231; duality of, 1, 5, 8, 20–1, 188, 215–16, 242–3; sacralisation of, 4, 20, 193, 197, 221
Bölükbaşı, Rıza Tevfik, 185
Borges, Jorge Luis, 'A Dream', 255
Bosworth, C. E., 165, 166
Browne, Edward, 185
al-Buhturi, 187, 190, 193, 197
al-Bukhari, 127
Bürgel, J. C., 127
burnus (monk's cloak), 168, 177, 178
Buyids, 215

Cahen, Claude, 202*n*41, 203*n*61
caliphal system, 209–10, 213, 215–16, 221, 230–1, 239
Capinha, Graça, 2
carpenters, 97–8, 102, 141–2, 157, 159
catalogues, 254
chains *see band* (chain)
Chakhrukhadze, Grigol, 165
Christensen, A. L., 215
Christian Qasida (Khaqani), 57*n*54, 114, 158–83
allusions to by other poets, 13–14, 18
autobiographical elements, 157, 160, 164
Christology in, 143, 160, 163, 165, 196
dhimmi regulations and, 166–74, 176–8, 181
religious ambiguity in, 167, 172, 176–7
as transgressive, 160, 182–3
Christology
in the Christian Qasida, 143, 160, 163, 165, 196
medieval European sovereignty and, 1
of Nestorians, 157–9
political theology and, 17–24, 135
chronograms (*maddeh tarikh*), 111, 183, 196

Clastres, Pierre, 208
Clinton, Jerome W., 206*n*94
Cohen, Mark, 202*n*45
Cohen, Ralph, 33, 47, 49
competitive poetry, 87–91, 95–100
complaint (*shikwa*) tradition, 5, 10–12, 101, 235
comprehensive discourse (*al-kalam al-jame'*), 68–9, 72
Conduct of Kings (*Siyasatnama*)
  authorship of, 210–11
  on *hukama* (philosophers), 228–9
  language of sovereignty in, 212–16, 221, 222
conversion, religious, 167, 172, 174, 177, 182
Coptic Christianity, 166
corruption
  of the ruler's body, 105, 187, 189–90, 191, 192–4, 197, 231
  of sovereignty, 184, 234, 238–9, 240–1
cosmology, 4
  in 'Aruzi's *Four Discourses*, 225–8, 236–7
  of Khaqani, 108–12, 116–17, 133–4, 162–3
  of Nasrullah Munshi, 75–6
  wheel of fate (*gardun*), 101, 102, 109
Croce, Benedetto, 8
cross, the (*salib*), 135, 136, 167, 181–2
Ctesiphon (Mada'in), 157, 158, 184–5, 186, 189, 195, 197, 198; *see also* Aivan Qasida (Khaqani)
Culler, Jonathan, 62

Daftary, Farhad, 245*n*13
Daniş, Hüseyin, 185
Danish, Hosseinkhan, 185
Danishyar, Morteza, 245*n*15
Dante, 1, 6, 7–8, 19–20, 236–7
Dashti, Ali, 256*n*6
dawlat (earthly sovereignty/fortune), 76, 80
  duality with *din*, 5, 19
Dawlatshah, 91–2
decay (*fasad*)
  of the poet's body, 3–4, 9–10, 47–8
  of the ruler's body, 156, 190–1, 192–4, 208–9, 229; *see also* corruption
  of the world, 219–20, 227
Dehkhodā, 'A. -A., 199*n*15
Delhi Sultanate, 13
desacralised sovereignty, 48–9, 52, 144, 227, 231, 234, 243
dhimmi regulations, 164–5, 166–7, 168–9, 170–4, 175–8, 181; *see also zunnar*
dice metaphors, 107–11, 157
Dickins, Frederick V., 61
din (faith-based authority), 5, 19
discernment (*'aql*) and erudition (*'ilm*), 214, 216
discourse (*sukhan*)
  as a dimension of genre, 33–5, 38–43, 47, 50–1
  Khaqani and the later phase of prison poetry, 106–11, 137–8, 148–52
  magic and, 127
  poetry as, 111, 220
  see also authority
divans (poetry collections), 46, 91–2, 99, 103, 159
dog metaphors, 98, 99, 113–14, 116
double entendre *see iham* (double entendre)
Dowlatabadi, Yahya, 185
dual address, 64, 176, 190–2
dualism of the body, 1, 6, 8
  Christology and, 18–19
  poets', 2, 7, 21
  rulers', 1, 5, 8, 20–1, 188, 215–16, 242–3
dubayti (quatrain), 65, 66, 67
Duncan, Robert, 21
duta (folded), 17–18

Eid al-Adha, 102
Eksell, Kerstin, 45, 46
elegies, 133
  for Lahore, 61–4, 79
  for Mas'ud Sa'd, 219–20
  for mourning the dead, 96
  urban elegy (*ritha' al-mudun*), 187
Elijah (Khizr), 141
Elsky, Stephanie, 2
emotions related to letters, 74

epilepsy (*sar'*), 135
evidentiary miracles (*mu'jizat*), 138, 218, 220, 221–2
exile topos, 64, 182

fakhr (self-praise), 91, 149, 181
falak (sky), 108, 162–3
Falaki Shirvani, 165–6, 191–2, 231
  Khaqani on, 96
  on Mas'ud Sa'd, 90, 91–5
  use of prison poem lexicon, 78
fantastic etiology (*husn-i ta'lil*), 100, 101
al-Farabi, 239
  Inhabitants of the Virtuous City, 232–3
Farid al-Din 'Attar, 151, 175
farrah/farnah/farr, 214–15, 222
Farrukhi Sistani, 234, 235, 242
Faruzanfar, Badi' al-Zaman, 88
fate
  dawlat, 76, 80
  ruzgar, 69, 95, 109
  wheel of fate (*gardun*), 101, 102, 109
Ferdowsi, *Shahnama*, 70, 189, 190, 214, 215, 217, 246–7*n*37
  'Aruzi and, 239–41, 242
  Khaqani and, 115
fertility imagery, 193–4
fitna (rebellion), 213
form (*anva'*), 49–50
  as a dimension of genre, 33, 34, 35, 36
  in modern prison literature, 252
  and topos, 36, 41–7, 49, 50–1, 67
  transgression of, 36, 38, 43, 78, 92, 93–4, 148–9
Foucault, Michel, 54*n*20
Fowler, Alastair, 53*n*43
fragments (*qit'eh*), 35, 36, 45, 50, 72–3
  of Khaqani, 133–5, 136, 181, 195
Frangrasyan, 217–18
Frederick II, King of Sicily, 4, 7
French language, 252, 253
Frye, Northrop, 182

gambling metaphors, 107–8, 112–13
  *zunnar*s and, 178, 179
genealogies, 159, 186, 215, 216–18
genre, 30–1, 32, 33
  genre theory, 39
  genre-subgenre typology, 45–6
  prison poem as a transgressive, 48–52, 118, 148–9, 252–3
  three dimensions of in Persian poetics, 34–48, 251
  see also form (*anva'*); topos/theme (*mazmum*)
Georgia, Kingdom of, 165–6
gham (sorrow), 78–9, 93
ghazal (lyric), 43, 45, 46, 50, 108
  defining as a genre, 60–5
  Khaqani's 'Language of the Birds', 151
al-Ghazali, *Molten Gold*, 211
Ghaznavids, 65, 70, 83, 105, 144, 209–10, 215–16, 242, 243
ghiyar (garment) codes in *dhimmi* regulations, 168–9, 175–6, 178, 180
Ghiyath al-Din Muhammad b. Malikshah, 211, 212
Ghurids, 65, 70, 80
Gibbon, Edward, 185, 210
gift (*tuhfeh*), 195
Gift from the Two Iraqs (Khaqani), 96–7, 98–9, 164, 194–5, 253
Gilani, Khan Ahmad, 15–16
God, praise for, 223–4
golden calf, 146–8
Goldziher, Ignaz, 170
Guha, Ranajit, 207
Guillén, Claudio, 45

habsiyyat, origins of the term, 2
hajv (invective), 37
al-Hamdani, Abu Firas, 42, 182
Harb, Lara, 40
Hasan, Hadi, 92
hasb-i hal (account of a condition), 9, 37
Hassan al-'Ajam, 102, 139
Hassan ibn Thabit, 101, 102, 139
Hayot, Eric, 45
Hegel, G. W. F., 7–8
hell, depictions of, 114
hierarchy of humanity, 'Aruzi on, 225–6, 228–30, 237
Hindi, 'Abd al-Rahim, 186
Hinduism, 179, 180

Hirsch, E. D., 47
historicity, in modern prison literature, 254
Holt, Kelly, 26–7*n*8
Homer, 7, 254
homonyms (*jinas*), 188
Horten, Max, 249*n*59
al-Hujwiri, 218
hunting poems (*tardiyyat*), 33, 46, 50
Hutson, Lorna, 2

Ibn Abi al-Yusr, 169
Ibn al-Abras, ʿAbid, 126
Ibn al-ʿArabi, 147
Ibn al-Athir, 173
Ibn Hanbal, 126, 171
Ibn Qudama, 171
Ibn Qutayba, 223–4
Ibn Rashiq al-Qayrawani, 47, 127
Ibn Sina, 108
  Book of Healing, 225, 230
Ibrahim, Sultan, 65–6, 76–7
ʿ*ibrat* (admonition), 191–2, 194, 195, 196–7
idolatry, 127, 146–8, 170, 179
iham (double entendre), 15–16, 139, 192–3, 219; *see also* multivalence; puns
illumination of the sun (*rawshan*), 129
imam's authority, in ʿAruzi's *Four Discourses*, 225, 232, 233–4, 236–7, 242, 243
imprisonment of *dhimmi*s, 175
Imru al-Qays, 126
Indo-Persian poetry, 35, 82, 95, 99, 111, 178–80; *see also* Lumaki, ʿAmid al-Din
inimitability, 138, 139, 220, 221, 233
innovation (*ibda*ʿ), 183
inscription (*naqsh*), 111, 135
intellectuals *see* philosophers (*hukama*)
intertextuality, 13–14, 77, 115, 172, 177–8, 187, 231, 254–5
Iqbal, Muhammad, 179–80
Iranshahr, Hussein Kazimzada, 185–7
ʿIsami, 255
Isfahan, 103–4
Ismaʿil I, Shah, 16
isolation and the prison poem, 94, 95

Jahansuz, Sultan, 234, 236
Jakobson, Roman, 254
Jameson, Frederic, 33, 36
Jarir, 177, 178
jawr-i zamaneh (tyranny of the age), 15, 74, 75
Jerusalem, 167–8
Jesus (ʿIsa)
  the cross and, 135, 143, 157–9, 182
  Khaqani on, 141–2, 143, 159, 163, 168, 197–8
  lips of, 160
  Masʿud Saʿd on, 11, 143
  Mujir Baylaqani on, 101
  needle of, 14, 17–18, 101, 164
  pen imagery and, 11, 143
  Vatvat on, 140–1
jewel (*gawhar*), 129–30
Jews, 168, 177, 178
jinas (homonyms), 188
jizya (poll tax on non-Muslims), 174, 175
Johannes-Obadiah, 181
Johansen, Baber, 208–9, 210
John the Baptist (Yahya), 141
Johnson, Samuel, 182–3
judgement, power of, 75
al-Jurjani, ʿAbd al-Qahir, 38, 127, 138
Juzjani, Minhaj, 80–1, *81*

Kaʿba symbology, 108–11, 113, 163, 164, 188
Kahn, Victoria, 2, 6, 48
Kantorowicz, Ernst, *The King's Two Bodies*, 2, 4–8, 19
karamat (saintly miracles), 138, 142, 218–19, 221–2
Karami, 198*n*1
Khan, Geoffrey, 201*n*30
Khaqani Shirvani
  Abu'l ʿAlaʾ Ganjavi and, 97–8
  Aivan Qasida, 111, 136, 157, 183–4, 185–8, 190–8, 231; *see also* Christian Qasida (Khaqani)
  animal imagery of, 113–14
  biographical context, 17, 97, 98, 157, 159–60, 164
  Christology of, 18–19, 135, 165

Khaqani Shirvani (*cont.*)
competitive poetry of, 87–9, 95, 96
cosmology of, 108–12, 116–17
Dante and, 19–20
depictions of hell, 114
dice metaphors of, 157
on Falaki, 92, 96, 100
gambling metaphor of, 107–8, 112–13
Gift from the Two Iraqs, 96–7, 98–9, 164, 194–5, 253
Ka'ba symbology, 108–10
'Language of the Birds', 151
on licit magic, 132
Mas'ud Sa'd and, 64, 88, 89–90, 91
Mujir Baylaqani and, 103
pivotal role of in prison poetry genre, 5, 12, 16, 105–6, 148, 156, 181, 196–8
poems modelled on, 13, 18
prison poem 1 *see* Christian Qasida (Khaqani)
prison poem 2, 114–16, 163, 198
prison poem 3, 107–8, 111, 116–17, 163–4, 227
prison poem 5, 116
prison poem 6, 146–8, 150–1, 194
on prophecy and poetry, 136–43, 146, 147–52
religion and, 167, 174
on Sana'i of Ghazna, 90
serpentine imagery of, 114–16
toothless mouth and mouthless teeth imagery of, 116
use of Arabic poetics, 139–40
Vatvat and, 89, 138–9, 140–1, 142–3
Khayyam, Omar, 187, 188, 193
Khismatulin, 211, 212, 245*n*15
Kierkegaard, Søren, 243
al-Kindi, 232, 239
kingship
changing Persian conceptions of, 12–13, 48–9, 52, 105, 243
Dante on, 6–7
Kantorowicz on, 4, 8, 19
Mas'ud Sa'd on, 66–7
medieval European, 1–2, 4, 19
see also padishah; sovereignty

Labibi, 130
lafz (utterance), 36
Lahore, 87, 131
elegy for, 61–4, 79
Leaman, Oliver, 249*n*59
letters related to emotions, 74
lexicon of prison poems, 76, 78–80, 93
light imagery in *Conduct of Kings*, 214–15
literary appropriation (*sariqat*), 89, 90
literary genres (*anva'-i adabi*), 34, 35
logic (*mantiq*), 233
Lumaki, 'Amid al-Din, 13–14, 35–6, 82
lyric *see* ghazal (lyric)
lyric ode, 24, 45, 61–4, 94, 133–6, 181, 196, 231, 235
lyric voice, 94

Mada'in *see* Ctesiphon (Mada'in)
magic, licit (*sihr-i halal*), 126–33, 132, 136, 150, 195–6
Mahmud of Ghazna, 65, 70, 175, 181, 239–41
Maimonides, Moses, 232
Majd al-Din Khalil, Imam, 138
Makdisi, George, 239
Malikshah, 138, 210–11
ma'ni (meaning), 36, 38, 41, 46, 61
Manijeh, 14, 15
March, Andrew, 207, 228
Mary (Maryam), 14, 17–18, 161, 164
masnavi, 252–5
Mas'ud Sa'd Salman, 81–3
'Aruzi on, 65–71
'Awfi on, 72
biographical context, 59, 65
corporeal poetics of, 3–4, 5, 235–6
discursive authority and, 216–17, 241
elegy for Lahore, 61–4, 79
first prison poem, 65, 66, 191
Khaqani and, 88, 89–90, 91
on licit magic, 127–31
as a lyric poet, 60, 94, 181, 231, 235
on Moses, 144–6
Mu'izzi's elegy for, 219–20
Nasrullah Munshi and, 76–8
on prophecy and poetry, 144–5, 148
serpent/dragon imagery of, 15

Shahnama and, 239
sky topos, 163
unpolitical early poems, 10–12, 95
use of apostrophe, 61–2, 63
use of *jur*, 75
use of prison poem topoi, 47–8, 79–80
zunnar and, 180–1
al-Mas'udi, 187
materiality of the prison poem, 4, 19, 34, 37
al-Mawardi, *Precepts of Sovereignty*, 212, 214, 234, 237
meaning (*ma'ni*), 36, 38, 41, 43, 45
Medvedev, P. N., 43, 45, 49
Meghrebi, Muhammad, 211
memoirs, 252
Messiah, 141
metaphor and metonymy, 32, 48, 101, 106, 156–7, 254, 256
migrations of prison poetry, 80–3
mihnat (affliction), 76, 78–80, 93, 95
Miller, David Lee, 2
mimetic model of sovereignty, 227, 237, 238
Miner, Earl, 60
Mingana, A., 199*n*7
Minorsky, 159
miracles, 138, 142, 144–5, 146–8, 218–19, 220, 221–2, 230
mi'raj (Prophet Muhammad's ascent to heaven), 114
mirror (*ayineh*) metaphors, 163, 191
Mongol invasion, 13, 105, 236
monk (*rahib*), 163–4
Moosa, Ebrahim, 216
Moses (Musa), 141, 144–9, 150
mourning poem (*marathi*), 46
mouthless teeth imagery, 47, 113, 116, 198
Mudarris, Muhammad 'Ali, 164
Muhammad, Prophet, 98, 102, 114, 127, 139, 195
Mu'in, Muhammad, 159
Mu'izzi, Amir Abdollah Muhammad, 95, 210, 211, 216–17, 219–20, 220, 234, 241
Mujir al-Din Baylaqani, 95, 96, 99–102
biographical context, 102–3
cosmology and, 112
on Isfahan, 103–4
multivalence
Bakhtin on, 39–40
band (chain), 35–6
dawlat, 76, 80
as a device used in the lyric, 61
gawhar (jewel), 129–30
in Mas'ud Sa'[d's first prison poem, 66–7
al-Muqtafi, 133–6
al-Mustanjid, 133–6
al-Mutawakkil, 173–4
muteness of the reader, 73–4, 116, 223

Najd, Shaykh of, 98
Najjar, Fawzi, 208, 209, 210, 232
Namsechi, Nila, 238
naqus (Christian church bell), 168, 169, 171, 172, 176
narrative verse, 252–4
nasib (erotic prelude), 45, 50, 223–4
Nasir Khusraw, *2–3*, 5, 10, 12, 162–3
Nasrullah Munshi, 71, 74–5, 76–9, 256*n*5
nationalism, and the Aivan Qasida, 185–7
Nay fortress, 65, 72, 76, 79, 146
nazm (poetry), 38, 40, 54*n*20, 128, 129, 220
needle imagery, 14, 82
needle of Jesus, 17–18, 101, 164
Neo-Platonism, 127, 225–6, 232–3
Nestorianism, 157–9, 161, 164, 166, 174, 185
New Persian, 9, 49, 210, 214
Nizam al-Mulk, 211
Nizami Ganjevi, 91, 131–2
Noth, Albrecht, 170, 172
novel genre, 37–8
Nur al-Din, 134

odes *see* panegyrics; *qasida*s
Omidsalar, Mahmud, 250*n*71
oppositional poetics, 47, 107, 125, 190
Orientalists, 45, 46

padishah, 212–17, 218–22, 233–4, 236, 237; *see also* kingship; sovereignty
pand (royal counsel/carrion bird), 192–3

panegyrics, 35–6, 37, 64
in ʿAruzi's *Four Discourses*, 223–4
and the Christian Qasida, 161
of *Conduct of Kings*, 212–14
Falaki and, 165–6
Khaqani and, 107–8, 133, 196, 231
Masʿud Saʿd's use of, 129–30
moving away from, 94–5, 117
relation between power and authority in, 234–5
*see also qasida*s
patronage, 67, 82–3, 91, 95, 129–30, 212, 224–5
pen imagery, 11, 143
people of intelligence (*ahl-i ʿaql*), 94, 95
persecution, religious, 160–1, 166, 169–74, 181–2
Persianisation of the Shirvanshahs, 165
petition (*ʿarz-i hal*) genre, 168
philosophers (*hukama*), 219, 227–9, 232–7
pilgrimage, 167, 168, 195
Pindar, Peter, 61
political theology, 1, 4
in the Aivan Qasida, 184, 190–1, 192, 193–8
in ʿAruzi's *Four Discourses*, 223–44
in the Christian Qasida, 160–1
Christology and, 17–24, 135
of *Conduct of Kings*, 212–16, 222
Dante and, 6–8
dhimmi regulations and, 175
Falaki and, 95
genre and, 33
Khaqani on, 116, 148, 150–2
licit magic and, 126–31
before the prison poem, 9
prison poem as transgressive, 48, 51
sign of the cross and, 135
use of *zunnar* in, 180–1
see also power
Pollock, Sheldon, 207
pope, prerogative of, 6
power
fleetingness of worldly, 75
increasing conflict between sovereign's and poet's, 5, 104–5, 117–18, 157, 190
in Masʿud Saʿd's first prison poem, 66–7
patronage and, 95
of poetry as a destabilising force, 70–1, 138, 208
of poetry's political discourse, 40, 41, 48, 49, 52
relation to authority, 207–8, 215, 216, 224–5, 230–1, 239, 242–4
transfer of from ruler to poet, 2, 125, 128–9, 133–4, 152, 194, 196–8, 234–5
see also sovereignty
praise poems (*madih*), 46, 223–4
prayer, direction of (*qibla*), 167–8
prison (*zindan*), 47, 48, 52
prophecy
in ʿAruzi's *Four Discourses*, 225, 227, 229–30, 242–3
al-Farabi on, 232–3
miracles and, 144–5, 218, 230
motifs relating to, 90–1
Persianisation of, 233, 242
poet-as-prophet: in the Aivan Qasida, 184, 187, 193–8; ʿAruzi on, 228, 230, 232–4, 242–3; Khaqani on, 18–19, 106, 110, 116–17, 136–43, 146, 147–52, 160, 182, 241; Masʿud Saʿd on, 143; Muʿizzi on, 220–2; references to Moses, 144–8
prose, in modern prison literature, 252, 253–6
punctuation, 253–4
punishment (*taʿzir*), and *siyasa*, 76, 94, 209–10, 214, 231
punishment (*ʿuqubat*), 213, 231
puns, 15–16, 18, 66–7, 72, 93, 192–3; *see also iham* (double entendre); multivalence
Putnam, Hans, 199*n*7

Qahqaheh (prison)/*qahqaheh* (laugh), 15–16
qasida, 45, 47, 50
of Falaki, 92–4
of Khaqani, 107–8, 151, 231
and the lyric ode, 61
of Masʿud Saʿd, 127–31
transgressive, 38, 43

tripartite structure of, 223–4
see also panegyrics
Qazwini, Mirza Muhammad, 85*n*29
qit'eh (fragment) *see* fragments (*qit'eh*)
quatrains, 76–8
dubayti, 65, 66, 67
ruba'i, 15, 35, 43, 50, 75, 160, 188
Quran
on Abu Lahab, 132
Khaqani and, 138–40, 142, 149–50, 151
on logic, 233
on magic, 126
on Moses, 144, 146–7
prison poetry compared with, 220–1
serpent references in, 145

radif (refrain), 35, 36, 61–2
Raduyani, 61, 85*n*25
rahib (monk), 163–4
ranj (suffering), 2, 4, 9, 78, 93, 106, 113–17
readers' corporeal experience, 71, 73–4, 116, 223
reproach, poem of (*'itab*), 46
rivalries, literary, 87–91, 94, 95–100
rosaries (*tasbih*), 179–80
ruba'i (quatrain), 15, 35, 43, 50, 75, 160, 188
rubies, as metaphor of poet's body, 3
Rubin, Uri, 147
Rudaki, 5, 9–10
ruins, poetics of, 187, 190, 191, 192–3, 196–8, 197, 231
Rumi, Jalal al-Din, 106, 161
Russian language, 252, 253

Sabet, Mahvash, 257*n*13
sacralisation
of kings' bodies, 4, 20, 193, 197, 221
of poetry's status, 141, 144
of poets' bodies, 4, 5, 118, 138, 148, 195, 231
Safi, Omid, 210
Said, Edward, 183–4
saintly miracles (*karamat*), 138, 142, 218–19, 221–2
Sajjadi, Ziya al-Din, 123*n*61, 133
Saljuqs, 65, 71, 209–10, 212, 215–16, 243
Ctesiphon and, 185
dhimmi regulations and, 166, 173, 175, 181
the Shirvanshahs and, 87, 95, 105, 109, 148, 157
Samiri and the golden calf, 146–7
Sana'i of Ghazna, 81, 89, 90, 175, 255
satire (*hija'/hajv*), 46, 98, 103, 126, 144–5, 177, 178
Saussure, Ferdinand de, 42
Sayf al-Dawla, 73
Schiller, Kay E., 6
Schimmel, Annemarie, 155*n*41
Schmitt, Carl, 4
Schoeler, Gregor, 42–3, 46
section headings, 253–4
secularism, 1, 4, 21, 76, 234
self-praise (*fakhr*), 91, 149, 181
sense *see* meaning (*ma'ni*)
serpent/dragon imagery, 14, 15, 113–16, 144–6
sexual references, 144–5
Shafi'i, *Kitab al-Umm* (*Mother Book*), 171
Shakespeare, 1
Shamisa, Sirus, 35
Shams-i Qays, 92
shari'a, 218–19, 234
Sharma, Sunil, 59, 64
Shavt'eli, Ioane, 165
Shayegan, 115
Shenoda, Maryam, 166
Sherwani, H. K., 210
shikwa (complaint) tradition, 5, 10–12, 101, 235
Shirvan
dhimmi regulations in, 171, 175
as Khaqani's prison, 151–2, 156–7
poets of, 25, 78, 87, 89–99, 104–5, 131, 133, 136–7
Shirvanshahs, 25, 87, 91, 93, 105, 109, 144, 165, 209–10
Shklovskii, Victor, 54*n*22
Shushtari, Mir 'Abd al-Latif Khan, 184
Siddiqi, Amir H., 246*n*30
siyasa (governance), 76, 83, 212, 231
as synonym for punishment, 94, 208–9, 231

Skalnik, Peter, 207–8, 227
sky (*falak*) topos, 108, 162–3
Solomon, King, 151
sovereignty
  corruption of, 184, 234, 238–9, 240–1
  dawlat (earthly sovereignty/fortune), 5, 19, 76, 80
  desacralised, 48–9, 52, 144, 227, 231, 234, 243
  language of, 221, 222, 224–5, 227–9, 236–44
  mimetic model of, 227, 237, 238
speech genres, 39–40
Spuler, Bertold, 209, 234
staff of Moses, 144–6, 149
'star of knowledge' (*akhtar-i danish*), 163
Stetkeyvich, Jaroslav, 45
style (*tarz*), 91, 95
subgenres, 45–6
suffering/wounds of the poet, 2, 4, 9, 78, 93, 106, 113–17
Sufism, 106, 161, 175
sukhan see discourse (*sukhan*)
sulb (loins), 142
sultanate
  Conduct of Kings on, 212, 215, 216–18, 221–2
  Four Discourses on, 223, 228, 229–31, 234, 237–9
  see also sovereignty
sun, the, 76, 128–9, 134–5
surud-i az zindan (songs from prison), 27*n*10
Syrian Christians, 170–1

al-Tabari, 141, 144, 187, 217
Tahmasebian, Kayvan, 57*n*48, 154*n*26
talent, natural (*tab*ʿ) and acquired (*masnu*ʿ), 69
Tamar, Queen of Georgia, 165–6
tarsa (Christian), 164
tarz (style), 91, 95
tasbih (rosaries), 179–80
tashbib-i sukhan, 223–4
tazkira (biographical compendium), 64, 91
tears, 10, 197
temporality, 107–8, 140–1, 190–1, 193–4, 198, 219–20, 238–9; *see also* chronograms (*maddeh tarikh*)
al-Thaʿalibi, 217
theme *see* topos/theme (*mazmum*)
theology, political *see* political theology
thread imagery, 82
  tasbih and, 179
  thread of Mary, 14, 17–18, 164, 169
Timothy I, 158
al-Tirmidhi, 126–7
toothless mouth imagery, 47, 113, 114, 116, 198
topoi/themes (*mazamin*)
  as a dimension of genre, 32–5, 37–8, 40–3, 46–7, 49–51
  of prison poems, 47, 48, 81, 91, 178
transgressive, prison poem as, 74
  ʿAruzi on, 71
  authorial fluidity and, 93–4
  Bahar and, 252–3
  of form (*anva*ʿ), 38, 43, 78, 92, 93–4, 148–9
  genre and, 48–52, 118, 148–9
  Khaqani and, 90, 182–3, 193
  Muʿizzi and, 220–1
  Mujir Baylaqani and, 103
  in political theology, 48, 51
tree of knowledge, (*dirakht-i dana*), 140
Turanians, 217–18
Turki, M. R., 57*n*54
Tuwa valley, 144
tyranny of the age (*jawr-i zamaneh*), 15, 74, 75

ubi sunt poetry, 187–90, 193–4, 197
ʿ*ud al-salib* amulets, 181–2
ʿUmar b. ʿAbd al-ʿAziz, 170
ʿUmar b. al-Khattab, 170
ʿUmar's Covenant, 170–3, 174–5, 177, 178, 192
ʿUnsuri of Balkh, 88, 89, 94, 234, 235, 242
urban elegy (*ritha*ʾ *al-mudun*), 187
Utas, Bo, 43, 44, 47
utterance (*lafz*), 36, 38, 41, 43, 45

van Gelder, Geert Jan, 53*n*43
Vatvat, Rashid al-Din, 68–9, 72, 74, 81, 131, 183
  Khaqani and, 89, 138–9, 140–1, 142–3
Virgil, 7

Wasil b. ʿAtaʾ, 189
Watt, Montgomery, 246*n*25
Weber, Max, 227
well, image of Bijan trapped in, 14, 15, 22, 23, 62
wheel of fate (*gardun*), 101, 102, 109
White, Hayden, 251
white hand of Moses, 144, 146, 147–8, 149
wine poems (*khamriyyat*), 32–3, 45, 50
wood of the cross (*ʿud al-salib*), 135, 181–2

Yavari, Neguin, 245*n*15

al-Zabidi, Murtada, 177
Zafari, Vali Allah, 51
Zahhak, 115
zajal, the, 32
zaman and *vaqt* (time), 140–1
Zarrinkub, 177
zindan (prison), 47, 48
zindanameh, 27*n*10
Zipoli, Riccardo, 88
Zoroastrians, 17, 25, 101–2, 159, 162, 215, 217
  under *dhimmi* regulations, 164, 168, 177
zunnar (belts worn by non-Muslims), 160, 165, 168–70, 173, 175–7, 178–81
  gambling metaphor and, 178, 179